TH

LEGE

JOE N

THE
LEGENDARY
JOE MEEK

The Telstar Man

John Repsch

First published in Great Britain in 1989
by Woodford House Publishing Ltd., London.
This edition published in Great Britain
in 2000 by Cherry Red Books Ltd.,
Unit 17, 1st Floor, Elysium Gate West,
126–128 New King's Road,
London SW6 4LZ

British Library Cataloguing in Publication Data
Repsch, John
    The legendary Joe Meek: the Telstar man.
    1. Pop music. Meek, Joe
    I. Title
    782·4'2'164'092
ISBN 1–901447–20–0

Typeset by Axis Europe Plc.
Printed and bound in Great Britain by
Biddles Ltd., Guildford and King's Lynn.
Cover Design by Jim Phelan at Wolf Graphics Tel: 020 8299 2342

Cherry Red Books would like to thank Mark Stratford and Terry Smith for
encouragement in putting this book out.

Contents

Introduction

N O ONE HAS EVER LIVED A LIFE LIKE JOE MEEK. SURROUNDED BY intrigue and controversy, he was Britain's first truly independent pop producer and set the ball rolling for the hundreds who envelop the scene today.

He was the man who against all the odds produced hit after hit in his flat in London's busy Holloway Road. In the pre-Beatles era when the British music industry was being run by the likes of EMI and Decca, and Britain was lying stranded in a sea of tepid cover versions of American teen idols, he decided to go it alone and battle it out with the giants.

From an Aladdin's Cave of dusty wires and ropey old spinning tape machines he developed a unique sound which made his records instantly recognizable. It gave them an exciting, spiritual feel which is still to this day so attractive that his discs are collectors' items and sell for very high prices. He even has a fan club!

Working from two bedrooms, his fine-fingered electronics wizardry was a wonder to behold, and the incredible sounds he created could make your hair stand on end. Like an eccentric scientist he worked all hours bending every rule in the book, turning music inside out and reconstructing it. He was the master of cramming everything onto one single track and for years was so advanced that no one in Britain could touch him.

However, behind all the success lurked personal problems and an ever shadier private life. Early in 1967, under mysterious circumstances, he was found dead. He was 37.

Joe was an enigma. His volcanic temperament and strange behaviour were never fully understood and were simply regarded as the trappings of genius. An intensely secretive man, no one really knew him or was even aware of half his peculiar story.

Consequently, researching his life has taken far longer than I expected, luring me along from one riddle to another.

Gathering facts has also been hampered in other ways. From time to time people have withheld information for fear of divulging how closely involved they were with him. Friendly smiles hide serious anxieties that sadly will always be with them. In a few instances I have even been given deliberate misinformation; to this day there are still singers and musicians harbouring grudges against Joe and against each other. Through constant verification of facts I am satisfied that any such false statements have been eliminated.

So, with this in mind, it will come as no surprise that this little volume is the result of four years' work, including more than 150 taped interviews and 500 hours of telephone conversations.

This is a chance to say thank you again to everyone who has contributed. Whether by answering my phone calls, replying to my letters or allowing me and my tape recorder into their homes and offices, they have helped make it all enjoyable and rewarding. I would have liked to acknowledge everyone but their names would fill two pages. I can mention just a few: Eric and Arthur for their wealth of memories and warm hospitality; Ena Shippam; Gerald Beachus; Allen Stagg; Adrian Kerridge; Jimmy Lock; Lonnie Donegan; Anne Shelton; Humphrey Lyttelton; Chris Barber; George Melly; Frankie Vaughan; Peter Cozens; William Barrington-Coupe; Marcel Rodd; Norman Shine; Lester Banks; Stanley Souter; Bob Kingston; Geoff Goddard; Robbie Duke; Terry O'Neil; Gary Hartnell and his mum of Polygram and Pye; James Deveraux of EMI; Pc James Ainsworth; E. M. Solomons; Ken Howard; Sir Joseph Lockwood; John Leyton; Michael Cox; Mike Berry; Clem Cattini; Heinz; Lord Sutch; Chas Hodges; Joy and Dave Adams; Pete Holder; Dave Dee; Lional Howard; Tony Grinham; Barry Lazell; Paul Pelletier; Brian Matthew and Radio One; *New Musical Express; Melody Maker; Record Mirror; Music Echo; Disc; Pop Weekly; Billboard; Cashbox; Daily Express; Evening News; Evening Standard; Psychic News;* Nigel Hunter of *Music Week;* West Hampstead Cemetery; Chris Charlesworth for his professional advice; Keith Waller for his internet assistance; David Pearce for allowing me access to the Meek Estate files; John Beecher and the Buddy Holly Appreciation Society; the RGM Appreciation Group's Alan Blackburn, Laurence Brown, Hinton Sheryn, Rockin' Tom Casey for playing me the music; Chris Knight for his reams of letters and the 30 interviews he had conducted with Jim Blake eight years before I started, and the latter who set me on the trail. A final thank you goes to the man himself for being such a bewitching subject; he would not have liked having his secrets revealed, but I think he would have appreciated his long overdue credit.

John Repsch

Prologue

February 2 1967. Evening. 304 Holloway Road. Meek's final hours, described by his office assistant, Patrick Pink: "He looked clearly sort of sick. He wasn't talking – writing things down. In the evening we watched some TV and had something to eat. That would be about 7 o'clock. I think I cooked it. He was writing on bits of paper; he was afraid the place was bugged and that he was being listened in to. He suddenly asked me after dinner, 'Let's go up, let's make your record. You're more or less up to standards now.' I'd only recorded demos before but this particular one was promised to come out in March, my own. I have a feeling he had it planned. That was *the* night. After all those years I'd been with him and I'd stayed sometimes the night – and that particular night: 'Come on, let's see if we can get a record out of you now'.

"About 9 o'clock we went up into the studio. He had some tracks already made up: the backing tracks. I just did a couple of old ones he had stored away and I'd learnt the words from the acetates – very quick attempts: about an hour. Then I did another one which I'd learnt. It was a backing that was laid down for Heinz; he had already voiced it and the voice had been taken off of it. Heinz had sung it years ago: "There goes my baby – look at the way she walks". Joe wrote it. Went on the radio once – Heinz did it 'live'. Nothing had been put out on record, and Joe said I could have it and get it released.

"Then all of a sudden he went really weird and told me to start miming to my own recording – said, 'Just stand there and mime – they're watching us through the walls. They're watching and listening'. I've no idea who these people were. Possibly EMI, because days previously he'd pointed out to me people in cars sitting down the road, possibly with listening devices, had his place bugged, and they were watching him every time he came in and out and following him everywhere. He got worse then and it started to play on his mind. It might well have been true and he wasn't nuts completely. I genuinely believe, even though he was going off his rocker, that there were people bugging his place. I genuinely believe it now; or whether it was the police watching his place, I've no idea. Maybe the police had it bugged; might have been the Drug Squad.

"I was recording the same song over and over and over and over again. I don't think he knew what he was doing at all. He was putting on a show basically for the benefit of earholes, people listening in. On the bits of paper he was writing: 'Sing it again', 'More coffee'. I had to keep going down to make coffee. The session would have been about three hours. I went to bed at midnight absolutely shagged out.

"I was in bed when he came up to get the gun. It was a single-barrel shotgun. He kept it under the bed for protection. He said, 'I'm taking this downstairs'. I never gave it a thought.

"At 8 o'clock in the morning he was still working, running tapes and things. I got up. 9 o'clock I made toast for breakfast and called him down from the studio: 'Breakfast'. He came down, drank the coffee. I don't think he ate the toast – pretty sure he didn't eat at all. He wouldn't talk at all. He wrote little notes, passed them over and burnt them after he'd wrote them. After he'd drunk his coffee he went out in the kitchen and had a burn-up. First of all he was burning a lot of documents, letters and things in the kitchen; it was in a small tin dustbin. He had a bonfire in that. Angry about something – no idea what; he was very angry. The previous day he had just been dazed. Now he'd changed. I think he had his senses – I'm bloody sure he had. He was absolutely paranoid but tense and angry. He wrote two or three messages: 'They're not getting this'. 'They're not getting these'. He went mad and he wrote: 'They aren't going to f—— get this', and he started to burn that painting on the wall: the one with the little black boys dancing naked round a fire. He put the painting on top of a fire – the two-bar fire – which scorched it all up. I thought it was strange but I didn't think it was coming to what happened. I thought at the time he was going out of his head and I was going to call Dr. Crispe and he stopped me. He was down for about half an hour. Then he disappeared upstairs to the studio for a little while. I thought, 'Crikey, I'll be safer to stay down here.' So I stayed downstairs. And he came back down to the living room. I think it was about quarter to ten. Give me a little note saying: 'I'm going now. Goodbye'. And I didn't know what it meant. I laughed. I thought, 'Where?' The note got burnt and upstairs he went. I thought,'Well everything's OK then.' 'Cause he was upstairs playing tapes – my stuff from the night before. That went on for ten to fifteen minutes.

"Then Michael arrives. Michael and Dennis – they'd just left school and they were looking for work, and Joe'd give them a job stacking tapes for a few days for a few quid. There was no set hours with them or whatever; they came and they were told to piss off – they went; that was the arrangement. One came, just Michael. I went up the stairs to tell Joe. Michael stayed at the door. I think he sensed there was something wrong straight away. Whether he'd been there the day before when I'd not been around, I don't know. Whether he knew there was something going on, I don't know, but he knew there was something wrong straight away. He said, 'Is it all right?' I went up to the landing and said, 'Michael's here.' I didn't actually see Joe at that point; he was in the control room. He called out: 'Tell him to f—— off – get rid of him', but I'd already started coming downstairs having told him that Michael was here. Then he came to the top of the landing and looked down on me, and said, 'Get Mrs. Shenton up here.' I in turn said to Michael, 'Joe don't want you today. Do us a favour, tell Mrs. Shenton to come up for me'.

"She came up and she came to me. I was in the room before the office, the waiting room, more or less at the bottom of the stairs. She said, 'What's up?' I said, 'I don't know. Joe wants you'. I took her two or three steps up. She said, 'Oh, hold this for me a minute. I don't like to smoke up there.' I took her cigarette off her, she went on her way upstairs and I went in the office. I think she said, 'Hallo Joe, how are you?' and all the usual rubbish 'cause she did ask me what sort of mood he's in. I said, 'He's in a bad mood again'. I thought everything's going to be OK now; she'll calm him down. Within about half a minute there was a lot of shouting. It was after I put the cigarette out. I was walking back in the living room when I heard him say, 'Have you got the book?' God knows what it was: probably the rent book or rates book or lease or something. He shouted it very sternly. They weren't both shouting, just him. I think she said, 'I haven't got it with me; I'll bring it in tomorrow', and asked him if

3

he'd like to come down for a cup of tea and a chat. The shouting went on for a couple of minutes, I think. It was all him; he was getting frantic. I was trying to eavesdrop on the conversation, being the nosy kind of person that I am, walking to and fro, but I didn't hear very much.

"I was in the office when I heard a big bang. I didn't know what it was. It was such a f—— big bang, I was stunned. I rushed out and she was falling downstairs and I sort of grabbed her as she came to the bottom, and felt her. I was sitting on the stairs with her flapped over me. I wondered what it was for a minute. Then I saw the blood pouring out of these little holes in her back. And she died in my arms – I'm bloody positive she went still. I had quite a bit of blood over me. Her back was just smoking. He must have been close range, he must have been right at her back. I held her in my arms; clearly there was nothing I could do. She was dead as far as I was concerned and I sort of pushed her over and I shouted out, 'She's dead'. Joe was leaning over the landing banister and I thought I was next. He just had a stony-faced cold look.

"A few moments later I rushed halfway upstairs and looked across the landing and caught sight of Joe outside the control room and I think he was reloading, and before I could get at him he'd pulled the trigger on himself, and there was Joe's body with his head like a burnt candle. Blood everywhere, including over me as well; I was treading in blood . . ."

1
Bumpy Beginnings

Newent is a small country town. It lies midway between Gloucester and Ross-on-Wye on the edge of the famous Forest of Dean. Nowadays it is more of a tourist trap than anything else, offering holidaymakers a bit of history and ample rambles, one of which climbs to the top of nearby May Hill where you can view ten counties.

Quaint, twisting streets with mellowed brick houses lead to the Market Square and Newent's prize attraction and symbol of the past: a 16th century Market Hall on oaken 'stilts'. In spite of its name Newent is old, dating back at least to pre-Saxon times, and during the Middle Ages it rose to fame as one of the main Market Towns in North-west Gloucestershire; Welsh farmers used it regularly as the next stop after Ross-on-Wye on their trek to the Gloucester cattle market. But that is all a long time ago, and apart from a few skirmishes in the Civil War and the church roof falling in soon after a service in 1674, not much has happened since. It has lost most of its former glory as a Market Town and, though the farming tradition continues, the town's revenue now depends on sightseers passing through rather than sheep.

The present population has swelled to 6,000 but the Newent of 1929 had less than half that and everyone knew everyone. At No.1 Market Square on April 5 that year Robert George Meek was born.

He was the second son of Alfred George Meek, better known as George, and Evelyn Mary, better known as Biddy. They were living in a rented 3-storey terraced house with George's mother. George was running a fish and chip shop but had aspirations towards owning property; although the Meek family had been settled in the area for the past 100 years they had never been landowners, and he had plans to change all that. His three brothers had been killed during World War I, whilst he himself had been invalided out a month before Armistice Day with shrapnel wounds and suffering from shellshock. His £400 disability grant had given him independence and paid for four acres of pasture-land and some cows; the milk he had driven around the village with a horse and cart, ladling it out of a bucket. This was to be the first of a long string of jobs for George. After a while he had grown bored with it, so decided to hang up his ladle and run a taxi service instead.

Then it was in 1927 at the age of 30 that he had met his bride-to-be at a local dance. Biddy Birt had been a 24 year old teacher from a large family in Huntley, in the Forest of Dean, and she had taught all subjects and played the piano in the primary school there. They made an unlikely pair: George, a tallish, stout fellow of 15 stone; Biddy, a frail 5′1″. He was a typical farming type, outspoken and free with his fists, whereas she was quiet and persevering. When she gave up her teaching career to marry him she could not have picked a more appropriate name for herself.

They set up home in Huntley with Biddy's father, whom she was nursing through the last months of a terminal illness. Then when he died, George brought her home to live with his mother at the Market Square.

It was at this time that they had had their first child, Arthur, who was named after one of the sons George's mother had lost during the War. A year later their next child Robert was born. He in turn was nicknamed by George's mother after another son she had lost: Joe. The name stuck.

As is the case with many mothers whose first child is a son, Biddy had set her heart on a daughter next. So when Joe arrived she tempered her disappointment by treating him as one. He was given dolls to play with, his hair grew long and he was kept mainly in dresses till starting school at 4. His mother had intended sending him as a girl but when he realized certain irregularities his protests to her got him into shorts just in time.

The first few years for the blue-eyed, brown-haired boy were marked by a series of moves as his father slipped ever hopefully from one job to the next. From postman to bookie to fish and chip merchant to butcher, he went on to move the family over to Bussage on the other side of Gloucester where he had five lorries hauling sheep flock up to London, and rags back down to the paper mill at Stroud. Then they moved to nearby Churchdown, and there was just enough time for Joe to start school at the primary before the family were whisked back to Newent for another round of fish and chips. By this time they had added two more children to the fold: Eric in 1932 and Pamela in 1934.

But for Joe, 1934 was more significant as the year he first showed an interest in music. Although the Meeks were hardly a musical family (in spite of Biddy's talent for playing the piano, the twin devils of no piano to play and no time to play it anyway had effectively put paid to that), Joe had heard enough on the wireless to warrant his clamouring for a gramophone, and mentioned it on a private recording of his life story several years later: "It was one of those toy gramophones with a celluloid soundbox and a key to wind it up. And I remember I'd seen it in a shop window and asked for it for Christmas; and as quite often happens my wish came true and I got this gramophone for Christmas with some children's records. I used to play this all the time, and it was quite obvious to my parents that this fascinated me, and when I was 7 years old they bought me a proper gramophone: a portable type that used to be very popular about twenty years ago. At this time I used to be fascinated with making things out of shoe boxes like puppet shows and slot machines and all sorts of things, and I used to try and experiment with my gramophone, and I discovered if you played the record at the end on the run-out groove you could shout down the sound chamber and the sound would be imprinted in the grooves. And I thought that I'd discovered something marvellous, and of course I was really doing just what Edison had discovered years before."

The following year his passion for messing around with bits and pieces brought him his first electrical success when he and a school-friend, Gerald Beachus, rigged up a light in his grandmother's garden shed.

Over the years, Granny Meek's house at the Market Square had often been a handy refuge in between moves, and they were now living with her on a permanent basis. She had given Joe the shed, a converted cowshed at the bottom of the garden, and whenever time allowed he would be hidden away in there wiring and rewiring. But at the age of 8 he thought of something that would put him right in the limelight.

From watching the local amateur dramatics he hit on the idea of staging his own Saturday afternoon shows for children in Newent. His only previous stage experience had been a fleeting appearance with Arthur, two years before, as a pixie: during an evening of singing and recitals at the Churchdown Mission Room they had been in a sketch called 'Daffodils and Pixies' in which they danced around some mushrooms. Now it was Joe who was calling the tune and he encouraged other children to bring along fancy clothes to the shed, where they would enact scenes from the plays they had seen or anything he had thought up. A neighbour of theirs, Mrs. Gladys Dallow, recalls: "He was always with girls, and whenever possible he'd be always dressing up in a woman's clothes. Sometimes his mother wouldn't allow him to have hers but his old granny would say, 'Don't you worry Joe, you can have mine.' He loved dressing up and having an audience, and he used to look quite nice. He looked like a girl and he used to prance about with a theatrical touch and flowing skirts." They often staged shows close by in the old cattle market, but with other youngsters around like John Bisco, who was certainly not a member of their guild of players, it could be a risky business: "He was always dressing up as a girl, pratting about, and we played hell with him. We'd try to mess everything up and pull his leg and chase him."

If there were rehearsals before the performance, everyone would be sworn to secrecy so neither the audience nor the John Bisco's would know what to expect. To compensate for the colossal entrance fee of a halfpenny, a large notice was placed outside advertising the main attraction: Free Refreshments. In the interval Joe would get out his wind-up gramophone and play records.

There was also a magician's act for which he would wear a tall black hat and perform conjuring tricks, and there were plays that he would make up as they went along, usually in the style of *Murder In The Red Barn*. Anything with a bit of stabbing in was especially popular; indeed, his two favourite subjects were mystery and witches, and he did not have to look far for inspiration.

It was a highly superstitious area, particularly in the huge Forest of Dean with its thousands of acres of woodland where witchcraft was rife. Perhaps due to the forest's relative isolation some parts have barely altered during the past 150 years, and in nearby Lassington Wood witches' covens are reputed to be around to this day. Witching in the Middle Ages was punishable by death, and there are said to have been hangings and burnings in the area – some as close by as Newent Market Square where Joe was now living. Stories of mystery proliferated, mainly of ghosts still keeping up regular appearances ever since the Civil War: the man in the old Tan Yard who was seen walking around without his head; the woman in white who caused a car crash on Ross Road; of nearby Conigree Court, where "all sorts of things have been seen". Besides those, there were also the more current goings-on such as the gypsy who had recently been found hanging in Highnam Wood and the headless torso that had been fished out of the river at Haw Bridge. And of course, there was the most famous story of all: that of Dick Whittington, three times Lord Mayor of London, who in 1371 had set off on his travels from up the road at Pauntley. Joe lapped it all up and it provided him with a rich source of material.

It was quite clear by now to whom he owed certain aspects of his character. Although he had inherited a singlemindedness from his father, as well as the fiery temper – "with a fuse so short it was nearly non-existent" – his father was nonetheless easygoing, whereas Joe would launch into each new activity with a passion bordering on obsession. And in contrast to his father he was shy and had a strong instinct towards being on his own; after school he would race home, not to play with friends as his brothers did, but to tinker and tamper alone in the shed. Even his mother who was a very hardworking woman lacked Joe's dedication, but it was to her that he felt closest. Unlike his brothers he was not turning out to be the robust son his father expected of him, and it was to her that he looked for love and affection. But he could not monopolize her time. There were three other children, a husband and an aging mother-in-law besides Joe, plus all the responsibilities that being a wife and mother entailed. And there was something else.

The £400 grant George received for his disability was little consolation for the suffering he and his family would have to endure as a result of his injuries. The horrors he had undergone whilst serving in the Royal Field Artillery in Belgium's bloodbath at Passchendaele, culminating in a terrifying experience when his horse was blown up beneath him while transporting a field gun, had profound effects which would stay with him for life. After the War, it was to be a full five years before he left military hospital to return to his mother, and then again he had to acclimatize. Violent outbursts of rage in which he would smash anything that came to hand were only gradually overcome by his mother's firmly tolerant understanding. Helping him out with his milk round and generally shielding him from life's trials she had been able to ease his anguish. And she was no stranger to such frowns of fortune. Her husband Charlie had emigrated to Canada just before George was born, leaving her behind with nine children and sixpence to feed them on. He had promised to send for her as soon as he had bettered himself as a lumberjack. He never did, but sent money instead. Bringing up the children alone as well as she did earned her the accolade of "a better woman never walked in a pair of shoes". She had hoped that when George got married he would stay in good health, and for a while he did, but he found he had to avoid jobs which entailed taking orders. It might have been a direct result of his other bitter experience in the War when shortly before receiving his injuries he had been ordered to step up and replace his dying brother on the field gun.

More significantly, as the pressures of family life grew, so once again did his problem. Joe's schoolfriend and confidant Gerald Beachus would sometimes hear about it from Joe: "Every now and again things would set him off. Maybe a door would bang and that

9

would take him back to the Somme, and he'd go a little bit crazy – shouting and raving. Joe's mother would get the brunt of that. I think she was like in fear of him because she didn't want to upset him to start him off. Either she'd manage to get him shut in the bedroom and everyone would get out of the way and leave him to calm down or the doctor would turn up and give him a pill or a shot in the arm. He could be violent. But he would never touch the old granny, his mother; the old granny could talk to him as her son and she could get him to do what she wanted him to do. Then if he didn't calm down within a certain period the doctor would come, who knew of course all about him. Sometimes he would be in this state for a week or ten days. Then once he'd come round he'd be perfectly back to normal. But it only took that little thing to set him off. I wasn't allowed to knock at the door in case it brought on another attack. Instead Joe would call round to me or we'd arrange a time for me to be outside his door. He used to say, 'You mustn't tell anybody because they'll think he's mad.' But it was virtually a war injury, so they called it 'shell-shocked'."[1]

On the other hand, unless he was crossed George was one of the most generous men around, handing out money to anyone in need or giving fruit away to children. But at home he was very much in charge. As one of their neighbours puts it: "He was the dominant lord and master; he'd speak and she'd jump." George's symptoms were not continuous but they did occur with sufficient frequency to warrant caution from the family. Although Biddy understood him and worshipped the ground he walked on, the children were often frightened of him. Their young, impressionable minds could obviously be affected in many ways: for Arthur and Eric, both hardy, down-to-earth lads, it served to toughen them up; Joe was softened. It alienated him from his father and pushed him nearer his mother. And very subtly he absorbed some more of the Meek temper.

He was a strange mixture of jovial Joe and melancholy Meek. When he was happy there was no one around who could laugh more. As one of his schoolfellows explains: "Joe found things funny. He had a great sense of humour and was quite a giggler. We would laugh at him rather than with him, but he'd take it in good heart." This feeling of being different, coupled with his determination to follow his own controversial pursuits, could not help but distance him from other boys of his age. If he wanted to play-act a wizard in his shed or parade in front of an audience, then all around him had a good time, but others said it was girlish and called him a cissie; if

---

[1] Refers to surplus detail in the Appendix, which would otherwise hold up the story.

he spent spare time pottering about alone in the shed, then he felt better occupied than playing marbles outside or running about with the boys, but this was deemed unnatural and labelled him an 'outer'. And even when he did make the effort to join them, perhaps for swimming, he would sometimes get scragged by other boys removing his swimming trunks and covering him in mud, baiting and baiting him till he blew his top. Of course, all this teasing, along with the obvious contrast between himself and his brothers, served to underline for him a fact he was becoming only too aware of: that he was the odd one out at home and one of the odd ones out in the town.

Being called a cissie naturally upset him, and for a sensitive home-loving mother's boy it presented all sorts of difficulties. He would go to his mother for comfort but could not always depend upon getting it. His mother was a sweet woman with a special fondness for him, but he sometimes put her in a tricky position. She had to exercise discretion when she gave him affection and soothing words, for should she be seen doing so in George's presence, this would be looked upon as namby pambying him, making him even more unmanly, and George wanted his sons men. Added to this, Joe was a little spoilt by her and though he was generally as good as gold and, unlike his naughty brothers, never caned in his life he sometimes behaved in a spoilt manner. Arthur would not always tolerate this behaviour, and being a strong, hardy youngster and the kind of country lad who walked around with a ferret in his coat pocket, was in a position to make his opinions felt. For this reason Joe did not usually get on well with him, and although Arthur got him out of many a scrape at school, he was just as likely to send him home crying to his mother. By the same token she could not take sides with Joe against Arthur in the presence of her husband for fear of upsetting him. In Arthur the firstborn, George saw himself, so Arthur was his favourite. Pam, being the only girl, was spoilt by everyone. So, if Biddy played the devil's advocate and her judgment swung in favour of Arthur, Joe would feel betrayed. He was becoming frightfully sensitive and would withdraw into himself and seek solace amongst his wires and batteries.

He had only two good friends and even them he saw little. Jean Trig, for a while his childhood sweetheart, and Gerald Beachus both shared an interest in his electrics and dramatics, and sometimes Gerald, another loner, would manage to get him out for more regular boyish exploits such as climbing trees and building dens in the woods, swimming and catching sticklebacks.

In spite of George's dark cloud hanging ominously over them the

11

family were happy together. However, work was the order of the day, and for Biddy in particular life was one long slog. Family outings in the Buick to Weston-super-Mare were few and far between and happy times together stemmed mainly from working together, and now they were all hard at it in George's newly acquired orchards.

George's itchy feet had walked him out of his fish and chip shop and into the fruit trade. From the farmers he had started buying up fruit crops in orchards sometimes 20–30 miles away, and employed half a dozen pickers to harvest apples, cherries, pears and plums, all of which he sold to wholesalers at Gloucester market. This took him through the summer, while the remaining months were spent competing with other locals in brewing and selling cider, and buying and selling at auctions, where he would pick up anything from farm implements and bric-à-brac to entire libraries. Such wondrous enterprise would have been highly commended by Winston Churchill's Conservative Party but did tend to worry Biddy who was less optimistic about her husband's varied ventures. After school Joe's job was to help weigh the fruit and load boxes on the lorry. He didn't mind fruiting but could think of better things to do and afterwards would race home to do them.

Besides organizing some singing in his concerts he was also singing in the church choir – no mean feat considering he was tone-deaf. His brother Eric had also been a member for a while, but due to his appalling voice had had to suffer relegation to 'organ pumper'; Joe's voice it seems was a shade less unbearable. Even so he was totally oblivious of any vocal deficiency he might have had because he possessed a Meek streak which made him think he was always right and no matter what he was doing he was infinitely the best suited for it! As Eric so succinctly puts it: "All the Meeks thinks they'm pretty clever at theirselves."

Being with the choir was quite a profitable proposition, as Eric calculates: "You'd get a halfpenny for singing and a halfpenny for attending; and double if you went twice on Sunday: you got tuppence. And you got fivepence for a wedding and fivepence if we had a funeral. So we'd all be hoping that somebody had died or somebody had got married, and the more the merrier as far as we were concerned."

Singing in the choir was one of the few interests Joe shared with his brothers. Apart from going to the pictures on Saturday after-noons and very occasionally joining them for swimming in the River Leadon, at which he was quite good, they had nothing in common. Understandably his brothers never bothered asking him along for cricket, football, fishing or rabbiting because his sporting inclinations started and ended with swimming. Worst of all in their opinion, he did what was little short of anathema for most lads of his age preferring the company of girls, and hardly endeared himself to his brothers by dressing up as one. Needless to say, they wanted no part of it and pointedly attended none of the performances. "Of course, we used to call him cissie,' says Eric. "We always said he ought to have been a girl. We told him that. And he would usually fly into another little tantrum and storm off up to the shed. He liked his own way; he definitely had to have his own way . . . He thought we were gross and mad. We thought he was feminine rather than a boy because he would rather dress up in some fancy clothes and be prancing about up the shed doing a play or something."

Christmas 1938 was to be one of the big turning points in his life. When asked what he wanted for a present, there was only one thing he had thoughts for: a *Practical Wireless* book. Suddenly with this book his abiding interest took on real meaning. He soon built a crystal set and this spurred him on to greater dedication, constantly experimenting with broken and secondhand wirelesses, cameras and gramophones.

Meanwhile at school he was busy gazing out of the window and showing little academic prowess. Since he was six he had been attending the local primary school, Picklenash, and his best subject was art – portraits and landscapes being his specialities. He did not, however, confine his art studies to the art class, and as a boy who sat next to him remembers: "He was good at drawing radios, and would draw them in *all* the lessons." As far as the other subjects were concerned his presence was merely physical, for when he was not drawing radios his mind had more than likely wandered off to ponder upon a piece of wire in his shed. As Eric saw it: "Joe was a dreamer. I mean, he'd sit and be miles and miles away, and the world was in oblivion to Joe, like. You could talk to him and he didn't take no notice. Joe tended to live and think in the different world he'd be in. He didn't live in our reality world as far as getting up to go to the fruiting. Joe lived for his little shed at the top of the garden, and as soon as we came home from work – it didn't matter whether it was 4 o'clock in the afternoon or 7 o'clock at night – he never came into the house. He went straight up the garden to his little shed, and that was his world."

When he was eleven he sat a kind of 11+ exam. That decided whether or not he was to go on to grammar school and what class he was to remain in till he left Picklenash. Surprise, surprise, he failed it and, of the three classes in the sixth form, he was to finish his schooldays in 'C'. This suited his father fine because he wanted all his sons working for him and it mattered not if they were dunces or geniuses.

Then one day something happened that set his school studies even further back and was so serious it nearly put paid to any hope of a career anywhere. His father kept livestock in the old cattle market and one Sunday Joe was sent in with some friends to tend them. The day before, with World War 2 raging, the Home Guard had decided to carry out a demonstration of their capabilities and those of the phosphorus bottle bomb in repelling enemy tanks; and with the market area cleared for them they had proceeded to throw their bombs about. After they had finished and the place had been cleaned up, the market was back in operation and presumably safe for Joe to feed the chickens. Any yellow phosphorus fluff that might have ended up on the railings had supposedly been washed away with high pressure hoses. Through prime Dad's Army incompetence, the underside of the railings had been missed and this lethal substance left exposed for anyone to chance upon. Joe did. He saw that when someone brushed against it smoke came off, so he placed some in his hand, and smacking it with the other one, was delighted to see it give off a small puff of smoke: ideal, he thought, to enhance his magician's tricks. Excitedly he took a larger helping and, hey presto, the result was even more spectacular. Then he started gathering up as much of this precious material as possible for future use and while he was wondering where he could put it all, he got a whole handful and clapped his hands together again. They burst into flames and his friend Gerald immediately pushed him flat to rub his hands in the dirt. He ran back crying to the house where his father bathed them in a bowl of milk, but the phosphorus was still active and had soon burnt both hands down to the bone.

In spite of painstaking care for six months the specialist in Gloucester did not think he would ever again have the use of his hands; they gave him constant pain and he could not move them. Fortunately the specialist had not reckoned on the devotion of the family practitioner Dr. Johnstone who, gifted with the patience of a saint, set about saving them. Every day for the first six months Joe went to him for two hours after morning surgery before the doctor set off on his rounds; then again for two hours after evening surgery. Tweezers had to be used to dress the injuries with medicated cotton wool and then his hands were wrapped in bandages.

Throughout all this he appeared less depressed at his plight than annoyed at the inconvenience. He was still going to school as usual but could do nothing with his hands, so spent a lot of time reading and collecting things to mess around with later. For those first few months Dr. Johnstone shared the doubts of the specialist but never disclosed them to his young patient. However, after six months, despite the specialist's continued scepticism, the doctor believed there was a growing chance of restoring movement. His encouraging Joe to try to exercise his fingers began paying off and slowly they began to stir. Six months later treatment was concluded. Not a scar was to be seen.

By this time he had accumulated a great deal of gear, so much in fact that the shed was filled to bursting point and the front room was being used for overspill. It was supposed to be the sitting room but one could hardly stand in it let alone sit, with equipment covering chairs, floor and window sills, and wires dangling from the pictures. The family had to be so careful where they trod that eventually Biddy prevailed upon her husband to give the room to Joe – officially. There were a few arguments at first: "If it's going to help him in any way," she said. "Help him be damned," he retorted. "He'll get my boot. I'm nearly fed up with it." The matter was eventually settled in Joe's favour, though Biddy had to make it clear to him that his "rubbish" must expand no further, or they would soon have to move out and sleep in the garden! As it was, any visitors calling by had to be received in the kitchen at the back. Immediately, he put up the 'barricades' so he could meddle undisturbed and would get very angry if anyone entered his new workshop without permission: "I don't want anybody in here interfering with anything," he ordered and once installed, come rain or shine, his friends needed dynamite to shift him. In Joe's words: "This became not only a hobby but used to take up most of my time. I used to go round old record shops in Gloucester and old sales rooms and buy up lots of gramophone records, a lot of which I still have at home in my attic. Anyway, this went on until I was about 13 years old and discovered that I wanted a magnetic pick-up which I connected to the gramophone. Then I wanted to amplify this and I made my first one-valve radio and then of course my first one-valve amplifier." And to what better use could one put it than playing music in the cherry orchards?

THE LEGENDARY JOE MEEK

When the cherry season came round he was never happy with his father's orders that the boys take air rifles to shoot birds so as to prevent them feasting on the fruit before the pickers got to it. So, as Eric recalls, he put his electrical knowledge to use: "He used to put speakers up in the trees all round the orchard and he did shout through the microphone to all the birds and play music to them all bloody day while they were sat eating our cherries! He also used to have a sheet of corrugated iron that he could bang with a big stick and then amplify it all over the orchard. It worked but they lived to come back and have another go; if you shot 'em they didn't come back. He didn't like us shooting the birds but it had to be done. Our father was in agreement with us that the best starling was a dead 'un."

The cherry season was especially tiring because it meant the boys being at their respective orchards by first light, 4 a.m., and back again at 4 p.m. till dusk. There was no time at all for Joe's garden shed activities unless he wanted to come back to an orchard full of cherry stones. When the weather allowed, it made sense to pitch a tent and with all his speakers in position he kept watch through the tent flap. Many were the times when the early morning stillness was shattered by his screaming into the microphone: "I can see you buggers!"

When he reached 14 it was time to leave school and he was glad to see the back of it. His father had bought a farm 24 miles away at Dinmoor Hill, and Joe went to join Arthur who had been running it alone since leaving school the previous year. There were about forty cows and a few chickens and horses to look after plus a small cherry orchard, but as Joe was not the world's finest farmer he did the cooking and cleaning. He was a good cook and Arthur's mouth would water when he thought of Joe's sausages: "Joe used to go to Hereford market on a Monday and he used to bring back eight pound of sausages; he used to go again on a Wednesday and bring back six pound, and he used to go again on a Friday and bring back another six pound: that's twenty pound of sausages. Me and Joe used to eat them in a week. Mind, they were beautiful sausages." Not so beautiful were his fatty fried cheese sandwiches. "Have another one," Joe told a lad helping out on the farm one day and offered him one more swimming in fat. The lad never came back again because he caught yellow jaundice.

Farmwork was not Joe's idea of a career but as the choice was not his he had to content himself studying and experimenting when he could. On the farm he had his equipment running off a 12 volt

16

battery, and with wires everywhere he played his music and probed and practised. His father was afraid he'd blow the house up. But his fortunes were about to pick up because with the sale of his most treasured possession, a cine camera, he was able to buy an amplifier for £7.10s.0d and offer his services to the local dance hall, playing records. He was a riproaring success and naturally when people noticed what a good job he was doing for the Newent swing scene the word spread and others in the area wanted a share of him. Armed to the teeth with 100 or more Vera Lynns and Victor Sylvesters he soon found himself supplying music to the masses with his wind-up gramophone and amplifier, and it was not only dance halls that were after him: "By this time I was about 16; I used to pro-vide music for amateur dramatic societies. I remember plays like *The Ghost Train* and *The Poltergeist*, lots of plays, and I used to go out of my way to provide the right sort of music for them and the right sound effects."

It was at this time he also built a TV set. Understandably the high esteem in which he was already held by the locals increased ten-fold when he proudly unveiled it: an actual, real live 9″ television. And it was not so much the fact that he had built it himself which set their teeth a-chattering as that no one in the Newent area possessed one. Unfortunately the only reception he could offer them was a screen full of interference because transmissions to the Gloucester region had yet to start.

During this time his father sold off the farm at Dinmoor Hill at a nice profit, thus beginning a series of buying up, renovating and selling off farms and at ever increasing size. On their next farm at Pendock, Joe was put in overall command of their 168 sow pigs, each with 6–12 piglets. According to Eric, it was a job to which he paid strict attention: "Whatever Joe done he liked to do well. Even cleaning out the pigs you could eat your dinner off the floors of his pigsties because they would be immaculate, spotless. And yet he knew within half an hour they'd be mucked up again." Besides that farm, there was another one to be looked after plus orchards to be minded and cows to be milked, leaving little time for matters dearer to his heart. However, keeping the birds and pigs happy were to be his final jobs on the farm because when he was 18 it all came to an end.

World War 2 had finished and the Meek family were able to look back and count their blessings. It seemed they had received their share of misfortune in WWI and apart from Joe's accident WW2 had hardly affected them. There had been blackouts but no bombs had dropped within ten miles and food rationing was easily compensated for on the farms. They had carried on fruiting and farming simultaneously, but with the War now over, the bottom was dropping out of the fruit market – too much was being imported from abroad. So in 1947 George decided to finish with fruiting altogether and as he was in the mood for a change he packed in farming too. He sold off the farms, gave up the house in Market Square (his mother had died just before the War) and bought up the Newent dairy in the High Street for Arthur and Eric to run. For Joe he had something else lined up. George wanted to continue investing in property, so was keeping connections with a Newent estate agency. Rather than send Joe out with Eric, Arthur and the milk, George decided he would be better suited as a clerk in the agency.

If Joe thought he had found farming boring, then office work must have charted new horizons: "I was radio mad. I just couldn't keep my hands off valves and wires, and working in that estate agent's office nearly sent me barmy." However, despite George's intentions to set his son on the road to an estate agent's career, Joe's life was moving inexorably in another direction entirely. He had had umpteen years to consider his future plans and they certainly included no estate agent's office. Early in 1948, after months of being shackled to a desk, at last came the manna from Heaven for which he had waited so long. It was his call-up papers for National Service and he had to choose whether to enlist for the compulsory two-year stint or, like Arthur, be exempted by doing farmwork again. But he had long made up his mind that it was the RAF for him and he was going to try for radar. His father was not at all pleased because he had seen enough of war himself and wanted his sons nowhere near the armed forces. Nevertheless Joe was determined, sat an exam with 1999 other hopefuls and to his delight was one of only two lads to be accepted. Now he was on his way to becoming a radar mechanic and getting a tantalizing taste of the outside world.

2
Picture-Painting In Sound

he training camp at West Kirby offered ideal conditions for anyone seeking 56 days' worth of hell. Those not relishing the rigid discipline and continual physical exertion had to grin and bear it. Top of the list of attractions was the assault course which he found sheer agony, and invariably held up proceedings to the rantings and ravings of the instructors. If that did not toughen him up – which it didn't – there was always the billet bully who regularly got his kicks tipping Joe and other timid creatures out of bed with their mattresses on top of them. Joe for his part met every new ordeal with a smile and without retaliation, knowing it would not last much longer.

When he was eventually finished there he took his eight weeks' supply of bumps and bruises along with him to Yatesbury, Wiltshire, where after two months of technical training he emerged officially as a radar mechanic and began his travels to various radar installations in the West Country. They were usually one-room buildings perched on hills in the middle of nowhere and filled with equipment, used of course to check out aircraft in the area and serve as an early-warning system in case of enemy attack. He sometimes found it lonely work when there was only one other man with whom to take turns keeping the long, desolate watches. But though he did not know it yet, it was to prove invaluable experience for the future by directing not only his attention skyward but also his imagination. The time would come when his interest in outer space would turn to goggle-eyed fascination, and have him creating spacey sounds so advanced for their day they would leave the music business gasping. Then he would look back on his RAF stargazing nights and remember how it all started.

He would also remember the other TV set he built. When he presented it to his parents it was ready for the first transmissions to the Gloucester area. Eric remembers it well: "We had the first television in Newent. Before even the radio shops in Newent had a television, we had one. It was in a virtual orange box; he built from scratch: he bought the cathode tube and built everything up to it. It was a little 12″ screen, and when it first came out they used to think everybody should sit in the dark and watch it. And it used to come on about half past seven at night, and we'd all get

19

in there in the dark, draw all the curtains, switch it on and sit there till the Epilogue at about 12 o'clock. And when we put the lights on, the house was full – chock-a-block, full of people! They just used to sneak through the door and nobody said a word – we used to be glued to this box."

After serving his conscription quota he had no plans to stay on. On demob in 1950 he returned home to find that his father had just died. George had carried on buying up property but the bitter legal wrangles following the sale of one of his houses aggravated some shrapnel which had all the while been lodged in his brain, bringing on a haemorrhage.

As for Joe, his father's death spared him any further opposition to his plans. Returning to Newent he knew exactly what he was going to do and that was to seek out a job at what he liked best: electronics. The radio shop in the High Street was small fry offering no more scope than he could procure for himself, mending neighbours' wirelesses, so he would have to try his luck in Gloucester calling on each of the electrical shops in person.

One of the big three at the time was a branch of Currys. Stepping shyly in he asked to see the manager, Ernest North, who told him that unfortunately all maintenance work was carried out by a firm in Worcester. And therein lay the rub. To Mr. North's bristling indignation he could see that such a policy meant more trade for his two great rivals: the MEB and Broadmeads. He had long been pondering the problem and now seeing Joe's disappointed face the temptation was too much. Violating the company's code would be a risk but one worth taking, so he offered him a post as shop assistant to camouflage the real business he had for him at the back, servicing radios and the eagerly awaited television sets.

So now Mr. North was on constant red alert with one eagle eye fixed on his two competitors while the other one monitored the movements of the inspectors from Currys' Head Office. As he explains: "Whenever a senior executive of Currys visited the branch it was always a flutter of heartbeats. Joe was aware of this situation, playing a predetermined plan of action by covering up any instrument he may have been working on in the rear part of the shop, removing any overall and presenting himself behind the counter as a salesman. This process went on for quite a while until my immediate superiors realized the situation and turned a blind eye to it."

Though he was an immense asset to the shop, he soon started getting restless. Besides working in the back room there were often forays to mend equipment outside, and this he disliked, seeing it as a waste of good bench time; not that time spent at the bench was such a precious commodity, for Mr. North kept a very tight rein on him and was not going to bend any more rules to let him carry out his own experiments during office hours. So, after nine months of valves and more valves he wanted some elbow-room and started coming into work late, saying he had been helping his brothers bottling in the dairy. (Actually it was due to late nights, staying up all hours building a tape recorder.) Then in October he decided it was time to pack up and move on. "He was ambitious," says Mr. North, "And made known his interests in advanced electronics and noises. His departure to London to seek a wider field was contrary to my advice, although he left with all our blessings."

He would have left with one blessing less had Mr. North known where that "wider field" really was. Not for another thirty-three years would he learn that Joe had in fact seen a local advert for a TV service engineer, and far from setting off for London, was now hot-footing it to Gloucester's MEB!

The Midlands Electricity Board ran a bigger service department entirely, with their workshop away from the branch and with three engineers to staff it. It was altogether more up his street than Currys, for whereas he had been used to spending a fair amount of time on the road, here he hardly went out at all. And fixing TVs was no longer the bind it had been, for the management was pretty lax. This, according to one of his associates, Geoff Woodward, gave him the opportunity of trying out his new tape recorder and mixing business with pleasure: "He was more interested really in sound effects than repairing tellies, because he always said to me, 'It's a dead-end job,' but he didn't mind mixing the two. He'd tape music and edit it as if he was a disc jockey. And he did it very, very well. In fact he lent me for a couple of dos some of his recordings he'd made up. He used to get the hits from the radio."

These tapes he would often play at fetes and Saturday evening dances where once again he was in demand. He only charged expenses though, being quite content with all the applause. There was no time for girlfriends and, unlike the string of girls his brothers took out, his own progressed no further in status than dancing partners. When at one local hop the girl he was dancing with suggested they slip outside to contemplate the Moon, he had gone before she finished the sentence.

When he was not dancing he would often introduce the records and may well have been one of the first ever mobile disc jockeys. For outdoor events he would use two huge speakers, and in Newent the sound could be heard all over town. On the sides of the speakers he had painted 'RGM Sound' explaining, "I thought of it from MGM, so why shouldn't I use RGM?" Those letters one day would initial millions of records.

It's a wonder he got any work done at all at the MEB because he was always messing around with tapes. Sometimes he would make up 3-minute comedy sketches with several voices, all his own, and sound effects. That meant using two tape recorders so he could first record something onto one machine, then play that recording plus a new voice or sound effect onto the other machine. As early as 1950 he was sticking sounds on top of each other, going from tape to tape three or more times. Odd noises went into 10-minute horror stories: a few suitably menacing words, intermingled with such homemade sound effects as the crunch of gravel, a knock at the door, an eerie creak and a scream. Actually he was in a way combining art, his favourite subject at school, with electronics, his favourite hobby at home. The difference was that instead of pencils and paints he was now working with voices and sound effects and painting pictures in sound. When he needed help in getting the sounds right his brother Eric was sometimes roped in: "He was always interested in weird sounds and had us doing all sorts to get them. He used to get up at 3 o'clock in the morning and put microphones out on the walls so that he could record the early morning birds singing; he'd have me spinning round the corners, ripping on the brakes and smashing glass to sound like a car crash. The shop was literally full of everything under the sun and he was never happier than when he could get somebody in to make a noise in there that he could record. The local people quite possibly thought that he was a nutter."

Recording was something he took quite seriously. It gave him a sense of achievement that he could not find in merely holding down a steady job or running around doing good turns for others. Composing stories gave vent to an imagination nourished on the silence of solitude; an imagination which like a best friend was always there to comfort him when times were tough or to whisk him away on spooky adventures.

By this time he had reached his full height and stood at a stocky, broad-shouldered 5' 8½". But still tucked away behind the chubby cheeks and the thick brown hair was the shy little lad of his boyhood: quiet, rather hesitant till he started talking about something that interested him; then his eyes would begin to smile, his mouth would curl and he would gain an air of casual authority.

The deep, quiet side to his nature contrasted sharply with that of the extrovert side, and never was it better characterized than when he was playing practical jokes, especially in the MEB workshop. Whilst cleaning the front of a TV cathode ray tube, rubbing it could generate a good deal of static electricity, but the person doing the rubbing felt nothing – as long as he was standing on a rubber mat. Any unsuspecting ear which happened to be within reach, and of course unprotected by the rubber mat, ran the risk of being tweaked by Joe's supercharged finger. The resulting squeal would be more than matched by Joe's shrieks of laughter.

He also took wicked pleasure in secretly recording the neighbours when they called round to gossip about each other. There were sometimes some red faces during their tittle-tattle when they would suddenly hear other previously recorded voices that were gossiping about *them*, as Joe played his tapes loudly down the stairs.

Over the next three years, life at the MEB continued in much the same shade of rosy red. During his time in the RAF he had experimented with disc-cutters, and now – thanks to the good old MEB – he was able to add another string to his bow by building his own. During the summer of '53 he cut his first record: a selection of sound effects. Producing the disc came as the high point of a period when life was going more his way than ever before. Here he was, a young man on the threshold of his career, free of responsibilities and a life laid out invitingly before him; he had a secure job which allowed scope for his own interests, and his skill at repairing electrical equipment assured him of a future in which he would never be short of work. He was popular in Newent and he was popular at the MEB and life had never been so good. But it was not to last.

Towards the end of '53, the icing on the MEB cake began to crack. He started suspecting people in the MEB shop of talking about him behind his back. He was also out-growing the firm, and his outside activities were demanding more and more of his time. What he could not fit into business hours he worked on at home – usually late into the night – so he was still asleep when the early bus to work went by. In the MEB workshop the way in which the hours were spent between clocking in and clocking out was of less concern to the management than the actual clocking-in and out itself. One thing they would not tolerate was bad time-keeping, and arriving for work at 10.15a.m. instead of 7.45 a.m. was precisely that, whatever the excuse. Mr. North at Currys had always understood the need for an extra pair of hands at the dairy, but at the MEB such an explanation drew a frosty response. As he got later, so their faces grew grimmer, until he was finally hauled before the front office and issued with an ultimatum: "Either get here on time or get another job." He chose the latter.

His next stop was Gloucester's largest electrical firm, Broadmeads. But the work here was not at all to his liking and as soon as he arrived he resolved to leave as soon as possible. He found himself on the road more now than ever before, and once they had pressed him into taking a driving test he was for the first time out servicing on his own, which pleased him even less.

Meanwhile his spare time disc-cutting activities were getting more ambitious. He had started recording local dance bands, and during the summer of '54 took a big jump forward when he cut his first vocal record. It featured a Newent schoolgirl, Marlene Williams, who was later to become Eric's wife. She sang along to a version of 'Secret Love' – one he may have recorded earlier by a troupe called the Melody Dance Band. He was so excited with the result – enhanced by an echo device he had built into a tape recorder – that he played it over and over at that year's summer fete, and like his other records he would turn it up full blast out of his bedroom window. He even sent it up for release to a record company, but unsurprisingly it was rejected, so there was no escaping Broadmeads yet.

However, pressure was mounting. After all these years he was still being teased and laughed at for not being manly enough, and had yet to find anyone with whom to share a close relationship. Besides that, he was facing competition on the disc jockeying front from two local men whom he saw as encroaching on his territory. Things reached boiling point one day when they all turned up at the same venue, provoking a scuffle on the vicar's lawn.

Then in the autumn of '54 the luckiest thing that could have happened did, when he skidded his van into a telegraph pole and ended up through the back and in the road with a pile of smashed TV sets. The accident left him unhurt but did give him the kick in the pants he needed to take a whole new initiative. Here he was wasting the best part of every day traipsing around the town and countryside fixing the same old televisions and radios as he had done since Currys in '50. His burgeoning quest to produce a commercially viable record was being hindered severely and he was now sick of the sight of valves and spare parts. He felt he was in effect being paid to waste his life and if that were the case they might as well give him his £50,000 now and lock him up for the rest of his days. He had to act at once or he would be with Broadmeads till he had knocked down every pole in Gloucester. The recording of 'Secret Love' had shown him where his main aims lay and he had to find some way of channelling all his energies in that direction. One thing was for sure: he was not going to find it at Broadmeads. In fact the only place that had any hope of fulfilling his dreams was that distant Utopia that had been beckoning for years and whose attraction was now irresistible – London.

An advert placed by a film studio in one of the national newspapers was offering posts in its London dubbing room, so he applied. He could use it as a stepping-stone till something better came along, so he caught the train up and passed the interview. Returning home in somewhat sombre spirits he told his family of his good fortune, trying to convince himself of it. It was a gamble. Supposing things didn't work out as planned, who would there be to turn to? He didn't know a soul, and it looked like being a re-run of the lonely radar days. For a shy young man uprooting himself from the country it was a fair step to take. On the bus coming back from work that last week he met their neighbour Mrs. Dallow, who says he still needed reassuring:

"I said, 'Oh, hallo Joe.'

He said, 'Hallo. I won't be doing this trip much longer. I'm off to London.'

I said, 'You're not are you, Joe?'

He said, 'I am, I've taken a job. Do you think I shall get on all right?'

I said, 'Yes of course you'll get on all right. What about your digs, because I've got a sister in London and she'd be only too pleased to put you up if you like?'

He said, 'Oh no. They're arranging all that for me.'

So I said, 'You don't want to worry, Joe. If you don't like it you can easily pack it in.'

He said, 'Well, I'm used to the open country; I like country life. I don't think I'm going to like all this busy life. I'm awfully worried about it. I don't think I shall settle down to it.'

I said, 'You'll get used to it. What's more, next time you'll be coming home in a Rolls-Royce.'"

Broadmeads were sorry to see him go and told him he could come back any time he liked. He left with mixed feelings; it was good to be finishing with repairing but then again, was the devil he knew better than the devil he didn't?

He thought of London with its car-clogged streets and forests of office blocks. It seemed a cold place: all those people, all those faces. It was like another world compared with Newent; beautiful Newent: the town he loved so much, with its friendly people, its Market Square, its woods, its May Hill, its sunshine, its rain and its memories; its jeers and sneers throughout his life and petty, pointed fingers; its failure to accept him as he was. Would they never understand? When it came to the crunch, all the work he'd put in, all the time sacrificed just counted for nothing. He still didn't fit in. He should have gone years ago as he'd once said he would.

Yes, it was indeed time to move on. This was the moment he had been waiting for and no way would he let it slip by now. At last he was in the mood to take his future by the throat and really show them, and nothing else mattered. The past ten months of deepening frustration had charged his dynamos up to full power and he was now ready to take London by storm. And even if the pavements were not paved with gold – damn it, they soon would be.

3
"His Job Of Balancing Was Out Of This World"

e caught the train to Paddington, and made his way to Queensborough Terrace, Bayswater, where the firm had found him a bed-sitter.

No amount of research has been able to trace who or where the firm was, nor did Joe have much to say about it: "I came to London and took a job for one week in a film-dubbing room, which I must say I disliked because there was nothing creative in it, and I left this to take a job in Stone's radio shop in Edgware Road." That meant TV servicing: back on the old treadmill again. How he must have felt is obvious, itching to find a foothold in the music industry, and getting no further than the back of a TV set. The one consolation was that the job was in London and paid the rent. In the meantime it was a matter of sitting it out at Stone's till something better turned up, and he had to gnaw his nails for two months before it did. But when it came, it was a bonanza!

One day he spotted a newspaper advert in which a company called Television Commercials (TVC) were looking for TV engineers. The main point of interest was that TVC were part of a larger organization called IBC, the Independent Broadcasting Company, who just happened to be the country's leading recording studios – ahead of even EMI and Decca. So, even if they were only after people to fix TV sets, it could still be a starting-block.

When he called round to their offices opposite Broadcasting House in Portland Place, he found they were in fact running a closed-circuit TV set-up and far from fixing TVs he would be operating film projectors. He got the job.

And so it was that he finally put his days as a repair man behind him once and for all. At last he let go of the apron string security of televisions and radios and set off on an adventure into the world of popular music: a world that seven years hence would be beating a path to his door.

Right now though, he was still beating a path to theirs because technically TVC had nothing whatever to do with music. It had been set up for the coming of commercial television and he was asked to run 16mm footage of American commercials to give British advertisers ideas for when ITV started. The facilities were not exactly breathtaking – just a few pokey rooms round the back with some bits and pieces of crude tele-cine equipment. The skill required was minimal for what was no more than a glorified projectionist, but if he could only bide his time . . .

Then after three weeks, out of the blue came an offer to join the staff on one of the Radio Luxembourg Road Shows: *People Are Funny*. Variety shows were recorded every week by IBC and were held in theatres up and down the country for broadcasting later on Luxembourg. This one, sponsored by Pye Radio, was Radio Luxembourg's top show and could also lay claim to being the first ever programme in Britain to actively involve the audience. His first assignment was at Bradford: "I went as the junior engineer and had to rig the microphones and run the cables, but I really enjoyed every minute of it. Well of course, the following Wednesday I sat up waiting for the programme to come on the air . . ." What followed was a frivolous mish-mash, with contestants on the show being expected to do daft things and dress up in ridiculous costumes, for which nonsense they would earn rapturous applause and prizes.

Thus after 25 years of hardly going anywhere he suddenly found himself being catapulted off everywhere, to all corners of the isle and with a pretty tight schedule: – Saturday: travel to the theatre and rig the equipment; Sunday afternoon: rehearse; in the evening: record the show; Monday: bring the tape back to edit; Tuesday: have the master recording ready. Then if he wasn't by that time sick of hearing it, he could sit back and listen to it being broadcast the following week.

When he had arrived back from Bradford it was to learn the art of editing: cutting out any stutters and splutters, then trimming it down to half an hour. The following Saturday it was the same routine again but the next show at Plymouth was different because he was promoted to the dizzy heights of control engineer and manning the machinery. For this he would proudly receive a mention from the commentator before each show, plus a round of applause from the audience as well as his photo in the March '55 edition of *Gramophone Record Review*. And the Joe Meek machine was still gathering momentum because after the programme had been edited: "I was put on some pop recording sessions. The first one I believe was for Pye; it was a Ted Hockridge record." Although it was not a position of responsibility, in the studio it made him officially a junior engineer.

"HIS JOB OF BALANCING WAS OUT OF THIS WORLD"

Now as he looked back over the past couple of months he could thank his lucky stars that things had gone well after all. Taking the plunge and coming to London had indeed been the right decision, for no longer was he throwing away precious time but being paid to do something creative with his life. And it certainly beat knocking down telegraph poles.

After that first Edmund Hockridge recording, the excitement began easing up. If his progress had carried on unhindered he might well have been IBC's managing director before the year was out! Instead he continued as a control engineer on the Luxembourg Road Shows, whilst back at IBC where studio work was far more complex his status was limited to that of 'tape monkey' (junior engineer).

Just now he had quite enough on his plate with *People Are Funny*, and took the job very seriously: "Of course, this was a great honour for me and I really did work extremely hard to keep the standard of recording up, which at times was extremely difficult." There were only two tape recorders: one to play the music and one to tape the show, and in the words of one of Joe's assistants, Adrian Kerridge, "It was a few Ball & Biscuit microphones and a few old drums of cable that would fall apart. It wasn't very technical."

Joe would have gnashed his teeth at that last remark for even if the equipment was in the last stage of rigor mortis, the show still got his full commitment. And he could be very difficult if he thought others were not giving theirs. Another of his assistants was Jimmy Lock, nowadays Recording Manager of the Classical Music Department at Decca, who worked with him on many shows and sometimes found the going rough: "It was nerve-racking to work with Joe because his demands of his expertise were so good – his ability to be able to keep the atmosphere of that show alive. If you didn't punch the music in at the right time you'd have a hell of a night at dinner because he would never let you forget it. But although his moods were sometimes purgatory to go through, it did set one's standards for the future, which at the time I didn't appreciate so much, but I certainly do now on reflection. I did go on other shows with other engineers and it was a much more easy laissez-affaire with them."

Joe occasionally found himself switched to other Luxembourg shows which were recorded during the week in London: *This Is Your Life* and *Strike It Rich* with Eamonn Andrews, *The Winifred Atwell Show*, *The Petula Clark Show*, *Sing-Song Time* and *The Candid Microphone*, and this enabled him to go home for the weekend.

THE LEGENDARY JOE MEEK

During the summer it was off to the Butlin's Holiday Camps for the talent show *When You're Smiling*, forerunner to TV's *Opportunity Knocks*, for which the winner could collect "This magnificent Pye table radio with five valves, three wave bands giving worldwide choice of stations and a host of other exclusive Pye features in the most handsome cabinet you've ever seen."

However as the months slipped by, the novelty of leaping around the country was fast fading and the old frustration returning. Once the show was in the bag he would be detailed to assist any one of IBC's half dozen balance engineers on their musical sessions before being bundled off again to some grotty little theatre in Barnsley or Aberdeen or wherever. He much preferred musical work but being a tape monkey, placing microphones where he was told and winding a reel-to-reel back and forth, was not satisfying his hunger to create and he was learning enough to now feel ready for a go himself. He longed for the job of senior engineer on a studio recording to show the world what he was made of, but there had been some recent changes in management, and Joe as sound-balance engineer did not figure in the plans of IBC's new Studio Manager, Allen Stagg. So he started petitioning the various producers with whom he worked to prevail upon Allen to give him a chance. One of them was independent producer Arthur Frewin: "I kept on to Allen saying, 'Look, why don't you give him a job – put him on balancing?' And he'd say, 'Some time.' And of course, when we had this big session at Conway Hall, Joe turned up to do it. We had a very expensive orchestra there. It was for an LP called 'Film Themes', arranged and conducted by Alyn Ainsworth. We had a complete showband brass; we had top rhythm: Bill McGuffie on piano and really top people on it and a 20-piece string section led by Freddie Sverdloff who was recognized throughout the country as the top string leader. It was a beautiful orchestra. And Joe had never engineered a session in his life. I thought, 'Oh, no!' It was Allen's way of shutting me up. I think he thought that it would stop Joe dead in his tracks; it didn't suit his book at that particular time from a personnel point of view. It was fantastic! Joe's job of balancing was out of this world and the musicians applauded the playback. Joe was over the Moon. We all went out and got drunk. The American financier who was over here for the record took us all out to dinner. We just talked and talked and talked about every track all over dinner. And Joe was so really pleased, not bumptious or anything like that, but he was really humbly pleased that he'd done it. His first one, and it was a big one and it was a good one."

That same month, October, keeping him high on Cloud Nine was his promotion to a senior balance engineer with a pay rise to £10 a week. Now he was more difficult to ignore. In between Road Shows he had more recordings including another big LP session. This time it was with the famous all female Ivy Benson Orchestra and was called 'Music For Lonely Lovers', for which incidentally, thirty years later Miss Benson was still patiently waiting to be paid! The best tracks of this particular session and that first one Joe had done were eventually put together under the fictitious name of the Mark Andrews Orchestra. Unfortunately, the LP was released on the American Gala label which promptly collapsed and the chances of Miss Benson, who spent hundreds of pounds on arrangements, or any of its other debtors being paid now are slim to say the least. Patience may be a virtue, but virtue can hurt you.

Then a few months later in April '56, he really came of age when he was responsible for the first jazz record to reach the Top Twenty in Britain. He was roped in on a session for independent jazz producer Denis Preston, and it was with one track of Humphrey Lyttelton's band that he made everyone sit up.

It was called 'Bad Penny Blues' and technically, not officially, it was also his first professional job in the capacity of producer. Combining the job of producer with that of sound-balance engineer is very difficult. It means dealing with intricate sounds and levels whilst at the same time directing the overall production, but as Denis Preston points out, Joe managed it well: "It was just sheer chance. We were supposed to have a 5-piece band, and the saxophone player had to leave before the end of the session – had a gig. So we're left with four guys: Humph on trumpet and three rhythm. So what can we do? We had a deadline, so I said, 'Well the best thing is – play the blues. What about one of those Harry James-type things, Humph, like 'Boo Woo'?' And it worked out a sort of boogie-woogie thing. I don't think, with due respect to the musicians, that it was the music we made. I think it was Joe's concept. He had a drum sound – that forward drum sound which no other engineer at that time would have conceived of doing, with echo. And it was the sound that Joe Meek created that made that record for Humphrey Lyttelton." It is also noteworthy for being one of the first instances where he applied the artificial effect of compressing-limiting. Used far more heavily than usual it gave the record extra boost, both soundwise, making it more forceful than other discs of the time, and chartwise where it reached the No.19 spot in July. [2]

♩♩♩♩♩♩♩♩♩♩♩♩♩♩♩

It might be assumed from this lengthy discourse on Joe's musical activities that he was having little in the way of social life, and that was indeed the case. His work was music, his hobby was music, he ate, drank and slept music; and when all those hours in the day were added up it was just about time to start again. His life was music. As far as anything else was concerned it was rarely more adventurous than the occasional meal out or a visit to the pictures to see a musical or horror film, and even then he had to be with someone or he would not bother going. Every few months he would catch the train home for some sanity and fresh air, fix a few radios, maybe wire up a dance, record a bird in a tree and catch the train back again. One of the main reasons why there was so little time to spare outside the music world was that there was such a vast array of attractions within it, and the big one at the moment was putting his gloss on potential hit records.

Not long after 'Bad Penny Blues' he spread the icing on the cake with one of the biggest selling records that year. This one was Anne Shelton's account of a soldier returning home to his sweetheart: 'Lay Down Your Arms'. To listeners the song was memorable for its stomping military beat, an ingredient which helped make it one of Miss Shelton's favourite sessions: "We had lots of laughs. We did a couple of rehearsals for balance and then the producer, Johnny Franz, decided that we needed marching feet and my husband who was also in the control box, suggested they went down to the Wellington Barracks to bring some soldiers back and have them marching up and down in the studio, and Joe said, 'And I'll make the tea!' Of course, we all started laughing and then he said, 'I can give you the effect of marching feet,' to which Johnny Franz replied, 'Yes, we can get a record or tape.' Joe said, 'No no, I can get you the same effect that you would get on the radio of real marching men.' Then he came back in with a box of gravel and someone [Adrian Kerridge] stood behind me shaking this box backwards and forwards. We did two takes and when the thing was finished the new black suit I was wearing was

"HIS JOB OF BALANCING WAS OUT OF THIS WORLD"

covered in white dust which had come out of the box."

Chartwise alongside 'Lay Down Your Arms' some very interesting things were happening. Since the War the music scene had been dominated by American artistes like Frankie Laine, Johnnie Ray, Doris Day, Frank Sinatra and Rosemary Clooney. This year America was still hogging the bestsellers but along with all the mushy ballads, it was now sending over the brand-new, red hot rock'n'roll. Bill Haley had started all the shaking back in '53 when he blended country'n'western with rhythm'n'blues on 'Crazy Man Crazy', and since then had recorded the first disc ever to sell a million in Britain and which triggered off the greatest upheaval in the history of popular music: 'Rock Around The Clock'. This year saw the meteoric rise to the top for Elvis Presley and the emergence of quite a few other contenders for the rock'n'roll crown. During Anne Shelton's month at No.1, Bill Haley had no less than five entries in the Top Twenty and Elvis had just gone out with two and come back in again with another. Meanwhile, all that we in Britain could muster were a few ballads from the likes of Dickie Valentine, David Whitfield, Alma Cogan and Jimmy Young – most of which were cover versions of American songs anyway – a piano medley or two from Winifred Atwell and the occasional Ying Tong Song. But we also had skiffle.

With all the energy and excitement flooding from Bill Haley's comet, the British music scene in '55 had turned for inspiration to a banjo player from Chris Barber's Jazz Band – Lonnie Donegan. Absurdly enough, even with skiffle we still couldn't get away from the Americans because they were the ones who invented it. It first appeared on the American jazz scene in New Orleans where it was played by poor blacks to pay the rent. A man behind on his rent payments would buy some beer and invite his friends round for a 'rent party' for which he would charge an admission fee. To make the party go with a swing the guests made instruments from combs and paper, stone jars and anything they could lay their hands on; words were added and that was skiffle. Thirty years later Donegan dusts off an old Leadbelly number called 'Rock Island Line' and skiffle is the greatest thing in England since false teeth. It was immediately dubbed the 3-chord-trick, because playing three chords on a guitar was the basic requirement to form a group. The rest was DIY with the rhythm section supplied by mother's washboard and the local grocer's tea-chest with a broomstick and string attached.

For the time being though, Donegan had that portion of the

33

market to himself. While everyone else was busy learning their three chords he was busy playing them, and to the tune of five Top Twenty singles and an American Top Ten hit. None of them so far had been engineered by Joe, but there were several on the way. In the meantime Joe found himself working with: Petula Clark, Shirley Bassey, Dennis Lotis, Lita Roza, Cleo Laine, Alma Cogan, Gary Miller, Harry Secombe, jazz singer Betty Miller, popular pianists Stanley Black, Winifred Atwell and Joe Henderson, classical pianist Daniel Abrams, the Eric Delaney Band, the Ted Heath Orchestra and Geraldo & his Orchestra.

Another big seller to be chalked up was with the young up-and-coming Frankie Vaughan and was called 'Green Door'. It actually started off on the B-side but proved so popular with disc jockeys that they ignored the other side. Suffice to say that anyone liking the 1981 version by Shakin' Stevens should try giving Frankie Vaughan's a spin.

It was now unbelievably only eleven months that he had been engineering music, but he had taken to it like a duck to water and was getting better fast. He was turning out to be rather more than an engineer who could do an adequate job and throw in a gimmicky sound effect for good measure. He had an understanding of popular music and what made it commercial; he realized that songs could not always depend on a good tune selling them and often needed something extra to grab the listener's attention. This was what some producers were quick to latch onto and the smart ones saw the producer in him trying to break out and used him as an ally like a producer's assistant.

Big commercial productions such as 'Green Door' and 'Lay Down Your Arms' owed some of their success to what can best be described as his revolutionary recording approach. He would try anything. If every other sound engineer in the world had told him, "You can't *do* that," he would have replied, "Can't I? Listen." As Arthur Frewin explains, he knew what he was after and was not going to let out-dated methods of recording stop him getting it: "He loved music, he loved sound and creating new sounds. And very often in the studio after a run-through you'd say, 'That's great, Joe.' He'd say, 'Look, I've just had an idea, can we have another run-through?' And he would create it there and get a fantastic sound. All of a sudden something clicked in his mind and he'd get, say, twenty strings sounding like sixty strings sometimes. And he'd come out with ideas which nobody else had at the time – well ahead of his time, Joe, soundwise, well ahead of his time. He'd have all sorts of ideas: throwing echoes in, but he knew how to control echo and make it work for him. Loved to put a microphone next to every instrument, but it couldn't always work, though; he loved to pick out instruments in the orchestra. A most creative man . . . He'd get a sound in his head and he would work and work until he got that sound. Some producers at that time didn't like it; they wanted bang, bang, bang – in and out. They couldn't understand what the man was after because half of them didn't know what the bloody hell they were doing, quite frankly. But he knew what he wanted. If you had the patience with Joe he'd get the most marvellous sounds for you; if you wanted the regular, routine stuff as most producers did he'd get it but he didn't like doing it. He'd need one or two run-throughs, then he'd play it back – 'What do you think of that?' Sometimes you had to say, 'No Joe, that's not what I'm looking for.' It *usually* enhanced it."

Nowadays there are all sorts of wonder-working gadgets to make a record more commercial, but in the mid-Fifties there was little scope. In fact the little that was available was largely frowned upon anyway because the English school of thought was such that except for adding a tiny touch of echo, editing out a few bum notes and using an equaliser to control the tone and a limiter to limit the dynamic range, all the commerciality should be in the performance itself. Consequently British pop records of the period were usually 'roomy'.

In those days before multi-track recording techniques, the whole record had to be made at once and went straight onto single mono-track tape. So nearly everything had to be done during the actual session – spending weeks and weeks on 'mixing' was ten years away! Amazingly, it was common practice to use one microphone for several instruments, so there was not much variation between 'live' and studio sounds. Joe on the other hand arrived on the scene ready to fabricate recordings from the ground up, so that the sound coming out of the equipment was very different from the one going in. His own pronouncement was that there should be more echo and limiting on pop songs and far more microphones set out.[3]

After the session, if he was not happy with what he had on tape he would sometimes finish off with limiters and compressors. These act as an automatic volume control, making all the quiet bits louder and the loud bits quieter; so this way he could quite correctly make shrill soprano singers less piercing and make up-tempo pieces more exciting. This however led him to discover a rather less orthodox means of generating excitement into the record. By simply turning up the power he could make the recording loud all the way through. And then, going even further down the path of unrighteousness, he found he could use the limiter not only as a machine to hold the level up but as a musical instrument itself! All he had to do was put it into overdrive and he could then induce distortion, forcing the music out like sausages with a 'woomph-woomph' pumping sound. This of course was not at all what they were built for, but he didn't mind that a bit.

However, he also had the sense to realize that pop techniques were not always suitable. On the contrary, Harry Secombe's classical arias and many big 40-piece, middle-of-the-road records with the Laurie Johnson Orchestra were another matter entirely. Out went the novelty attention-grabbing gimmicks and in came a natural richness of sound. The sound he much admired and used as a yardstick was the one he heard on the Capitol label featuring the work of the Nelson Riddle Orchestra. By using a minimum of microphones to lift just a few instruments here and there he was able to measure up to Riddle's sound without copying it. It was no mean achievement.

But life was not easy. He now wanted to devote all his energy to music but that was impossible when three or four days each week were often lost on Luxembourg shows. Road Shows and music had to go hand in hand and made for a pretty hectic life, especially since he often worked on days off. The studios were not booked solid but when the engineers were busy they were like ants at a picnic, and with all the repertoire of Pye and most of the independent companies to cater for, plus surplus sessions for Decca, Philips and EMI, an 18-hour day was common.[4] In those early days there was no overtime pay either, but apparently the engineers were so happy in their work they didn't care!

Such an industrious climate might have been good for breeding success, but for Joe it was also breeding enemies.

4
"Rotten Pigs! Trying To Take My Secrets"

over versions were made at the speed of sound. Everyone was copying American records, so the trick was to rush your own version into the shops before the original arrived and before anyone else had the same idea, and that meant getting the skates on. Last minute sessions were sometimes held at 9 o'clock at night for a song hot from the publisher's; then at midnight the tape was raced down to the disc-cutting room; two hours later it was cut and off to the factory to be on their doorstep that morning and on sale twenty-four hours later.

The question of cover versions was one that bothered him a lot and was one that cropped up often. There was a strange situation at IBC since more than one record company were using their facilities. He could be recording one artiste with one song in the afternoon whilst in the evening he could very well find himself doing the same song all over again with another artiste. This was bound to happen when he was becoming increasingly sought after but once when it did, he kicked up such a stink that the job was handed over to someone else. That was after recording the Gary Miller version of 'Garden Of Eden' for Pye, complete with his own personal thunderclap, and being asked by Philips to do the same again with Frankie Vaughan. In future he would just have to grit his teeth and do it. But it was always an important matter of principle to him, and made no easier by his showing favouritism towards some producers; so he was hardly likely to revel in working closely with one producer to achieve a particular sound only to hand it all over to the next one who walked through the door. It was tantamount to trading secrets with the Russians, and the number of secrets he now had up his sleeve was swelling. People were intrigued by his use of echo and limiting and they had to stay intrigued. "Rotten pigs!" he would say. "Trying to take my secrets."

This attitude won him no sweet smiles from the boss, Allen Stagg, and not much in the way of honeyed phrases either: "The guiding force in Joe's life was selfishness; he was ruthless in his selfishness. He could never ever work as a team man. It was essential at IBC that people were very team-minded because it was necessary for everybody's success to be able to rely on somebody else, and Joe was a loner. You could never rely on Joe to do the right thing in the essence of teamwork; Joe would only look after himself – entirely selfish person. I met his mother during one of our annual Open Days and she was very interested in a motherly way. He was naturally very proud to be showing her what he was doing, but that was the only hint I ever had that he didn't exist solely for himself. I could never describe Joe as a nice person because he was much too selfish and he became virtually impossible to deal with as he became more successful. He wanted me to lock studios and I absolutely and downright refused. When he'd set up ready for a session he wanted nobody to go in there at all and I said, 'Don't be so bloody ridiculous.' It would be while he went out to lunch or had a bit of time in between then and the recording session. He'd say, 'I want the studio locked,' and I'd say, 'Well you're not damn well having it locked.' And of course, I wouldn't allow him to stay in the studio and keep everyone else away. He had to understand that if a member of staff wanted to go in and discuss anybody's session, they always had to be free to do so. That was the atmosphere I tried to create and I wasn't having Joe destroy that."

This kind of reaction to Joe's one-man-band style can also be explained rather differently. Success in one person often breeds resentment in others, and when that person starts squirrelling away secrets he is bound to be branded selfish by someone. And that word selfishness can easily be used to misrepresent self-preservation. It should not be forgotten that the music business is the biggest rat-race of them all. If an engineer establishes himself he will be in demand; if other engineers know his ideas, they will too. Allen Stagg was right – up to a point. The fact that he was maintaining IBC's reputation as Britain's Number One recording studios was no small achievement, for unlike the other giants the company could not afford to sit back and rely on its equipment to see it through. IBC was being run on a shoestring and therefore depended upon his influence over the staff in insisting on flair and fine quality. Moreover, it improved engineers' performances working in an independent studio where they were competing with each other, and if a client walked in saying he didn't want so and so, then that engineer did not get the job nor perhaps the salary increase later, and was relegated to something like a Road Show.

Allen Stagg was meticulous to a degree in preserving standards and tip-top efficiency. But he was no innovator and it was unfortunate that his orthodox teamwork approach allowed little room for individuals, however brilliant they might be. Also high on his list of grievances were Joe's lengthy sojourns of experimenting: such a practice was fine in small doses (maybe twice daily before meals) but not something to get hooked on: "Joe would be there all hours. Now this was rather difficult for me because I used to actively encourage people to do experimental work. But I used to rely on people being above board enough not to do it financially at the studios' expense. He had to convince me he was furthering his own experience instead of his own pocket. I couldn't say I was convinced he was doing this, but I was as sure as hell suspicious." In order to guard against any of the tape monkeys picking up Joe's wicked ways he impressed upon them that "Joe Meek is a shining example of what you must never be." Two Joe Meeks at IBC would have been just too much of a good thing.

And there was something else about Joe that Allen couldn't stomach. It was apparent to some people that Joe had a slightly effeminate manner, and to those he trusted he was now openly admitting being homosexual. It's worth mentioning that although in today's freer-thinking society homosexuality has a moderate acceptance, in the mid-Fifties it did not. There were another ten years to go before the public would even consider the prospect of 'gay liberation'. Until then any person of that ilk who did not conceal it stuck out like a knife in the back and was liable to suffer all sorts of traumas: either from general persecution or from the knowledge that even homosexual acts in private constituted a criminal offence, one carrying a maximum *life* sentence.

His mild manner and soft, medium-pitched voice often suggested a girlishness about him, and this was further hinted at by the care he took in his appearance. Much time outside was spent combing his hair in doorways and shop windows, and his face was so closely shaved that it looked like the hairs had been plucked out. (He had up to half a dozen electric shaves a day.) As for any shiny noses, they would disappear under a touch of pancake make-up as they always had done since his RAF days. But despite these little idiosyncrasies and the strong scent of after-shave that followed him around, nothing was ever blatantly obvious until he lost his temper and let rip with all the elegance of a Portuguese washerwoman. He had accepted where his proclivities lay when recently moving lodgings to share a large room at 15 Leinster Gardens, Bayswater with Lional Howard, a young fellow of similar age and persuasion. Usually he locked such matters away with his host of other secrets but was not afraid to confide in those he thought more open-minded. In fact he once brought into work some photos of the athletically bare-chested Lional, and was quick to point out that their relationship was no secondary substitute for the real thing but something in its own right.

He had only become fully aware of himself on leaving Newent for the first time to join the RAF and meet others in common with himself. Still coming to terms with his sexuality, he was far from happy about it. In one open-hearted moment whilst travelling by train to record for Luxembourg, he told a colleague how he desperately wished he were "normal" and could lead an ordinary domestic life; how he would like a home with a loving wife and children. The one tragic thing he said that stood in his way was that women did not appeal to him. The nearest he had arrived to marital bliss was in co-habiting with Lional, a weight-lifting chef. Generally they got on splendidly together, though as individuals they had a few contrasts: Joe, average height, burly build, totally music-orientated; Lional, waltzing in tall and trim "stinking of kitchens". Never did Lional interfere in Joe's musical activities, preferring instead tactfully taking a back seat and playing the role of onlooker while Joe busied around with his bits and pieces in their ever-shrinking bed-sitter. He was fascinated by it all and Joe valued his opinion, but it was elsewhere that Lional really came into his own. The flamboyant humorist in him relished attention and made him the life and soul of any socializing they did. It would also get him scolded by Joe for embarrassing him in public because despite Joe being assertive inside his own environment, he was still reserved outside it. Many were the vitriolic tempers Joe would unleash on him, but Lional's admirable composure in times of stormy weather was the best of tranquillizers and usually saved the day. Lional could be hilariously funny and possessed the invaluable ability to make Joe break down with laughter in the middle of a temper; then no matter how much Joe strove to regain his rage he would just find himself coming unstuck again laughing. So Lional would merely sit back, the picture of innocence, while Joe battled his way through a staccato series of angry giggles.

Lional was actually the first really close friend he had ever had and certainly did him a power of good by not only providing slap-up cuisine but security and companionship, and the latter to Joe was gold dust. There was a great deal of warmth in their friendship and nearly always when Joe went away on the Road Shows he would bring back a small present like a watch or souvenir. Lional was well worth it and, although the same age as Joe, looked after him in an almost motherly way.

Although Joe's personal life was now much improved, there were still deep discomforts. The general public attitude towards him and his particular situation was not so dissimilar to the one he had left behind at Newent. He had hoped Londoners would be more open-minded, and indeed they were more so than the insular country folk back home, but not enough. As for the well-known claim of the music business that the love of making music is the great leveller that transcends all barriers, be they of class, creed, race or whatever: it sounds fine in theory but in practice, at least during the Fifties, it fell somewhat short of expectations. He found to his anguish he was still getting the "whispering in corners and looking over the shoulder" treatment. Help and advice were offered by like-minded people, of whom the Arts attract an extra high proportion, but no one could reconcile him to accepting prejudice or criticism of any kind. He was upset most, as assistant engineer Jimmy Lock recalls, when he heard about it indirectly: "When it came to what was being said behind his back, that's the one thing that he couldn't tolerate. It used to drive him crazy. If somebody said something and he heard it secondhand by somebody else, whether derogatory about his work or home life or anything else, this used to freak him out. He was in the wrong slot at the wrong time. There's no doubt about it that there was a certain madness always within Joe – there's no question. This delicate balance between Joe in a happy mood and Joe just becoming impossible was a thin thread."

The manager kept an eye open for any possible misdemeanours in the studios, and his thorough dislike of homosexuality made him doubly watchful: "Although Joe was always at first glance effeminate he was too shy a person to flaunt this around. I would have called Joe effeminate but not outrageously so: little girlish. Certainly he wasn't a raving poof. But if he fancied somebody, then he wanted them to work with him. This was the problem. I had issued instructions to change second engineers quite frequently; it was a good thing to change people around so that they didn't get set in bad habits. There was constant trouble about his assistants: 'I don't want him.' Great sort of scenes about: 'Joe doesn't want me to work with him on sessions.' Joe would absolutely and utterly ignore somebody he didn't want to work with. I had these sort of things once or twice a week. I would get to know of it when somebody would say to me: 'Allen, can you go down to Studio A, I think Joe's got his periods.' And so I'd go down and there Joe would be – all flushed and angry. As he got more and more experienced, he became more and more impossible".

It is worth hearing how other contemporaries saw the situation: Alan A. Freeman, producer, Pye-Nixa Records: "Although I was aware of his effeminate outlook I never found it interfered with his work, which was always of an inventive and highly professional standard." Arthur Frewin, independent producer: "His mind never ever wandered on my sessions – he was a complete professional." Ray Prickett, senior engineer: "There was no indication or any sort of embarrassing situation at all in the studio; he was quite well behaved in that sense." Denis Preston, independent producer: "All I can say and Adrian [Kerridge] . . . that as far as we were concerned, that was his personal life which never intruded on his business life, on his professional life, on his creative life."

Allen Stagg's statement can be partly explained by Adrian Kerridge who nowadays, as one of Britain's leading sound engineers, is running the well-known Lansdowne Studios and was then assisting Joe over half of the time: "On the sessions that I worked with him he was very highly temperamental. But he was also very talented and it was artistic temperament rather than any other area. In that day and age homosexuality was strictly taboo and I think there were a lot of people at IBC that had blinkers on and therefore they would perhaps look for some meaning that wasn't there. Joe never approached me; never once did he make an approach. I think there was a lot of prejudice towards Joe and he'd make the scenes because he couldn't get some technical thing. Somebody would antagonize him – they'd know he wanted to use a piece of equipment in the 'Assembly Room' – for example, a compressor which he needed on his session; perhaps somebody else would use it and Joe would say, 'Well I've booked it.' I remember scenes like that. People would actually go out of their way to make life obstructive for Joe, and therefore he would create an artistic scene because he didn't have the tools of the trade, which were very limited in those days. 'Those rotten pigs!' he'd say."

Other times he blew his top at producers, especially those who hadn't got a clue. They were then called A & R men (Artistes &

Repertoire – the word producer had not yet been assigned) and some had got the job by simply being ex-musicians. Usually their forte was in matching the right song with the right artiste, but they were sometimes out of their depth finding not only songs and artistes but arrangers and engineers, and then producing the record. Naturally, such non-technical people were bound to make a few stupid decisions in the studio, and Joe was hardly likely to congratulate them on their incompetence.

As if being homosexual were not considered corrupt enough, he now started sinking deeper into the den of iniquity by meddling with studio equipment. All of it was built by Noah (or at least, one person thought so), but it was not there to be abused, which was the accusation being levelled at him. In the clean, clinical atmosphere which the management had created, knobs were not to be interfered with but left in the same position in which they were set. So the cheerful feeling he got from running around in the busy setting of an independent studio was all rather spoiled working in an environment where it was more like a hospital.[5]

As his success was growing he was pleased to find himself acquiring star status as IBC's biggest client puller and arguably their biggest hit-maker, if such a distinction could befall an engineer.

Allen Stagg was even less likely to invite Joe round for tea when he found his own position as one of Denis Preston's engineers usurped by that man again – Joe Meek. In the wake of Humphrey Lyttelton's 'Bad Penny Blues' success, Denis made it clear in no uncertain terms that there was only one engineer he wanted from now on, and it wasn't Allen Stagg. He told him that if his wish was not carried out he would take his custom elsewhere. So Allen, fully aware of Denis's importance as IBC's biggest independent client, wisely agreed. From this point on, unless Joe was already booked elsewhere, he engineered all Denis's sessions and there were plenty of them. It is no overstatement that Denis Preston was the king of British recorded jazz because the vast majority of it was filtering through him in the guise of such giants as Chris Barber, Ken Colyer, Alex Welsh and Humphrey Lyttelton.[6]

THE LEGENDARY JOE MEEK

As for Joe, such an impressive talent linked with such dedication and brazen contempt for rules and regulations could hardly fail to notch up a few firsts. In becoming Britain's first really contributive sound engineer, he was breaking new ground in recording methods all the time, and Denis Preston's comment some years later that "Joe had a concept of sound I really and sincerely think ten years ahead of its time" was already beginning to hold some truth. To the shocked disbelief of his colleagues he was actually recording sounds on top of one another and sticking microphones all over the place – even inside the musical instruments. Such unorthodox practices have since been hailed as important innovations, and one of his 'phasing' effects has been described as "the greatest thing in Heaven!"[7]

It did not however sound like Heaven to Allen Stagg, in whose books Joe Meek was scaling ever great heights of disapproval. "I don't think Joe was a good engineer. He was good enough and better than most when comparing with what EMI and Decca were able to do. He was an inveterate fiddler. He did it because he didn't know any better, which underlined my mistrust of him technically." Both men would regularly take it in turns to complain to each other about the state of Joe's Luxembourg Road Show equipment. It was often cracking up – valves make notoriously bad travellers – but the maintenance of it was not entirely Joe's responsibility, especially when he was so busy in the studio. He once arrived in Scotland to record the Jimmy Shand Band the next day, only to find that the tape recorder had broken down in transit. The "inveterate fiddler" stayed up all night fixing it and was able to bring back a first-class recording after the show.

But it irritated people that he would not toe the line and there were those around ready to make life hard for him. On top of that his temperament was worsening in direct proportion to his success, and he was indeed becoming very successful. This was clearly demonstrated by his wish to have his own way. At that time a recording engineer's job officially was to translate the producer's ideas into music and not make suggestions unless asked and certainly not to "have his own way". His influence if any was subtle, but Joe saw his role rather differently. Every engineer knows that even translating a producer's ideas should be an art form and it is one that can be likened to the art of acting, where there is only a certain amount of directing the actor can take and the rest is up to him – unless he prefers being a puppet. According to Arthur Frewin: "He'd annoy a producer by saying, 'Perhaps we should have one more take.' Probably the producer is watching his clock because he's on a budget, approaching overtime. Joe says, 'I really think we can get one in.' And the producer is saying, 'No Joe, sorry,' Joe turns and says, 'If you can't bloody well do the job right, don't do it.' The producer says, 'Look Joe, we haven't the time.' Joe says, "We can get one in in time if they all start now.' 'All right Joe, let's do it.' He'd get one more done: the best. They'd be pleased but they don't like being told because Joe was just there to press buttons."

And producers were not the only ones to feel the rough edge of his tongue, as Arthur Frewin continues: "He'd suddenly switch off and could be very cutting: 'That's the *fifth* time you've cracked that note!' he shouted at the lead trumpet. You don't say that to top brass. He knew what he wanted but there's a way to talk to them and you don't talk to them like that. You'd have a quiet walk in the studio, call the lead trumpet on one side and say, 'There's something wrong with the arrangement. We haven't got the pitch right.' Not Joe. 'That's the *fifth* time you've cracked that note!' He told the man off so everybody knew. It often happened. Joe was a perfectionist. To Joe, musicians were rebels. He treated them the way they treated the music. They came in, did the job – mechanically. I mean, they're fantastic musicians: they sight-read. It's showed up in front of them; never seen it before and they're 'beat' in and they play it. That's why they get all the work; they're playing the notes and they're doing their job. But it used to hurt Joe because it was a beautiful arrangement. And Joe'd say, 'You've got to feel it.' I remember him saying one day, 'That piece is marked MF – mit feeling!' . . . In fact he'd buy them a bottle of booze sometimes to get them in the mood. He'd try any gimmick to get them in the mood."

Those who had the hardest time were the tape monkeys and because of the pressure to which they were subjected, some refused to work with him. If he gave an order and the fellow's finger pressed the wrong button, then disaster struck and there was the devil to pay. The split second between pressing the right button and the wrong one was also the split second between one mood and the next, and engineers had to have the stamina not to be fazed by him or they would go under.

Meanwhile the Luxembourg shows were still trundling along. Now though, he was less involved because of big demand on the music side. On the occasions when he was called upon to sound-balance shows nearby at Conway Hall, he was only a stone's throw away from a café which his friend Lional was running, and he could pop in for fun and free meals. Always guaranteed to send him into fits of laughter were his candid tape recordings of the restaurant staff, especially those of the cashier. The trick was to hide the recorder out of sight and try to keep a straight face whilst niggling the poor woman into as bad a mood as possible, extracting from her what wrath one could before bursting a blood vessel fighting back the giggles.

One of his favourite pastimes was rummaging around markets, stocking up his electronic supplies. Having had to depend on a few secondhand shops in Gloucester for most of his life, in London there was suddenly a whole new range of junk available to him. And it was all brought within easy access by a rickety old Flying Standard he and Lional had bought for £35. There were also his two rooms over the dairy at Newent which were filled with as fine a selection of "rubbish" as one could hope to find anywhere, and every few months his mother's heart would leap for joy when he drove home to take some more away. He usually brought Lional along with him plus a boot full of gateaux and goodies, and would be received by his mother like some kind of prodigal son. No expense was spared in making his weekends as happy and comfortable as possible, and the pride she had in her son was there for all to see.

In London time out was never a strenuous affair and was for spending quietly in a restaurant or watching a film or show. As for sports, kicking a ball about offered all the fun of a day at the dentist. Sports were of course for others and though he still liked swimming he got his exercise thinking about it rather than doing it. Thinking was something he did a lot of on train journeys, and in between scribbling technical notes he dreamt of the future: of inventing some new gadget, of having his own recording studio, of being super-successful.

He was still basically the same old Joe. All the past characteristics were there: the soft Gloucester accent, the shyness, the warm-heartedness, the acute sensitivity to criticism and the resulting temper. And all the while the lone wolf was still there growling deep within. But his years in London had not passed without bringing a few changes.

Although he still loved a good joke and would laugh at the most insignificant things, he was losing some of the happy-go-lucky country boy charm that people had recognized in him at first. Taking its place was a much harder headed determination and mounting ambition. This was no doubt nourished on the amazingly fast and furious success he had so far achieved, but perhaps helped along by his realizing that the world was turning out to be a pretty tough place; things had not been easy this far and didn't look like getting any more so. Thankfully he had come some way to finding the two main things that were fundamentally important to his happiness, neither of which he could ever have found in Newent: friends to whom he could relate and the glittering promise of self-fulfilment.

Now in 1957 England found itself in the grip of skiffle fever and the undisputed leader was Lonnie Donegan. Joe had already engineered Donegan's 'Showcase' LP, the first British LP to reach the Top Thirty singles charts, and before the year was out would have had a hand in four other skiffle standards: 'Don't You Rock Me Daddy-O', 'Cumberland Gap', 'Gamblin' Man' and 'My Dixie Darling'. This last one was made in a British Legion Drill Hall at Plymouth, and to get some of his beloved echo into it he recorded the sound 'live' in the Gents' lavatory with a speaker at one end and a microphone at the other. Most of the skiffle records were turned out at full gallop, and Donegan's 'Cumberland Gap' was put together in such a rush – one run-through and one take in eight minutes – that there was barely time to tune the instruments . But the Donegan magic still took it to the top of the charts.[8]

By this time would-be Lonnie Donegans were springing up all over the place. Meanwhile Joe was still stuck in a bed-sitter wishing he had his own recording studio so he could personally exploit this new fad before it fizzled out. So he and Lional set about a frantic search for a flat, and in July that year came up with one on the ground floor of 20 Arundel Gardens, near the famous Portobello Road Market. It consisted of a bedroom, kitchen and a large lounge, offering scope for a studio and control room. Needless to say, when everything was moved in, there was hardly enough space for the bed and furniture, let alone the disc-cutter, gramophone, tape recorders, Binson echo unit, speakers made from tea-chests, amplifiers, microphones, a £10 honky-tonk piano from Portobello Road, piles of records, a floor full of cables and tapes spreading into the hall and kitchen and an assortment of junk. Where the musicians were expected to play was anyone's guess.

Now it was a matter of getting a demonstration record together. With this he could tempt Denis Preston into allowing him his first recording session officially as a producer. He had just composed a song called 'Sizzling Hot' with a 17 year old office clerk, Charles Blackwell, so all he needed was someone to play it.

The hottest act in Hammersmith were an outfit calling themselves the Station Skiffle Group, and one evening he dropped in to investigate them at the Boileau Arms where they were playing. What he was looking for was a competent skiffle band. What he found was a nutty bunch of 18 year olds: one crawling about the stage with a washboard strapped to his legs, another was standing, rocking on his beer barrel bass while the singer, guitarist and accordion player were jumping about pulling faces. And the sound was terrific! The audience was full of it and he knew that if he could capture this atmosphere on disc he would be onto a winner. After the show he introduced himself and took them out to a nearby coffee bar. They told him they had already made some records without success, and he in turn dived straight in offering them a chance to make some more, with him as their personal and recording manager. The recording management they eagerly accepted but as for personal management, that was already going to a girlfriend's father. Before they parted, Joe insisted on a change of name and after some head-scratching he noticed a sign on the counter saying Bar-B-Cue. Since their lead singer's name was Jimmy Miller, he would call them Jimmy Miller & the Barbecues.

Over the next couple of weeks all his spare time was spent at the flat rehearsing the group playing 'Sizzling Hot'. They also practised it at West Kensington Underground Station where the stationmaster had given them their own room to rehearse in. There, playing on the platform at the end of 1956, they had got their original name, the Station Skiffle Group, and when guards had invited them aboard they were the first skifflers to perform on the tube.

At last he was able to play Denis a rough recording of it, and one August evening, into the IBC studio they all trooped. Denis went along as well to keep an eye on where his money was going. The adrenalin was high because they all knew Joe's credibility as a producer was on the line, and indeed it was not long before he lost his temper. The problem was the washboard: it was so deafening that it was drowning out the washboard player's voice – and he represented half the chorus! Joe had resolved it at the flat but here the acoustics were different and he could get no balance at all. At first he simply flew into a rage and told the fellow to hit it less hard. But that failed, so he got him to hold the thing away from the microphone whilst playing it, but then again, craning his neck over to the microphone was making him sing flat! It was getting touch and go whether the recording would ever happen but eventually Joe pushed him right away to scrub on his own and dubbed the voice on separately afterwards. They then scrambled through the B-side, and that was the official start of his career as producer, songwriter and recording manager.

He was delighted with it and played it over and over. And with 'Sizzling Hot' he had made his own little bit of pop history by becoming Britain's first producer-engineer. Until then it was unheard of for the producer to also man the controls, and he would be doing it a lot in future.[9]

A week later he again recorded the group, but this time 'live' at the Edgware Road's famous Metropolitan Theatre, where they won the Great National Skiffle Contest, started a near riot and got their shirts ripped by feverish fans.

Several other people called round to try out his homemade facilities, including Petula Clark, Lonnie Donegan and Johnny Duncan & the Blue Grass Boys (whose superb 'Last Train To San Fernando' – probably the best skiffle record of them all – was another piece of Meek engineering). The noise was a wonder to behold. The old house had never before had such a swinging time, with its windows a-rattling and doors and floorboards a-shaking in time to the beat. There were soundproofing tiles on the ceiling which were fine for the people upstairs but not much consolation for the old man in the basement flat below, who would often shout up: "Stop that noise!" and other less savoury phrases. Such requests would be ignored till the man turned nasty, threatening to set his Alsatian onto him, whereupon Joe would seek to dampen the old fellow's fiery temper by running a hose pipe down the stairs and turning the tap on. The house had few quiet evenings. When Joe sang, recorded or listened to music he would stamp his foot in time and the old man would thump back on his ceiling with a broomstick. (The man is also well-remembered for the times when he would stand outside in his bit of garden with the dog in the pouring rain, carrying an umbrella whilst watering the grass with his watering can!)

Never was a moment wasted. As if to make up for lost Gloucester years, life was now for living at a rush, and he would finish work in the IBC studios to hurry home and start again in his own. The same principle applied to spare time as to working time and he squeezed the sap from every second. In developing his new songwriting sideline he took full advantage of train journeys for Road Shows. Climbing aboard perhaps at King's Cross he would arrive up North five hours later having written the lyrics to three or four songs and committed the tunes to memory. Most of them never progressed beyond scribbles in notebooks or warbles on tape, but as luck would have it a certain Mr. Denis Preston half-owned a certain music publishing company called Allegro which had already accepted 'Sizzling Hot', so it might take some more. Evenings he would sit hour upon hour prodding at the piano, digging for tunes and desperately trying to master the instrument, but as with learning to read and write music it eluded him. [10] He was still composing during the night, getting up all hours to hum and la-la into the tape recorder.

Though it might to an outsider seem an unnaturally one-track-minded existence he was leading, to Joe it was thrill-a-minute stuff! The music business was tightening its grip on him by the session and he was happy to let it go on tightening. Every day presented new goals to aim for, new ideas to try out, new recordings to make, another artiste, another producer. Quite simply he was doing what he liked best and being paid for it. True, there were ups and downs: some days went like hot treacle pudding, others like cold curry. But never was it boring. Perhaps that was what he needed: time to sit still with nothing to do; for his problem was that despite spending his time on the things he wanted to, there seemed to be more and more things on which to spend it. The need to cram it all in was becoming a drug, bringing on nervous tension, headaches and a greater tendency to fly off the handle. So, wherever he was, be it gazing out of a train window or sitting in Lional's café, he always found it difficult not fidgeting or thinking about his one topic of conversation: music. Give him a spoon and he would tap everything in sight in his quest for new sounds. And underlying all the joking, jollity and dashing and darting about, one sensed a touch of melancholy about him as though something besides music were on his mind, and no matter how much he laughed and joked it was always there.

Meanwhile back at IBC all was far from well. Towards the end of August, despite the financial rewards he was bringing the company and the high esteem in which many now held him, opposition was mounting. There was constant friction between him and the management, as Lional recalls only too well: "He had personality clashes all the time with Allen Stagg. Joe was always on about him. That name cropped up day and night – it used to get on my nerves."

It's a wonder he had so far avoided the sack, and were it not for the inevitable outcry from a pack of snarling A & R men his position would have been less stable. He had an uncanny knack of getting up Allen's nose and his "inveterate fiddling" was a prime offence, for not only was it considered unsporting by IBC standards but he never readjusted the equipment after use. Thus any engineer on the next session was saddled with an extra half hour's work setting up for it. This was one 'fault' that really was a fault and finally led to the whole practice being squashed when the manager had the machines fixed with special locks.

As if he had not already enough drama surrounding him, there were also the regular studio assemblies to discuss business and air grievances. Battle lines would be drawn up in defence against his bombardment of demands for new or modified equipment. Adrian Kerridge was there as well: "He fell out with them at IBC because it wasn't very happy times for Joe. The reason being was really his dedication. There were some horrendous things used to take place at IBC. Every month there used to be a staff meeting, where all the staff were put together in Studio A, and the Studio Manager used to make particular comments about performances and goodness knows what else. And usually they'd have a go at Joe because of the way he was, because he was homosexual. I used to defend him because I didn't give a damn, I mean, he never bothered me. I used to see Joe reduced to tears at some of these meetings; in fact they had me reduced to tears at one stage. And I remember one particular morning, I'll never forget it, when we were working till 3 in the morning. I was in the corridor and there was the Studio Manager – after Joe having worked with Joe Henderson or Petula Clark till 3 in the morning – pointing at his watch like this. Joe walked in all smiles. The Studio Manager said, 'You're late. It's 11 o'clock,' tapping his watch. Of course, it upset Joe. I think he had a row with them because of this attitude and because of the way they were treating him."

Someone else saw it differently. In Allen's view: "Joe was becoming quite impossible to deal with and was getting paranoid in every possible direction. He definitely wasn't worth the trouble. Joe before he left us was a pain in the arse, because Joe was Joe and Joe had to be the most important thing on God's earth."

THE LEGENDARY JOE MEEK

At last Joe could stand it no longer. Early in September, when he told Denis he was washing his hands of IBC, the latter was understandably staggered. He depended on Joe for the bulk of his sound-balancing and no one else around could satisfactorily replace him. Denis reflects: "He said his favourite expression: 'Rotten pigs! I'm leaving next week.' I said, 'What am I going to do, Joe?' "

5
The House Of Shattering Glass

t was a good question for which Denis had a good answer and promptly offered him a job. Joe could be his personal engineer and have his own tape-editing studio. Joe was thrilled and agreed. He had always got on well with him, especially since Denis appreciated his ideas and allowed him scope to experiment.

However, things did not work out at all right. The plan had been that when he left IBC, the new job would be no more than a variation of the old one: Joe now working for Denis instead of IBC and still engineering there. This was not to be. Now that he had left them they would not allow him back to engineer there at all, and would only let him in the door as producer or producer's assistant.

So, it was decision time for Denis. He was already forking out £6,000 a year hiring studios, a sum he thought grossly extortionate. Money would soon be pouring into his company, Record Supervision, from production royalties on the big selling 'Last Train To San Fernando', so he decided to set up his own recording studio. What was more, he intended having a second studio too, solely for hiring out. Where they would be was another matter, but work could start as soon as premises were found, and Joe could be both engineer and studio manager. That was just the kind of news Joe wanted to hear. It had been a nasty shock suddenly finding himself banned from IBC, and this would more than make up for it. He was meanwhile engineering occasional 'live' performances, mainly at the Humphrey Lyttelton Club in Oxford Street, but most of the time he was lumbered editing in Newman Street and urging Denis to hurry up and find somewhere for his studios. At the same time he started keeping a look-out in his own neck of the woods around Notting Hill.

Now it was party time! The biggest one was the publicity launch of 'Sizzling Hot' at his flat. The publisher and record company organized the invitations while Joe and Lional organized the rest. Whilst Lional was preparing the banquet, Joe had the group working flat out filling the place with balloons and Christmas decorations and fitting cods' heads on a fishing line in the bathroom, so whenever anyone opened the door, the line was stretched and up to greet them popped several fish heads from the blue bath water. During an evening at the end of September, somewhere in the region of 150 people appeared with their notepads, cameras or smiles to add to the hot air Joe was circulating about his wonderful Barbecues. How they all squeezed in is one of life's mysteries, but every new face he saw he pounced upon, not letting go till all the Barbecues had been introduced to it. Record producers, singers and journalists all heard the fanfare for his super new group, and while Lional fed them his sandwiches and kept a huge roast sizzling hot on a spit, the band gave them a zippy, zany and much praised performance. That night he went to bed a happy man.

With more evenings to spare, he had time for some social life. The Barbecues' jaunty lifestyle appealed most strongly and he accompanied them to many parties where they were invited and coffee bars where they played for their coffee. There was something about joining in with his band of merry minstrels, whether performing in a crowded train or on top of a bus, that made it all worthwhile, as if he really belonged. Nothing could be better as they strolled back from a gig, playing guitars down the middle of the street and singing their heads off, while the people of Earl's Court threw coins to them. Feeling more and more like a personal manager, he arranged various appearances for them, including the *6-5 Special* TV pop show, a Woodbines cigarette advert, the Hammersmith Palais and even a Masonic function. And there were session-parties at his flat too, with Lional supplying the spread.

It was through these get-togethers that he started taking a serious interest in spiritualism. He had already dabbled in seances without success, and so had Jimmy the lead singer, who found sittings at his own ouija board handy for impressing would-be girlfriends. However, seances are not guaranteed light entertainment, as they found to their horror one evening with some friends at the flat. A new scheme Jimmy had brought along involved a Bible and mortise key. First one end of the key was laid on a certain passage. Then the Bible was bound tightly with string and the participants rested their fingers on the protruding key handle. The final part was to read the passage aloud, and it was then that something happened. The key turned completely, and because it was held so firmly inside the Bible, it tore the pages. For those present the experience was nothing short of stupefying, effectively scaring Jimmy right off his jolly pastime and sharpening up Joe's appetite for more. Joe was suddenly convinced that together they had the power to make all sorts of things happen. Over the following weeks he was to continue holding seances himself, with no success at all, whilst in vain pestering the awestruck Jimmy to join him.

Recordwise there was a disappointment. Despite its receiving plenty of airplay (due perhaps to the stack of requests he had had the group send in to the BBC using different names, addresses, handwriting and notepaper), 'Sizzling Hot' was not hot enough for the charts. There was too much atmosphere and not enough music! Apart from a funny noise at the start which he had recorded with his 'mystery' echo chamber, the record had little to offer, and he told them they would have to change their sound. Out must go the washboard for drums, so too their booming one-string beer barrel bass for a proper bass guitar.

While he left them open-mouthed at this unexpected bomb shell, he was branching out in search of new treasure trove. The first of two fresh discoveries was a dance band called the Jackie Davies Quartet. They had just the right feel for some romantic ballads he had written. Jackie Davies, nowadays known as Chico Arnez, was to spend a lot of time at the flat and says Joe's recording techniques were unlike anyone else's: "Normally if you go in recording studios you're booked three hours and that's it. With Joe you'd do ten, till you got it right: five hours one day and five the next. He was a perfectionist, so he'd go on and on till he got what he was aiming for; some of this was during the night. Sometimes we'd work at a club till one in the morning, then go round to his place 2 till 7. He had a weird way of working like that, but sometimes that gets the best results. A really smoky, sweaty studio; the windows were covered up – no fresh air, but plenty of coffee and drink. It was a very old-fashioned room and the equipment was all a complete hash, but we had a lot of fun doing it. It was a good atmosphere and he got some fantastic results."

Denis gave the demo the thumbs-up again. Then for Joe it was back to his old hunting ground at IBC, where he produced but did not engineer two slow, slushy love songs, neither of which was to sell well.

The other act to catch his fancy was a brother and sister harmony duo, Joy & David. The teenage pair, aged 19 and 16, were singing once a week in a pub when someone recommended they phone "this recording engineer I know". They soon passed an audition at Parlophone that Joe arranged. But Denis suddenly started objecting to recording non-jazz artistes and so, much to Joe's annoyance, they had to be found an agent and sent off touring with Alma Cogan and Cliff Richard.

Then in December, by luck he stumbled upon an actual licensed recording studio being used by an amateur cellist, 100 yards from Holland Park tube station in Lansdowne Road. It was no recording fairyland, but offered scope for converting into two studios – if Denis was ready to spend the money. And he was! He went in like a shot, bought the lease and started calculating how he could turn what was little more than a cellar into the most advanced recording studios in Europe.

To Joe went the job of designing all the equipment. He was in his element and mixed his editing commitments with frequent visits to EMI's factory at Hayes, setting his wits to work constructing it to his own specifications. Denis sometimes went along too: "Joe designed the original mixer we used in this studio himself – 'I want that scarlet and gold trim and all the faders silver' – the most fancy looking thing you've ever seen! But he was right and insisted on what he wanted. We were the first studio to equip specifically with stereo. It may not have been the best but it was stereo. Joe went in head first. Now it sounds ridiculous when you talk about 24-track, but the problems one had in getting twin-track stereo to work in those days. He saw to the installation and literally, I'm not kidding, he worked 24 hours a day." What is more, he worked for nothing fixing the studios so Denis would afford the best. His plans with their hitherto unheard of levels of equalisation were so advanced that the boys at EMI had trouble carrying them out.

Getting the studios ready finished off the year and was to take care of most of 1958 as well. Time was getting scarcer now and his social life had gone to the dogs, but in January '58 he squeezed in one more record with Jimmy Miller, only this time without his fellow Barbecues. In spite of heavy battering by Joe they had stood firm against a change of sound and only Jimmy had agreed; so for his latest song, 'Jelly Baby', Joe replaced them with some session men. Unfortunately, coming at the tail end of the skiffle craze it did not sell at all, and the Barbecues broke up soon afterwards.

Although 'Jelly Baby' flopped, it prompted a most significant occurrence in Joe's life. It was in mid-January, soon after the recording session, that Jimmy says Joe coaxed him back to the seance table for a Tarot cards sitting, where they joined an Arab friend of Joe's called Faud: "This was the first time I had handled Tarot cards, and even now I am getting tingles down my spine as I recall the events. Joe to my knowledge did not drink and we all had coffee, otherwise I would question my own thoughts on what transpired. At one point Joe asked that I shuffle and turn the cards with the left hand; in the right I held Joe by his left, in turn he held Faud by the left. Faud's right hand was to mark down on a writing pad whatever message came through. We had done this twice already and nothing at all had happened. This was the first time I had actually handled them. They felt strange. I felt nauseated but somehow I was being pulled into something from which I could do nothing except continue to slowly turn the cards. It was like I was outside of myself looking in on the group, and sounds became non-existent. Halfway through the pile of cards I started to grip Joe so hard my fingernails broke the flesh on the underside of Joe's knuckles. And Faud was caught up in whatever happened and wrote down a date of February the 3rd followed by the name of Buddy Holly and the word 'Dies'. After all the cards were turned, Joe let out a yell as he now felt the pain in his fingers, and when he read the message on the pad he paled visibly and let out another yell. The whole affair was amazing because the message was written in what looked very much like my handwriting."

Buddy Holly was the singer-guitarist with the American group, the Crickets. In the past few months he had quickly become recognizable by his large horn-rimmed glasses and the distinctive 'hiccuppy' voice which had graced three straight Top Ten hits: 'That'll Be The Day', 'Peggy Sue' and 'Oh Boy', the first of which had reached No.1.

Any interest Joe had in Holly through his music was now redoubled by the anxiety his 'message' gave him. There were only a couple of weeks left in which to warn Holly of February 3's danger and he lost no time in advising the relevant record companies and publishers to do so.

Be that as it may, February 3 passed without a sound, and a few weeks later Holly and his group arrived in England for a month's tour. The prediction, Joe felt, was just as valid as ever and at one of the London venues he made a point of meeting him, emotionally explaining what had happened and delivering the handwritten 'message'. For someone confronted by an excited stranger warning of his impending doom Holly displayed admirable calm, accepting the note and thanking him for his concern.[11] The tour went on to be a memorable success, and the infectious love songs Holly was writing, enriched by his highly original style of singing and guitar playing, continued charming millions.

Back at Arundel Gardens meanwhile, more passions were being roused. Early in the Spring Joe found himself living alone since his good friend Lional had upped and left after having an armchair slung at him. It was by no means the first instance of flying furniture and was more a case of the straw breaking the camel's back. For long-suffering Lional it was one armchair too many and so he moved out, leaving Joe to smash up the flat in peace.

Although Joe had not yet turned up trumps with Jackie Davies or Jimmy Miller he had high hopes for two more discoveries he had made. The first was ex-London Army middleweight boxing champion-turned-singer, Jack Davis. Decca were enchanted by his Pat Boone-ish voice and during the Spring Joe was able to get him a record contract. The only little snag was the name, being too similar to that of his other star, Jackie Davies, so they arranged a competition to find one. He mentioned this plus other things on his mind in a letter home in May '58. The reproduction of it here is as it was written. (The tax that he speaks of at the end refers to that of his father's estate.)

Dear Mum

Thank you very much for your letter I love to hear from you and the news.

Well lots of things have happened since my last letter, first Jack Davis – the boy I put on Decca records was in last week's Daily Mirror and they asked everyone to name him, very good publicity for him, he will be making his record soon, I will let you know what it is.

Now some more new's two sundays back another singer was brought over to my place three people had phoned me up and so, I thought "he must be worth hearing".

THE HOUSE OF SHATTERING GLASS

So he came over and I gave him a test, and I was very impressed, so I made a Disc took it to Dennis Preston who said we had to many singers, so I sent him to Parlaphone with the record and they singhned him up right away for two years, Now here's the nice bit, he was so greatful he has given me 5 per cent of all his record royaltys for two year's, but best of all the day he was at my place I recorded one of my songs "Put a ring on her finger" well he played this to Parlaphone chief George Martin and he said thats perfect for you we will record it on your first record which he is making this week, so all I can say is it pay to be kind and help other's as much as you can, some let you down but you are rewarded in the end.

This singer's name is "Edie Silver", I will let you know when the record come's out. Ron Goodwin is doing the arrangments.

Edie has been over since and recorded two more for me to help me sell my songs, but in there contract They say that Edie must have first chance of my songs, I think this is a great complement because they think so much of my work., of course if he dosent like one or two I take them else where, I have over 50 songs all written by my self and I will release, them, when I feel when I feel the time is right.

I want to write a musical to use up some songs, "I have started", but need a script written.

I'm sure your Son is going to be famous one day Mum, as things are going I am very well know in the whole record world and have a very good name too.

Our Studio is in progress and it will be the most up to date in this country, I have desined and

59

modeled the mixers studio etc, and will have a share in the company we hope to go into operation in about two months.

Dennis Preston gose on holiday in two weeks and once again I take over, but this time I wont work behind his back I think to much of him and the wounderful premotion he has given me, the money will come along soon, he has given me a free hand with the studio and alowed me to record my songs and push my artists.

Well Mum its rather a long letter I had so much to say, Lionel sends his love and regards to all he's a good Pal and calls round a few times a week, but lets me get on with my work, if Im writting or recording.

Still at the same place I may stay its so handy, work etc. Sorry to hear about Peggy and Arthur, but "thats the way it gose", all my love to every one including Jimmy Meek, now dont forget Mum you have to get up here for a week or two this year, I have so many people for you to meet and you can fit it in with the date we have the party at the studio, Ill let you know but any time of the year suits me, Mum. So all the best with everything Im always Thinking of you, in all I do I would love to help pay that tax I may one day who knows, so all my love, look after yourself

From your loving Son
Joe

Joy & David's first crack at the charts came at last with some teenage fodder titled 'Whoopee' which David had written on the back of a cigarette packet. Denis finally succumbed to unremitting pressure and the 'Whoopee' session was held at EMI's Abbey Road studios with Joe producing and A & R man George Martin overseeing. But when Joe asked George if he thought the duo would have a hit he replied, "Yes, about their eighth record." That was not quite the reply Joe had been looking for, so it would be a long time before EMI were offered any more Joy & David masterpieces. It did however give them a chance to appear on TV and project the overly cutesy, saccharine-sweet image he had given them. Escorting them to studios he would insist they go round afterwards thanking and shaking hands with everyone while he stood by like a proud mother. Their totally innocent naivety he saw as a big selling point and should never be shattered by their breathing a word about Joy's 2 year old son. As for their record, it was well put together but despite the gimmicky effect of 'suction-pump' kissing, failed to make whoopee.

Instead his sun was shining 5,000 miles away on the other side of the Atlantic, where he was about to have his first success as a songwriter. Eddie Silver's 'Put A Ring On Her Finger' had seen scant sales but had been heard by the American duo Les Paul & Mary Ford. In September their cover version of the song went into the US Top Forty, prompting our own Tommy Steele to use it on the B-side of his latest record, 'Come On Let's Go'. That got it into the British Top Ten. The song was just a simple, happy, Moon-and-June type piece which he had written some time back on a tatty scrap of paper whilst travelling on the train for Radio Luxembourg:

Just put a ring on her finger,
A kiss on her cheek,
And you can bet your life she'll marry you
In the best side of a week.

Just say you love her,
Be faithful and true,
And there's nothing in this great big world
She wouldn't do for you.

And there was another success for him in the States. This one was by his new protégé, Jack Davis, who thanks to a Daily Mirror reader was now going round calling himself Mike Preston. Joe had produced 'A House, A Car And A Wedding Ring' for him which, although doing nothing in Britain, reached a useful No.57 on the American Hot 100. Unfortunately he had not written that one, and producer's royalties were going into other pockets.

On the music scene British rock'n'roll was at long last starting to take off. Tommy Steele had already been manufactured two years earlier as Britain's answer to Elvis, but then his manager had whitewashed him into an all-round entertainer. Now Cliff Richard and Marty Wilde had arrived to share the rock'n'roll crown. Meanwhile, Donegan was still strumming on, oblivious of the fact that the skiffle craze had long since gone. As for ballads, there were still a fair number of American ones around but the voices of Frankie Laine and Co. were being replaced by Pat Boone, Perry Como and Vic Damone amongst others; the British ballad front was headed by Frankie Vaughan, Petula Clark and Michael Holliday. But it was rock'n'roll that now reigned supreme and Elvis in his third year was indisputably top of the bill, having just proved it in style with 'Jailhouse Rock' – the first record to hit the charts at No.1. At the same time the atomic rock'n'roll approach of the master rockers like Chuck Berry, Jerry Lee Lewis and Little Richard which had taken over from Bill Haley, was itself being modified into the milder, melodic delivery of groups like the Everly Brothers and Buddy Holly & the Crickets.

The Fifties' scene from a more general perspective was looking pretty turbulent too. Since Joe's move to London, Britain had joined the rush to 'go nuclear', building nuclear power stations and testing H-bombs near Christmas Island. Ever more anxious petitions for an end to nuclear energy and the accelerating arms race were in vain; leaders of the superpowers, Khrushchev and Eisenhower, carried on glaring at each other and the best that could be banned was dark factory smoke in Britain, third class travel on British Railways, licensed prostitution in Italy and Japan, rock'n'roll in Iran and Egypt, and America's practice of fingerprinting foreign visitors. 1956 had seen Winston Churchill's successor as Conservative Prime Minister, Anthony Eden, battling it out with Egypt's President Nasser in the Suez Crisis, and while most eyes were watching the outcome the Russians were watching Budapest, where they saw a tasty anti-communist uprising and, quick as a nun's kiss, moved in and crushed it. The Suez Crisis cut short Eden's term in office, so now it was Harold Macmillan leading the 'modern, go-ahead' Conservatives and giving Britain in '58 its first tower block, motorway and Transatlantic jet airline.

In the meantime, closer to home, the long hours were at last beginning to pay off. In August Lansdowne Recording Studios Limited was set up. Although there were still some months to go before they were ready, Joe signed a contract making him Studio

Manager/recording engineer and giving him £1,000 a year plus 5 percent of the profits – a pretty penny in 1958. He was also given an open cheque to buy himself a decent car, and picked up a sporty, red and white Sunbeam Rapier.

By late '58 one studio was at last ready for experimental sessions, though it was still far from finished and a matter of the red light being switched on to cue out the workmen and cue in the musicians. Yet there were ominous signs that the lengthy spells of sweat and toil were affecting more than the shape of the studios. Frequent nights without sleep were creating a terrific strain on Joe's nerves, and Joe's nerves were creating a terrific strain on everyone else's. Denis's advice to him was to "lay off" but he ignored it. He felt like a pilot at the helm and, come what may, intended steering them full speed ahead to a position of pre-eminence in the music world. To "lay off" was the last thing he was going to do.

One of the first people to record there was the regenerated Chico Arnez, formerly Jackie Davies, who now had a new Latin-American orchestra to go with his new Latin-American name. The session was for his first LP, 'This Is Chico', planned as a co-production by Denis and Joe but marred by lack of co-production. In between the hammering of the workmen and the wrangling of the producers, it's a wonder Chico's record was ever made: "We got it done in two sessions which was six hours. We'd have got it done sooner if there hadn't been so many arguments between Joe and Denis. We couldn't hear them because they were in the box; we could only see them yelling at each other. There was a hell of a hassle going on the whole time. We'd hold it a minute while they had an argument, then we'd carry on. They just couldn't get on, especially when I put the vocals on. Denis didn't want them on because he'd rather have just band numbers. Joe said, 'No', and there was another big argument, which Joe eventually won."

It was at this time they also received their first complaint, which was from one of the residents upstairs. As it concerned the studios' acoustics, which had not been designed by Joe, he for once was innocent. One of Denis's critics, and indeed an objector to all his artistes, was a little old lady three floors up. Whenever she opened her oven door, music came out! She could if she wanted sit at her gas stove all day listening to Lonnie Donegan and Humphrey Lyttelton but obviously that didn't appeal to her. The music in fact was travelling up to her through gas pipes from

63

the studio; the building's gas meters were all situated close by the studios' echo chamber and had not been properly insulated, thus offering the lady her undesired luxury. Of course, had anyone actually wanted a musical gas oven they would have had to pay a small fortune for it.

The year was still young when it threw up one of the biggest tragedies ever to hit the pop world. Buddy Holly, Ritchie Valens and the Big Bopper were all killed in a plane crash. The date: February 3.

At the time, they had been playing on a long American tour with the Platters. By this stage in the tour they had become very weary, trekking by coach from state to state and city to city, snatching sleep between stops. At their latest venue in Mason City it had been snowing hard when they arrived and when it carried on after the dance, making it so thick they would have to wait till morning before setting off for their next one-night-stand at Fargo, North Dakota, Holly decided to save time by chartering a small plane from a local airfield. It was still snowing when the plane set off that night, never to be heard from again. Hours later a search plane spotted wreckage on a farm ten miles away. The pilot had had no qualifications to fly on radar.

Understandably Joe was very shaken by the news. Besides recalling the seance of a year back, he also thought of the sporadic nightmares he had suffered during the months that followed, and the one recurring segment that had always mystified him, where at the conclusion to each nightmare a pile of dirty clothes was being stuffed into a box, a cupboard or perhaps a car boot. The explanation he was looking for was given that day in a *United Press International* despatch from Clear Lake, Iowa:"The singers, members of a rock'n'roll troupe touring Midwest cities, died because they wanted to make a fast hop between dates so they could get their shirts laundered."

That night a tearful get-together was held at Joe's flat, playing the Holly records. At this point the admiration he had for the man and his music suddenly became a mild fixation, and was richly nourished on seances he began holding to contact Holly's spirit. Whatever authenticity they might have held, he was firmly convinced that the singer subsequently visited him, thanking him for his warning of the previous year and promising that he, Buddy Holly, was going to help him with his career as a songwriter. Joe's faith was further strengthened by the fact that his songwriting actually did improve! He found himself never short of ideas and his style grew more melodic, with a better choice of words drawn now from his own feelings.

Not surprisingly, the whole experience was to have some bearing on how he saw life from here on. For some time now he had adopted a fatalistic attitude to life out of which had sprung the morbid belief he would die before reaching 40, and violently. So the events of the past year, culminating in Holly's untimely demise at 22, had not only bolstered this idea but to some small degree made him identify with the singer as a person.

The widescale effect of Holly's death was to send his latest record 'It Doesn't Matter Anymore' to No.1, and with a legacy of top-notch pop music still unreleased, make him even more popular than when he was alive. Over the next few years, write-ups about him in the music press were to crop up as regularly as the apparently inexhaustible supply of unissued recordings, and for a long time he would be voted into the World's Top Ten Singers. All of which bore witness to a great lost talent.

Rather happier news came that month when 'Petite Fleur' by Chris Barber's Jazz Band provided them with their first Top Twenty hit since moving to Lansdowne. Ironically it was off an LP Joe had balanced at IBC over two years earlier, but that didn't matter. It was to pull in two Gold Discs and turn out to be 1959's biggest seller for Britain worldwide.

When it came to adding his magic touch to recordings, without doubt his favourite effect was reverberation. Some people said he was echo mad! At home he was forever sniffing out new places to echo up sounds. When singers were not being pushed into the bathroom to get their resonance right, they would sometimes have to sing across a jug or cigar box. When he had a sound already down on tape the scope was wider. Not content with just sticking a speaker and a microphone in the bathroom he would try them out inside a dustbin or down a drainpipe and record what came out the other end.[12]

He had also built two echo devices of his own. The first one surprisingly was just a garden gate spring, wired up so sound could run through it: simple but effective. The other one was his 'mystery' echo chamber. He was sure no one else had one, and had been intending getting it patented ever since using it on 'Sizzling Hot'. Built into a small metal case it was taped up so nobody could look inside. If it was accidentally knocked, it made a loud, resonating 'yoing-yoing' sound. And he had made it out of springs from a busted fan heater. This little piece of Top Secret information was only revealed when Adrian Kerridge, still his assistant, risked life and limb untaping it to peek inside. Fortunately Joe never found out.

This secretive behaviour actually seems a little excessive in view of how closely they had always worked together. And that was exactly how it was becoming. He had always been one for covering up his tracks but as the months slipped by, this practice was taking on grim proportions. Lional was the first to notice it: "He was always secretive but he was getting even more so. He was always wondering if people were listening in on the telephone to his conversations and his records that he was doing. He used to have a microphone where he could stick it onto the wall – suction – and listen to the next room, and he had things plugged into the keyholes. He would go round and look under carpets in case anybody was recording or listening to his music with bugs. He didn't want to let anyone know what he was doing because he was hurt by people letting him down, running off or backing out of verbal deals: deals with artistes who hadn't turned up at his flat or had pinched a song. He'd play a song to me and say, 'Oh don't let anybody know.'"

One of the many under suspicion was Chico Arnez: "He didn't trust anybody. You could tell by the way he looked at you. He still didn't trust you even after seeing you about 20 or 30 times. He probably thought Denis Preston was listening to everything he was doing."

♪♪♪♪♪♪♪♪♪♪♪♪♪♪

Naturally, most of the action was on the jazz side. By the time of the official opening of Lansdowne Studios in May '59, people like Humphrey Lyttelton, Kenny Ball and Acker Bilk had all been in to lay down tracks. That month Joe travelled abroad for the first time to Berlin's huge Deutschlandhalle to produce a 'live' album of one of Denis's top artistes, Chris Barber. His work was really cut out for him on that one because he had to balance the sound by ear whilst sitting in the front row with a tape recorder perched on his lap. The record, 'Barber In Berlin', later won golden opinions from jazz fans who had hitherto declared that the quality of the great pre-war jazzmen had never been attained since then.

There were though a number of Denis's flock who were far

from impressed with the sounds he and Joe were capturing on their recordings. Chris Barber, for instance, did not like either Denis's style of producing or the studio where he was doing it. In his view Denis was pandering to popular demand at the expense of pure jazz and not taking British jazz musicians seriously enough.[13] Similar concern over Denis's commercial leanings is voiced by Humph: "I didn't always agree with the sound he'd get. He was gingering up my albums to make them sell, and was not after the sound we got on gigs. Jazz purists like myself tried to resist. Denis Preston was striving to be a producer and jazz people were striving against being produced: 'This is our music, we are the experts, we know how it should sound.' There was a built-in collision point between him and the jazz die-hards. There's no doubt that Joe Meek had a big hand in it and was a great influence on Denis as well as being encouraged by him. Joe was the first person, I think, to use echo on jazz records. I reacted a bit to heavy drums and echo and we'd have a little tug-o'-war. Sometimes I won the argument and sometimes he did, which is why some had a more produced sound, like 'Baby Doll'. But Joe now I think was right with a lot of his ideas, and at least one of my albums he engineered, 'Triple Exposure', is now looked back on as a classic."

The commercial aspect was the price jazzmen had to pay in gaining the wider following that Denis wanted for them. It also gave them the opportunity of regular work. Evidently the price was not too high. And despite Barber's claims to the contrary, Lansdowne were rated the best designed and equipped studios in the country, at least when they opened. They were ultra-modern compared with all the others, and EMI were turn-of-the-century. IBC dubbed them 'The House Of Shattering Glass' because of the clarity of their recordings, and had to smarten up to keep in the running.[14]

During these late Fifties a fair share of Lansdowne's success was due to Joe. The studios were flourishing and this was because many clients had followed him from IBC. Joe for his part was proud of what he had accomplished in helping set the place up, and as for being Studio Manager in what was technically his own studio, it was just terrific! Thanks to Denis he was now the first engineer in Britain to have become a producer and the first to be doing both jobs together. All he needed at the moment was more leeway in adding his own touch to jazz productions and freedom to record more of his own artistes.

He gave an idea of his general thought pattern in October when he wrote to his sister Pam wishing her well on the arrival of her baby boy. (The recordings, incidentally, that he mentions at the start were by the Black & White Minstrels; they would pre-record their songs at Lansdowne and mime along to them on their TV show. Also, the treatment for his mother that he speaks of is to help her arthritis.)

Dear Pam

Congratulations, Im very proud to be Uncule to your littel boy and girl, and brother to such a lovely sister.

I hope everything is OK and you are well after having such a big baby, I will get home to see you as soon as I can safley leave the studio Ive never worked so hard in my life, and its made me rather run down but I know its been worth it, and the studio is now a very great success.

By the way Pam its not our studio you see on TV its only the sound you hear they record at my Studio and then next day mime to the recording. Clever isnt it, the studio is very lovely, morden and very smart I will send some photo's, it is the best without a dout in Britian.

No I havent been in the papers very much lately but I expect I shall return, to some peoples Ideals of a succesful song writer they havent given me much of a chance lately its like selling a bottel of milk to Mrs Meek, she has already got plenty, but Pam I will succeed I know it, but everything takes time.

I have just got home from a recording with Ted Heath what a noise, you know how loud I used to play the music in the shop, well when I am recording I have to lissen much louder to hear seperation between each section, of the orcestra, so at the end of my day, 10 -1, 2 - 6, 6.30 - 12 (thats the times I have worked the last two months) I feel quite dead, its rather like the feeling I used to get when I got up at 4 in the morning to go cherrie minding, only diferance is I cant hear.

I still have not had any cash from the song writting but I think any week now, I shall bring as much as I can home to Mum to spend on the house and help her out with the expence's, that would make me very happy, and then all the strain and hard work will be worth it.

There are a lot of plans I have made Pam, at the moment I am just getting my foot in the door, I know I will make a lot of money, and I am doing work I realy love.

Well its been all about me in this letter but theres so much to say and Im such a big head?

Im very sorry Mum is not well still, and suffering, I hope the treatment will be able to make her well she must think me a bad boy not writting, but I feel so ill at times I just seem to sleep when I get to my flat. please give her a big kiss for me and say Im sorry, also one for you, Sandra and the new baby.

I will give your regards to Lional, he will be pleased to think my folks havent forgotten him, he's a fine friend. all my love Pam thanks for having a son I will do my best to be a good Uncle to the two littel Angels, if he turns out to be ¼ as wounderful as Sandra Ill be happy. she's got a place of honor on my mantelpiece here, and in my heart. look after yourself love, I be thinking about you

From your loving
Brother

Joe

One vital piece in the Joe Meek jigsaw was his introduction in October to the electric organ. It came through the music publishers Southern Music who were amongst the growing ranks of clients being attracted to Lansdowne. One of Southern's directors, Bob Kingston, had just returned from New York where as usual British publishers were forever popping over to check on current music trends and snap up recordings worth covering in England. What he could hardly fail to notice there was that the big new thing happening was the organ; every major store was displaying one and practically every recording session he attended was using one. Bob in fact was the right man to notice for only the year before he had helped form the dance band, Lord Rockingham's XI, providing it with its distinctive organ; their marvellous 'Hoots Mon' had topped the charts but since then organ sounds had all but died. However, a modern style organist called Dave 'Baby' Cortez had just topped the American Hit Parade, winning the instrument legions of new fans, and when Bob arrived back in England he was well stocked up with 'Baby' products. He at once gave them to Joe to hear and brought in the organist Harold Smart.

Their attempts failed to recreate that sound and nothing came of their joint venture; nothing that is, except for making Joe so eager to capture it by himself that he went and splashed out £40 on a new style electronic keyboard. Even then nothing came of the Dave 'Baby' Cortez sound, for he ended up being completely sidetracked by other qualities he found in the instrument. These he was to put into effect sooner than he thought.

One person he had not mentioned in his letter to Pam was Denis. The relationship which had started so fresh was already turning sour. Easygoing Denis had had plenty of experience handling temperamental artistes and had so far managed to keep Joe sweet by spoiling him, both with regard to rigging Lansdowne and with giving him much more than an engineer's say in jazz productions. As a result the studios were thriving. But Joe was never satisfied; the more his demands were met the greater they became. Besides badgering Denis to use his songs for B-sides, he was beseeching him to let him record his singer Mike Preston, who had not so far that year recorded one song. Minor points like these were becoming major issues in what was effectively turning into a power struggle, and the boss was slowly but surely losing. As Chico Arnez explains: "Joe's back was up because he felt he was the one producing all the art and Denis Preston was getting all the glory. He had a little bit of a Denis Preston 'hate'. He said he couldn't get on with him: 'Denis thinks he knows everything and knows nothing.' Denis gave him so much leeway that Joe ended up thinking he owned the place and that he was the boss: 'You're just here for a suggestion which I may listen to if I want to 'attitude'.' "

His tricky temper was further aggravated by his flagrant misuse of slimming tablets. Whilst seeking to restrain the size of his stomach he discovered that, taken in sufficient dosage, they did more than suppress appetite. They were called 'Preludin' and a couple of them acted in the same way as pep pills, producing a few hours of nervous energy. He was now taking them frequently, especially in the evening, and often sent Adrian Kerridge off to buy them at the chemist. When the effects started wearing off, the high would be replaced by the low and he would get irritable; then was the time for another couple.

Something else to give him an even bigger high was the £3,000 nestling in his bank account as royalties from 'Put A Ring On Her Finger'. And it was giving him ideas. First his mother would have what money she needed, then if he saved up a bit more he could afford to get right away from Lansdowne with its boss/employee format and go for the pot of gold: independence. At last he would set up his own management-studio-record label, where he would be answerable to no one. He would not, unlike Denis, be pinning his faith on faceless bigwigs in the record company hierarchy but dealing directly with the public. And he would be channelling some money into his own pocket for a change instead of other people's. He would even out-Preston Denis by taking control of every aspect: discovering talent, writing songs, managing artistes, engineering and producing their records, distributing them on his own label and serving up the tea and biscuits afterwards.

With this in mind, he was gradually gathering round him a roster of artistes, all of whom were contracted to him, their recording manager. The latest act to join the fold was a band of part-timers he had seen called the Cavaliers. He had written a couple of songs for them to record and these he intended leasing out himself and not through Denis. That meant resorting to cloak-and-dagger tactics and recording them at Lansdowne during a weekend when everyone else was at home. No one would suspect anything because he often worked weekends anyway.

That was how 'Magic Wheel' and 'Happy Valley' were made. Complete with Hawaiian guitar the country'n'western style 'Magic Wheel' marks the first appearance of such a guitar on a

British pop record. The flip-side, 'Happy Valley', is notable more for the session itself. The end of the song had to be speeded to represent Chipmunk-style 'Happy Valley' people running along a railway platform. The weird manner in which he came by them would have won him an award in any training school for prospective lunatics. Anybody stopping by to look in on the session would have seen six men bounding dementedly around a microphone and bellowing with laughter – slowly! To add to the confusion no one except Joe knew what on earth was going on and they had to wait till the recording was cut and dried before all was revealed.

In similar fashion another of his songs, 'Just Too Late', was recorded soon afterwards. This one was by singing decorator Peter Jay, about whom he had heard whilst having his hair cut. Again it is of more interest for the session itself which, unknown to the musicians, was performed as quickly as possible (just one take) in case a certain Mr. Preston happened to drop by and raise the roof. In the event he didn't drop by, though even so, 'Just Too Late' was made just in time. It was Joe's burgeoning interest in songwriting which a few days later cooked his Lansdowne goose.

So far Denis's publishing company had only accepted nine of the 80 or so songs Joe had offered, and as these included 'Put A Ring On Her Finger' he felt it was high time they took some more. Denis reports on what was to be the final confrontation: "We had a most difficult session for America: Kenny Graham with Joe Harriott – 'Jazz Cha-Cha'. A very difficult album, big orchestra, all brass and saxes and big rhythm section, and working in a tiny control room with the temperature probably about 85°F, because we didn't have air-conditioning at that time; and inadequate mixing facilities really for the sound we were aiming to make. And Joe's written a song. He'd scrawled something on the back of an envelope, and I'm trying to get this session through for MGM and Joe keeps saying, 'Look, I've written a marvellous song. I think that my song is much better than what you're recording now.' He keeps showing me. And I said, 'Joe, for Christ's sake, if you want to talk about songs – later. We're trying to make a record.' 'Oh, rotten pig!' – and he got up and walked out." It was November 4 1959 at 11.15 am in the middle of the morning session and there was still the afternoon one to get through. Joe's assistant, Adrian Kerridge, who was busy upstairs leaning on a broom suddenly found himself taking over the session and the job. They phoned Joe the next morning to tell him not to bother coming in again.

THE HOUSE OF SHATTERING GLASS

He was thunderstruck. It was one thing to leave voluntarily, which was what he had intended doing soon, but to be sacked was unthinkable. Not even Allen Stagg had done that to him! He was outraged and the more he considered how much he had put into Lansdowne, the less he thought he had got out of it and the more shoddily he felt he had been treated. Spitting fire he resolved to take them to court and get his money's worth out of them and went straight home to Newent, raging over how he had been dumped and determined from now on to go it alone.

But the trouble was that he had been in the wrong. Although it was the first time he had ever walked out of a Lansdowne session, he had acted irresponsibly and chosen a bad time to do so. To cancel the session would have meant paying 20 musicians all over again as well as slipping behind on the production schedule. Given those circumstances his dismissal was valid. Denis, whilst being interviewed some 17 years later about his time with Joe and their eventual break-up, rounded it up: "I met him at an EMI party with my wife and he came over and kissed her and was as friendly and delightful as ever and never really held it against me. But I think that if I'd continued to work with Joe I'd have had a nervous breakdown. You can't have two creative people. I believe myself to be creative when I'm producing records; as an engineer he was a creative engineer. And there comes a point where producer and engineer, if he's creative, must clash. Whether this temperamental problem arose from his personal problems is not my concern. I can only say that, as I found, when things were going well, when he had no personal or emotional problems, that he was one of the most creative men I've worked with – and I was the first man in this country to insist that engineers' names went on sleeves. He was in a sense a split personality. He came to my house one Christmas and my son was probably 3 or 4, and Joe was marvellous with children, and he was a different man from the man under pressure. You could have times with Joe when he could be the nicest, most lovely, friendly, beautiful guy in the world, but if something crossed him he was like a jealous woman: quite impossible to deal with. Working with Joe when things were good, when he didn't have his personal problems or he wasn't writing a song, when he was concentrating on the job in hand, was a most rewarding man to work with."

Looked at in perspective, it is clear that the partnership was doomed from the start. Putting it bluntly, he couldn't stand having anyone in authority over him, and the only terms under which he could conceivably have remained at Lansdowne would have been his own, running the show.

Actually, his dismissal from Lansdowne was not half so intolerably calamitous as he at first thought. Instead it was to herald as significant a change in his career as the one that followed his fateful car crash into the Gloucester telegraph pole.

6
Records Made For The
Hit Parade

Now he had one objective: to set up his own record label!
Obviously as he had insufficient funds to finance himself he
would have to find a backer. That meant checking out
record and publishing companies.

Things looked good. On top of all his past achievements,
there were three records he had recently worked on that were
right now in the charts for all to see, and halfway through
November they were all sitting pretty together in the Top Ten:
Emile Ford & the Checkmates' 'What Do You Want To Make
Those Eyes At Me For' on its way up to No.1, co-produced by Joe
and Emile Ford; Marty Wilde's 'Sea Of Love', engineered by Joe;
and his biggest success so far as sole producer: Mike Preston's
'Mr. Blue'. Credits like these should, he felt, prove irresistible.
However, it was not until a lot of writing, phoning and walking
had been done that he realized his temperamental reputation had
already overtaken him. In what was then a fairly small music business, one only had to cross up the Inner Circle and within a couple
of days no one wanted to know you. They had all heard of his
storming out, and none of them was ready to risk it happening to
them. For all the chance he now had, he might just as well turn
up wearing a leopard skin and wielding an axe. The weeks slipped
by without spawning any offers and, all things considered, the
Fabulous Fifties were ending on a rather flat note. And it didn't
look like the Swinging Sixties were about to offer much improve-
ment, for at the end of December '59 he sued Lansdowne Studios
for compensation, thus promising all concerned another generous
dollop of gloom to tuck into.

His case was based on moonshine. The way he had his solicitor understand it, the blame lay entirely with Denis. He claimed
that he himself was in charge of the production and that Denis
was interfering with his artistic control; that Denis was trying to
tell him how to produce the music and Joe, being a temperamen-
tally artistic man, would not stand for it. How much of this he
actually believed is unknown, but from what his solicitor saw, Joe
felt he had a real grievance. All of which is an indication of how
much authority he had seized by the time he left Lansdowne.

Now it was up to the solicitors.

He mixed his job quest with his most ambitious project to date. It was at a time when he was growing more and more fascinated by outer space and now firmly believed in the existence of alien beings on other planets. He had no more proof than anyone else, but his belief was bolstered by the great mass of news coverage on the exciting Russian-American space race. The Russians had got in first when a couple of years back they had launched man's first satellite into orbit, Sputnik 1. That one had marked man's entry into the Space Age. Since then a dog had been up there flying around and exclusive photographs sent back of the dark side of the Moon. Now both countries were battling it out to be first with their feet on the Moon. The merest mention of their respective high jinks had Joe's eyes popping out with wonder and now he wanted to get in on the act in his own way. He intended producing something no one else had yet done: a musical LP about people on the Moon, and all in stereo. He would call it 'I Hear A New World' .

The whole project had been prompted by the electronic keyboard he had bought back in October. Called a clavioline, it was the primitive forerunner of the synthesizers that are so popular today, having but two octaves and notes that could only be played one at a time; it produced a sound like that of an organ but with a rougher quality. He also detected in it the slight air of mystery one often finds in electronic music, making it well suited to depicting the mystery of outer space.

The Cavaliers agreed to play the tracks and for six weeks they called round to rehearse and record, taking away with them his grotesque singing demos. These featured a voice badly in need of tuning up, accompanied by a fork banging the beat out on a table. The opus was a long labour of love utilizing his sound-on-sound method together with a crude stereo technique. It was also mixed up with bizarre sound effects: running fingers down combs, tinkling washers on a bolt, vibrating a knife on the edge of a table and simulating waterfalls by blowing bubbles in a glass of water. So they often worked at it all day or night.

No one knew when or even if the finished work would ever be issued but (slipping silently into the future and back) part of it was, in the form of an EP (an 'extended play' disc with 4 tracks). Judging by the fact that only 99 copies were ever pressed, to avoid paying purchase tax, it seems that the expected public demand fell somewhat short of a stampede. In the event that proved right:

it was highly acclaimed critically but not by the public. The LP is even rarer, and anyone possessing one of the 20 or so pressings should rush it to their nearest bank vault.

It was the world's first concept album but is so unheard of today that the credit is generally given to Phil Spector's 'A Christmas Gift For You' of 1963. It demonstrated an exceptional ability to feel and understand space in terms of sound, and the whole lot was in stereo! Although it was not a perfect balance, sounds were separated and moved about which was more than any of the other studios were doing with pop music LPs. In a nutshell, the tracks were comprised of simple tunes put over on the Hawaiian guitar, clavioline and various other less orthodox instruments, processed (echoed up, speeded, played backwards, etc.) and set amongst some curiously celestial sound effects. Most of it was ahead of its time and it is no exaggeration that a few of the sounds would not be out of place on a Kraftwerk or Tangerine Dream record of the Eighties. Its only real blemishes were a couple of uninspired Chipmunk-style tracks which were garbage but mercifully short; ironically those tracks were probably the only commercial ones on the LP, the rest appealing solely to a few moon-ogling astronomers.

Naturally he was very proud of the recording and loved playing it to those he thought might like it. While the record was on he would chatter about it as if they were actually there on the Moon. Brimming with childlike enthusiasm he would describe a huge ball of water rolling along an otherwise dry river bed till it reached a precipice, fell over the side and plunged to the bottom with a great splash, from where it would gather itself up again and continue its journey; and there were the hovercraft people who flew effortlessly about in machines over an area unaffected by gravity. At these times, he was in his Utopia.

With regard to more earthly matters things were about to start happening. At last in January he heard that a company called Saga Films was hoping to start up a new record label. By this time his hopes of finding anybody interested were at a pretty low ebb and he would gladly have signed a deal with the Devil himself. The tip-off led to talks with the firm's director and subsequently the topsy-turvy Saga saga. Saga Films had kept the name despite by now having little to do with films, being almost entirely devoted to classical LPs. They were now in need of some extra push; someone had had the bright idea of forming a parallel pop label which could later be used to do just that.

THE LEGENDARY JOE MEEK

The brains behind the scheme was a William Barrington-Coupe, a tall, smart, public school-type of Joe's age. Coupe was a classical man and had started off promoting concert artistes at the Albert Hall. When the going had got tough he had been forced to take a less glamorous job as a clerk in a toy importing company; but back he bounced, helping set up Saga and producing several classical recordings. Although a quiet, tight-lipped man who would never use two words where one would do, he made up for it with a full, booming laugh loud enough to wake the dead, plus his exceptional skill for publicity, with a handy gift of being able to "charm the birds from the trees"; no doubt he would have been in big demand in Newent's cherry orchards.

When he explained his plans for a new record company called Triumph Records and suggested they take equal shares in it, Joe leapt at it like a trout for a fly. He was bursting to make his presence felt on the scene again, besides which he had in fact already worked with Saga when they brought along to Lansdowne the star of the current hit show *West Side Story*, George Chakiris. Furthermore he recognized in him a man with big ambitions like himself with all the answers to back them up.

They each agreed to put £1,500 into the company, Joe's share coming from his 'Put A Ring On Her Finger' royalties. Recordings would be held in small studios and rehearsals at his flat. Also, arrangements were made for various pressing plants to stand by ready to manufacture the discs, which Saga would help distribute. Of all places to operate a record company Saga had their offices in a toy warehouse at Empire Yard, 538 Holloway Road, N7 and Triumph were to share them. So much for the theory, the practice was another ball game.

As for being a British independent label, it simply meant you were not one of the Big 8 – Decca, HMV, Parlophone, Columbia, Pye, Philips, Fontana and Top Rank – and unless you either had pots of money or pots of luck it was often not worth the effort. One of the biggest headaches was distribution. As if circulating discs all over Britain were not tough enough, they were not wanted anyway. Most of the small traders stocked no more than the Top Fifty and, to add insult to injury, a glance at their chart list would tell them what they already knew: there were no independents on it. It was a Catch 22 situation: how for Pete's sake could the independents' records be on it if nobody stocked them? And this in turn got the reply: "What shops want to be lumbered with records they don't need by artistes they've never heard of?"

RECORDS MADE FOR THE HIT PARADE

According to the *Record Mirror* charts, apart from the phenomenally successful Nixa label, there were only two British independents since listings began whose records had ever reached the Top Twenty: Oriole and Polygon each with four. What that made Triumph's odds on collaring a hit record is a job for a mathematician but they stood about as much chance as finding the Lost Chord in a hangman's handbag.

Another headache was disc pressing. A big company like Decca could afford to be over-optimistic predicting public response to a record and end up with 10,000 surplus copies all going down the chute. The philosophy was: you win some, you lose some; the next record might crack the million. A little tuppenny-halfpenny outfit like Triumph only had to make a couple of mistakes like that and they would be down the chute as well.

With these plus a multitude of other obstacles in their way, the future looked as rosy as a Scottish weather forecast; two men singlehandedly squaring up to the music industry, and with only two weapons between them: one man's ability to conjure up the right noises and the other man's flair for selling them.

Finding talent was easier than they expected. News in music circles spreads fast, and singers and groups were soon dialling in for auditions. One of them was a 21 year old actor named John Leyton. Currently he was appearing as Ginger in the popular children's TV series *Biggles*, and was brought to Joe by his manager, the up-and-coming Robert Stigwood. His voice wasn't much to sing about and he had already failed auditions at Pye and EMI but to Joe the voice was secondary. As long as the singer bore good looks, Joe could, as John recalls, soon twirl the voice into shape: "I think Joe loved a challenge . . . and I think somebody that came to him that had no idea about music and even better still, who couldn't even sing a note, I mean, Joe loved that, because he could play with his machine and do all this amazing electronic mixing that he did. I went into his flat and Charles Blackwell was there . . . Charles played the piano and I sang a song. And when I'd finished, Joe immediately went to his small machine and twisted half a dozen different knobs and played the song back and I was absolutely amazed at what I heard. I couldn't believe it was my voice. I thought, well maybe being a singer isn't such a bad idea after all!"

Someone else Joe decided to take on was Ricky Wayne, a 22 year old West Indian singer. Ricky, a future Mr. World, was really more interested in bodybuilding but was getting some good reaction singing in clubs. One of the songs Joe had for him was a rock'n'roll number he had written, called 'Hot Chicka'roo', and he was delighted when Ricky came up with the right fast-belting rock'n'roll attack to put the song across.

Besides working with him in the studio he gave him an extra boost by polishing up his image. As Ricky points out, Joe knew exactly how to market him: "Joe was obviously impressed too with my personality and physique and so on; he saw it as a package. Soon after he recorded 'Hot Chicka'roo' he didn't like my clothes; took me to a hairdresser in Soho who changed my whole look and gave me this kind of flat-back hair. It was totally new – it's the rage now! And got me shirts that were open length down to here, so I could show my chest off. It was strictly a look with clothes and open shirts and wearing them all the time both onstage and in the street, so it drew attention. Joe was doing all this from his own expense. Shoes: he didn't think I should wear heavy shoes and so we went out and got a whole load of moccasins; and very tight pants – no underwear. He got me a bunch of pants. I remember one particular pair: white with stripes on; I could barely breathe in the damn things! Joe was punk. And yet he was in his suit and everything . . . And he would tell me how to behave, how to deal with interviewers and so on, because I was totally green. I was very, very shy; he was very, very shy. And he was making a point that I shouldn't allow it to impede what I was doing. If what you had was physicality, show it! That was my gimmick; nobody else had it. His idea was: 'Project health, project vitality and use your body'."

When they signed the contract on February 25 1960 and announced to the world the birth of Triumph – "Records made for the Hit Parade" – it seemed to Joe like the day he signed with Denis Preston all over again, only better. If it gave others the desk work and allowed him poetic licence to record what he wanted, it was a flawless situation.

The label got off to a sparkling start with a press party in 'The Lotus Room': a top London Chinese restaurant and a favourite haunt of showbiz folk. Here journalists could meet the new Triumph artistes and Barrington-Coupe could air his gift of the gab: "Triumph is the first label to produce discs exclusively for the Juke Box Generation. We shall be producing new discs at regular intervals and, with the support of the press and trade, I think we have excellent Top Ten material." There was some waffle from Joe too: "I've built stars before for other record companies and I can do it again. I've been looking out for suitable material for the last six months with this company in mind. Because we're young we know what the pop fans like. I'm a pop fan myself, so I should be able to tell. I don't think the big companies do know what the youngsters want . . . It's more a case of hit and miss with them."

Two records were released to a flourish of posters along the London Underground's Central Line and adverts in the music papers and teenage magazines. A few of his 'space' albums were also sent out to reviewers. By this time they had signed up a dozen acts. Most of them were almost total unknowns like Joy & Dave, Joy's 4 year old son Smiley, Peter Jay, Ricky Wayne, trad jazz band Chris Williams & his Monsters, the Cavaliers and a Cingalese jazz singer called Yolanda. He was also engaging the services of Charles Blackwell, his co-writer of the Jimmy Miller epic 'Sizzling Hot'; at 19 Charles was being made the youngest musical director in the business. And slap-bang in the middle of all the hubbub was Joe, the king pin, busy as ever, full of confidence in the new venture and enjoying life immensely. Here he was, at last producing for his own label and playing the big studios at their own game. If he could make a success of this he would never have to answer to any of them again. Coupe would be happy as long as they turned out a few hits now and then, which shouldn't be too difficult.

In April a weekly 15-minute spot *It's A Triumph* was bought on Radio Luxembourg. Ricky Wayne's dulcet Caribbean tones sounded just right to Joe, so for most shows he had the job of disc jockey. On one of them Joe revived memories of his own disc jockeying days in Newent when he played host under the name of Johnny Watts. Also lined up to show off their artistes was a 'Triumph Pop Package' tour of seaside resorts and a stand at the first ever British Teenage Fair, and there was even a TV ad campaign being considered.

They now had records to please all tastes, including a slow, almost thunderous lovesong he had written for the jazz singer, Yolanda, called 'With This Kiss'. This long forgotten gem was the first to encapsulate the unique Joe Meek sound. Plenty of the ingredients were there: heavy beat, angelic choir, piano, strings and tons of echo:

With this kiss our love will grow
Through the years, this I know,
Till the end of time when skies grow dark
And the sun will fall and the rains will start.

His lyrics showed a marked shift in style from his lovey-dovey, prune-in-June influences. Significantly, its arrangement was by Charles Blackwell. His first disc as arranger was Joy & Dave's 'Let's Go See Granma' but it was with his contribution on 'With This Kiss' that Joe's sound at last blossomed into an instantly recognizable quality. Charles was worth a king's ransom because on the recordings he arranged he was also the musical director, gathering the session musicians together and with Joe's assistance, conducting them in the studio.

The two men's way of working together followed a fairly fixed pattern: Joe making up a tune and humming it onto tape in his hazy, half-baked, melody-mangling way; Charles coming in to decipher it at the piano with Joe looking over his shoulder, supervising; then, before letting Charles take it away to write an arrangement, Joe telling him what kind of sound he was after and suggesting likely instruments and backing vocals. The mass of ideas he had collected from hundreds of past productions stood him in good stead, and with Charles pitching in his own the system worked well.[15]

Occasionally he forced himself to go out and see his artistes onstage. Such luxuries were never high on his agenda but he did like giving tips, as Ricky Wayne recalls: "He would come and watch me perform at the Lyceum Ballroom and then he would later criticize it. I was a heavy Elvis Presley fan and there were a lot of Elvis influences in my stuff and Joe never once tried to kill that. In fact he would say, 'Elvis wouldn't do it like that.' And so he'd demonstrate whatever way. Little gimmicks that everybody else was afraid to touch; and Joe would heighten them deliberately. He was a very tomorrow guy; he was ahead . . .

"He wasn't afraid of controversy. Ultimately I was singing 'Whole Lotta Shakin' Goin' On' at the end of my act, and would do this kind of striptease of just the shirt. In the middle part where the song goes down, I would take the shirt off gradually like a real stripper and move muscles in time with the music. That was Joe's idea and always used to go down very, very well. Nobody had seen muscles like this on a guy who sang. I'd be talking to the audience and start unbuttoning the shirt and very often some woman would scream something, so I'd stop and reply to her; so you'd encourage exchanges all the time, holding back the stripping. And that was all Joe's idea. You didn't just take the shirt off. And at one point, just at the end of the strip, I would then do a muscle pose routine, making the muscles move to the music: stomach, chest, arms. That was the highlight of my cabaret act."

In May, with no less than seven singles on release, they decided to add another sure-fire hit to their teenage repertoire with Stravinski's 'Concerto In E Flat – Dumbarton Oaks'. One might be tempted to wonder how on earth 'Dumbarton Oaks' or indeed anything by Stravinski could be considered a 'Record made for the Hit Parade'. In case such a thought did not readily spring to mind, perhaps two LPs following soon after which included Chopin's 'Nocturne In F Major, Opus 15' and some Russian songs by Moussorgsky might raise an eyebrow.

The fact of the matter was that these recordings belonged originally on the Saga label and with all the hoo-hah now surrounding Triumph, the time was deemed right for Saga to move in and share the spotlight. Joe was not at all keen on the idea and felt that for a label whose gimmick was youth appeal they were now aiming for some rather old teenagers. But that was the policy.

Then suddenly they had a hit on their hands! It wasn't 'Dumbarton Oaks' but a rocking instrumental version of 'Greensleeves' by the Flee-Rakkers called 'Green Jeans', and in mid-May it entered the Top Thirty.

With the good news, he took time off to help solve their crippling distribution problems by finding out which were the top shops selling chart material. There was no way Triumph could supply all the country's 7,000 dealers, so the next best thing was to concentrate on the main ones in the larger cities. One of the jokes going about centred on the difficulty in finding shops selling Triumph discs; when you asked the record dealer for one he would say, "Sorry, have you tried the chemist?'

In the meantime, company funds were beginning to dwindle and Joe was adding his own share to the trouble by burning up the budget as if there were no tomorrow. It seems that the sudden freedom to do his own thing and having access to an apparently vast fortune with which to do it, had sent him session silly. At least a dozen sessions were held whose recordings came to nothing. Many of them, like Charles Blackwell's pizzicato LP, mischievously named by Joe 'Those Plucking Strings', were using twenty musicians. Perhaps he thought Saga had a hidden oil well round the back of Empire Yard or that Coupe could charm cash as well as birds out of the trees. He couldn't care less where the money was coming from as long as it kept coming and he could keep hiring the musicians and making the music. But he was making it too fast and Coupe was scared stiff of flooding the market and ending up with thousands of unwanted discs. Inevitably there was a confrontation between the two but though it made Joe ease up on his workload it did sow seeds of discontent.

He was also bitterly disappointed that nothing had come of his 'I Hear A New World' opus. That was the record he had banked on winning him standing applause from the music fraternity, but hardly anyone had even heard it. The EP had received a few good write-ups but in the event it looked far too risky and only the 99 copies were pressed.

As the weeks passed, Coupe's aggressive advertising in all the music papers was working. Someone else who was selling a few was George Chakiris who jumped into the Top Fifty one week and out again the next; but no one was interested in him.

All eyes were now turned towards the next superstar on the Triumph assembly line. This one was Michael Cox, an unknown protégé of Jack Good, mastermind of the TV pop show *Oh Boy* and one of the most powerfully influential men on the scene. Good had already produced two Cox records which had flopped, but having broken in the likes of Marty Wilde, Cliff Richard, Adam Faith, Terry Dene, Joe Brown and Lord Rockingham's XI on his TV programmes, it was just a matter of time. The quarter page advertisement read: "Cash in on the sensational hit of the ITV show *Wham*, 'Angela Jones' by Michael Cox." They could have saved themselves the price of the advert because within a week of release the record had sold out and orders were coming in so fast that the second pressing soon sold out too. The song itself was a rather soppy teenage ballad, a cover version of an American hit, but Joe and Charles Blackwell's beautifully light production treatment was ideal and actually improved on the original.

'Angela Jones' entered the charts early in June. Within two weeks it was in the Top Twenty and with the Flee-Rakkers still hovering round the No.30 mark retailers were squealing themselves silly for immediate supplies. Most of them were to be disappointed. The saying goes that it never rains but it pours, but this time it would be cats and dogs.

In readiness for the big pay day Coupe decided on an expansion programme. A new branch called Triumph Electronics was set up employing over 100 people and manufacturing cheap, tatty tape recorders and record players. Coupe moved his Head Office into an advertising agency in the City's Carey Street, perched somewhat defiantly next to the offices of the Official Receiver. Triumph then broke clear of Saga, who with the sudden unexpected loss of Coupe as well as the ill-timed departure of their main client Great Universal Stores, promptly fell apart at the seams to the tune of £1/4m. Behind the scenes much fuss was made over the ownership of the Saga repertoire, and one of the eventual losers was Marcel Rodd of Allied Records who found himself buying it twice over! At the same time he was also pressing most of Triumph's discs and he had even less to laugh about when soon after his first shock he fell in the soup again: "Coupe, under the name of Triumph Records, gave us his cheque in advance together with the lacquers to press some records for him. The records were pressed by error before the cheque had cleared. The cheque bounced and I decided I was bloody well going to get that money. It wasn't a large sum – something like £500 – but it annoyed me that he'd taken me for a second time. He had an address in Balls Pond Road and there was a girl there and I brushed her aside, as she said I couldn't come in because Mr. Coupe was not there. I walked through this factory; it was a long, narrow room with benches on either side and half-assembled tape recorders and gramophones. And there were mammoth quantities of orders from record shops all over England for 'Angela Jones'. There was a large number which he'd invoiced out, but the pile of orders which he hadn't invoiced out was much bigger than the pile which he had. And they were the records we'd delivered, for which we'd never been paid. Having no money, nobody would press for him and he was running around like a chicken with its head chopped off finding someone to agree to press them. I sat around for 30 minutes for Coupe to appear, hopefully, but he didn't." Nor did his £500.

It would have helped if shops had sent cash with their orders. Instead it was the usual parasite story about building up their own businesses with other people's money, and then taking months paying debts.

THE LEGENDARY JOE MEEK

As if Triumph had not enough on their plates circulating records around the country, there was also the ludicrous palaver of composers' royalty payments for each record sold. The Mechanical Copyright Protection Society would not trust them to pay royalties later like larger companies, so instead a stamp had to be stuck on every disc. Sticking stamps by hand is quite feasible if it's a few hundred but not so funny when dealing with tens of thousands; all of them had to be bought in advance and licked by a paid workforce. Triumph managed a few thousand and in a manic attempt to somehow appease the M.C.P.S., stuck stamps and half stamps here, there and everywhere. It was all enough to send you haring up the nearest lamp-post, only there wasn't time.

As they sank deeper and deeper into the swamp, the advertising agent with whom Triumph were sharing offices and who was paying for much of their publicity took to arriving at the office early so as to allow him an hour on his knees praying for an end to their troubles.

By the time Coupe eventually arranged a deal to ease the distribution worries, Joe had had enough. He wanted his records where the public could get at them: in *all* the shops. Moreover, he was sick of a situation which dictated that the more money they made, the less they had, and though he knew how to scrimp and scrape – which was exactly what he was doing with his own recording equipment – he was never one to watch the pennies in the studio. He had to carry on until he got it right, even if it meant running over time and then warring with his partner. Making things worse as usual were personality conflicts, a point illuminated by Arthur Frewin, who knew both men quite well: "You had to *know* Joe to work with him, and you had to know what to say and what not to say. You could always tell what sort of mood he was in. Sometimes you had to pussyfoot round him, sometimes you could really hammer him; if you hammered him on a day when you had to pussyfoot you had a raging tiger on your hands . . . Coupe was an intellectual and they are very hard to handle. He could throw a few shafts into Joe which would reduce him to a quivering jelly of fury. Coupe would be as cool as anything; he was a very intelligent man – no fool."

Joe was fed up. By mid-June there was nothing within the sphere of mortal man that Coupe could have done to induce him to stay. Their relationship had slumped from bad to worse and Joe had grown to hate him, suspecting him of stealing his songs and ideas. Now all he wanted was to get away and start afresh.

RECORDS MADE FOR THE HIT PARADE

'Angela Jones' was to be his final record on Triumph. During his travels he started keeping his eyes peeled for any new openings, and one company he discovered that was itching to get its hands on him was the music publishers, Southern Music. By this time they were all well acquainted, Joe having known them since his Lansdowne days when he used to call round to their offices in Tin Pan Alley's Denmark Street regularly offering them songs they regularly turned down. At the same time he had been engineering recordings for them and it was one of these called 'Be Mine', sung by Lance Fortune, that had suddenly riveted their attention on him. It owed its style to that of the big Buddy Holly hit 'It Doesn't Matter Anymore', whose pleasing pizzicato strings had prompted them to try the same effect on a British record. However, though 'Be Mine' was the first song in Britain to sport that style, its release was delayed several weeks and the pizzicato effect was destined to find more fortune without Lance, notably on Adam Faith records like 'What Do You Want'. Still, it made the Top Ten and its sales had Southern Music planning to set up a label of their own. So, with Joe now available they prevailed upon him to join them for a 50-50 share in the company. Had they made their offer when he first left Lansdowne they would have got him and the Joe Meek story would have turned out very differently. Instead they left it too late, and while he was umm-ing and ah-ing over what might turn into another Triumph tragedy, someone else appeared on the scene.

One man had all the while been lurking in the shadows watching and waiting. He had known all about the founding of Triumph, its business affairs, its artistes, its records, its tours, its promotions and had been following the label's progress to the last detail. And well he might, for he was the owner of Saga Films as well as the toy warehouse where it was based. His name was Wilfred Alonzo Banks, better known to the world at large as Major Banks. And now he pounced. While 'Angela Jones' was still safely moored in the Top Ten he proposed a joint partnership where Joe would provide the music and he the money.

♪♪♪♪♪♪♪♪♪♪♪♪♪♪

The Major was an imposing figure, or at least thought he was. Upright though portly, he liked to be looked up to and would say that if you are tall you make more impression on people. Being only 5′9″ he would often comb his thick, gingery hair up to give him another two inches; that way he believed he could strut smartly into a room, stand by a 6-foot man and no one would notice the difference. His regimental manner was immediately apparent. Some would say he was too regimental, like an actor playing a major, which naturally begged the question whether he really was one. In fact he was and had hung on to his rank since the War when he served as a major in charge of transport in the Royal Army Service Corps. Now aged 46, his clean-cut military bearing complemented a brisk, well-drilled efficiency and a bloodhound's nose for business. It was his work and his hobby night, day and weekends, and for him a 14-hour day was routine. This way he had built up the country's biggest importing and marketing company of Christmas decorations and had his fingers in four others besides. His soldiering days had stood him in good stead; he had grown used to bossing men about in the army and was now bossing them about in business – and it worked. On top of that he was both a hard bargainer and, like many of the best businessmen, trod a very narrow path between right and wrong. So far it had earned him few friends but plenty of business acquaintances, who to him were the ones that mattered.

This obsessive interest in one thing drew a parallel with the singlemindedness of Joe, for whereas Joe's all-consuming passion was the sound of music, the Major's music was the sound of money. His interest in music went no further than wrapping it up for sale; his knowledge of it was zero, but zero was ample when he could sniff it out in others. One of these was Joe Meek. It would be a travesty of justice if this young man's brilliant music-making ability could not be put to proper use, and listening to his past successes and future plans, Joe's voice sounded like coins cascading into a sack and his name seemed to change to Joe Mint. When Major Banks watched him working at Arundel Gardens he was, as Marcel Rodd recalls, especially impressed with the effects Joe got out of his homemade equipment: "His great interest in Meek was that he had invented a thing no larger than a cotton bobbin, which had two wires coming out of it and if you put the sound through these two wires, somehow or other it came out of the loudspeakers with a delightful echo; and it was wired up so he could get all sorts of remarkable sounds. This led Banks as a layman to think Joe Meek was a genius. He believed in Joe Meek. He used the word genius to me many times and told me that classical music was a flop compared to pop; the big money was in pop provided you had the right people to make the right noise, and Joe Meek was just such a one. Banks spoke about Meek in a rather affectionate sort of way: nice young kid, on his way up, very innovative, tons of ideas, great musical talent."

Between them they discussed a new option. Instead of running their own label they could do what Denis Preston was doing: run a production company and lease recordings to any of the major companies that wanted them. Although this method did not guarantee a release with every recording they made, they could at least rest assured that the ones that were accepted would receive fair distribution throughout the land. As Joe had no money left, Banks would pay him a salary of £20 per week. In a nutshell, Joe would deal with everything but money.

However, Banks was no soft touch. He had seen what happened at Triumph when Joe was given an open cheque book to go out hiring studios instead of owning one himself. So, he would have to operate from his own. But there again, although the Major was a wealthy man and understood the need for facilities less primitive than those at the flat, he was not about to slip into a tutu and do a fairy godmother act. He was only prepared to find him a larger studio-flat, pay the rent and furnish it with Saga's unwanted equipment, the cost of which would have to be paid back once enough profits were made.

Joe found the idea very attractive, so between the two of them they started checking out the area around the Major's toy warehouse in North London's Holloway Road. Naturally he was far from impressed by the surroundings in that part of the world. Holloway is one of the many drab and dirty districts for which London is renowned, and was a big step down from the more elegant Notting Hill which he had grown used to over the past few years. But it was convenient, rents were low and it was there, only five minutes walk down Holloway Road, that he came across the kind of place he was looking for: a three floor flat. This one was over a leather goods shop at No.304.

His choice seemed an odd one. Setting up a recording studio over a shop on one of London's busiest roads does not immediately strike one as the wisest of decisions. As part of the Great North Road it was the main route serving lorries between the North and London's docks and markets; and again, he might be in for some stick from neighbours, since the house was set in a terrace. None of the rooms was particularly large, so he would have to use the biggest one as the studio. That was on the second floor and would mean climbing two flights of steep, narrow stairs – not much fun for musicians with drum-kits and other bulky instruments. Of course, he would much rather have been setting himself up in a quieter part of London, on the ground floor, away from neighbours and with a car park nearby, but that could all come later when there was more money in the kitty. For the time being this place offered distinct possibilities, and at least there was an Underground Station handily placed 200 yards farther down the road. So, in spite of all the snags, he arranged to take over at the end of June and eagerly looked forward to getting cracking. Banks was pleased too because the rent was only £7.10s.0d per week.

However, adding more tremors to the upheaval was Joe's Arundel Gardens landlady. She served him with Notice To Quit under the pretence of having the house restored, though it was peace and quiet she really wanted restored. The eviction was annoying but he agreed to go without a fuss as long as he could leave behind some of his furniture till the new flat was ready to move into. Until then a roof over his head was granted him by his old buddy Lional, at this time living at 3 Clifton Villas, Paddington. That though was on condition he behaved himself and did not treat the furniture there as if it were his own.

During the next few weeks his thoughts were on both the business side (discussing contracts with Major Banks) and on having the new flat redesigned. Compared with his old one there were plenty of rooms here and he knew exactly what to do with them. On the first floor would be his living room which already had a kitchenette partitioned off; he could eat there and entertain guests. The room at the front over the shop would be partitioned down the centre to make an office and waiting room. The next floor would be devoted entirely to recording. The studio itself would be the former bedroom overlooking the road, but without the bed this time! Although only 13' x 17', it was well served by a small back bedroom adjoining it which would be the control room. Of the three rooms at the top of the house, the back one would do as the bedroom while the others could harbour surplus junk.

Every day he would pop in to delight in seeing it all taking shape, impatiently directing singer Dave Adams who, as a skilled carpenter, was dealing with most of the alterations himself. Work had not been going on long when he decided to start installing recording apparatus. It was at this time, as Dave recalls, that Joe was first introduced to one of his neighbours: "Before I had the windows blocked up and soundproofed Joe and I were in the control room one day testing out equipment, when an irate neighbour on the street that backs onto Holloway Road started banging a stick against a dustbin lid in retaliation to the din that we were kicking out. Joe opened the window and stuck a microphone out recording the sound and then played it back six times as loud! Soon after, the windows were fixed and we heard no more about it."

Apart from having the flat renovated and soundproofed, he was most concerned that no one should be able to spy on him. Over the living room was a skylight, so he instructed Dave to place venetian blinds across it; this should foil any attempts by people who might climb onto the roof to peer through and try somehow to steal his songs.

He also felt a slight mistrust of Major Banks. The Major wanted him to sign some very wordy contracts before agreeing to any partnership and did not look like a man keen on parting with money. On the other hand, Banks was offering to finance the whole set-up, and if he let Joe get on with his work in peace and provided the funds with which to do it, the future looked fairly bright. So on July 25, six months after signing himself into Triumph,[16] he signed himself out again and banked his chips with Banks.

Their agreement gave him complete artistic control within the scope of the Major's budget. All income would go straight into the company, and Joe must stay fully committed to this one and get involved in no others.

It seemed fair enough. On the face of it, joining up with Banks looked like the smartest move he had made to date. He wanted an outsider with money who had faith in him: someone who was not going to tell him what, when and how to record, but who at the same time was sharp enough to cope with music business costs. What he did not realize was just how sharp Banks really was.

7
The Sound Of RGM

ext on the agenda was tape-leasing. He now had to set about farming out the Triumph master recordings to major companies. This opportunity was only thanks to an extremely astute, if not downright deceitful, practice in which he had throughout his Triumph days made sure that all artistes signed themselves not to the company but to himself. Apparently William Barrington-Coupe had known nothing about it and says he was shocked to see almost all the assets, i.e. the artistes and recordings on which Triumph depended, disappearing before his very eyes. All this time he had been running a record label with no artistes signed to it! He didn't do too badly though and was to accept a £1,300 handshake from Major Banks.

However, Joe's new task of tape-leasing was very risky, and he knew it. As yet it was far from common policy for major companies to accept recordings from independent producers in England, because they expected their own staff to produce the goods. That was after all what they were being paid for. If though, the quality was up to scratch, it was obviously in their interest to take them; the record company was onto a bargain for they were being handed finished product on a plate and only had to deal with pressing, distribution and promotion. And of course, they could take it or leave it. Denis Preston was by far the main exponent of this system in England and the other lesser mortals could be counted on one hand.

The first man to see had to be Dick Rowe, latterly of Decca, but now running the A & R department at Top Rank. Dick was handing out contracts like confetti since all of Top Rank's product was coming from independent companies, mostly American. And both men were well acquainted through Joe's engineering works at IBC and Lansdowne. Their meeting at the end of July went like a dream. Dick was so pleased with the recordings offered him that he not only accepted most of them and paid him a few hundred pounds as advance royalties, but also signed him up as an independent producer for Top Rank!'[17]

One curious fact to arise from all this was that when he handed over his Triumph recordings, he started another new phenomenon: independent producer-engineering. Now that he had broken clean away from Lansdowne and Triumph he was a free agent,

THE SOUND OF RGM

able to lease out recordings to anyone who wanted them. Admittedly, it was a freedom which itself depended on people wanting them, but before Joe arrived on the scene no one in Britain had ever leased tapes that he had both produced and engineered.[18]

One of the Triumph recordings which had not yet been heard was a sorrowful number sung by the *Biggles* actor, John Leyton. Titled 'Tell Laura I Love Her', its release had been postponed because he was singing as a man killed in a racing car accident and this brought to mind a recent spate of British motor racing deaths. However, now that a tactful period of time had elapsed and before the original US hit by Ray Peterson arrived, Top Rank decided to risk putting it out. Then a few days later on August 6 at Baker Street's Olympic Studios Joe taped his first recording as an independent: the Michael Cox follow-up to 'Angela Jones' – 'Along Came Caroline' – another pot of syrup as similar to its predecessor as to be easily mistaken for it. Both discs were set to go out very soon, and would have done so but for one minor hiccup: on August 10 Top Rank collapsed! It was sold off to the mighty EMI, already owners of HMV, Parlophone and Columbia.

Michael Cox was shunted over to HMV (his fourth label inside a year), where 'Along Came Caroline' provided him with his second hit when it reached No.41 or No.20, depending on whose chart you followed: *New Musical Express* or *Record Mirror*. The John Leyton disc did not fare so well. Unfortunately EMI now found themselves with two recordings of 'Laura' so John's was scrapped in favour of the other one, sung by someone on the Columbia label calling himself Ricky Valance (filched from that of the late American singer Ritchie Valens). That actually turned out a wise move, seeing that it was the better version and went on to reach No.1.

But that was the least of Joe's problems. With the collapse of Top Rank he suddenly found his contract in tatters, as did all the others connected with that firm, and once more had to start seeking new deals for his artistes. Some of them he managed to off-load upon Alan A. Freeman of Pye, and once again Dick Rowe, who was now back at Decca after his eighteen months' absence.[19]

Now things were very different. He could find no one prepared to do a generous Top Rank style deal with him. Independent product from British producers was usually viewed down a high held nose and even if accepted, rarely received advance fees. So from here on, he would be paying for all his recordings out of his new company's funds. And some might never see the light of day.

♭♭♭♭♭♭♭♭♭♭♭♭♭♭♭

After spending a month at Lional's the time was ripe for moving into the new flat. While Dave Adams was busy making changes there, Joe had also been making changes in Lional's flat. Already during his short stay he had kicked the door off its hinges and smashed various pots, cups and glasses, and with Dave Adams getting on so well at Holloway Road it seemed like an ideal time to move in. But moving was to be a long-winded process. He was not prepared to entrust the safety of his hundreds of records, tapes and other assorted treasures into the hands of some thieving removal firm, so over three days in September everything except the kitchen sink was stuffed in and strapped down on his Sunbeam Rapier and Lional's Austin A40. On the first trip all went well until the little procession took a short cut through Hyde Park, where the sight of Joe's bed and armchairs sailing stately across crown land earned them a reprimand from the Parks Police for committing an offence to the Queen and an order to take the longer route next time.

He began practice sessions right away, testing and re-testing the studio's acoustics and his hotch-potch of equipment. At the same time Dave Adams continued building and decorating around him. When the windows had been blocked in with carpeting and he was sure the studio was safe enough from traffic noise, he could at last revel in a happy satisfaction with the whole set-up. He felt as if he were concealed in a cocoon where he could only be reached via the one door and into which he could retreat deeper and deeper. Now he could entertain people when he liked, and when he didn't he could climb up the stairs away from them all and the rest of the world. Here he could be alone in his own little universe, oblivious of the one outside and free to turn his sounds upside down and inside out. When enough hits had been made and something better cropped up he would move out, but till then this would do just fine and was where he intended making sounds every bit as good and better than those emanating from the big studios.

THE SOUND OF RGM

The tone of the control room was soon set. Joining the yards of electric cables draping the floor were great strands of reel-to-reel recording tape. Anyone looking in would see a jumble of Heath Robinson-style machinery and a mass of apparently tangled wires with barely space to walk. And yet he could reach down amongst this mess and join two wires together to immediately produce a sound he wanted. If it happened that he made a mistake he would first listen a few times to the new noise and then file it away in his head somewhere for future use.

Some of the equipment was new, some homemade. Much of it had been completely reassembled from old EMI and Saga cast-offs and secondhand stuff from junk shops and army surplus stores. His main tape recorders were a Lyrec twin-track stereo recorder and an EMI TR51 mono recorder.

As for the famous Meek method of recording, compared with modern multi-track techniques it sounds as out of date as whalebone corsets, and even then was generally despised for being slow, complicated and losing clarity. But unless everything was recorded at once, as was traditionally done in the large studios, there was no other way.

His technique was almost exactly the same as the one he had started back at home in 1950 using two tape recorders: over-dubbing. By layering one sound on top of another – sometimes up to half a dozen times – it meant in effect that when you listened to a Meek record you were hearing not one but several recordings! He much preferred this way because it allowed him to concentrate on one section of the recording at a time, getting the performance he liked best and giving him the chance to change his mind as he went along. Now though, life was much easier with the aid of the Lyrec twin-track. The finished recording would end up on its two tracks – songs having the backing on one track and the voice on the other – and this gave him much more leeway than ever before.

First of all he would deal with the backing. The rhythm section would go into the studio and play while the singer sang along as a guide, unrecorded behind an old screen. While this performance was going on, he would be recording it onto the one track of the TR51. He might record 20 'takes' before deciding which one he wanted and moving on to the first overdub. This time he might want to add an extra drum sound; so he would simply choose the rhythm 'take' he liked best and relay it out into the studio for the drummer to play along to. Thus the two sounds combined would be channelled onto one track of the Lyrec. When he again had a 'take' that satisfied him he would perhaps overdub a guitar and do exactly the same again, playing the last recording out and collecting both sounds together on the track of the TR51.

Depending on the sound he was after, he would gradually add more and more instruments, spinning spools back and forth until his backing track was done. And while all that was going on he had other machines running. Apart from feeding sounds through echo units he had to watch out for loss of quality; each time he transferred from one track to the other, a little of the original sound was lost. So he had to use limiters and compressors which gave him a louder signal. They could also give him the sound of pumping. This he would often use to add to the overall excitement, besides which it played an integral part in his unique Joe Meek sound.

When all the backing was happily on one track of the Lyrec, he would have the vocalist sing along to it. The only difference this time was that he liked to keep the singing separate, so would give the singer headphones and play the backing through them instead. Then eventually, probably after more messing around on his own adding sound effects and so on, he had two finished tracks on his Lyrec.

Off he would go with them to one of the outside cutting studios where facilities were better than his own. Surprisingly in the months to come his choice of studio would usually be IBC. Engineers there were still the best and now there was less reason for him and the Studio Manager, Allen Stagg, to be at each other's throats. There he would supervise having his two tracks mixed down to one – the 'master tape'. Ten shillings in the engineer's pocket assured him of an extra good cut and helped make it the "loudest in the juke box"; and preserving his thick, solid bass drum beat meant that some should get through to the kids who were listening on little portable radios. He would also have two or three demo acetates made with varying levels of bass, treble, etc., and the one he judged best he would hawk round the record companies. If he found a taker he would give that record company his 'master tape' and help cut the 'master disc', so it kept most of its original quality. This practice was not to be 'on' at the prudish EMI and only grudgingly permitted at Pye and Decca. After all that it was clean out of his hands when it went off to the factory for the pressing process.

THE SOUND OF RGM

On September 12 the new production company was registered. Aptly titled RGM Sound it gave equal shares to Banks and Meek who roughly put in £5,000 (including £2,000 worth of equipment) and 24 recordings respectively, many of which were destined never to be pressed.

Recording tests were offered to literally anyone off the streets! It was a distinctly dodgy practice for someone like Joe running a one-man-show, since those who failed to measure up were not always agreeable to being bluntly shown the door.

Choosing solo artistes hinged as always on three factors: youth, good looks and an assurance of blind obedience. To anyone calling at the door with these credentials he would always lend an appreciative eye and an attentive ear.

Choosing bands depended more on musicianship, and while good looks in lead singers could sometimes sway him in favour of their shabby backing, it would always brew up stormy sessions.

Soundwise he had to keep up to date on the charts and a watch on the Americans, who still ruled the scene. The original rock'n'roll greats like Chuck Berry, Jerry Lee Lewis and Little Richard were fading fast and via the softer more tuneful approach of the Everly Brothers and Buddy Holly, they were now being replaced by a new glamorous generation of clean-cut teen idols like Ricky Nelson, Bobby Darin, Paul Anka, Johnny Mathis and Neil Sedaka. Collaring so much of the market these were the ones making rock music respectable; not that a lot of it could really be classed as rock, having by now become so diluted into teenbeat pop as to bear virtually no resemblance to the real thing. Even Elvis had watered down his act.

His choice of material also demanded that he give more thought to his budget than he had of late. So the artistic freedom he enjoyed was a freedom set within rigid limits. Major Banks had learnt enough from William Barrington-Coupe's mistakes to keep his finger firmly on the till, so that meant 20-piece orchestras were out for a start. Calling round daily with his nose in his wallet, the Major insisted on keeping a strict note of all costs. Of course, such frequent visits were not at all to Joe's liking and when they began souring the relationship they quickly grew rarer.

THE LEGENDARY JOE MEEK

Working days were long and tiring. Visiting record companies and publishers, testing and experimenting in the studio would usually take him through to 10 o'clock at night when he would go downstairs for a meal and unwind by listening to the radio or watching TV. Then with relaxation would come inspiration for songwriting. More precisely it was record-writing because usually when he wrote a song he had the whole production at the back of his mind plus the person who would sing it. First he would simply hear a vague overall sound in his head; then grabbing some paper he would start scribbling, and before he had finished eating, would be hurrying back upstairs to get something onto tape. Once he had got part of the melody out he was away; the shred of theme would attract words about it and expand into a basic verse while he doggedly sang it through again and again, honing it into shape. Composing by day he would add his own rhythm accompaniment by stamping his foot and tapping whatever object came to hand. By night the sounds of tapping and stamping do not always bring joy to the hearts of one's neighbours, so then instead he would sing along to his growing stock of rhythm tracks.

When feeling particularly inspired, songwriting could take him through the night. While A-sides usually took an hour or more, B-sides he would knock off in 10 or 15 minutes; they could not be allowed to distract disc jockeys from the main side. All in all, these were extremely private moments and anyone hearing him composing would have a sense of listening at the keyhole. At these times he was not to be disturbed and, as Dave Adams says, "If someone had interrupted him to say that Elvis Presley was at the door he would have told them to wait."

Up until this point he had been placing most of his songs with Essex Music. Now he chose to break clear of them and join two others in Tin Pan Alley: Southern Music and Campbell Connelly. These two were to receive the bulk of his songwriting output, the lion's share going to Campbell Connelly's newly-formed Ivy Music. They had one carrot to offer that no one else had: Radio Luxembourg.

Apart from Holland's Radio Hilversum which hardly anyone had heard of, the only popular music stations for British listeners were the BBC's Light Programme and in the evenings Luxembourg. At the time there was a stark lack of teenage pop music being broadcast from the BBC, for in between the interruptions from programmes like *Woman's Hour*, *The Archers* and twice daily helpings of *Mrs. Dale's Diary*, most of it was middle-of-the-road *Housewives' Choice* fare. And that was the way it would stay for another seven years before pirate stations forced them to take teenagers more seriously. So, at a time when all the publishers relied on a handful of programmes like Sam Costa's *Record Rendezvous* and Jimmy Young's *Twelve O'Clock Spin* to put across their up-market stock, as well as on record companies buying time on Luxembourg, Campbell Connelly hit on the bright idea of actually tying up with Luxembourg to form Ivy Music. As Luxembourg would thus be getting half the publishing royalties on any song placed with Ivy it was in their interest to play them.[20] So they guaranteed songwriters a quarter-hour programme five days a week called *Topical Tunes*. Happily in due course it would be RGM records that were given most airtime.

Southern Music had something else to offer. Although he did not realize it at the time, September 1960 held one card that really was to turn up trumps: a 22 year old musician from Reading called Geoff Goddard. He had just graduated from the Royal Academy of Music fully qualified to become a concert pianist but had decided that the competition was too great. So, having left the Academy one Thursday he had got himself a job playing piano in one of the Reading hotels. Seeing himself as another Russ Conway he had then spent the weekend glued to his radio and had composed three Conway-type tunes. On the Monday he had plucked up courage to hawk them around the London publishers. At 5.30 that evening he had crept timidly into Bob Kingston's Southern office with the three pieces he had written. Like a latterday Beethoven, with his thick, black mop of hair he then sat down at the piano and proceeded to outplay all the popular pianists. Bob, after taking a quick whiff of smelling salts in case he was dreaming, advised him against competing with the likes of Russ Conway and Winifred Atwell and to try songwriting instead. "I'll have a go," said Geoff in his broad Berkshire accent and went away leaving Bob fully expecting never to set eyes on him again. But back he crept a few days later with a handful of what Bob described as "brilliant" pieces, and this time as he reached for the smelling salts he had him sign a year's contract.

Since then five months had passed. Bob, wondering what Joe might make of Geoff, arranged for them to meet at his office so Geoff could play him some of his tunes. At the end of the recital Bob and Geoff turned to Joe and waited for his reaction. After a few moments' silence he looked at Geoff and solemnly announced, "I shall call you Hollywood." Geoff, realizing he was now being considered as a performer, quickly piped up, "Well, I quite like the name Hollywood, but I'd prefer the name of Anton." Thus Anton Hollywood was born and the door opened ajar for an immensely successful songwriting-production partnership.

Then a short while later, with Dave Adams's three months of renovations to the studio completed, Joe was pleased as Punch to find himself an 18 year old 'answer' to Buddy Holly. He had been given a demo disc containing four tracks by a band calling themselves Kenny Lord & the Statesmen. While it was playing he showed no interest at all until the last song: one made famous by Buddy Holly called 'Peggy Sue Got Married'. When he heard it he couldn't have been more excited if Peggy Sue had come in to tell him herself. The singer's voice sounded just like Holly's and at once Joe started making plans for an LP and single all to be sung in Holly style.

Soon afterwards they all arrived for their session and he swung into action with what he intended as the group's first single, 'Set Me Free', and the first recording to come out of his brand new studio. And it was a big anti-climax! Kenny's Statesmen were hopeless and would have to go. Fortunately Kenny knew of another band, and these Joe auditioned without their lead singer, who with admirable timing fled off to get married. Then he renamed them the Outlaws to give them a Western image. Kenny found himself renamed too and via his real name, Michael Bourne, and the *holly* berry Joe came up with Mike Berry.

It was November before Joe got them all together in the studio but this time the session did the trick. Mike's voice came across well, the Outlaws proved to be a very competent backing band and Joe was absolutely delighted. It seemed like ages that he had been straining at the leash to get the show on the road and now it really looked like the studio was to be christened with a hit. This was how to put Holloway Road on the map: with a bang! This one would show that you don't need big over-priced studios to get results; as he said himself: "It's not what you've got – it's the way that you use it."

As soon as the recording was ready he made a beeline for his old ally at Decca, Dick Rowe, and sat tingling with excitement as he watched him listening to it. But alas, the tingles turned to trembles when Dick said he didn't like it. The singer was okay, he thought, but not the song. Joe didn't know whether to burst into tears or fly into a rage, but Dick was quick and promised to take Mike if he sang the right song – the right song being a new American one called 'Will You Love Me Tomorrow'. The original version of it, performed by the Shirelles, had just been released in the States but was definitely not coming out over here, so he wanted it covered at once before someone else did, and with the same musical arrangement. If Joe recorded it, Decca would release it. Inwardly seething, he agreed. Copying other people's records had never interested him but at least he had got a deal, and with the mighty force of Decca behind it, was virtually assured of a hit before he had even recorded it.

The session was to be a difficult one. The arrangement called for violins, heralding a full house at 304 because his little studio would be pretty well crammed to capacity with just the backing band and singer; the orchestra would have to play elsewhere in the house. The session took up most of the day. Simply conducting it with Charles Blackwell was something of a dilemma, with Joe bounding in and out of the studio issuing orders to Mike and the Outlaws and up and down the stairs into the living room where the orchestra (four violinists!) were stationed. Everyone was nicely miked up but he refused to use cue lights or talk-back systems, saying that this way he could get a more homely, relaxed atmosphere. Instead the violinists were wearing headphones and taking their cue from the band, who were in turn taking theirs from Joe popping his head round the door shouting, "Ready". The biggest headache was getting a good voice out of Mike Berry: "I sang it in this high clef and we did it so many times, in the end I couldn't get up to the note. If you listen to the record I sing terribly off in several places – it's really diabolical! On that session, by the time we'd done the 20th take the violinists who were downstairs in another room linked to upstairs were saying, 'What a singer – *Jesus!'* And I didn't blame them. And Joe heard them over the system and he went mad and nearly threw them out saying, 'If you don't f—— well like my singers you can get out!'"

Still, Dick at Decca liked it and said the disc would be on sale in January.

Another actor whose record had been destined for the Triumph label but whom Joe had since off-loaded onto Pye was Ian Gregory. Like John Leyton he was a Robert Stigwood protégé. Stigwood, a young Australian whose empire at the time extended no further than a small casting agency and a ballet group, had cleverly recognized that recording success for his clients could be a means of boosting their chances of acting roles, so regardless of whether they could sing or not they now had to start trying. It was a philosophy for which many a future Meek fan would be enormously grateful, for without it they would have been denied one of the most atrocious singing voices ever to be pressed into vinyl. With the benefit of hindsight it is clear that of all the scores of voices Joe released on disc during his career this one bears the distinction of being the worst. Ian Gregory sounded like he had taken lessons from a clapped-out alley cat and gone out and found an alley. For his recording of 'Time Will Tell', Joe had the inspired idea of putting Ian in headphones to help him keep a minimum of pitch singing along to the voice of Dave Adams. But that song plus the one on the other side were still painful and could only be recommended to penance-seeking sinners. Even though his voice had some of its inadequacies masked by echo and a bravely cheerful backing, the problem was that you could still hear it, and that meant the record stood about as much chance of reaching the charts as a Russian recital on the 1917 Bolshevik reform laws. But it did! In mid-December it climbed to No.17 on the *Record Mirror* chart, giving renewed hope to tone-deaf singers everywhere and showing that Russian recitals might be in with a chance after all.

It is to his credit that at the time Ian confessed: "I don't want to be a singer really. If by some chance I really got ahead through singing I can assure you I'd drop it fast. All I want to be is an actor." Whether his record sales earned him more acting roles is unknown but he was to carry on playing his part on disc well into 1963.

1960 had been quite a jamboree bag. The year which had seen such events as the wedding of Princess Margaret, the election of Senator John Kennedy as US President, the launch of Britain's first nuclear submarine, the end of British rule in Cyprus, Nigeria and Somaliland, plus the last of *The Goon Show* and the good old faithful farthing had also seen the spectacular rise and fall of Triumph and Joe's latest appearance on the music scene as a freelance producer. Since leaving Denis Preston he had recorded a Top Ten hit plus a handful of minor ones; twenty of his records had been released and though much of his Triumph stuff had been rejected he was super-optimistic, and next year he intended consolidating on 1960's groundwork. Christmas he spent at Newent in preparation for a busy 1961.

8
"It Sounds Like He's Singing At The Bottom Of An Empty Well"

Joe was hopping mad! In the middle of January, Mike Berry's 'Will You Love Me Tomorrow' was released – and so was the original version by the Shirelles! In spite of Dick Rowe having given his assurance that it would not come out, there it was on Top Rank speeding up the charts. Dick maintained that he had been told on good authority it would not be released in Britain, but that had been back in November long before it had reached the No.1 spot in the States. He explained quite reasonably that someone at EMI had obviously seen it selling like hot cakes over there and figured it might do the same over here. Decca, he reminded Joe, were also missing out on their investment whereby thousands of their Mike Berry discs were now gathering dust in record shop shelves. All of which was a fat lot of consolation for Joe.

On top of that, his disc had had all the guts taken out of it! Decca's pressing engineers had left it just as tinny as all their others and a poor substitute for the American version.

As January proceeded into February he grew angrier. Decca were hardly promoting it at all, and while the Shirelles' record was moving up the Top Ten, Mike Berry's was still nowhere to be seen. And the American record was taking on new meaning. To him it began to embody the attitude of the music business towards him, and the higher the record went, the lower he felt in their esteem. It was as if they were telling him, "If you want hits, make them in proper studios like ours, not tinpot outfits over leather shops." Soon it became clear that all his sky-high hopes for a lucky disc to launch the studio had not been worth a bean; that after all the time, effort and expense, all he was left with was egg on his face.

And then he had another thought: that maybe Dick had known all along of the American record's British release; that even though Top Rank was now an entirely new company, Dick might still have contacts there who had given him a snaky tip-off, so as to force him out of business before he became a threat. This might even explain why Dick had turned down his first Holloway Road recording, 'Set Me Free'. And if that were the case, then maybe the dirty tricks had started months ago – with 'Tell Laura I Love Her'. Again on that occasion he had been pipped to the post when the Ricky Valance version climbed to No.1 while his own, sung by John Leyton, had done nothing. And who was the man to accept his recording that time? Dick Rowe. As his thoughts pursued their path, so his eyes narrowed with ever more suspicion, and Dick zoomed ever faster up his list of undesirables. The way he now saw it, not only had Dick three times made a monkey of him, but had tried to scuttle him too. However much Dick might protest his innocence – and he had good grounds on which to do so – Joe decided on the sentence: Dick and Decca had to suffer. Their little conspiracy had failed so far to shut him down and they now had to be punished the only way he knew how: by being ignored. In future he would hawk his wares elsewhere.

The only glad tidings came at the end of January. The Lansdowne lawsuit which had been dragging on since the end of '59 was at last settled, out of court. The Denis Preston camp had been getting a bit sick of it all and perhaps a pinch pessimistic as to the outcome. So the issue was wound up with Joe agreeing to accept £200. He was not overjoyed with the settlement but felt that justice of some sort had been done.

All things considered, it was a super result for him. But that was just about all the good news he had. Apart from the occasional cash-in-hand job such as recording TV commercial jingles or just balancing the sound for other people's groups like Carter Lewis & the Southerners, there was not much to write home about. HMV were taking some product but as the weeks slipped by, things were getting tougher and tougher and his records were not even selling enough to cover costs. On top of it all Major Banks was nagging him to pull a hit out of the hat and everything was getting depressingly frustrating. This was also the period when he was learning the struggles of the tape-lease game: getting the wheels of these organizations grinding. However terrific it might feel having a recording accepted, that was just the start of more hassles. He would find himself chasing the company first for a pressing date, then a release date and later when he found that the record was not selling, it might either be because their promotions department was not pushing the thing or because it was not even in the shops – not enough discs had been pressed! Keeping his records' chances high meant fighting, fuming, ranting and raving right down the line – otherwise he would get nowhere.

In March he briefly broke out of the doldrums by conjuring up some light relief with the Outlaws. To launch their first solo record, 'Swingin' Low', he thought himself up a publicity stunt: in keeping with their Western image, he decided to have them dress as cowboys and ride a stagecoach around London's West End. So they got their gear and a stagecoach was hired, bedecked with posters proclaiming the record to have been voted a hit on the pop programme, *Juke Box Jury*. Then the newspapers were informed and off they galloped down Oxford Street with Joe inside playing the music and Mike Berry running along behind handing out leaflets. On the way, they pulled up at the HMV record store and rushed in to hold up the staff; pointing their aluminium guns menacingly at an assistant, they demanded a copy of their record. As if their behaviour were perfectly normal she didn't bat an eyelid. "Oh yes," she replied. "That will be 6s.4d." They paid their dues and shuffled out, wondering if cowboy hold-ups were regular events round there. The ride continued up Oxford Street and down Shaftesbury Avenue with Joe blasting shoppers and traffic constables with the record. Their reign of terror was briefly interrupted at Leicester Square where police told them they were breaking some old by-law by advertising within a mile radius of Piccadilly Circus. As he gave his name and address Joe agreed to take down the posters, at the same time putting on a sour face for their cine camera. Then away they all dashed again, with Joe dangling a poster out of the window. The whole event would have been a tour-de-force but for one thing: hardly any newspapermen turned up. Better luck next time.

Then it was back again to harsh reality and records, records, records. As usual he was catering for all tastes: ballads, rock'n'roll, guitar instrumentals and even some trad jazz but most of it was falling on deaf ears. Hopes were high for one called 'Can't You Hear My Heart', sung by his own 'answer' to Cliff Richard, Danny Rivers, but it only reached a luke-warm No.36.[21]

Then there was Michael Cox who still seemed to have plenty of hit potential left in him but his songs didn't. There could be no complaints though about the American style productions which Joe could hit spot on, and of the latest Danny Rivers record, Jack Good was moved to write: "It's an outstanding achievement. Joe Meek, the independent recording genius, has got closer to the

105

elusive American pop sound than anyone over here. It's called 'Once Upon A Time'. One small moan, though. I had the privilege of hearing Joe's original tape on this record. The bass sound he achieved was quite incredible. When the Decca pressing arrived I was somewhat disappointed. For some very obscure and extremely misguided reason the balance had been altered. Result – a phenomenal record had been transformed into something that is merely excellent." It flopped.

As for Joe's Anton Hollywood recordings, he might just as well have been selling last week's newspapers: no one wanted to know. It seems that Anton's main stumbling block was not so much the tunes he was playing as the rather irregular accompaniment he was giving them, beating time by stamping his foot on the floor and letting out from the back of his throat "an uncanny, groaning, wailing sound". When he was asked to play without stamping or groaning he found he couldn't. Eventually poor old Anton was getting nowhere so fast that Joe forced him to give up the ghost in favour of Geoff Goddard, songwriter.

What Joe needed was a good, solid hit to really get him off the ground but it seemed as elusive as a wig in the wind, and come July his 1961 output had managed only two minor chart scrapings. That was not too bad a tally out of only nine releases, but there were that number again he had not found takers for, and it highlighted a new and very real battle he now had on his hands.

It is said you can always tell a pioneer by the arrows in his back, and Joe Meek was no exception. Like so many others who have broken down barriers, he was realizing there was a price to pay. He now found himself competing with the same A & R men who used to bring their work to him at IBC and Lansdowne, and it was not a sportsman's rivalry. The esteem in which some of them had held him a few years earlier when they had been climbing over each other in their efforts to have him grace their records, now turned to scorn as they jealously guarded the marketing and promotion of their own in-house product. They ridiculed his use of echo and compression, slating his productions as "souped up". This was even though he had used the same effects, albeit to a lesser extent, on their own records. Others merely laughed at his work, snobbishly dismissing it as sub-standard dross. But laughing time was almost up.

A real whopper of a record was about to hit them for six and infuse some Great British vim into the charts. The ball started rolling when manager Robert Stigwood booked his client John

"HE'S SINGING AT THE BOTTOM OF AN EMPTY WELL"

Leyton an appearance in a top TV series called *Harpers West One*. Appropriately he was to play a pop singer and would be seen opening a store's record department. The shrewd Stigwood had quickly counted on his fingers the average number of viewers expected to be watching and this, like the other two big soap operas of the day, *Emergency Ward 10* and *Coronation Street*, came to 10 million. He then pulled off perhaps the biggest publicity stunt a British disc had yet enjoyed by arranging for Leyton's character, Johnny St. Cyr, to also perform his latest record during the episode. Stigwood didn't know it, but the song that was to be sung by Leyton had not yet been written, and one Friday while he was tearing around the publishers frantically searching for it, the man who was to write it was making phone calls from Paddington Station.

It was the new songwriter Geoff Goddard, and he was at the station because he found that telephoning people in London from his home in Reading worked out expensive, especially when they were like Joe and took ten minutes to reach the phone. Geoff reckoned he could knock a few pence off his bill by catching the train for the 40 miles up to Paddington and making his calls there from a kiosk. On the Friday when he eventually got through, Joe explained the situation asking him to try and write something for Leyton over the weekend. Geoff had not as yet written any songs at all and it was hoped that when he did he would have more luck than with his instrumental tunes, which had so far seen only one release: 'Lone Rider' by the Flee Rekkers (new spelling). On the Sunday he was inspirited to compose a song about a man hearing the voice of his dead lover calling him from the Beyond: 'Johnny Remember Me'.

The final choice rested with Robert Stigwood. When he listened to it on the Monday he decided it was the best of the bunch he had heard, thoughtfully remarking that "it's about time for another death disc." All the same, 'Johnny Remember Me' could easily have suffered the same fate as the great majority of the genre. Death discs issued in the Fifties and early Sixties were considered tasteless by various moralizing clergymen and teacher-parent groups, and by thus usually being refused airplay by the BBC, were almost invariably doomed; tragic irony! Hopefully the high turnover of Ricky Valance's 'Laura' might have softened the hearts of a few Victorian prudes.

Anyway, the song captivated Joe and its spiritual lyrics lent themselves perfectly to his childishly fertile imagination. First he

organized with Geoff and Charles Blackwell the kind of arrangement he wanted. Then come the day of the session, when he got
his hands on the words and music he had at them greedily, fairly
blowing life into Geoff's beautiful imagery – 'singing in the
sighing of the wind, blowing in the treetops' – injecting it with a
zing and wanton yearning reminiscent of Emily Bronte's
Wuthering Heights characters, Heathcliff and Cathy. John Leyton
gives his own account of the session: "We were all in the studio;
I was behind the screen and right next to me was Geoff Goddard
playing the piano. And Geoff, when he played the piano, he
always used to make strange noises through his teeth. He was
always singing; if the microphone had been a bit more to the left
you would have picked up Geoff singing as well. The Outlaws
were doing the rest of the backing. We did it over and over. Joe
wanted plenty of exciting atmosphere in it, and it was a really
exhilarating sound with the galloping, driving beat. He was
getting all excited, slapping his leg and combing his quiff. I was
singing along but my voice was dubbed on afterwards with those
of the session singers, which included Lissa Gray. Originally the
lyrics were: '. . . the girl I loved who died a year ago . . .' and that
was all recorded and finished. And then I went back in the studio
and put that one line in again to: '. . . the girl I loved and lost a
year ago . . .' I think somebody had said that the BBC didn't like
that bit!"

Geoff was as pleased with the end result as Joe: "It just
clicked. It just sounded exactly as I wanted it to sound, as I'd
conceived it."

Certainly no pop video today could hope to better the kind of
pictures in sound that the Goddard-Meek-Blackwell triumvirate
inspired with that one or indeed its follow-up, 'Wild Wind'. Even
if such visual aids had been around then, they would have been
redundant in this particular case, for who can improve upon the
ultimate video: the imagination?

Joe was elated by it, and the promise of a good hit record in
the coming weeks after all these months of disappointment
christened the Meek-Goddard musical bond of friendship.

These two shy, retiring loners were plumb on the same wave-
length, for as well as their love of making music they were both
acquiring a growing intrigue in the psychic field. Bob Kingston,
who had by now come to know both men fairly well, puts Joe's
spiritual side in an interesting light and also shows its importance
in the budding Meek-Goddard relationship: "I think basically he

must have been a religious man because he was searching constantly. He was not a devout church-goer but within himself I think he was very much a lost individual. I always thought he was a very lonely person but you could never really get to know him. Crossing this barrier between knowing Joe and being close to him was something that rarely happened; it didn't happen for me except on rare moments. He responded tremendously to kindness. It wasn't always easy to feel kind towards Joe because he was very aggravating in many ways but when deliberately a little thing was done, such as giving him a little gift on odd occasions, he would be embarrassingly emotional in his response. And I believe that this inner loneliness he had was also with Geoff Goddard. They became *really* close. These two very strange personalities worked like magic together. I think they were very similar in make-up and temperament; both very mystical. They didn't think and live on normal planes as the average person. They were constantly searching for something and I believe that this is very largely the reason why their sensitivity was so attuned to outer things that they were capable of creating what they did. I believe one can mentally attune oneself to an infinite knowledge or this unknown thing in infinity. It can be done. I believe that inventors, scientists, great creators in the Arts are really totally devoted people who work this single course in life and totally attune themselves to becoming receptive to available things from outer space somewhere. I believe that Joe was, like Geoff, one of these very sensitive people, lonely people – complete loneliness, total individuals; totally different sets of values in life, but nevertheless had great creative ability and this mental attuneness which enabled them to draw on something to enhance this creativity, and therefore do what they were doing."

Besides their deep interest in psychic research, the two men found their ties further strengthened by a common fascination in the contribution to pop music of Buddy Holly. Both of these subjects for Joe at least had long held an almost unnatural attraction and were inextricably linked. So now it was sometimes with Geoff he would try 'contacting' the lost giant. Joe's dabblings with a glass, letters and numbers had carried on since his Arundel Gardens days but now with Geoff's influence he was taking a more active interest, often holding seances twice a week. At one particular sitting, one of the Outlaws and his manager had walked into the living room to find Joe apparently talking to his father, with whom he was getting on much better now. It seems that his father was well informed on the Hit Parade, and it was after Joe had extracted information from him on next week's positions that the two newcomers replaced Joe's two friends at the table. Neither of them believed in such things but agreed to rest their fingers with Joe's on the edge of the glass while he asked the questions. During the hour that followed, the glass erratically spelt out the name Mario Lanza, a 'sign' of whose presence being a rather obscure rapping noise from elsewhere in the house. A little more encouraging was their next 'contact' with Al Jolson who asked them to play one of his old records. Someone was then sent upstairs to find it but came back empty-handed. Instructions where to look were then spelt out and gave Joe's two partners quite a scare when they proved correct.

Geoff Goddard's involvement in spiritualism was more serious than Joe's for he was attending a weekly development circle in the hope of becoming a medium. He had first been attracted to spiritualism when reading a book called *My Greatest Story* by the 'Pope of Fleet Street', Hannen Swaffer. (Swaffer, the top journalist of the Fifties, had earned the nickname through his love of what he called 'the three isms': spiritualism, socialism and journalism.)

Turning such talents to songwriting obviously afforded Geoff access to vast untapped resources, making him ideally suited to composing a 'tribute' to Holly, which he did. After one of these Holloway Road sittings, Geoff went home and dreamt of him which induced him to write a song, 'Tribute To Buddy Holly', in his memory. Set to a slow melody, it told of the singer's untimely death and his songs lingering on: 'We'll always remember Buddy Holly'. Geoff says that when he played it to him, "Joe raved over it and said Mike Berry must sing it."

Since October, Mike's total output had been but one forlorn version of 'Will You Love Me Tomorrow' on which as Joe's 'answer' to Buddy Holly he sounded just like someone singing nothing like Buddy Holly. To add insult to injury Mike's backing band, the Outlaws, were having success in their own right, releasing two instrumentals which had both grazed the charts. After recording the song it seemed only natural to get Holly's opinion on it, so one evening when Geoff and another friend were there, Joe got out his glass, letters and numbers, switched on the red bulb inside the electric fire and turned off the lights. Geoff goes on: "We sat round the table in his sitting room and he put a long playing record of Al Jolson singing on the record player. And we sat and put our hands on the tumbler and it started moving round and spelt out Buddy's name and mine. And Joe asked if 'Johnny Remember Be' would be a hit, and it spelt out that it would go to No.1. And he asked if the tribute to Buddy Holly that I'd written – would that be a hit, and the answer was: 'See you in the charts'."

By this time Joe was of course very pleased indeed with 'Tribute' but not so sure that the Buddy Holly Appreciation Society would be. In case they might find it in bad taste, he invited along the club's president, John Beecher, and the Holly fans to hear it. (The song 'My Baby Doll' that he mentions, is the B-side to Mike Berry's 'Will You Love Me Tomorrow'.)

Dear John

May I introduce myself, my names is Joe Meek and I run a company called RGM sound, I have made many hit records for Artists and have on my books Mike Cox, Danny Rivers, John Leyton etc.

Now one young singer I have, and you may have heard him is Mike Berry, his first disc was MY BABY DOLL, he has a voice so much like Buddy Holly that at times you would think it Buddy singing.

At first I was against recording him but his performance's of the Buddy Holly songs were so wounderful that I made his disc's.

He loves Buddy Holly and his songs, so do I, he was and still remains to me, the singer that realy gets to the heart, sincerity in his voice made him Millions of friends.

After a lot of thought I decieded to make with Mike Berry a disc which is a tribut to Buddy this has turned out to be a realy lovely disc, please believe me when I say I have not done this to make money but to make more friends for Buddy Holly, I am going to keep Mike Berry singing similar songs and if there not hits I don't care, you see this way I can keep Buddy Hollys name alive, because you must realise that after a while people would begin to forget him

111

and his songs when no new records came out.

I would like you to come along to my studio and lissen to this disc befor I send it through to Decca for release, I do not wish to upset any of Buddys friends and will regect the disc if you dislike it in any way, but Im sure you will love it can you come along to see me as soon as you can, by the way I would be greatful if I could become a member of your society also Mike Berry look forward to hearing from you soon my kindest wishes

yours Sincerely
Joe Meek

It was very important to him that the recording should be approved. He had studied every Holly track issued and what he didn't know about the man's music wasn't worth knowing. If they were to object to the record he would definitely withdraw it but would be deeply hurt, seeing this as a personal attack on his sincerity and his ability as a producer.

Come the big day, Holly photos and album sleeves covered the walls and a crowd of young enthusiasts called around in the evening to receive the VIP treatment and hear 'Tribute'. It was a success. Any fears that the fans would condemn it were thankfully wiped out when they not only gave it the thumbs-up but stayed for more. Mike and the Outlaws then ran through a string of Holly hits and Joe, mixing the sound as he went along, played them back afterwards. He had wired up the house with speakers and was delighted to see fans all over the place: either running up and down the stairs or jam-packed in the living room, looking very serious in their Buddy Holly glasses. There was a party and he had a whale of a time discussing the late singer, and John Beecher gave him his opinion of the evening's tape recordings: "He got the Norman Petty-Buddy Holly sound on those tapes that night. People were impressed with the sound that Mike Berry & the Outlaws got, which meant the sound that Joe got. It *did* sound like Buddy Holly & the Crickets. He really had worked on it to get that sound right. He really was a Holly fan. He was aware what the B-sides were to each record and he knew album tracks that people weren't really that conscious of. He'd say, 'Do you remember the B-side of 'Think it Over'?' or something like that. He idolized Buddy Holly's music; he'd talk all night long about those records and the way they were produced and how fantastic they were and how wonderful Norman Petty was for producing them. He genuinely wanted everyone to accept Holly and what he'd done."

When it came to putting up 'Tribute' for release, it was not to Decca that he took it this time. Instead he offered it to EMI.

Meanwhile 'Johnny Remember Me' was living up to all expectations. After its TV airing the audience reaction was immediate. ATV were besieged with enquiries as to its availability and next day a crowd of girls gathered on the pavement outside 304 to see John. On its release it was played on BBC TV's celebrated pop programme *Juke Box Jury*, where every week a new panel of television personalities would be lined up to air their ignorance of pop music and judge records that completely mystified them. Needless to say, they were not at all impressed with it and unanimously voted it a 'miss'. However, at least there was one intelligent comment from a member of the panel, comedian Spike Milligan, who thoughtfully likened it to "the son of 'Ghost Riders In The Sky'." There is certainly a similarity since both songs feature a rousing rhythm less related to this world than the next, but the "son" had obviously learnt a lot from the "father", and Lissa Gray's haunting harmonies would have scared the spooks out of Frankie Laine's ghost riders.

The music critics' reaction to it was scathing, saying of Leyton's echo-laden voice that he sounded like he was singing at the bottom of an empty well. But unlike all the other British productions of the day it had a dramatic atmosphere about it which only the Americans seemed anywhere near capable of achieving. Since then though, attitudes towards it have changed and it has been hailed by various pop connoisseurs as a classic.

Anyway it went straight into the Top Thirty. At the end of August it was at the magical No.1 spot notching up 250,000 sales within four weeks of its release, so earning a Silver Disc.

Joe was all of a twitter and fairly skipping about with delight; he felt absolutely top of the pops and recharged with recording zest. All he wanted now was to pull out another No.1 and another and another. He knew that things had to be easier from here on – no more could the record companies ignore him. Every production he put their way had to be a potential Top Ten hit and now he had shown them that in black and white. This was where the gear change came; this was where the big time started. The heat was on.

'Johnny Remember Me' was to remain at the top for five, six or seven weeks, depending on the chart. High sales of any record automatically attract attention from the music press, and while it was at No.1, two interviews with him appeared which were quite interesting. He talked about his work but, reading between the lines, one can see how conscious he had become of his unusual working conditions and what people might be thinking of them. Reporters, he thought, were bound to view his amateur-looking studio with amazement and compare it less than favourably with others they had seen. So, what he had to do was underline its virtues: "I don't use any talk-back, no cue lights at all. They're completely on their own in the studio and I think it helps a lot. There's nothing to distract them . . . All they have to do is produce a sound. Which is what I'm interested in. When I want them to start a number I go into the studio and tell them. I then go back to the control room and by the time they've started I've got the equipment ready. This is where I like to record. And this is the way I like to record. I stress 'informality' because you get the best out of an artiste in this business in that way."

Actually, much of it did indeed suit him. Apart from the domestic surroundings of the studio helping with its absence of white coats, commissioners and canteen staff to create a relaxed atmosphere, he was also glad to be working at home, cutting out time-wasting journeys to work every day. So tapes and recorders were always on hand when he felt a tune coming, and none of the time limits governing major studios were his, where a 3-hour session had to produce both sides of a single and a 15-minute tea break! He could take as long as he liked and was free to work the only way he could: as both producer and engineer; already he had quite enough problems getting musicians to play what he wanted, without having to explain it all to engineers as well.

But there were drawbacks. Running it all on half a shoestring so he could not afford more up-to-date equipment or even a secretary to help him was a curse. He would also have preferred having a larger studio altogether, so musicians no longer had to squeeze out onto the landing, and to have the whole house to himself a million miles away from traffic noise and neighbours. Then there would be no more rows with the Shentons – the landlady and her husband – and the people with a baby next door who would bang on the wall during sessions; no more threatening letters for him to tear up and no more complaints from the fish shop lady when he walked in to buy some fish and ended up whacking it round her face. (His detractors did score a partial victory around this time though when they joined hands to present a petition at the Town Hall demanding less noise from 304 and prompting a Health Inspector to call round and ban him from recording after 6 and at weekends. Naturally he carried right on recording whenever he pleased but during curfew hours he would generally, mood permitting, tell drummers to drum quietly and would 'direct inject' all the other instruments so their sounds bypassed the loudspeakers and were fed straight into the tape recorders.)

One rumour that used to get him very het up, although it was perfectly justified, had it that the bathroom was also used for recording. "No, it just isn't true," he exclaimed to the *Disc* reporter. "I don't make recordings in the bathroom." Of course, he did. The tiles on the walls were not just for decoration: they also happened to produce just the right acoustics for girl choruses, session violinists and some of John Leyton's and rock singer Cliff Bennett's vocals. He also used it for separation (to prevent 'leakage' of sound from certain instruments) and to help him wheedle out exotic new sound effects. But he hated people finding out about such unethical methods and felt quite rightly that to many in the business it was very funny. What he should have done was capitalize on it rather than conceal it because it made a mockery of the superstudios with their vastly dearer facilities. Instead he preferred playing down the role of the bathroom and to concede only that it was sometimes used for making tea: "I suppose that's how the story of my using the bathroom started. But I don't mind what they say, it's the results I'm interested in. Some musicians, particularly string sections, ask me if I want them to sit in the bathroom or kitchen when they first come here. But they take everything more seriously when they hear the results."

Likewise a photo of the studio carried in the *Record Mirror* showed no mess of cables, beer cans and cigarette ends, but a few neatly placed instruments and microphone stands. He went on: "To survive as an independent A & R man I've got to produce records that are different. This is the only advantage I have over the big companies, and working as a small unit like this I can do it. When I first get a song sent to me I know exactly what sort of sound I want, who is the best person to sing it, who I want to back it and so on. I can only look after all these things if I do it myself.

Sometimes I use Charles Blackwell to write arrangements but I'm not using him much these days as he's so tied up with other work. Anyway, I seldom use complete arrangements. I get a group in, usually the Outlaws, and let them work it all out in the studio. That way they get more punch and feeling into their music. I'm after a sound, and to get results you have to experiment. That's how this flat started . . . as an experiment. Then I thought I could get better results here. I still think so. The B-side of John Leyton's hit was achieved in only two takes but 'Johnny Remember Me' took longer. It was very difficult to get the correct balance. The follow-up was also recorded here and we are starting work on a Leyton LP this week for release about October.

"I suppose I average about one disc a week. And I don't think I could work any harder than I do. But I do have time to think about new ideas. And usually when I record I put the singer's voice on a separate track and don't join it up with the backing until a few days after the session. That gives me even more time to decide on the sound.

"I've never reached the perfection I wanted, but every time I hear one of my discs for the first time I get the same thrill as I did eight years ago when I made my first record. People are surprised when I say I like this kind of music but I genuinely do."

𝄞𝄞𝄞𝄞𝄞𝄞𝄞𝄞𝄞𝄞𝄞𝄞𝄞𝄞

By this time 'Tribute To Buddy Holly' was in the shops. The song of course was controversial and he was helping stoke up more with absurd comments about Mike Berry like: "He looks like Buddy Holly", "It's impossible to tell their voices apart" and "This resemblance in Mike is a gift, not mimicry. He even talks like Buddy." But he was not so pleased about the things Geoff Goddard was saying.

As 'Tribute' climbed into the Top Fifty Geoff was busy chattering away to the press about the inspiration behind 'Johnny Remember Me' and his own links with Holly. The *Psychic News* were very excited about it, making Geoff their top story of the week. Alongside his photo went their banner headline: " 'JOHNNY REMEMBER ME' SENSATION. Does Dead Rock Star Guide Songwriter?". He told them, "I am sure I receive my inspiration from the spirit world. When I wrote 'Johnny Remember Me' it was early morning and I had just opened my eyes. I always keep a tape recorder by my bed, and I sang that song into it without working on it at all . . . I was always a great fan of his [Holly] and play his records all the time. I did the rounds of Denmark Street publishers because I received a strong impression that I should go there. Strangely enough none of them were interested except the one that published Buddy's music – and I ended up by working for a freelance recording manager the way Buddy did. I intend to go on with my songwriting although it seems I must wait for inspiration from the spirit world. I find I can sit at the piano for hours without being able to write a note of music – and yet after a dreamless sleep I can produce a bestseller in practically the time it takes to sing it!"

To the music paper *Disc* he explained that since receiving his first message from Holly in March, the late singer had been the guiding hand behind his career: "Every Monday night I attend seances with a development group and this first message was passed on to me from someone who received it and who knew I was a songwriter. Since then I've had several more, this time directly to me from Buddy, and these talks with him have given me the encouragement and inspiration I need. Buddy said he would help me and soon after that I started getting better ideas. I wrote my first recorded song, 'Lone Rider', which was cut by the Fleerakkers and then I wrote 'Johnny Remember Me'. I remember writing that song. I woke up on a Sunday morning and within ten minutes it was completed, words and music. Buddy said it would reach No.1 – I believed him; he said it was a great song and would be the start of good things for me. He is a constant inspiration to me . . . When I wrote 'Tribute To Buddy Holly' I had Mike Berry in mind. He too is an avid fan of Buddy's and wanted to do something to retain his memory. When I had written the song I asked Buddy what he thought of it. He thanked me for the honour and said, 'See you in the charts'. He seems to have an amazing foresight as far as my career is concerned."

None of it cut any ice with the BBC though, who promptly banned the song for its "morbid concern over the death of a teen idol". As for the Buddy Holly fan club, they were most displeased about Geoff's revelations, so Joe had to write apologizing to them, fervently denying any interest himself in such moribund activities.

The sight of 'Tribute's' healthy chart showing brought a letter of heartfelt sorrow from Dick at Decca. He asked why 'Tribute' had not been offered to him first, saying they would definitely have accepted it. Joe let them eat their hearts out.

Meanwhile 'Johnny Remember Me' was already bringing in benefits. For a start there was more work coming in: publishers offering songs; singers offering talent. Then there were money matters. The promise of royalties ahead persuaded Major Banks to loosen the purse strings and let him share out his increasing workload by employing an 18 year old office boy, Tony Kent. By sheer coincidence Tony just happened to be the founder member of the Buddy Holly society but had long since broken all ties with it. Calling round looking for work, he told Joe of his plans to become a recording engineer. However, giving all his valuable secrets away to an assistant engineer did not appeal to Joe at all, so instead of taking him on he arranged an interview with Allen Stagg at IBC. Tony failed it, but returning to Joe, managed to convince him he was handy with a typewriter. His pay, he says, was £7 per week: "Most of my job with Joe was essentially making coffee for the artistes, answering the telephone, typing his letters and trying to get some sort of semblance of order in the office as far as contracts were concerned. I had to type contracts out from a standard form. The whole thing was totally disorganized. I hadn't had any experience of office procedures or legal procedures about contracts but occasionally he'd say to me, 'Do you think we should put a clause in there; do you think I should get a bit more percentage?'"

During all this the John Leyton circus was still on the road. John was suddenly being touted as an all-round showman: actor, singer, song-and-dance man, impersonator, comedian, and he was making quite a good job of it. At Chester's Royalty Theatre he was described as "a very accomplished and stylish performer". Immaculately dressed in his silvery suit he looked a star and projected all the sex appeal and loneliness the girls could wish for. Thanks to one hit record he was now earning £200 per week, with film and TV work lined up plus possible dates on American TV.

While 'Johnny Remember Me's' swelling sales were keeping John shining in the limelight, his manager was out earning his 40 percent commission campaigning for the next one. Following up a debut hit record is never easy especially if it's a chart-topper, so the safest option, they decided, was to stick to the winning formula. Joe, as if to proclaim that his first No.1 as an independent was no flash in the pan, hammered it home with the more ferocious 'Wild Wind'. Also penned by Geoff this one was virtually a manic rehash of the first; again there was the intriguing touch of the supernatural about it, with eerie voices swirling around the melody line. It was an exciting sound built round the beat of sticks on the cymbals, with Geoff pounding away at the piano as if his life depended on it and Joe echoing everything up, urging everyone on like Nimrod gone musical.

Robert Stigwood's publicity campaign was doing everyone proud. An unprecedented 44 million TV viewers were expected to watch 'Wild Wind' performed on just about every pop programme in Britain, and the word was going around that "John Leyton's handlers have every intention of building him into a British parallel to Elvis". Such a remark was extravagant to say the least and sounded as if the poor man who made it had let a No.1 record go straight to his head and had become confused. True, Leyton had plenty going for him: good looks, stage presence and a fine songwriting-production-marketing team to back him up, but as he admits himself, he was never any great shakes as a singer; his voice was merely adequate for the job. Like some of Joe's other artistes he tended to sing flat and as Stigwood confessed: "It takes John about two hours to warm up completely for singing. By that time he's really with it."

In October 'Wild Wind' blew some more fresh air into the Hit Parade when it shot straight into the *Record Mirror's* chart at No.8 below 'Johnny Remember Me'. A couple of weeks later while they were still in the Top Ten, the appearance of Mike Berry's 'Tribute' made it three in the Top Twenty. All that was needed now was for 'Wild Wind' to reach No.1, but that was where Helen Shapiro was 'Walkin' Back To Happiness'. All in all it was turning out quite a good month because following hard on the heels of 'Johnny Remember Me' came another No.1 – in Sweden! This was 'Sweet Little Sixteen' by Michael Cox and was to be the first of many big sellers for him in that country. Perhaps the Joe Meek sound, described by one English reviewer as "overloaded by excessive echo and electronics", struck the right chord in Swedish ears. Michael Cox just clicked over there, and while his future releases were to be all but ignored in England, they were to make him something of a national hero in Scandinavia.

Before October was out Leyton was dashing off to Billy Cotton's *Wakey Wakey Tavern* TV show to pick up a Silver Disc for 'Wild Wind' and one for 'Johnny Remember Me', which had now sold its first half million.

However monotonous Joe's way of life might appear to the average onlooker, it was to him absolutely gripping! This was his world. In one way or another music matters now accounted for around 16 hours of any given day. He lived and breathed every detail: every chart placing, sound effect, knock at the door, telephone ring, every new gadget on the market, every mention of his name in a music paper, every spin on the radio of one of his discs. In fact most of it he loved. What he did not like was being short of money to buy fresh equipment; he hated hawking his recordings round, especially when they were turned down; he mistrusted all those with whom he did business and always jumped at the chance of getting his own back on them. In general, despite his need for and generosity to people, he had no great liking for them. Strange as it may sound, little by little he was coming to the conclusion that the world at large was against him and that his only means of survival was to fight back and prove to them how brilliant he was and how brainless they were.

That meant music-making more or less full time. Not for him were discussions or even thoughts on life's broader issues: how marvellous or disastrous a job Harold Macmillan was doing as Prime Minister; whether the Double-winning Tottenham Hotspur of 1961 was the greatest football team ever; whether the new Polaris submarines were a good thing; whether Ena Sharples of *Coronation Street* really was a dragon. None of it interested him. The multi-faceted music business answered nearly all his needs, even if it did give him a narrow outlook on life, so he was not going to waste time on other subjects which foxed him and revealed his ignorance, causing him embarrassment. Taken away from his abiding interest he was like a fish out of water. Far wiser, he thought, to stick to what he knew best, where if anyone was going to look stupid it wouldn't be him.

Then there was his habitual hot-headed problem. Although his fortunes had changed dramatically for the better, there was alas no change in his Jekyll & Hyde temperament. The mistrust he had in those around him was as deep as ever, as was his resentment towards those he unwillingly depended on. To add to his unease he felt as much an 'outer' now as when he was a child. Still he was acutely sensitive to any adverse criticism and always conscious of hostility towards him whether real or imaginary. Thus, as Southern Music's Bob Kingston recalls, it could take him by surprise when in the middle of his usual sense of rejection he received a slight spark of goodwill: "Everybody basically liked Joe; you may have been in a state of war with him at any one time but you couldn't help but like him. I remember that when we had this big No.1 hit with John Leyton I organized an evening out to celebrate. It was in the days when the Edmundo Ros Club was still open – Bob Stigwood, John Leyton, they had some girlfriends in the casting agency, Joe, my wife and myself. And I had bought them all a gift: gold cigarette cases with an inscription thanking them, and Joe who didn't smoke, something ornamental for his flat – I forget what it was. And Joe was so overcome when I gave him this thing he burst into tears. The next day he was screaming at me like a fishwife down the phone over something that didn't please him. Incredible man. Very, very talented and so temperamental."

That temperament was something you had to live with. It came all in with the talent and you could not have one without the other. As Bob continues, it was a nerve-racking combination: "Like everybody else you went through phases of not being in favour with Joe or being so in favour it was embarrassing at times. Extremist. You are either completely in or completely out. And one walked a tightrope with Joe all the time. When you walked into a recording studio where something exciting is happening – a good song and a good artiste is now going to be recorded beautifully by Joe – and you walk into a temperamental situation, as a result of which he clears everybody out of his studio and scrubs the session regardless of the responsibility involved, this is a frightening situation. So one walked a tightrope all the time: is this session going to be completed? Is he going to retain his enthusiasm and good humour or is he going to destroy everything right in the middle of it? And this happened many times.

"We were at his studio one evening with my wife and Bob Britton, the ex-Ted Heath singer. What happened was: Joe had a lot of trouble with his wiring. We simply had to pop over there to do some testings and demos, and things went wrong with his wiring and he was in one of his short-tempered moods. And he stopped a real packet: he picked up something and got the full charge, threw it, screamed and jumped. The face that he pulled, his whole reaction physically, was so hilarious that we laughed; it

THE LEGENDARY JOE MEEK

was so funny. Everything that he did was like something in a film that is designed like Laurel & Hardy to make you scream with laughter and it had just that effect. Only for a few seconds and realizing how hurt he was – not only from the shock but the fact that we were laughing – I put my arm on his shoulder and said, 'Joe, I'm sorry.' But he swept my arm off, he swore at me, he stamped out of the room and slammed the door. We looked at each other and said, 'Oh my God, now we've got a problem.' Knowing him as I did, we just stayed there and waited five or ten minutes because he'd be stamping around somewhere else swearing out his anger. Suddenly the door opened and back he came, very contrite, nice little smile on his face and quietly said, 'I'm so sorry.' And it was all forgiven. Now that could have been one of those situations where we didn't hear from him for six months because that was a real hatred thing that just happened to reverse itself on that particular occasion. But he was so generous when he had one of his good moods on. We couldn't stop gifts coming at us; my wife would get bouquets of flowers, I got a beautiful wine trolley – for no reason at all. He would just suddenly feel terribly warmhearted: we'd had some success maybe six months or nine months ago and this was still in his mind and he had to do something for me, giving him the song or the artiste or whatever it was. And gifts would start arriving for two or three days. And then probably the next week he wouldn't speak to us."

In the meantime, while 'Johnny Remember Me' was still high up, there was some more welcome encouragement from Jack Good in *Disc*. Good was a useful ally and but for the frequent mentions he gave Joe in his weekly column hardly anyone outside the music business would have heard of the Holloway Road studio. Being a fellow independent producer himself, he understood some of the problems Joe was up against: "Like Charles Blackwell with whom he works hand-in-glove he is, to say the least, unorthodox. He creates sounds that have never before existed – not even in your wildest dreams. Needless to say, this again causes trouble. Not infrequently his imagination has brought something really wonderful into being and the record firm has rejected it, because they haven't understood it. But Joe persists in making records for teenagers rather than record bosses. This has taken courage, for if the company releasing Joe's record doesn't really have faith in it, it understandably doesn't get the exploitation it deserves. And nothing sells without getting plays. Maybe, following 'Johnny Remember Me', Joe's ideas will be taken more seriously. They should be."

After the success of that first Leyton hit, it was definitely becoming less difficult finding homes for his productions. His biggest client, HMV, were now viewing him with very wide eyes and the charms they had not seen in him before were to double their takings off him. But it was still turning out a pretty barren year on the other labels. Although things had much improved on his pre-'Johnny Remember Me' output and overall nearly two thirds of his recordings were now being accepted, it was still not enough. That rejection of a third had him suspecting that the real reason was not simply their dislike of it but a fear of cutting their own throats. Perhaps they thought that accepting more might make him too successful and have him starting up another Triumph; that would mean competition from him and from heaven knows how many others following suit.

Whatever politics he thought he understood, record rejections always struck him as personal rebukes. He was firmly convinced that every recording he offered was bound for the charts and when his charmingly naive style of salesmanship failed to have effect, he could well switch to tears or temper. Cheerlessly he would slam out but would be back again right as rain within the next few weeks, sometimes offering the same recording to someone else in another department – a practice that was frowned upon and rarely worked.

As always he loathed going the rounds but it was either that or sending recordings by post and he wasn't having them mysteriously lost on the way. Besides, he felt he stood a better chance if he was there in person. It also speeded things up a bit, because stimulating interest in one man was only half the battle. That man had to present the recording for approval to a selection panel consisting of staff from both A & R and marketing departments. Joe knew it was the A & R men defending their own territory who offered the strongest resistance to his work, and they were the ones for whom he reserved his most bitter contempt. In his eyes they were nearly all totally incompetent: a bunch of white-coated morons making records of which they knew nothing for a public of whom they knew even less. His sentiments are echoed in knife-edged tones by Marcel Stellman who worked for thirty years at Decca, and was International Manager and an A & R man there: " It's an old fact, and I can speak from experience, that anybody who is an independent producer or who comes to a record company with finished product and has to talk to the A & R man in that company, is going to be criticized, is going to be downed, is going to be having everything that will make him feel that he's no good, because this guy's supposed to know better. The only time this A & R man is going to gloat all over is if he's bought something and it's a hit – then he's going to claim all the credit for it anyway. I mean, even today you see those A & R men – they know sweet FA most of them; very few know what they're all about. And what happens? They listen to product by independents and they sit there in their plush offices as the arbiters of good taste and 'what are going to be hits' . They don't know more than anybody. In fact there was an old story that some of them couldn't start a piss-up in a brewery."

Meanwhile back at Holloway Road he was up to his ears in it. While 'Johnny Remember Me' was adding to its half million sales and 'Wild Wind' passing the 300,000 mark, he was sweating blood in a Herculean effort to get 13 weekly record shows produced for Radio Luxembourg by December as well as two LPs ready in time for the Christmas market. Sessions had to be held all day nearly every day, and the task was made no easier by antagonism from neighbours, irked by the constant thundering vibrations within their midst. But he had to stand firm since the LPs would suffer loss in sales for every day over schedule.

The first one was by the Outlaws, whose singles had been selling well enough to merit an instrumental collection, 'Dream Of The West'. However, apart from liberal doses of his whooping Wild West sound effects, there was little to distinguish the Outlaws' style from that of dozens of other guitar groups and to make their task that much harder, like the Flee Rekkers, they were suffering from an acute attack of Rotten Tune Syndrome. Both bands had built up a small following but if they could only come up with some good tunes like the Shadows, who seemed to be pulling them out of a bottomless bag, they might just join the big league.

The Leyton LP, called 'The Two Sides Of John Leyton', was a much bigger project and well worth the effort. It's one of the best things Joe ever did. Blessed with the combined talents of the three backroom boys – Meek, Goddard, Blackwell – this album is a superb example of the unique RGM atmosphere for which he was fast becoming known. Nearly everything that became synonymous with the studio is on it: Geoff's jangling piano playing, ethereal girl chorus, echo, compression and big orchestral sounds with swirling violins and horns. The dozen tracks, three of which were written by Geoff and three by Joe, are split evenly between hearty, galloping numbers and dreamy ballads to show that John was not always singing out on the moors. The sleeve notes written by Robert Stigwood may have come across at the time as everyday publicity blurb but there was a hint of truth in them: ". . . recognized as Britain's most adventurous and talented disc producer, Joe Meek has developed a world-beating production team with the country's youngest musical director, Charles Blackwell, who has won well-deserved acclaim for his clever and exciting arrangements, and Geoff Goddard who is surely the most commercial hit writer to emerge for many years."

Finally there was the Radio Luxembourg series. Called *It's The Outlaws*, the Saturday evening slot was given to him by Ivy Music, each show running 15 minutes, which was just time enough to play some Outlaws tracks and one from a guest artiste. The guest also gave a quick chat which he read from a script, and written by Joe it was about as revealing as Page 3 of the Church Times. The shows were being recorded at Holloway Road, and somehow he managed to finish them all plus the LPs bang on time ready for Christmas.

For his next trick he turned to horror and found it in a group calling themselves the Raiders. They were a bunch of part-timers who impressed Joe when he went along to a North London church hall to hear them rehearsing a few instrumentals. He was not so impressed though when they came up soon afterwards to record a horror rock instrumental titled 'Night Of The Vampire'. After continual stopping and starting he at last called for a tea break, and that was when he asked about their new vocalist, a 16 year old Rod Stewart, who had come along hoping to sing in his first recording studio. "What's your singer like?" Joe asked. "Rod's very good," they replied, so Joe asked them to run through a few numbers with him. The singer whose voice was later to rasp him in a fortune sang some Elvis Presley and Eddie Cochran songs, but after ten minutes Joe had had enough and gave his considered opinion of Rod's singing by bursting into the studio waving his arms from side to side and blowing a raspberry. Following that promising start to his recording career, Rod would for the time being have to stick to sand-machining poster frames and singing with the group part-time around pubs and clubs.

In spite of all the stoppages 'Night Of The Vampire' eventually turned out quite well, opening with wailing winds and a creaky coffin before breaking into an eerie guitar instrumental. There was even a guest appearance by Mr. Meek himself as the scream at the start and the finish.[22] Because the group, now called the Moontrekkers, were unknown and the record was banned by the BBC as "unsuitable for people of a nervous disposition", EMI cautiously pressed only the minimum 5,000 copies. Luxembourg on the other hand went to the other extreme and literally plugged it to death, for it sold out as soon as it reached the charts and further pressings arrived too late because of a factory dispute.

But it was to be another character who was destined for the real horror honours; and with the help of Joe's grisly productions and lots of irrepressible publicity he was to become one of the master monsters of the rock age. He called himself Screaming Lord Sutch and had started playing in pubs in '58. At that time he had found everyone modelling themselves on Elvis, Buddy Holly and the fresh-faced wave of American idols, so to be different he moulded himself on American horror man Screamin' Jay Hawkins. Hawkins's act featured him emerging from a flaming coffin carrying a skull he called Henry and singing 'I Put A Spell On You'. It only needed Sutch to watch a few old Boris Karloff movies and before you could say Jack the Ripper, he had grown his hair down his back got himself a coffin, some fire, an axe and a few heads and was giving British audiences their first taste of rock'n'blood. It was the most macabre act Britain had seen and Joe loved it.

As soon as he could he got Sutch into the studio to record his debut disc. This was "Til The Following Night', a gruesome graveyard piece, totally outrageous for its day. Sutch wrote the song but it takes nearly a minute of atmospherics – thunder, rain, wailing wind, piercing shrieks and a creaking coffin lid – before he can get to it; in fact it opens like a night out on the set of one of those old monster movies. Then he lets rip with his story of a horned creature that gets out of its coffin in the cemetery to strangle people then gets back in again "til the following night'. It's a good, thumping rock'n'roller and the sound effects are excellent. The song was first called 'My Big Black Coffin', but that title gave HMV the shivers and had to be changed to something less risqué. This was going to be the problem with most of

"HE'S SINGING AT THE BOTTOM OF AN EMPTY WELL"

Sutch's releases; lyrics and sound effects which would by present day standards be considered tame were then called obscene, getting little radio exposure and therefore low sales. That was a pity since his ever-changing backing group, the Savages, sported some of the top rock musicians, and were to put a lot of worthy music on the market. To compensate for lack of airplay Sutch needed more news coverage than most and was not too fussy how he got it.

The early Sixties were a good time for publicity stunts because they were novel and supplied the media with news and pictures as they happened, brightening up the boring stories. Sutch, hollering like a man possessed as he fled through Shepherd Market dressed as a Viking, was a reporter's dream and this got him noticed and if he was lucky got him arrested too. If he wanted to pull the Sunday headlines, he had only to get near the cameras on a Saturday and there he would be in the papers the next day in his new role as a demented Indian chief with hair down to his waist and a lavatory seat draped around his neck. Other proficient publicity seekers like Stigwood or Barrington-Coupe were inclined to use more subtle methods but the objective was the same, and Sutch's inelegance appealed to Joe.

Unfortunately, however much Joe praised it, the Lord Sutch brand of stark, staring sensationalism was only suitable for the career of Lord Sutch, and not at all right for the clean-cut, boy-next-door image of his other artistes.

The singer least suited of all to that kind of promotion arrived on Joe's doorstep in November. Don Charles was the type of old-style balladeer Joe had left behind at IBC. For around five years he had been crooning away, and without a hair or romanticism out of place he looked and sounded as if he had just been airlifted from 1956. Recently he had had a record released on Parlophone but, as Don remembers well, he was not at all happy with his voice on it, and nor was the producer George Martin: "George said they were having trouble recording me. And I was very upset when he said that I've got a woolly-edging voice: the centre was fine but the edges used to drift out; they weren't flat or sharp but he found trouble getting presence. Somehow George and the engineers just couldn't get it, and he said that they weren't taking up the rest of my contract – which they'd only just acquired! I was a bit upset and I went downstairs. And I always got on well with a Canadian guy there and he said, 'This is the guy you need'. And there was a clipping in *NME* or something like that about Joe Meek. So I rang Joe and he said, 'Come up'. George Martin had said he couldn't get the sound that I knew was there: the sound that I seemingly produced on a cabaret floor. I went up to Joe and Joe got it the first morning! He played a back track of something and asked me to sing to it. And the ridiculous thing was he recorded me about 10 o'clock in the morning when I was walking about like a bunch of seaweed!"

The next record that everyone had high hopes for was John Leyton's latest, 'Son, This Is She'. Again it conjured up images of life in the world unseen – "And a voice from above said, 'Son, this is she'" – but this time broke clean away from the frantic pace of its two predecessors and had a stronger melody. It also had a deep, expansive quality about it as if Joe had crammed a full blown symphony orchestra into the studio. In what is one of the prime cuts to come out of 304 – and also in retrospect one of the best British records of the Sixties – Geoff's song, Joe's production and Charles Blackwell's arrangement all come together in one sweeping, majestic mass of sound. Throughout most of the production the big accompaniment simmers menacingly underneath the vocals as if ready to rise up and shove John right off the record; then it erupts in a marvellously over-produced middle-8 before allowing John to safely finish his refrain. All of which goes to show what one can do with a four-piece rhythm section plus four violins, a harp and French horn! The rhythm section was courtesy of a new session band Joe had mustered by advertising in the *Melody Maker*, and who were designed to be no more than a nameless houseband quartet providing backings on disc. Their day would come.

Joe was very pleased indeed with it, and the record set everyone up ready for another Top Five hit in the New Year.

Things were really going well. It was hard to believe that only five months ago he was desperately pulling out all the stops for some faint ray of chart sunshine. Now here he was at the start of December with two LPs just released, two of his singles suddenly selling in hundreds of thousands and another one all set to follow suit. At this rate the record companies would soon be clamouring for everything he put their way. Multiplying his delight was the letter Buddy Holly's parents had sent Mike Berry, thanking him for the "wonderful tribute" to their son, while Holly's producer Norman Petty had praised it as the best memorial disc there was to the late singer. It all showed that the only thing in the music rat-race you can really be certain of is the uncertainty; no sooner are you down than you are up again smelling of roses.

"HE'S SINGING AT THE BOTTOM OF AN EMPTY WELL"

Unfortunately the reverse is also the case. Perhaps the safest philosophy is that of the realist who hopes for the best and prepares for the worst – like the pessimist he is never too disappointed. Joe on the crest of a wave was now a Utopian optimist hoping for the best and expecting it, so when it didn't come it was a hard blow. There is no doubt that the massive coverage received by the first two Leyton hits did much to increase their sales, and this was clear when the luxury was not afforded 'Son, This Is She'. There was to be no charging straight into the Top Ten this time, and any hopes he had of a hat-trick of Top Five placings were dealt a knock-out punch when the actors' union Equity suddenly went on strike.

As usual with industrial action, the union was seeking pay rises. Until these were forthcoming all Equity card holders were barred from accepting any more dates on ITV programmes. The BBC were not involved in the dispute, though that was little comfort when pop musicwise all they had to offer was *Juke Box Jury*. (The panellists on that programme, incidentally, showed their usual lack of imagination and foresight by voting 'Son, This Is She' a resounding 'miss'.) It meant that no pop fans were to see Leyton perform it on TV. It also meant their being deprived of Ian Gregory.

Apparently seven Ian Gregory TV dates had to be turned down and he needed them even more than Leyton, depending as he did entirely on his good looks and Joe's artful dodges. Ironically, at this time he could be seen every week in the popular children's series *Richard the Lionheart* playing, of all things, a singing minstrel. Fortunately, whenever the character he was playing opened his mouth to sing, it was someone else's voice that came out. According to Ian, somebody had already recorded the songs before he even got the part. No doubt that saved a few problems.

The end of the year found Joe comforted that Leyton had been voted by *New Musical Express* readers Britain's 'Best New TV and Disc Personality', and 'Johnny Remember Me' – 'Disc Of The Year'. As for the record's progress in the States, the Americans had reacted to its release with all the fiery gusto of a bowlful of geriatric goldfish. That had put paid to any thoughts of John's TV appearances over there. Joe however was more concerned about the plight of 'Son, This Is She' and hoping the strike would hurry up and finish so everything could be right again.

9
Up, Up And Away

1962 got off to a flying controversial start. The lead story in the first week's *Melody Maker* was printed under the headline: "POP SINGER DENIES GIMMICK CHARGES". There are no points for guessing who the singer was – John Leyton. The rumpus was caused by a growing number of old fogies getting hot under the collar about the increasing use of studio techniques on recordings. In their opinion it was not musicians who were making the records, but engineers; that hardly anything musicians played or singers sang came out accurately on disc. "A great many singers seem to be manufactured by studio sounds today," declared one of them, pointing his finger at John Leyton. Only two desirables were named, Matt Monro and Cleo Laine, who apparently were never ever tarted up, and as Leyton was the one singer who sounded least like either of them, it was judged only right and proper that he should pay the penalty for such a vile outrage: he was denounced as an "electronic product".

All things considered though, the old fogies had a fair case. Were it not for Joe's merry meddlings Leyton would have been reaping far less fame and fortune than he was. Still, it was bad for the image to admit to things like that and much wiser for John to fan the flames a bit: "My critics say all my records are just electronic – that I wouldn't succeed without echoes. But no record succeeds through technique alone. Even Frank Sinatra has echo effects. Pop records today must be as exciting as possible."

And what, might one ask, had a certain Mr. Meek to say about all this fuss? "Utter rubbish. Certainly I try to inject punch and drive into my productions with John. But he is basically talented. He would have made headway with whoever put him on record."

He had a bit more to say though three weeks later. Martin Slavin, arranger of the Helen Shapiro hits on Columbia, had obviously been reading his *Melody Maker* because he wanted to get in on the fun too. In a defiant column in the *Record Mirror* he said what he thought of a remark of Joe's that sounds were often altered on disc: "I don't agree with Meek that there are a lot of doctored recordings around today. I'd say it was quite the opposite, unless you allow that the microphone distorts the voice to a certain extent anyway. And a singer like Craig Douglas has a voice that is virtually untampered with on record. Helen Shapiro? Anything vaguely resembling tampering just doesn't happen. Nothing is really done to her voice . . . I would agree that it's impossible for John Leyton to sound the same on stage as he does on records unless he sang down a very deep hole." He also made a veiled reference to the 304 studio: "A recording studio is the place to record. They are there for that specific purpose and have the best technicians in their employ. If they can't get an intimate sound then it isn't there in the voice."

Joe's reaction was to pull in his stomach, draw himself up to his full height and put every ounce of his 11½ stone behind his counter punch: "Why did Martin Slavin slate me in that column? Who is he to say what he did about a studio he has never entered? First of all, what is a recording studio? It is basically a room with acoustic treatment, fitted with mikes, play-back speakers, chairs and music stands. My studio is equipped with the best type of mikes available, together with carefully balanced acoustic treatment and all the material I need for recording. The only difference to any other studio is that I use some units I designed and built myself. They add an extra something to my recordings. Fair enough, my studio was originally a large bedroom, but it is now a first-class studio in which I have made many hit records – and no one will tell me that it is wrong. If Martin Slavin had dug deeper he would have found that most studios started as a room, basement or bedroom in a town house. My studio is just that.

"As for Helen Shapiro and Craig Douglas or indeed any artiste I record, that is bunkum. I use echo, yes; equalisation, yes. That is to enhance the artiste's voice and is used for every worthwhile artiste the world over. A voice recorded flat, without any reverberation at all, would not be accepted by the public. If Norrie Paramor took away the echo from Cliff Richard and Helen Shapiro, Norman Newell from Shirley Bassey and Danny Williams, Alan Freeman from Petula Clark, and Dick Rowe from Billy Fury, I doubt if they would have any more hits. As for Helen Shapiro and Craig Douglas using no echo, that is rubbish. Helen's 'Please Don't Treat Me Like A Child' had the voice first squashed up with compression, echoed, fed back and equalised – so who does Slavin think he's kidding?

"I would be a fool to listen to an arranger with a bee in his bonnet. I make records to entertain the public, not square connoisseurs who just don't know."

Meanwhile back at the ranch, no one knew it yet but 'Son,

This Is She' had signalled the slowing down of the John Leyton show. RGM Sound was almost wholly dependent on the Leyton records for its revenue and in January, instead of racing up to the top, 'Son, This Is She' clambered only as far as No.15. Geoff Goddard, seeing what he thought to be the writing on the wall, suggested a change of tack for the next one: "I felt after the first three they were too much of a muchness and I said to Stigwood, 'John should record someone else's song.' They rang me up one Sunday saying they were stuck for a song and therefore 'You must produce one by Monday'. I was going mad and in the end I stuck another lonely lyric onto 'Lone Rider'."

This time Joe, as if to grab hold of his critics and rub their noses in it, made 'Lone Rider' even more provocative than the previous ones. It marked a return to the old 'Johnny Remember Me'-'Wild Wind' formula and again was exciting stuff. But perhaps this time it was a bit too exciting, because people were now taking their discs back to the shops thinking they were warped! In typical Goddard fashion the song centred on a dead motorcyclist riding the country in all weathers warning other riders not to take 'risks for kicks'. When it reached the girl chorus, the violence of the groove wiggling about inside the disc was such that on many record players the needle couldn't keep up with it and jumped. It was all so over the top that it made the original version by the Flee Rekkers sound like 'Lone Rider On A Tricycle'. However, creating what was certainly a masterpiece of overproduction failed to impress the record buyers, and what had seemed a temporary setback with 'Son, This Is She' was turning into a temporary nightmare as the John Leyton handlers watched their parallel to Elvis climb in the charts to the very un-Presley-like position of No.40. Although some of the blame for that can be put on the Equity strike, which was still biting deep, 'Lone Rider' was to be the last of Leyton's 'dynamic' recordings.

One bit of hopeful news came in February with the supplying of his houseband to tour with Billy Fury. Billy's manager, Larry Parnes, had sacked the previous backing band, the Blue Flames, and when Joe heard of it he was quick to offer assistance. Parnes at that time was a very important figure on the scene, for along with Jack Good he had played a big part in shaping British pop music during the late Fifties and early Sixties; he was the country's top impresario and Joe was thinking he could well turn out to be very useful.

Then there was Billy Fury. Nowadays it is generally thought that he was the nearest thing to Elvis that Britain ever had; his voice was good for both rock'n'roll and ballads and, like Elvis, his movements onstage were highly suggestive. Along with Cliff Richard and Adam Faith he was one of the top three singers of the day. This was an opportunity Joe could not resist. Furnishing a backing band to tour with Billy would not only bag the boys a hefty hunk of publicity and increase their chances as recording artistes in their own right but would almost certainly present him with Billy on a plate. Joe could get him the No.1 hit Billy had so far failed to achieve with Dick at Decca, while in the popularity stakes he could turn the lot of them into another Cliff Richard & the Shadows – quite a mouthwatering prospect.

Everyone involved duly trooped up to the studio for the audition to which Joe was delighted Parnes and Fury gave their seal of approval.

A lot of their rehearsals were held at 304. The tour itself was one of those many multi-star packages so popular in the Sixties in which Billy and John Leyton were topping a bill that included Eden Kane, Karl Denver and another of Joe's groups, Peter Jay & the Jaywalkers. A month into the tour he decided the backing band were ready to cut their first disc and had them back in the studio on one of their days off. The tune he had written for them was an instrumental, and in dedication to their lead singer the title would be 'Love And Fury'. What he wanted was a passion-ately wistful sound, so resurrected the clavioline which had been gathering dust since the 'I Hear A New World' album and brought in a keyboard player to join them. They also needed a name and he came up with something suitably turbulent in a John Leyton B-side spoof he had written called 'Six White Horses': 'There was laughter and love, we were happy, till a tornado swept her away' – the Tornados.

Unfortunately 'Love And Fury' didn't offer much suggestion of either love or fury or even a decent tune, so never saw the charts. The keyboard player didn't turn out a success story either because he soon fell out with Joe and was replaced by ex-Household Cavalry Trooper Roger LaVern; LaVern had offered himself up as a solo pianist in the Russ Conway mould, so was quite surprised to suddenly find himself backing a top rock star.

With the change in the Tornados to recording artistes came a change in the colour of their German bass player Heinz Burt's hair. As the youngest and the one whose Nordic features were expected to drive the girls wild he needed no persuading to help give the band an image and become its fair haired focal point.

After all, if Elvis could dye his hair black, why shouldn't Heinz dye his blond?

Joe got the idea from a sci-fi film called *Village Of The Damned*. It centred on the mysterious birth in an English village of twelve children, all of whom had disturbingly staring eyes and . . . fair hair. He was so enchanted by it all that he immediately wanted a whole band of blond boys.

However, the real reason for dyeing Heinz's locks was more deep-rooted than it looked. It stemmed from the fact that as sure as night follows day Joe was in love with him. He was absolutely besotted with this baby-faced, happy-go-lucky 19 year old, defiantly ignoring all the gossip arising from having Heinz now sharing the flat with him, and come hell or high water intended making him a star. The first step of the plan was to delicately instil some ambition into him: by simply making him eye-catching on stage he knew he could leave the rest to the girls. He had seen that Heinz was already getting some attention during the act when he and the rhythm guitarist would briefly join Billy Fury in the spotlight for harmonies, but now the new-look Heinz was bound to provoke an even better response.

As expected, the response was excellent – in fact as good as Larry Parnes's wasn't. According to Heinz, Parnes wanted only one star a-twinkling onstage and that was not Heinz: "Parnes was moaning all over the place. He got onto Joe and he said, 'He's had his hair done – it looks like cotton wool on his head! People are laughing sat at the back when he walks up to the mike with Billy; and people are saying, 'He's a poof'. It looks bloody ridiculous. Get him to dye it dark.' 'Cause Parnes knew whenever I walked in that spotlight the girls would scream their heads off. And Joe said, 'If you don't like it, stick it. I'll pull the band out.'" So Parnes stuck it and the band stayed. However, Joe was to be constantly informed by him that he was being granted a huge favour by having his group used. His reply was always that it was Parnes who was getting the favour by being allowed to use the group; that they were promoting Fury, not vice versa.

Inspired by continually good receptions to Heinz he set about getting a record made to launch his solo career. Mike Berry's first success had come with a tribute to Buddy Holly, so maybe one to Eddie Cochran, another American rock singer who had suddenly died at the height of his career, could do the same for Heinz. But Heinz didn't like the song he was given, besides which he felt things were happening just a little too fast and was not quite ready yet for stardom. So Joe didn't force him.

It was about this time that an event occurred, exposing both Joe's uneasy financial position and his complete lack of self-control in times of stress. It came about as a result of the sacking some months earlier of the Outlaws' lead guitarist, Bill Kuy. Bill thought he had been booted out simply for giving someone in the band a black eye, though it was actually because of a letter his wife had sent in to the *New Musical Express*. The letter bewailed the fact that during all the excitement surrounding the success of 'Johnny Remember Me', no mention had been made of the Outlaws' contribution as Leyton's backing group; each of them had received their £7.10s.0d Musicians Union fee for the session but no publicity whatsoever. When Joe noticed the letter, he saw red and made sure there and then that Bill was given his marching orders. Now, several months later, Bill got in touch with him again: "I phoned Joe and said I'd had no royalties for the LP. It sold eight copies and I wanted my fourpence! Outlaws singles – and I hadn't had a penny. And he's giving me all this about Major Banks not paying up yet. I said, 'Look I'm coming round and I want to see some money.' So I went round there and we went into the office, and he's giving me all this Major Banks shit. I said, 'Well that's not really my concern.' And then he just went berserk. He started this windmill fighting – flailing about. Then he picked up a long pair of scissors and I ran out and he chased after me as far as the stairs, and I ran on down while he stood at the top yelling profanities. I was very frightened. I got a cheque for £30 some weeks later."

If Joe's slight effeminacy gave people the impression he wouldn't say 'boo' to a goose, they could be in for a shock. In a temper he was probably capable of taking on anyone who came into the studio and, by fair means or foul, coming out on top. Although he was far from being in peak condition, as borne out by the much resented layer of flab around his stomach, his farming days had given him a fair broad shouldered strength. This strength plus the uncontrollable eruptions of rage, which some-times saw him screaming white with wrath, body quivering, cheeks twitching and eyes starting out of his head, presented an awesome combination. Angered once at hearing a bad guitar solo being played upstairs, he brought his fist down on the telephone so hard that bits flew out to all corners of the room. Though these incidents were mainly no more than blasts of hot air that blew themselves out after a couple of door slams and a cup of coffee, they rendered him completely inaccessible to reason, and on a bad day could have him slinging a hundredweight's worth of tape recorder across the studio at someone as if it were a box of matches.

♪♪♪♪♪♪♪♪♪♪♪♪♪♪♪

The next John Leyton disc was made at IBC. Until now, Joe had always resisted pressure to record John at bigger studios, but following his way-over-the-top recording of 'Lone Rider' they had all been getting stick from the BBC and EMI for the high level of distortion, and Robert Stigwood was anxious to cut it down. The result was a more subdued 'Lonely City' which, thanks to the lifting of the Equity strike, rewarded them with another Top Twenty entry and time to find a fresh horse to flog.

Then Charles Blackwell suddenly left. Up until this time he had been a much sought after independent arranger working here, there and everywhere doing all the arrangements at 304 that called for orchestral backings, and those accounted for nearly half of Joe's releases. The end came when Charles was wooed away onto the payroll of the by now high-flying Robert Stigwood, who was branching out on his own. Although Joe's official reaction to it was: "There's plenty more where he came from," it was a bitter blow for he had relied heavily on him since recognizing his potential and giving him his big break as arranger for Triumph.

To top it all, as if it wasn't bad enough having your arranger walk out on you, the man was actually signing up with one of Joe's least favourite business associates, Robert Stigwood, for it was around now that he was becoming increasingly suspicious of Stigwood's intentions.

His misgivings found much substance in what he believed to be the loss of the John Leyton recording contract. As a rule he always had artistes sign a contract confirming him as their recording manager. So, when Stigwood declared either that it was invalid or that it had never existed, Joe immediately turned the office upside down in a frantic search for it, eventually finding everything but the document in question. Suspecting treachery in the ranks he rounded on his office boy, Tony Kent. Tony denied all knowledge of it but Joe sent him on his way with a phone in his face. Anyway, it seems odd that Joe, who was so well practised in having artistes sign on the dotted line (as he demonstrated to such advantage at Triumph), should get it wrong in Leyton's case. Whatever had happened, he never ceased to believe that Stigwood had cheated him.

What it meant in effect was that Stigwood was now in a position to make himself Leyton's recording manager and take him away to record elsewhere. Thus future Leyton discs would involve Joe less and less. They would mainly be produced at Abbey Road, with Joe merely offering advice on the first few.

But the matter did not rest there. In June Leyton flew off to Munich to start on a leading role in the blockbusting war film *The Great Escape* alongside Steve McQueen and Richard Attenborough. With Leyton away, Joe watched in dismay as Stigwood took Mike Berry under his wing, becoming his personal manager. Although Joe was only Mike's recording manager and was not guiding his career, he disliked the way Stigwood seemed to be poaching some of the people he had gathered around him; singer Billie Davis had also left him to join Stigwood, and he was even having to share Geoff Goddard's songwriting skills with him. Adding insult to injury Charles Blackwell had written a song for Mike Sarne and not brought it to him to be produced. It was called 'Come Outside' and much to Joe's disgust went to No.1.

Losing Charles could have turned out a disaster. Freelance arrangers were pretty thin on the ground, especially the ones he could trust to keep secrets. But the gods must have been smiling on him because almost at once another talented one dropped into his lap. This was Ivor Raymonde, a man who had worked with him on and off during the IBC and Lansdowne days, arranged and directed hits for the likes of Frankie Vaughan, Marty Wilde and Billy Fury, and who would soon be adding many more for Dusty Springfield, Kathy Kirby, the Bachelors and the Walker Brothers. Ivor says things went well from the start: "When he called me up to Holloway Road – to the Bedroom, as I used to call it – immediately I seemed to hit it off quite well with him. I can't say that I know many people who did like him; I know at the time a lot of people had a down on him I think mainly because of what he was, but I used to get on very well indeed with him. He never gave me an ounce of trouble. I just found him a very nice, easygoing guy who let me get on with what he asked me to do. I'd go up to him and he'd give me a tape of a rhythm section and a singer, and he would always play me what he had and just say he'd like to put strings on it and a choir, or could we use a tenor saxophone and a trombone and strings, or can we use four cellos, did I think four cellos would be good. And he would just say to me what he thought he'd like to hear; and sometimes he'd say would I follow the melody line with the strings. I'd take the tape away and book probably just four violins and either three girls or two girls and two boys or whatever it suited. And I'd do an arrangement around the existing track and go up into the Bedroom with musicians. We'd then play, with Joe playing his track to us, and that as far as I was concerned was it. In actual fact we had such a good rapport going between us that – if I can say this without sounding big-headed – he used to think the sun shone out of my arse. Because he'd have spent hours and hours with some of these unknown boys getting rhythm tracks down and I'd go in with say, 6, 7 or 8 musicians and do three or four titles in three hours. And this so pleased him."

All the same, for Ivor the unconventional studio setting must have come as a shock after the prim efficiency of the major ones to which he was accustomed. After wending his way through speakers and gaffer tape littered around the hallway downstairs, he had to navigate the rather alarming staircase where, as one person said, you were in "grave danger of falling down and breaking your neck, with your feet tangled up in six miles of wire."

On his first session up there, sitting together with three other violinists, all shivering in their overcoats, hats, scarves and gloves and trying as they played not to poke each other's eyes out, he must have wondered if he was dreaming! Peering around the dimly lit room he could see the choir (a few girls similarly clad) in one corner, a drum-kit in another and a battered out-of-tune piano against the wall; over the walls and ceiling was the sound absorption: a mixture of egg boxes, cork tiles, pegboard and cardboard packing whilst on the floor, laced with cables, were the remains of a carpet. Then rooted to his seat, praying no live wires sent him flying up through the roof, he would wait for a shout from the next room to start and away they would go.

As for the group musicians, most had never seen inside any other studio so were none the wiser. Nevertheless, they were naturally intrigued by the concept of running a recording studio in a room overlooking a main road, where heavy lorries would occasionally disrupt proceedings and where on hot summer days when the windows were briefly opened, music would blare out to people passing by.

For all the group musicians knew, his style of running a session might have been perfectly orthodox but they still found it peculiar. Often he would be prancing in and out, sometimes with edited tape draped round his ankles, and either giving confidence or criticism or re-setting microphones. A typical sequence while the band were playing would have him suddenly rush in to pull out a wire, dive back again into the control room and then back again shouting, "Stop, stop, stop!" They would wait while he shifted one microphone here and another one there, switched two cables round, picked up some bare wires to change a drum sound, then raced back into the control room: "Go on then, start!" – "Oh, didn't know you were ready." – "'Course I'm bloody ready." Away they would go again till they heard him yell, "No, that's not the way I want it." He knew what he was after and would usually get it, whether by charming or terrorizing it out of them.

Meanwhile from where they were standing or seated they would hear him slamming his machines on an off, sending tapes screaming back and forth. Were they to dare follow the trail of the dozen or so wires back into the control room they could marvel at the most amazing sight of all: Joe at work in his Inner Sanctum, darting about like a mad scientist in the organized chaos of an electronics laboratory. Earnestly seeking to put onto tape what he heard in his head, he would be taking the music apart and reassembling it, adding and extracting here and there, sometimes concocting sounds hitherto undreamt of. Great spinning tape machines, amplifiers and echo units would be working around him, half a dozen or more at a time, and the incredible speed with which his fingers ran the tapes and changed the plugs had the grace of a virtuoso pianist. Then suddenly the elegance would disappear when one of these weary old machines broke down and he had to start coaxing it back to life, first with some surgery and then with his foot.

The whole room was an unmitigated electrical mess with an inch or more of anonymous dusty black wires, cables and tape edits carpeting the floor. If, for example, he ever needed an empty spool he would simply run a tape out onto the floor and leave it there! But untidy as it was he didn't mind at all because he knew every lead and plug and it was only finding the odd tape edit that had him foxed. Then he would call in the band and have them on their hands and knees grovelling around for a thunderclap or something, while instructing them not to touch his spring echo unit – a garden gate spring, stretched out on a piece of wood and nailed to the floor – and certain naked wires being held into sockets by matchsticks or chewing gum. These wires were mostly in his homemade 'mixer': like an old style telephonist's switchboard with jack plugs and sockets serving microphones and little booster amplifers.

With none of today's multi-tracking conveniences the vital need was to get the balance right there and then. The moment the band left the premises, that was it – the balance was there forever. It has been said that he achieved sounds in two hours that people nowadays, using computerized mixing and 24-track recorders, spend weeks getting which gives an indication of the ear he had for balance. Precious time was also saved by clever positioning of microphones and an intimate awareness of the capabilities of each. He knew his equipment.

Perhaps as Ivor Raymonde sat in the studio gazing incredulously at the old screen by the drum-kit (the type that women used to change behind in films of years ago) with the ragged army blanket nailed up to help isolate the drum sound, he was discouraged from expecting much in the way of marvels but, as he recalls, he was in for a surprise: "There were some sessions where he got fed up using these group musicians, and I did quite a few records with him with what we called a 'legitimate' rhythm section: people like Kenny Clare or Ronnie Verrell, Jim Sullivan on guitar, and so on. And Kenny Clare, I remember this very clearly, he's a pretty loud drummer and this room was quite a small room. A choir mike was open, the drum mikes were open – one on the bass drum, one on the tom-kit; there'd be a string mike open – I remember this particular session – there were two trumpets and a trombone: that's six microphones were open. And I went in to talk to Joe in the back room about something, and everybody was chuntering on. Kenny Clare, I remember, was really hammering. And Joe turned off Kenny Clare's drum mikes and not a sound – I know that Kenny Clare was carrying on playing – and not a sound of it came out of the string mike or the trombone mike or the brass mike or the choir mike, which technically is almost unbelievable in this tiny room. It meant that his separation in this room was quite phenomenal. How he did it I don't know – it was just the guy's genius."

His skills were no doubt stretched still further on his 'big' sessions. In an effort to get a different kind of sound he would sometimes have a recording take place all over the house with perhaps the rhythm section in the studio, the singer in the living room, the choir in the bathroom, the brass in the bedroom and the strings on the landing and up the stairs! Anything was worth a try.

On many sessions it was the Outlaws who provided the backing. For this he would pay them the Musicians Union rate for three hours, though the session would usually drift way over the time and he would end up treating them to a round of fish and chips on top. Their competent musicianship helped avoid some of the tantrums that often blighted other groups' sessions and left people playing nervously. An idea of what it was like playing in that studio is given by bass player Chas Hodges, nowadays one half of the famous Chas & Dave duo: "The main thing when we went up there was the sound that he got from the playback. Everything else don't matter – if it's dust or crap all over the floor, you don't care what it is; and our first feeling when we went in and Joe said, 'Come and have a listen,' and we heard this sound coming out of this speaker, we just felt 50 feet high. And even though Joe could change just like that and suddenly lose his temper, the feeling of the great sound that was going to come out of them speakers topped it all. In general we got on all right with him and he said we used to play well and we put over what he wanted. It was quite hard really 'cause he sang out of tune and also his timing was a bit out, but we did enjoy the sessions. But when we started doing loads and loads of sessions backing like 20 different artistes auditioning a day, with a pretty face and no talent, it wasn't so good. When we were doing Outlaws stuff or with Mike Berry they were exciting and it was a good atmosphere. You can play better in a small area anyway; you get a little four-piece group in a small front room – it sounds great 'cause you can hear everything acoustically perfect."

♪♪♪♪♪♪♪♪♪♪♪♪♪♪

Apart from John Leyton's hits there was still little happening chartwise. But he had much to be proud of when he performed a minor miracle by getting Ian Gregory back in the Hit Parade. However, this time on 'Can't You Hear The Beat' it sounded suspiciously like the miracle relied on a little cheating because either Ian had had his vocal chords re-strung or it was someone else singing over him on the record. In fact it was the latter. Geoff Goddard had been singing along through Ian's headphones to help keep him on the right track, but it was not until the record came out that Geoff recognized his own voice on it: Joe had been re-directing it from Ian's headphones and onto the tape!

He was after recognition which meant selling records, and he couldn't care less how he got them to sell, so long as they went. The record charts were another useful ploy. Originally compiled for a bit of fun by the *NME* in 1952, they were fast taking on a vital role, gaining influence over the whole industry and in turn becoming highly vulnerable to those less virtuous. Besides showing record popularity they also help radio programmers choose material. A record in the listings is more likely to be played than one out of them, especially if it is on the way up; it also has a better chance of being bought, given the added prestige of simply being there.

The various charts were and are to this day based on a sample of record shops' sales returns. A different selection of shops is used to compile each one. Obviously no Top Fifty can hope to be 100% accurate until it is based on the sales of *every* record outlet in the country, and in today's age of the micro-chip this possibility is not so far off. In the early Sixties the lists of sample record shops were readily available to all the people who should not have had them, and buying records into the charts was commonplace. If other people could do it, Joe saw no reason why he shouldn't too, as saxophonist Peter Fleerackers explains: "Joe'd rig the record shops and would buy 10 to 20 in each. It was so easy. The agents got the list, and the 60 or so record shops in London were common knowledge. You could buy 100 copies to get it into the charts; buy a few more the following week to push it up a bit more; then get onto deejays to say it's in the charts. I remember Joe doing it; it went on all the time I knew him. If he could promote a record that way he would, but if he went in a shop and bought ten they wouldn't mark it; he couldn't buy them all at once or they'd realize and not mark it down. He'd have to get a fan club or band to go in one after the other. Sometimes if you crossed the guy's palm with silver you didn't have to buy any."

Meanwhile, early in the year he and Dick Rowe had buried the hatchet. In February they were rewarded with a minor hit when Don Charles warbled his way in with a very pleasant, slushy ballad Joe had written called 'Walk With Me My Angel'. It was the Fifties revisited and beautifully captured. It was also symptomatic of the wide variety of styles the early Sixties were evoking, and now in '62 it was more or less a case of 'anything goes'. Hit Parades had jazz from Kenny Ball and Dave Brubeck, guitar instrumentals from the Shadows and Duane Eddy, ballads from Frankie Vaughan and Matt Monro, piano ditties from Russ Conway, comedy from Bernard Cribbins and Mike Sarne, a bit of rock'n'roll from Elvis and Jerry Lee Lewis, twisting from Sam Cooke and Chubby Checker, syrup from Bobby Vee and Neil Sedaka and yodels from Frank Ifield.

Given his relish in pandering to all tastes the pop scene could not have looked brighter. For instance, on the instrumental front, come March he had no less than five bands tucking into that sizeable slice of the market. Instrumentals had started off back in '58 when an unknown South African group rejoicing in the name of Elias & his Zig Zag Jive Flutes released a torturously catchy penny whistle piece called 'Tom Hark'. With undiluted rock'n'roll losing its commercial appeal, that record heralded a final strong-hold against the toothpaste teen idols and paved the way for Duane Eddy and later groups like Johnny & the Hurricanes and the Shadows. As the watering-down process of rock'n'roll continued, so did the demand for instrumental groups, for they were the ones keeping the rock pot hot. Joe's contributions to the scene were the Flee Rekkers, Moontrekkers, Tornados, Stonehenge Men and, top of the list, the Outlaws, who were gathering a substantial following.

But apart from them and Michael Cox, whose records were selling in Sweden by the kilogram, most of his artistes were barely paying their way. Record companies receiving his material might be making a small profit but he wasn't. Any royalty cheques he received had to subsidize all the other recordings which were rejected. For example, session musicians (backing all solo singers) had to be paid at the end of each session, release or no release.

Furthermore, funds from the Leyton discs were rapidly being swallowed up. In spite of 'Lonely City' getting well promoted on TV, the record left the charts in July having only reached No.14, and it was looking more and more as if the John Leyton gravy train was running out of steam. Of course, you could never be sure in this business, and given the right disc plus a bit of luck, the next one might bounce straight back in at No.1 . One thing was certain though: John was going to have to cast off his lonely image to get it, and how would his fans react to a happy Johnny? Hopefully a good deal better than they were reacting to the current array of talent Joe had lined up for them. During the year up to mid-July they had had 21 releases between them but only managed one Top Twenty entry and two sniffs at the charts. The hits were drying up again.

One of the main problems was in coming up with good tunes. Compared with the current scene when melodies have lost much of their importance to production techniques and the image of the artiste, in the Sixties no matter how well it was all presented, if the melody was below par then the record stood scant chance. No amount of tarting up would sell a poor tune and a lot of poor tunes were coming out of Holloway Road. Perhaps because he was composing so many, plus dozens more unheard of, they were getting low on quality. And with his head alive with music, tunes and songs would spring on him at any moment of the day or night: whilst having a meal, buying some steak, running a session, holding a seance, reading the music papers, driving his car or giving an interview; even a chance remark could set him off. Sometimes at night he would sit alone in the studio at the piano with the lights turned off, and here he believed Buddy Holly helped him write songs by telling him what to play or actually plonking tunes out on a guitar that leant against the wall.

One tune came about in a similarly unusual way. His new instrumental group who were now backing Billy Fury in a summer season at Great Yarmouth had recently called in at the studio to record their second disc, a guitar piece titled 'The Breeze And I'. On a Sunday a few days later their drummer rang up anxiously to tell him that another group called the Fentones (the band that used to back Shane Fenton before he became better known as Alvin Stardust) had also collared the tune and were about to have it released. With three weeks' head start the Fentones would have the market to themselves, so Joe had to shelve his version and come up with something else. That something else was to be his greatest work.

As luck would have it he got all the inspiration he needed three days later on July 11. That was when, soon after its launch into orbit, an American communications satellite picked up signals and for the first time beamed 'live' TV pictures across the Atlantic to England. There had been plenty of media coverage leading up to the event and he had already determined to settle down some time and compose a tribute to it. Past midnight he sat alone in the living room glued to his little black and white television. Then, just after 1a.m., there emerged on the screen the blurred, ghostlike shape of a man in a dark suit sitting motionless at a desk. The pictures lasted no more than 30 fleeting seconds but Joe was entranced by them and felt impelled to put something down there and then. His understanding of television technology and his fascination with the stars sent his imagination spinning into orbit too, and that was when he knew what kind of sound he wanted. With the satellite whirling along on solar energy at thousands of miles per hour, circling the Earth nine times a day, there had to be about it a sense of power, speed and . . . space. He was back on 'I Hear A New World' territory once again, but two and a half years on, and now eager to find out what he could do with his own advances in equipment and expertise. The group's first record had featured the clavioline, and only through recent experiments had he come to realize the enormous scope it offered when used for recording. Along with the air of mystery that he had recognized in it in 1960, he had since found it could produce a sense of aloofness which he could get with no other instrument. For both of these qualities, he intended using it to its full potential.

At this moment, though, there was one thing only that he wanted and that was the right tune, but eventually he had to go to bed all keyed up without it. He fell asleep but woke up again as usual in the early hours and lay there in the dark picturing the satellite speeding around the world, relaying its earthly messages from a very unearthly 3,000 miles out in space. Suddenly a tune started coming and he dashed downstairs to la-la it onto tape. For the next hour or so he steadily improved it, wailing it through cathedral-like echo over an old rhythm track till the melody in his head was more or less the one on the tape. On this occasion it was starting life as "loo-oo-la-da-dee-da-deedle-ah" over the backing track of a recent B-side he had written for Geoff Goddard called 'Try Once More'. In honour of the satellite he was calling it 'The Theme Of Telstar'.

After breakfast next day he translated the wailings onto the clavioline; this time he had Dave Adams playing the tune over the backing of a Mike Berry record, 'Every Little Kiss'. Then he rang the group and arranged a recording session. A few days later, after their Saturday night show they drove down to London in their organist's little A35 van and on the Sunday called in at the studio.

The session itself is of interest because it gives an idea of how he would conduct them, and Clem Cattini who was drumming

145

offers a brief account: "Joe played the demo a few times, and then Alan [Caddy] worked out the chord sequences. Joe wanted a moving rhythm; he sang the beat – like dum-diddy-dum – and imitated the guitar sound and bass, and then we just kicked it about and he'd direct each individual into the shape he wanted it to go. He knew what he was after but if someone did something he liked he'd say, 'Keep that. I like it.' Then he'd say, 'Right, that's it up to there', and it went on like that until it was more or less ready. Then he'd record it and change a couple of things here and there. I played the basic beat with brushes on the cymbals and it was almost exactly the same as 'Johnny Remember Me' and 'Wild Wind'."

Their session took a day and a half. As usual the melody and rhythm were recorded separately. For a start all of Sunday was spent laying down the two rhythm tracks, one for each side; the day was finished off with the one on the B-side, 'Jungle Fever', only taking an hour.

The group left after 12 hours at 10 o'clock to return the next day and overdub two guitar breaks on the A-side. But there was no time for them to finish the job and put the main melody line down. They had to get away by 2 o'clock to be back onstage in Great Yarmouth that afternoon, so Joe told them that Geoff Goddard who had been lucky for him on 'Johnny Remember Me' could come in and be lucky for him again.

Geoff duly arrived to take over on the clavioline and for the next six hours sat wearing headphones playing Joe's tune over and over. At the same time Joe was fiddling around in the control room, as usual compressing the music while bouncing it back and forth from one machine to the other; this way he overdubbed it in the high and low octaves to thicken the sound, echoing it all up as he went along with a concoction of tape delay, Binson, spring and echo chamber. The clavioline, just a small battery-operated keyboard, was all the while clipped onto the piano making life easier for Geoff, playing both instruments. During the tune's guitar breaks, Joe had him softly tinkling the piano's high notes giving, with the benefit of drawing pins in the hammers, a harp effect. Then Geoff rounded the piece off with some airy, out-of-this-world aah-ing. The tune on the flip-side, 'Jungle Fever', was laid down rather quicker; to bless the record with even more luck he let Geoff compose it, and with a rhythm track as a guide, it took him as long to make up as to play: two minutes.

After the session they stood in the control room listening to

'The Theme Of Telstar' as Joe played it back again and again. Geoff felt a cold shiver run down his back on hearing what Joe had done to his simple bit of keyboard playing. Perhaps it had something to do with the thunderstorm that was raging at the time, a fact that oddly enough convinced Joe he had a hit on his hands. Ever since the vocals on 'Johnny Remember Me' had been recorded during a thunderstorm he had always been pleased when musicians brought rain with them.

Next the whole thing had to be speeded up about half a tone to give it more of a sense of urgency. To help create an atmosphere and catch attention he also added some bizarre sound effects at the beginning and end, the ingredients of which he kept secret. The only clues available today are that they were recorded backwards and speeded and part of them had already been launched on the 'I Hear A New World' LP. Anyone with the right audio equipment who fancies unravelling an electronic hotchpotch could be in line for the undying gratitude of Joe Meek fans everywhere, if successful!

Having made up an acetate he took it along to the Ivy Music publisher Roy Berry to hear how marvellous he thought it was. Roy's only reservation was the title: "I thought that 'The Theme Of Telstar' was too wordy and I suggested to him with a little trepidation that we change it to 'Telstar' – because he was proud of his own ideas. And he thought that was not a bad idea." Decca were the ones to see next. Dick Rowe liked it, the selection panel accepted it and the engineers – although horrified at its unheard of levels of limiting and compression – agreed to cut it, and all went fairly smoothly till the top twit in the sales department rang to politely ask why the disc was scratched at the start. The air was blue in the few seconds before Joe slammed the phone down on him.

Now it was out of his hands. He had put together a classic which nowadays ranks as one of the finest pop records ever made. Here he was at his best and as close to artistic perfection as damn it. Here was the quintessential Joe Meek sound where his concept and production had fused together on one extraordinary 3-minute recording. Basically 'Telstar' is a catchy tune in a punchy package but the sound was unique. Nothing like it had ever been heard before and, as intended, it conjured up the very image of a television satellite racing through space: stuttering to life with the noise of generators it built into a pulsating blast-off to the main theme, surging forward with the electronic clavioline, then easing into a calmer, cruising, silvery guitar break and finally soaring resolutely away on a crescendo of rampant energy and freedom. Not bad value for 6s.6d.

In the meantime he had another record on his mind that he considered just as important: the latest one from John Leyton. In order to win back flagging support the Leyton camp had decided to take a whole new initiative with a different composer, producer, engineer and studio, and if the write-up in *Record Retailer* was anything to go by, 'Down The River Nile' stood a good chance of getting it: "This is one of the most commercial and possibly the best the artiste has made." Unfortunately the reviewer was either deaf or daft because 'Down The River Nile' was in fact the *worst* he had made and probably the worst of his whole career. John sums it up: "When 'Johnny Remember Me' came out we got a lot of criticism because everyone said it's so distorted, and some of the early songs there really was a lot of distortion and we had to ask Joe to make them less so; he really did tend to go over the top sometimes in his mixing. The problem was that 'Johnny Remember Me' was such an enormous hit and it was at that time such an unusual sound. I was automatically typed with that sort of song. And then of course when we came up with 'Wild Wind' I'd got into a rut. I wasn't like Adam Faith or Cliff Richard singing pretty songs; I was singing a certain type of song with a certain type of sound – we had trouble finding songs for me. And then with 'Down The River Nile', which I think is the poorest song I ever recorded, I think panic had set in: got to get out of this rut – send him down the River Nile!"

With 'Down The River Nile' they did get out of the rut but landed in another one. The record only made one chart and that was at No.42. From here on, Britain's highest paid pop singer would be singing lots of pretty songs, and with dwindling success. It would not be until 1964 when he had broken right away from music and moved to Hollywood that his career would take off all over again. Major roles in films like *Von Ryan's Express, Guns At Batasi* and *Krakatoa – East Of Java* would keep him busy to the end of the Sixties.

Even though 'Down The River Nile' had had little to do with

Joe its poor showing did mean he had not had a record in the Top
Forty for nearly two months, and it was a full nine months since
his last Top Ten hit. Perhaps he had been spoilt by 'Johnny
Remember Me' but it did leave a dry taste in this latest RGM
sales drought. Nor was it fun hearing sniping comments about
himself on the grapevine: that people in the business were
describing him as a has-been, saying he was over the hill; that the
Joe Meek show was finished. It was depressing and made him feel
the whole world was waiting to see him fall. He could not let them
have that satisfaction but wondered how he could avoid it.

He was firing on all cylinders and getting nowhere. In his eyes
if there were any justice in the world, the cheques should have
been pouring in. Considering how many 'answers' to other
artistes were on his books, one of them should surely come up
with something soon. There were the Outlaws: 'answers' to the
Shadows; Michael Cox: Ricky Nelson; Mike Berry: Buddy Holly;
Danny Rivers and Andy Cavell: Cliff Richard; Joy & Dave: the
Everly Brothers; Alan Klein: Bernard Cribbins; as well as Gerry
Temple, who if he was not an English version of Neil Sedaka,
certainly sounded like he was and Don Charles who was singlehandedly taking on all the olde-tyme ballad merchants; and Jerry
Lee Lewis was saying that Cliff Bennett & the Rebel Rousers
sounded more like him on record than he did! But maybe Joe
stood more chance putting his money on originals like John
Leyton, Geoff Goddard (who had now taken up singing after, as
he says, Buddy Holly had told him to start) and his new bunch the
Tornados. Unfortunately the last one was an ultra long shot, the
market being almost totally geared to whatever America flung
this way, though at least the Tornados' name and disc title were
American, so with any luck the public might be fooled into thinking
they were another US import.

Towards the end of August he had something worth writing
home about. He had not written to his mother for several weeks
but 'Telstar' was now just outside the charts. In the same way that
his visits home depended on things going fairly well for him in
London, his letter-writing relied upon his having some shred of
success before he would put pen to paper. So months could pass
without a word.

Dear Mum

I am ashamed of myself for not writting for
such a long time, Ive been waiting for something good to
happen and hopping I would come up with a hit.
The weeks seemed to fly by and then the

cherries came, I kept meaning to write but again left it late, please thank Arthur for them Im very greatful.

I had a letter from Pam today its upset me a great deal, I think someone should have phoned me when you had the nose bleed so badly, I feel left out of my family life so much, I seem to work my guts out for others, others get rich not myself, I would dearly like to send some worth while money home, but things have changed alot now I do not get any extra, but I will tell you Mum Im all set now for a steady littel extra it will take a few months to work but then I should be OK.

I hope you like my record Telstar I wrote it and its going to be a hit, I need it so badly to put me back in the public eye again.

There are some nice disc's coming out soon "Stand Up" by Mike Cox "My Littel Girls Come Home" Geoff Goddard, Sept 7th and 14th, Geoff's will be a hit.

I badly need a rest my brain is so over worked at times I just dont hear what people are saying to me but with Telstar about to take off I must stick to it. I will do my best to come and see you in the next few weeks, I may bring Heinz with me he keeps saying he would like to meet you, please look after yourself Mum, I don't know what I would do if anything happened to you, Im working to be a susses just so that I can give you the things you deserve, Im growing to hate Major Banks he's a very greedy man and lives for no thing but money.

I have told myself I will own RGM sound in four months by hook or by crook.

Well give my love to everyone, please forgive me for not writting look after yourself Mum all my love

from your loving Son
Joe

UP, UP AND AWAY

The Banks problem was a big one. As might be expected Joe's relationship with him was sinking fast. It was the same old story: he couldn't bear being answerable to anyone and where money was concerned he was indeed answerable to Major Banks. Every cheque had to have Banks's signature too; every time he used a session band he had to phone him for the £7 cheques. As Heinz remembers, the Major would always send his son Lester down with them: "Joe called Lester the 'Poodle': 'The Poodle will be here in a minute with the cheques.' Little Lester Banks would come running down with his glasses on and all the bits: 'Here we are – frightfully. Here's your four cheques. Who are they made out for?' Joe couldn't stand him. Lester would often take the piss out of him and Joe'd send him out with a flea in his ear. Financially, Joe didn't have a say; they ran the whole show. He needed someone for finance but he was open. I won't say Major Banks took him for a ride but others did."

However, though Joe always ran Banks down something rotten and amongst his artistes made the name Major Banks synonymous with that of the Devil, he was not half as black as he was painted. He was a businessman, period. Without him to keep tabs on where the money was going there would have been no money to keep tabs on. The man naturally wanted the business to thrive and he knew it would not if he gave him a free hand. But there was only black and white with Joe, nothing in between.

Making him sorer still was the Major's intention of drawing out his investment before sharing any profits. And with no sign of profits within telescopic range he looked like being hampered for quite a while to come. The bitterest pill was having Major Banks helping himself to his composer's royalties. When in 1960 Banks had signed the cheque to finance RGM Sound, Joe had signed away half his own wealth. Everything he worked for, all profits, must be for the good of the Company and go into the Company. That seemed fair enough at the time when he was on his knees but now it was a millstone. Thus every time he got out of bed in the middle of the night to go downstairs and compose a song, every time he broke off from lunch to hum into a tape recorder he was doing so for Major Banks as well. It was not enough that he should be working all the hours God gave putting recordings together; striving with all his time, energy and creativity to make the company a success. He was shackled ball and chain to the man and felt hard done by.

On the other hand it was of no significance to him that it had been Banks who had risked £5,000 in getting the company off the ground. To his mind, investing in such a gilt-edged proposition as himself constituted no risk whatever; Banks had merely wangled himself an easy ride from where he could sit smugly

151

back and watch the money rolling in. Nor was he soothed by the £20 a week salary he alone was receiving and the company's payment of his rent; that was all a pittance he thought when comparing his own input into the company with that of the Major. He would not have minded quite so much if he had felt that Banks was putting in his share, but all he seemed to be doing was claiming very high office expenses and tightening the budget on his only real expenditure in life: equipment. He had little money of his own so it had to come out of RGM Sound. Consequently Banks had to be persuaded as to its necessity, and since he knew as much about recording equipment as a hippo squatting in a mudbank it took some doing. Banks even kept a supply of new tapes at his office and when Joe wanted them he had to send his office boy round with a prescription.

As a result of all this he had realized he had one saviour: the composer's pseudonym. The one he had been using for years, Robert Duke, was thanks to his grandmother who had once proudly told him as a little boy building his crystal set that if he continued like this he would one day be a duke. That one appeared on the B-sides of all the Leyton hits, amongst others, and was a nice little money-maker, seeing that B-sides bring in as much from record sales as A-sides. Banks unfortunately knew of Duke, otherwise that money could have been gushing into Joe's coffers instead of RGM Sound's, but he knew nothing of Dandy Ward, Peter Jacobs or Robert Baker – yet. And all these served a dual function. Not only did they get round the Major but saved explanations when he placed his music with publishing companies other than Ivy. Though he would sometimes fall out with Ivy he was scared stiff of offending them, and time and again when he called round next door to Bob Kingston at Southern he would plead with him not to tell Roy Berry. Sometimes, as Mike Berry recalls, he dispensed with assumed names altogether, putting a real person's name on his compositions, with 304 as their address for royalties: "There was a song that I was credited with that I didn't write and I actually signed the contract. It was one of my B-sides, and it was because he didn't want Major Banks to have the money. I didn't get the money for it. He said words to the effect of: 'Bloody Major Banks and his bloody companies! I'm having to pay them all this bloody money and I'm doing all the bloody work. So I want to put this song in your name and then I won't have to pay RGM Sound.' 'How Many Times' it was called."

Naturally it was always very hush-hush and no one else should be let in on their secret. Major Banks suspected this underhand dealing and hardly endeared himself to Joe by taking out various of Joe's record company contacts to top eating houses and

UP, UP AND AWAY

surreptitiously fishing for details of his pseudonyms and business affairs. It got the Major nowhere and just left him thinking that every one of Joe's artistes whose name appeared on the label as composer was swindling him.

Aggravating things still further were their opposing personalities. What the Major needed above all if he had any hope of holding their partnership together was a firm friendliness in dealing with Joe, with an appreciation of his highly sensitive temperament as well as an understanding of the music business and Joe's position within it. He didn't understand any of it. What he knew about music could be painted in large letters on the back of a postage stamp. Worse still, he was used to calling a spade a spade and bossing his colleagues about to good effect, but it didn't work with Joe. Joe may have buckled down to that brusque, no-nonsense attitude in his RAF training days, but since then he had gained ten times the confidence and no one but no one was giving him orders now. So the Major was hardly ever calling round to the studio now and would be met by a tidal wave of ill feeling when he did.

On the Tornados front, Larry Parnes was growing very keen to manage the group; he wanted them as Billy Fury's permanent touring band. Joe had been dreaming of a co-management tie-up with Parnes for months, so when Parnes suggested a discussion on the subject he gladly obliged.

The ideal arrangement, they decided, would be one whereby each retained full control over one half of the group's activities. Joe's naturally would be in the studio where he insisted that he continue to rule supreme without the interference of Parnes or anyone else. Parnes for his part assumed responsibility for the group's public appearances and was equally defensive over his own territory; Joe would have no say whatever in choosing venues but could demand priority over them if an important recording session cropped up. To Joe the idea of joining ranks with Parnes to boost the Tornados' gunning power sounded super. Not only should it brighten their and Heinz's chances of success but also bring Billy Fury that bit nearer Holloway Road. They signed the deal.

Then Parnes saw the group at Great Yarmouth and asked them to sign it. If they didn't, he warned, Billy would get a new band. So they all signed – except the drummer, Clem Cattini. He had worked for Parnes before and thought he could afford to pay more than £25 per week. So then Joe had to drive up and meet them both, and was soon "doing his bananas" threatening to sack Cattini, with Cattini threatening to inform the press if he did. At that, he saw his Billy Fury stepping-stone sinking in front of him, but was relieved to see it helping Parnes decide he could afford more after all. Cattini left the meeting several pounds a week happier. Curiously that made the Tornados the first act to be signed by Larry Parnes for personal management since Joe Brown three years back.

A few days passed. And then the beginning of September saw 'Telstar' loom into view at No.50 on the *Record Mirror* chart. Even as it entered the listings Joe knew exactly how far it was going to climb having enquired at one of his seances and been told No.4.

When the Tornados themselves heard the disc they must have wondered where they were on it! They had after all departed for Great Yarmouth leaving behind only the rhythm and lead guitar tracks, and having no idea the recording would end up sounding like it did. They got their second surprise two weeks later when the record, instead of petering out around the No.35 mark, moved into the Top Ten. At the same time in the middle of September the Great Yarmouth summer season ended, giving Joe the chance to hook them back into the studio for two weeks before the next tour started. Once again work was piling up and he had them recording more tracks and backing other artistes, for they were still his main session band.

All at once everyone wanted to know who these Tornados were. They had reached the Top Twenty without a single TV or radio appearance and had received hardly a mention in the music papers, apart from a few poverty-stricken adverts; much to Joe's annoyance, Decca had as usual been too mean to spend more than peanuts on publicity.

The story of how they all came together in the first place differed somewhat from the one given in the papers. It began in the autumn of '61 with the sacking of the Outlaws' lead guitarist, Bill Kuy. No replacement could be found, so their bass player Chas Hodges had decided to switch over and play the lead himself. A new bass player had to be found, and the first one to try for the job was Heinz. He had travelled up to Holloway Road from his home in Southampton with a band of part-timers and was the only one Joe didn't dump. But, as Chas remembers well, when Joe picked Heinz as his replacement on bass his thoughts were not on musical ability: "I rang up Joe and he said, 'Well I know a good bass player.' And I said, 'Who?' He said it was Heinz from Southampton. Typical Joe: I said, 'What's he like?' He said, 'Oh, he's nice looking, he's very smart . . .' I said, 'No, what's he *play* like?' Anyway, he got Heinz down and I wasn't very impressed with his playing. When Heinz came down Joe really fell for him in a big way. So I thought, 'I know Joe's really hot for this Heinz, like. I can't go to him and say I don't think he's any good.' Well, I could have done but I didn't have the bottle to. So I went to him and said, 'I don't think I'm good enough for the lead guitar; I want to go back on the bass.' He said, 'All right then, go back on bass and we'll get another guitar player.' So he put an advert in the *Melody Maker*."

Pirate Alan Caddy, who had grown tired of 'Shakin' All Over' with Johnny Kidd, auditioned but by then Joe wanted to form another group solely for sessions. It made sense because the Outlaws were often away performing with Mike Berry, besides which he felt sorry for Heinz who had just packed in his job bacon-slicing in a Southampton grocer's. By this time the Outlaws had dwindled to one, leaving Chas by himself! Pirate drummer Clem Cattini and rhythm guitarist George Bellamy were then snatched from the Outlaw's grasp to complete the new session band.

Much to Joe's amazement, at the beginning of October, 'Telstar' knocked Elvis's 'She's Not You' off the top spot. Within a week at No.1 it had sold over 250,000 copies, holding off all competition for five weeks and keeping him deliriously happy pinning up telegrams.

For a while it was difficult to avoid hearing it because for two months it was the most played record on radio and whistled wherever you went. If this helped sell it, it also helped spoil it. Whilst for some it was electronic bliss, for others who were sick of hearing it day and night it was the lowest form of musak – even Ian Gregory singing it could not have been worse. One *Melody Maker* reviewer had already commented: "With topicality the only thing to commend it, the Tornados romp through 'Telstar'. Billy Fury's backing band ought to be able to produce something less monotonous than this." To no one was it greater anathema than to disc jockey David Jacobs, who hated it with a vengeance, seizing every opportunity he could to condemn it. When introducing it on his *Pick Of The Pops* radio show he would make remarks like: "I'm sorry I have to play this. It sounds like music from a third-rate ice show." Joe was so incensed the first time that he rang Roy Berry at Ivy Music demanding he get an apology. None was forthcoming but Jacobs was destined to eat humble pie in the humorous conclusion that cropped up some months later.

As for his A & R rivals, their reaction was different entirely. Considering how 'Telstar' has still not dated and sounds as crisp today as if it had just been produced, it's not hard to imagine the question running through their minds when it appeared way back

155

in '62. Here was this Joe Meek disc with its peculiar sound which no one could fathom, and it simply towered above all their own stuff. What would the man come out with next?

Curiously, while 'Telstar' was powering from strength to strength the Tornados were limping along painfully slow getting off the ground. With the record at No.1 all the promoters were after the group to appear on solo tours and TV, but far from laughing all the way to the bank, the lads were still scraping together extra pennies recording backings for artistes like Don Charles and Andy Cavell, none of which apparently said much for Larry Parnes's abilities in managing them. But it went deeper than that.

The trouble was that they were technically still no more than Billy Fury's touring band, and that contract more or less bound them to him hand and foot. A gruelling 2,000 miles a week, 49-nighter tour had already been arranged with very few days off. It also created the scandalous situation whereby their solo spot on the show was just long enough to get through 'Telstar': 3 minutes! That was all they were allowed before having to fall back out of the spotlight and once again become an accompanying group. They were not even billed. Yet they were playing their part in packing houses at every performance, for outside the theatres they were facing long lines of autograph hunters and in their dressing rooms were answering 400 or so fan letters a week. And the rest of the acts – Billy Fury, Mark Wynter, Joe Brown, Karl Denver – couldn't muster a No.1 hit between them! The excuse put forward was that the package show had all been mapped out long in advance; no spot had been given to the Tornados, and with so many stars already in the line-up, no more than three minutes could be spared.

And Joe could only look on seething. If he had had his way they would have topped the bill and gone on last. Regrettably he had no say. Obviously he should never have allowed it to happen in the first place, but when he signed the co-management contract his thoughts had been on Billy Fury and not 'Telstar' as the passport to the Tornados', and ultimately Heinz's, success. 'Telstar' had not at the time promised the super-popularity that Fury had. He was already a gilt-edged performer, so wherever he appeared on tour, there too could be Joe's blond bombshell, basking in a little of the attention and publicity being afforded one of the top three singers in the land. Now of course things were different and he realized his mistake. Now Heinz was only reaping a fraction of the adulation and media coverage that should have been his had the Tornados been free. Every booking agent and promoter in the country was dying to get his hands on them but they were untouchable.

And that was just the way Larry Parnes liked it. He was smart enough to realize that by keeping them pegged down as a support group their glory would be vastly enhancing Billy's. As far as he was concerned, that 3-minute spot was ample, and the less audiences saw of Heinz and the others onstage with Billy, the less they would be distracted from him. Parnes had already lost one battle with Joe over the bleaching of Heinz's hair, and the ever present threat of someone else's protégé upstaging his own was one he wanted minimized. This was the way to do it. At the same time he didn't mind sending the group off alone to play dance halls during the odd break in the tour. To confirm their popularity their first solo gig at Oxford's Carfax Ballroom was a sellout with 300 being turned away at the door.

Joe consoled himself by resolving to groom Heinz into a star as soon as this cursed 49-nighter was over. Fan mail looked like turning Heinz's head and Joe was ready to set to work on him right away.

Once the Billy Fury tour was over, one might have assumed that for the Tornados everything at last would start coming up roses; that without the complication of having Fury around, Joe and Parnes would finally pool their recording and entrepreneurial skills and find a winning formula. Instead it was tug-o'-war time! Joe wanted the group in the studio but primarily he did not want them on the road at all. As a result the boys did a lot less touring than Parnes might have planned for them, as Heinz explains: "We should have been out in the public eye but Joe didn't want that. No, Parnes would have made the money; he'd love to have put us out every night of the week, but Joe had this thing: 'Whenever I want them in the studio . . .' He had first rights and that's what he made sure of: that we were in the studio regardless. The deal was: Parnes paid us £25 a week; he paid nothing to Joe. And of course, when we'd finished with Billy, Parnes then really cashed in. The moment the Billy Fury tour was finished he put us out on our own. And Joe saw all these bookings coming in and he sussed. And Joe said, 'I'm not having this.' And he kept stepping in saying, 'I want them in the studio. They've got an LP,' and so on."

Thankfully it was not all gloom for the group because on the plus side a spot in the new pop film *Just For Fun* had cropped up. At the same time Joe was breathlessly busy working on a Tornados series for Radio Luxembourg as well as all sorts of Tornados singles, EPs and LPs. The best news came at the end of October when Larry Parnes announced that there had been a "very good offer" for a 10-day visit to the USA in February with three major TV shows lined up.

Even this early, reporters were asking about the Tornados'

next single, 'Globetrotter', which he already had awaiting release. "I'll tell you it's NOT an outer space thing; I think that would be a mistake. But it is a colourful type of thing. I went out of my way to try and create a picture again. I like playing with sounds. The story is that 'Telstar' was written and recorded in a hurry . . . which is true. But a couple of years ago on the small Triumph label I had a stereophonic long player and an EP out called 'I Hear A New World'. That was full of what I call outer space noises, so the idea of 'Telstar' isn't exactly a new one." Much to his annoyance Decca were keeping 'Globetrotter' under wraps until the New Year due to 'Telstar's' continued heavy selling, thus thwarting his plan to fill the top two places.

Meanwhile Billy Fury & the Tornados were being touted as a new Cliff Richard & the Shadows. Naturally with the Shadows having been hogging the instrumental limelight for so long, music papers were having a field day with headlines reading: "TORNADOS GO ALL OUT TO CHALLENGE SHADOWS" and "SHADOWS BEWARE – TORNADOS COULD TOPPLE YOU". In that latter part of '62 it seemed quite likely that they would, but anyone looking back on those headlines from a mere six months hence would have seen how trivial they really were. Even while 'Telstar' was at the top another group were nosing into the charts for the first time, who were to become famous the world over for their haircuts – amongst other things. They were of course the Beatles. Inside Liverpool they were already an institution; outside they were virtually unknown. Now thanks to the fact that their first single, 'Love Me Do', was an unimaginative production of an equally unimaginative song which had only reached No.17 – despite their manager Brian Epstein buying 10,000 copies for himself – those acts currently in the charts were unwittingly enjoying a few months' grace.

With 'Telstar' riding high came the inevitable offers from the major companies. These were for him to join their own staff or to work at their studios, giving them first option on his output. He didn't want to know. "I'm not going with those bloody peasants," was his attitude and he spurned their charms. What he wanted was total freedom and was still yearning for the day he could buy out the Major.[23]

Early in November another overdue letter went to his beloved mother. (The name 'Tiger' that crops up is that of the family dog.)

Dear Mum

Thank you for your letter, the other letter has been found, it was with a batch of others and I put it on one side and it got covered up, I get about 12 letters a day, my buessiness has become so hecktick I have great hope's for the future, of course it means very hard work, but thank God I don't mind that.

My plans for a visit this weekend seems to look dim, on monday I resighn from RGM sound and have meetings with my Solicitor satarday, and sunday prepare my case, but if its only for a few hours I would love to be with you so I may be home, but please dont worry Mum, If Im not there in body I am in spirit, I knew someone had died I had a strange vission about 2 on sunday morning last, was this the time you think Tiger died.

Heinz had this weekend all sorted out, for he will be in Gloucester sunday, and was coming back to meet you afeter the show and stop the night, he will be a bit upset about it, but I cant help it, this boy is a great insperation to me he's so full of life and go, and has great respect for me, which is a change from a good deal of my Artists, since he came along my luck seem's to have changed, and given a littel time I will start making worth while money.

There are several record to watch one I go for, its by Peter Jay and the Jaywalkers "Can Can 62" it will be a hit, Andy Cavell has a chance, Don Charles may make it, the Packabeats with my tune "Evening In Paris" on Pye could click but a realy big hit will be, by a new boy "Neal Christian" the song "Road To Love" it comes out 23rd Nov, and he's going to get star treatment, I have made a wounderful record of the vocal version of Telstar the boy is named "Kenny Hollywood" its the best name Ive dreamed up for along time and one of the best records Ive made too it will be a hit there's no release date yet, it will come out when the Tornado's version drops below eight in the chart's, of course I wrote the lyrick.

As you see I get through a huge amount of work but nows the time to make hay while Telstar shines, I have changed my car I got 500 for the other which was so expensive on repairs, Ive got a new Zodiac its loveley all I need now is the time to get out in it, I bought it because I have to pay off the rest, and this will make me keep searching for money which is so important, I have to be mean and gready its the only way.

Give my love to everyone keep lissening to Luxembourg and most important of all look after yourself dont catch cold keep off the stone floor eat like mad and keep the cold out, if you neglecket yourself now youl be run down all through the winter.

Thank Arthur for looking after you I hope he's well, he will like the car, but its much bigger than the other.

Thats all for now please look after your self all ways thinking of you
your loving Son
                    Joe

His resignation was followed later in the month by his reinstatement. An agreement was reached regarding an eventual split. The new terms were far more favourable towards him than the original ones, and it was a shame they had come so late. From now on, all royalties from his songwriting would be his. So, along with his latest winning streak, they should speed up payment of the Major's loans and share in the profits and soon see him safely on his way.

Supposedly to help maintain the winning streak the "wonderful" vocal version of 'Telstar' was released early. Sung by the 15 year old he had named Kenny Hollywood, it was called 'Magic Star' or rather 'How to ruin a good tune in two easy minutes'. As for being wonderful it was anything but, and unfortunately for Joe the public thought so too, staying away from it in droves. Said Joe at the time, "He is a boy with a tremendous future and will do well." He was never heard of again.

That month 'Telstar' earned its first Gold Disc on passing a million sales and on December 15 the group could be seen receiving it on ITV's pop show *Thank Your Lucky Stars*. It is unknown what Larry Parnes's thoughts were at the sight of Billy Fury presenting it to them but Joe's could be summed up in one word: glee. It was a real smacker in the eye from him to Larry. Billy had never even had a No.1 record let alone a Gold Disc and, according to Heinz, when Joe saw him handing one over to the Tornados he declared, "That's how it should be!"

His best record to come out of late '62 and one of the best of his entire career was a song he wrote for country'n'western band Houston Wells & the Marksmen, called 'North Wind'. It was one of his own favourites and reminiscent of 'Wild Wind', though more melodic. The doom-laden lyrics hasten along to a driving beat amongst a wonderfully atmospheric chorus and a very effective undulating organ representing ethereal breezes:

> *Blow North Wind and tell your story*
> *Of my love, its hates and glory:*
> *How I loved and lost my baby, lost my head as well,*
> *Tell them how I killed her lover, broke my heart as well.*
> *Blow North Wind and tell your story.*
>
> *Blow West Wind, yeh, let it thunder.*
> *Tell all the angels way up yonder.*
> *How I loved and lost my baby, took her life as well,*
> *Tell me I'm forgiven now, don't send my soul to Hell.*
> *Blow West Wind and tell your story.*

His lyrics had come some way since 'Put A Ring On Her Finger'! Perhaps their fearful sense of tragedy was what relegated it to a B-side, though it would richly deserve featuring in a Top Twenty of Joe Meek tracks.[24]

As for the rest of his stock, apart from a very pleasant number written and sung by Geoff Goddard called 'My Little Girl's Come Home' and Michael Cox's 'Stand Up', both of which might have fared better with a modicum of airplay, they were all rather routine affairs.

Less routine were the nail-biting discussions in progress at 304, where Joe was plunging into his latest venture: a new film and a new star! With the Tornados' records selling by the lorry-load, a lot of attention was being centred on Heinz. Getting most of the band's fan mail had finally turned his head and Joe was excitedly setting the wheels in motion. Obviously the basic requirements for any solo pop singer are a reasonable voice, moderate looks and stage presence. In Joe's book if you had the looks you were in – the rest could be arranged. Now he was impatient to put Heinz on show and the sooner he made him presentable the sooner he could get onto the booking agents to pull in some stage and TV dates. For a start Heinz had to learn some songs, and to allow him more time for them Joe had one of the latest gadgets fitted into Heinz's new Ford Zephyr: a car record player.

Plans were also underway for a B-movie to be financed by an outside concern. Called *Farewell Performance* and featuring the Tornados, the story was described as a raw-edged drama about an unpopular singer who gets murdered; towards the end of the picture Heinz replaces him as a new discovery and sings a song. Already Joe had written all five of the film's numbers, and in December he announced that the film's release was set to coincide with the launching of Heinz's solo career. All of which goes to show the wonders concealed in a bottle of peroxide.

A slight disappointment presented itself at the end of the year when he read that not only had *NME* readers had the gall to vote 'Telstar' No.2 behind Frank Ifield's 'I Remember You' in the 'Best Disc Of The Year' list and made the Tornados runners-up to the Shadows as the 'Best Small Group' (self-supporting), but had voted David Jacobs best disc jockey! Was there no justice in the world, he wondered. Happily other things were going on to keep his spirits high.

For a start there was 'Telstar'. To the surprise of everyone but Joe it was not slackening its pace. Far from sliding down the charts into the cobwebs it was still hovering in the British Top Ten and getting bigger and bigger around the world. Come Christmas 'Telstar's' sales were booming, with overall figures nearing two million. But his biggest Christmas present was smiling at him from the other side of the Atlantic. The album had just broken into the American LP chart at No.45. The single was at No.1.

10
"I'm Still The Bloody Governor!"

A nd that was the way 1963 opened: in style at the top of the American charts. It gave the Tornados the distinction of being the first British group ever to do so and they held the position for three weeks. What was more, the very fact the disc was British gave cause for wonder. Whereas well over half of all the records that had ever reached No.1 in Britain were American, only four British ones had ever done so over there: Vera Lynn's 'Auf Wiedersehen', 1952; Laurie London's 'He's Got The Whole World In His Hands', 1958; Acker Bilk's 'Stranger On The Shore', 1962; David Rose's 'The Stripper', 1962.

In the first week of the year it was announced that the record had earned a second Gold Disc. Now he was really away! Decca's interest in his product had already trebled; with dollar signs shining in their eyes the Decca hierarchy had pushed his overall output up by a third. What they had yet to realize was that 'Telstar' was to give him a measure of power over them with which he could hold them to ransom. Charming them with the promise of another 'Telstar' on the way, he would be able to insist that his product was not only released but given the amount of push he wanted; otherwise if they did not behave themselves they would get three duff Tornados follow-ups, each of which would be so shabby it would not be worth pressing. That way he could end the contract and take the group to other bidders. Things were also hotting up elsewhere on the record company front, where Columbia for the first time were accepting recordings and Parlophone were increasing their takings off him, all of which meant that his entire output was now being accepted!

There was less peace than ever at 304 with groups, publishers, record companies and the rest phoning and knocking at his door at all hours. And the media were bursting to make him a celebrity, trying in vain to get him on TV and radio chat shows. He loved it! These were flash, bang, wallop times and life had turned into one long firework display.

Working at full throttle there was little time for social life, and as long as the records kept selling, that worried him not a jot.

THE LEGENDARY JOE MEEK

Starting work at 10 in the morning he would often go on through to 2 o'clock the next morning, with only a meal break and a gallon of coffee in between. Sleep, like bills, was something to be put off as long as possible. When he ate he ate well, which meant a pound of rump steak and chips nearly every day. But time was tight and besides steaks his ravenous appetite for music-making had him munching greedily through the hours on a daily diet of singers, songs, sessions, phone calls and fan clubs. He was bestriding the British music scene like a Colossus. This was what he had been hungering for since first arriving in London: having the industry at his feet with everyone hollering for his attention, and publishers and record companies dancing to *his* tune rather than vice versa. And at last he had it and it felt good.

On top of that, all this success underlined his standing in the profession. At 33 he was unequalled either as a producer or as a sound-balance engineer and he knew it; he had known it for years. There was no one in Britain to touch him. As producer Jack Good pointed out at the time, nobody else except engineer Terry Johnson of IBC could satisfactorily duplicate the popular sound from America and, with all due respect, the British sounds being turned out for the home market Joe could whip up standing on his head. As for his own sounds, they might just as well have been wafting in from another world; nobody but nobody knew how he got them. The so-called experts would waffle about his endless overdubbing and manic echoing and limiting but however strongly they professed to know his secrets, they were as much in the dark as a mole in a hole. They hadn't the faintest idea to what degree he was using these techniques, how he was modifying his equipment, where he was sticking microphones or what gadgets he was employing to alter drum and guitar sounds and he was not about to tell them. In fact right up until the day a recording of his reached the record company he would be beside himself ensuring that they didn't even find out what was going on it, let alone how it got there.[25]

Not surprisingly he soon detected more jealousy amongst the music fraternity. Many resented the fact that not only was he free to have his own way in his own studio, but was reaping success as well! And whilst studios were astutely accepting all his product the bosses were rumbling and grumbling about the lack of inspiration coming from their own A & R departments. If Joe Meek could create his own identifiable sound and record big, original, money-making productions costing nothing in a dirty old hole over a leather bag shop with live wires dangling all over the place,

164

why the hell couldn't they, with their hundreds of thousands of pounds' worth of technology, do the same? They didn't know. And while they were trying to fathom it out Joe carried on regardless, bettering his sounds and making them more unusual so no rotten pigs could thieve them off him.

His attitude towards his contemporaries is clearly outlined by Don Charles, in whom he sometimes confided: "After 'Telstar' he was very thrilled indeed because they were all writing him off and they said he'd shot his bolt and he'd finished. He would say, 'That'll show 'em. I'm still the bloody governor!' He thought he was the best A & R man in the world – always. And I think that's what made him produce things. At one time he *was* the governor, certainly in this country. They always said about Joe that he was ten years ahead of anybody else. He was way, way ahead: his techniques were incredible. What he did with those machines were nobody's business – the sounds he made! I remember he did something with a kettle; and there was some weird sound on a record. And I said, 'What's that?' And like a child he fell about laughing. And it was made from the steam of a kettle lifting a lid up, and it keeps plopping. He always used to ask you to guess what the 'Telstar' effects were but would never tell you and piss about laughing. He was doing phasing on tapes before anyone else was ever doing it. He just slowed the track down: he'd stick his thumb against it; he'd play two, one against t'other, and hold one back, minutely behind each other, giving a swimming-type effect. I think with 'Telstar' he was thrilled to pieces that he'd proved to others that he was way ahead and still ahead, basically . . .

"They always used to knock him: everybody knocked him. Every A & R man knocked him. They always did because they couldn't produce what he produced. I remember vague conversations of the rows he had when he was an engineer because he used to hear A & R men cock-up things and he would suggest things and they'd just tell him virtually to shut up and produce the sound they wanted. And he wanted to say, 'That's wrong; that is not right. This is – it's screaming at you!' He used to walk out of sessions in sheer bloody frustration."

With riches flowing in from far and wide the inevitable question now was whether he planned staying on at Holloway Road, and he did: "After selling about two million and making £26,000 I can stop watching the pennies. I'd like a handsome ground floor studio so the artistes don't have to lug so much up and down stairs. But then again I like it here." Despite the traffic noise and cramped conditions, he had well and truly settled in. In fact the previous June after much deliberation he had signed an under-lease on the three floors, which would take him to June '67.

At the beginning of January the Tornados' next magnum opus, 'Globetrotter', was released. He told the press he felt "quite confident that it will be a No.1, but I could be wrong. Personally I think it's as good as 'Telstar' and it should appeal to the same people – that includes the adults." Actually he didn't think it was as good as 'Telstar' but he wasn't going to tell the world that. By any standard 'Telstar' was no easy act to follow but regrettably 'Globetrotter' came as a complete anti-climax. Taken on its own merit it was a superb record, this time presenting the clavioline in a spacey, laid-back style but after the aggressive intensity of its predecessor it sounded wishy-washy. Furthermore 'Telstar' was not the only record with which it invited comparison.

The opening bars bore a striking resemblance to a recent hit by Mark Wynter, called 'Venus In Blue Jeans'. When he took 'Globetrotter' along to Ivy Music, Roy Berry was also surprised: "I couldn't believe my ears. When he first played it to me I looked at him askance because I thought it was too much like 'Venus'. And I said to myself, 'What's he recording this for?' I suggested this to him with the same cautiousness I usually employed on these matters with him and he said, '*Nothing* like it!' So we proceeded. But I was afraid we'd be sued by United Artists – it was so similar." When Joe asked Tornados drummer Clem Cattini what he thought of it, Clem was less tactful: "I thought we should have stuck to the 'Telstar' formula; I didn't like the record or the sound. I said. 'Well, I don't really like it, Joe – it sounds like 'Venus In Blue Jeans'.' The next moment all hell was let loose. He stormed out, which he normally did, come storming back in with this stool which he threw at me. I ducked. It hit the top of a tape recorder and shattered the tape holders. He hadn't even used the machine yet; it had only been delivered the day before. It was an Ampex and cost over £1,000.[26] He was yelling away: 'How dare you criticize my work? Get out!' I said, 'All right, fair enough.' As I was walking down the stairs I heard Joe coming behind. I shot down the last flight. Suddenly I heard 'clatter, clatter, clatter' and I looked round and this tape recorder's following me. I got out of the door at the bottom just in time as it came crashing down against it."

Someone catching Joe in a calmer moment managed to get a more productive response on the subject: "I wrote this tune long before 'Blue Jeans' was released. I know it's only the opening that is similar, the rest of the melody is completely different, but still I'm a bit worried that people will think I've lifted the idea. I honestly didn't. It's just an unfortunate coincidence, that's all."

The 'Globetrotter' story in America was something of a non-event. Disc jockeys had been listening in closely to the Tornados' album and within a week of 'Globetrotter's' release they got an LP track 'Ridin' The Wind' out as well. It seems they were knocked out by the thunderclap effect at the beginning, and indeed the whole production was a more commercial one. Of course, any meagre hope 'Globetrotter' had of emulating its predecessor's success went straight down the pan taking 'Ridin' The Wind' with it. Had they both appeared in a blaze of publicity it might have been another tale; both singles in the Top Ten would have been some coup and won laurels galore for Decca's man in New York responsible for their dual release. Instead hardly any publicity was forthcoming. Each sabotaged the other, with 'Ridin' The Wind' fizzling out at No.72 and 'Globetrotter' lasting one week only at No.93. The man in New York lasted a further week – then he was out too.

Over here in Britain both records were faring much better: 'Ridin' The Wind' on a very good Tornados EP at No.2 in the EP chart and 'Globetrotter' at No.2 in the *Melody Maker* singles chart. Of 'Globetrotter' some people were saying its release onto the market had been too soon, taking the wind out of 'Telstar's' sales, but Joe was more than happy. 'Telstar' and 'Globetrotter together in the Top Ten were repeating the 'Johnny Remember Me' - 'Wild Wind' double-act of '61; whilst further down, there once again was a Mike Berry record freshly in to make it three in the Top Twenty, just like before. At the same time, coasting along at the other end was 'Can Can '62' by Peter Jay & the Jaywalkers, giving him four in the Top Thirty. He would have hogged the lot if he could. 'Telstar' at last dropped out of the Top Twenty at the end of January after a five months' run, handing over the baton to the 'Telstar' EP on which it was to grace the EP Top Twenty for a further five months.

Meanwhile taking over from 'Telstar' in the Top Ten was Mike Berry's bouncy 'Don't You Think It's Time', co-written by Joe and Geoff Goddard. At first glance their co-writing efforts hardly look worth mentioning, since during the four years they were together only four releases claimed their combined talents. Actually their total output was prodigious, and it seems that were

THE LEGENDARY JOE MEEK

it not for Joe tricking publishers, their names would have appeared together on many other titles. Instead he would give authorship to either one or the other, depending on whose concept the song was based on.

Harking back to his songwriting days with Joe, Geoff says that one of their methods was to work separately, assembling a quota each and later taking turns in presenting their own: "I would take the initiative on one and he would come in and join me and finish the song off. And the next one he'd take the initiative and the same thing would happen. We produced several like that in a batch." Between them they turned out dozens of songs, many of which were to end up unpublished. Their rapport was much enhanced by the fact that they wrote the same kind of lonely lyric, easy-to-remember melodies. Continuing, Geoff says he often worked better with him than on his own: "I could sit at home all day and not come up with anything, but it seemed when we sat together at the piano we could just knock 'em up one after the other. A lot of them would be rubbish but there'd be a potential hit or two amongst it."

Songwriting times together were happy times, and judging by some of the tape recordings of these sessions which have come to light in recent years the two men relished every second. Along with the usual melancholy songs there was everything from rock-'n'roll to evangelical to bawdy with broad accents. Sometimes they worked on through the night, each acting as a catalyst on the other, intoxicated by their love of making music in an atmosphere electric with prospective Top Ten hits. Joe had a highly attuned sense of detecting something magical in a phrase and would have Geoff ad-libbing hour upon hour on the piano. Now and then he would suddenly say, "Stop, that's great, let's develop that." And all the while a tape recorder was running so nothing was lost.

When both were satisfied with their collection of compositions the next stage was making demos. Geoff goes on: "I'd play the piano and Joe might bang on the door to put on some rhythm accompaniment to it. Then he'd play the tape to whoever he thought it would suit, then I'd come up for the session. A lot of the arrangement was already there on the demo. We'd usually do the backing tracks first and then the singer would go along on another day, then they'd finish off." It sounds pretty straightfor-ward the way Geoff tells it, and the demos he was involved in generally were. But the demos Joe put together alone of his own compositions were another matter entirely, presenting 304 with its most notorious melodramas: an equal source of mirth and heartache.

It seems that just about everyone who had anything to do with recording at his studio has memories of him flaring up during sessions. And it was his demos that were often the root cause. They were a major problem for him, offering the fearful possibility of treble trouble.

The first peril lay in the way he made them. Their diabolical presentation highlighted one of his biggest hang-ups: lack of communication. He was severely limited in what he could personally commit to tape, for whereas he only had to hum a phrase to Geoff to have it immediately played back with harmony, the best he himself could manage was an old backing track or just a bash on the door along with the melody line – and what a melody line! His completely tone deaf la-la-ing had to be heard to be believed, for as Saints guitarist Roy Phillips explains: "His demos were the greatest in the world. He says, 'Right, I've got a demo upstairs I've made.' *He's* made. And he's used no musical instruments. All he's done is get hold of a microphone and hum out of tune and pound on the floor and there is a tune in there somewhere and you have to find it." Andy Cavell, the singer Roy Phillips often backed, elaborates: "Most of the songs he'd written were based on him singing into the microphone and just banging away. It was comical to hear him – always very high-pitched. He used to play to you and say, 'This is the song I want you to sing,' and while he did it I wanted to laugh and he'd say, 'Well, you can't do better than that anyway, so what are you laughing for?' That's how the tunes were; there was no music. And then Dave [Adams] would come along and start playing it and the rhythms were all wrong and Dave would say, 'You can't do that, Joe, because it just doesn't go. It's either 2-2 or 4-4 or 12-bar this or that, but it can't be one minute this and the next minute that.' Because half the tunes would change the beat halfway through. That's how he used to write them: it was just a bare voice with him banging. He used to bang on the piano and stamp his feet. That floor – you could see it sinking, but he never took any notice of that."[27]

It was unfortunate he could not have someone like Geoff or Dave Adams there full time to lay down his compositions for him. But if friends were not around, people had to be paid and that kind of luxury was not acceptable to Major Banks. Therefore much of his work had to go through the vocal chord mutilation process first, saving money and wasting time.

The amazing thing was that despite having such a well tuned ear for a commercial sound that ear could not tell him how out of tune his own voice was. So of course, when the tune was finally harnessed, the delay had been due to the incompetence or bloody-mindedness of the musicians rather than any vocal deficiency on his part.

Sometimes he would treat the band to a backing track by picking out one of his old records with a similar tempo and singing along to it, regardless of the tune already on it. Then again musicians were sometimes faced with his singing along to the wrong beat entirely with a slow melody like 'Son, This Is She' on the back of a fast rhythm like 'Johnny Remember Me'. And if that didn't confuse them enough there were other occasions when he would perform alone, simply walking into the studio to whine or wail in front of the musicians: "What do you think of this one?" and with his hands in his belt and his feet stamping the floor, away he'd go, banging and shrieking, his face lighting up as if he were in a fantasy world. He thought it was all there – and sometimes by fluke it actually was; usually it wasn't. Then it all had to be interpreted, with Joe leaping in and out of the studio, getting ever more frustrated with himself and everyone else while he struggled to put across what he thought was a perfectly obvious tune. These kind of proceedings can be likened to those of a cook who spends half the morning searching for a saucepan. Meanwhile the musicians would be growing more and more restless, and at any point Joe could suddenly erupt and disappear downstairs.

His imitations of guitar sounds were hysterical! No wonder so many sessions broke up when musicians were expected to take such hilarious affairs seriously. But serious they were, and time and time again a happy atmosphere would be destroyed by the second crisis.

Playing or singing one of his homemade efforts would trigger off a predictable chain of events: someone would grin, Joe would sweetly enquire why, tension would mount to be broken by a fit of giggles from the group, whereupon he would throw an instant tantrum and anything else that came to hand. Although he realized he was no Caruso he saw nothing in his voice that could possibly be construed as funny. That kind of reaction could only stem from scorn, and reminded him of the catcalls he had faced as a child, dressing up in his plays.

Cliff Bennett & the Rebel Rousers made a lot of recordings

up there, and Cliff gives a vivid description of the situation: "He'd come in during a session and say, 'No, no, no, no, no. It goes like this: dee-dee-dee-dee-dee-dee.' We'd all break up because it was so funny to hear him singing his heart out in that terrible strangulated way of his. He'd stamp his foot: 'I'm not going to stand for it; if you're all going to piss about I'm going to go downstairs. I'm not going to put up with this silly laughing.' He'd stomp out slamming the door and off he'd go downstairs to make some tea or something while we sobered up a bit. Then he'd come back half an hour later: 'Now, are you all going to behave yourselves? Right, let's get on with it. It goes like this: dee-dee-dee-dee-dee-dee.' And no one in the band dared look at each other; we had to look at the wall or something. Otherwise if one of us caught someone else's eye they'd burst out laughing and we'd all explode. Then it would just go on and on and on like laughing gas, until your sides ached and you just wanted to stagger out of the studio before you fell apart. And there was Joe standing there looking so angry and it was like being back at school: he was the schoolteacher and we were the naughty pupils. And the angrier he became, the more we tried to hold it back and the funnier it was. We'd just laugh and laugh until it became quite impossible to work and sometimes he'd start laughing too – he couldn't help it. Twenty minutes later we'd forgotten what we were laughing about – we were absolutely past it. When we'd all cooled off he'd say, 'You might as well go home now. You're a real bunch of bastards. You know what I'm trying to do and you send it all up. I'll tell you this: it's just as well you're good musicians. When you boys behave yourselves you're great to work with.' Then, come the next session, we'd all be there in the studio ready to get on with the recording and he'd come in and say, 'I hope we're not going to have any stupid antics like last time.' Of course, at once we could feel it coming back again. I'd say, 'Oh Joe, why did you have to mention that? We'd forgotten about it.' He'd say, 'Well I haven't.' "

In future instead of giving them his infamous impromptu performances, he took some time properly preparing demo tapes for them to copy.

Thirdly there was always the danger that the band would not like his composition anyway, however well it was presented. This happened when he offered the unruly Rebel Rousers a song of his, ironically titled 'Poor Joe'. The timid melody and lyrics were at odds with the band's own rock'n'roll style and, as Cliff Bennett explains, Joe was very unhappy with their reaction to it: "We were doing the session and we were just f—— about; we didn't like the song, and he knew. He came in and really got upset. I actually saw him in tears: 'If you don't want to do the song, pack your stuff and get out.' He could get hurt very quickly if somebody criticized his work. But even so, every time we went back for sessions he'd say, 'I still think you should do it.' He was so persistent, in the end we gave in and recorded it, but never played it at gigs. We would also clash if we didn't like his approach. He would say, 'You're doing it this way because it's my time and money.' We'd say, 'Fair enough.' "

11
Operation Heinz!

" **I** think he's got tremendous potential, very individual," Joe told the press. "By this time next year, or even before, he could be one of the biggest names in the pop world." Although he had decided Heinz was to sing "the quieter type of ballad", he stressed that the young man was full of enthusiasm and so often dreaming up ideas that "he seems to have some new ones every time he comes round to see me."

Heinz's debut disc was to feature in the new pop film. Called 'Dreams Do Come True' its title was a pinch from a telegram Joe had received when 'Telstar' reached No.1 in America. He had dreamt it would get to the top over there and when he was sent that line he put it aside as a useful title. The lyrics were suffering from writer's cramp but that did not matter, if the overall sound was right.

> *I've been told and I'm sure it's true*
> *That when two lose their hearts, dreams do come true.*
> *I believe that out of the blue,*
> *Someone will fall for me and make my dreams come true.*
> *I drift on a big, white cloud, over the house-tops high above,*
> *Dreaming there must be someone, a certain someone for me to love.*

Heinz was getting the full treatment. Throughout January when he was not on tour with the Tornados, Joe spent hours and days on him polishing him up like a brass button, practising the song, arranging every move and inflexion to the nth degree. With eight years of firsthand experience to call upon he knew what he wanted, darting about like a TV director eyeing him through camera-shaped hands. He loved it all and saw himself in the young man but the perfectionist in him made him a hard taskmaster who took a lot of satisfying. With time fast running out he was far from happy with Heinz's voice, so when he put the recording together he did an 'Ian Gregory' on him by blending the voice of another singer into it. That voice would feature strongest on the record, with Heinz's drooping delivery safely out of harm's way underneath.

During February their scenes in the film were shot in the old Metropolitan Music Hall where Jimmy Miller & the Barbecues had had their shirts ripped, ironically the last use to which the hall was put before being bulldozed. He went along as well to make sure his stage directions were followed to the letter. Once that was safely in the bag Larry Parnes whisked them off for another of his bumper package tours, this time billed second to Joe Brown above Susan Maughan, Jess Conrad, Eden Kane, Rolf Harris, Shane Fenton and Peter Jay & the Jaywalkers.

That month the Tornados' American LP peaked at a respectable No.22 and there were a couple more awards for 'Telstar'. One went to the Tornados from *Cashbox* who had decided to start presenting a new trophy of their own to anyone topping their American chart. The other was a special Gold Disc which was to be presented to Joe himself, who the papers stated was the first A & R man ever to get one. The following month he received it from the Tornados on *Thank Your Lucky Stars* and promptly burst into tears.

February also brought an announcement that 'Telstar' had the highest certified British sales of 1962 at 850,000, and as composer he was to be presented with Britain's top music honour, the coveted Ivor Novello Award. (The worldwide figure had passed $2^3/4$ million outstripping 'Stranger On The Shore's' $2^1/2$ million plus to become Britain's biggest seller ever!)

At this time 'Telstar' was still figuring well in Top Tens around the world. It had topped the charts in many countries, and dozens of cover versions were floating around too, apparently with the most absorbing variations being Latin-American, Hawaiian and Chinese.

Midway through March came the release of the Tornados' next disc, 'Robot'. After 'Telstar', 'Robot' was arguably the most inventive and commercial track they were to put out. Joe had given it a very strong runaway melody line set to a heavy beat with little this time in the way of space connotations, unless you were looking for them. It was interesting to note that a year had passed since the release of their first disc, the instantly forgettable 'Love And Fury'. At that time it had looked like the Tornados were set to be stuck in the same rotten tune rut as his other groups. Instead they were now basking in the sunshine with a harvest of good tunes, and being given a boost by Public Relations man and gossip columnist Keith Goodwin, who Joe was hiring at £40 per month to say all the right things in all the right places.

Soon after 'Robot's' release Joe flew over to Paris with the Tornados. While the group were being filmed by the Scopitone juke box company, miming to 'Robot' as they walked out of some woods wearing space helmets, he was visiting a French promoter in the hope of booking Heinz some dates in France. The band also had time to mime footage for 'Telstar'. In the evening he rushed back to join Heinz in a studio where the juke box company were filming him miming 'Dreams Do Come True'. For the next four hours until 3 in the morning he was busy telling everyone how it all should be done. As always he knew what he wanted and was ready to fly Heinz home if he did not get it. And so followed the farcical situation where Joe, as director, was directing the director who was directing Heinz, who was being redirected by Joe. Eventually, against all odds it was actually finished, and all three filmstrips were juke boxed.

Three weeks after the Tornados' day-trip to Paris they were back again for their first foreign venue: a fortnight at the acclaimed Paris Olympia. The show was a sellout. The only trouble was that the Paris Olympia ought never to have been their first foreign venue but their second and could be little compensation for the cancellation of their February dates in the States. In fact they should have been able to go to America, and with any other management they would have done.

In a nutshell the Larry Parnes/Joe Meek partnership was a dead duck. About the only thing they could agree on was the time. They were forever rowing about the group's affairs: where they should play, what they should wear, how they should move onstage.

As soon as the contract had been signed it became obvious that to Parnes the Tornados were of no importance whatever compared with his golden boy, Billy Fury. That "very good" US offer had not been quite good enough, because Parnes had merely seen it as a chance to get Fury in on the act too, and as the Americans had never heard of Billy Fury they didn't want him. So the Parnes ultimatum was: "No Fury, no Tornados". Thus everyone failed to capitalize on the disc's enormous sales in what was and still is the world's largest pop record market. While 'Telstar' was chalking up 2 million in that country alone, instead of the Tornados riding on the back of it to a small fortune they were stuck over here tied to a succession of weekly venues and one-night-stands; besides which they were still bumming around doing session work backing Joe's artistes in the studio. And all the glamour in being Britain's first group to top the American listings ran silently to waste.

THE LEGENDARY JOE MEEK

Naturally the lads were very disappointed with the American fiasco, and none more so than Joe who had dearly hoped they would perform on TV over there and perhaps even give him the thrill of a lifetime with a 'live' transmission of 'Telstar' via Telstar. Fortunately he never allowed himself long for disappointments. A whole pot of goodies was on the boil, including a blue-eyed boy of his own.

The latest good news was that he had managed to get Heinz a TV spot on *Thank Your Lucky Stars*. A promoter had also placed him on the forthcoming Jerry Lee Lewis-Gene Vincent package tour, and the Outlaws had grudgingly agreed to back him. Thanks to a multi-millionaire heating company manager they let themselves be bribed with an open cheque book for new instruments. There was also a new teenage film in the offing called *Live It Up*, starring David Hemmings, and Heinz was to play a part as a member of a pop group who go through the usual hassles before getting their big break. In fact Heinz was set for a busy week's filming and touring because the two were due to run concurrently.

As zero hour drew closer so the excitement grew. With the other film *Farewell Performance* about to be screened, as well as his solo debut on disc, TV and stage all timed to coincide in the first week of May, some showbiz folk, claimed the music press, reckoned Heinz was on the brink of the big time and were rating him as "the hottest property to erupt onto Britain's pop scene since Cliff in 1958". Four fan clubs had sprouted up, with one in Wolverhampton mustering 1,000 members already; the London branch was being manned by a certain Dave Adams of 304 Holloway Road, N7; telephone NORth 4074. For Joe and the one who fans called 'The White Tornado' the countdown began.

With the 'Telstar' thousands now pouring in, no expense was to be spared in launching the blond bombshell to the highest height in the pop galaxy. The beginning of May saw the release of 'Dreams'. Adverts were splashed all over the music papers whilst colour photos and a Heinz biography were sent out to teenage magazines, disc jockeys, record reviewers and Uncle Tom Cobley and all.

Joe held his breath for the screening of Heinz's first TV spot on *Thank Your Lucky Stars*. Though a little wooden his performance was not too bad, thanks to the fact that on pop programmes singers always mimed to their songs. Now with that show in the bag he felt that Heinz had more than enough going for him, with his girl-grabbing looks, flashy pop star outfits, well rehearsed act, widespread publicity plus all the fan mail and Tornados success to give him added confidence. Two extra venues, which had been booked in small halls elsewhere to warm him up, did not come off as well as hoped, though that was hardly surprising since barely a dozen people bothered to turn up. Joe needed no reassuring now; his faith in Heinz had been supported thousands of times over by sackloads of letters, and the first full house was bound to prove him and them right.

But it didn't. The week of one-night-stands started a disaster and ended up a nightmare! Even with the Outlaws to back him, sticking Heinz on a bill with two giants of rock'n'roll made as much sense as sandwiching Screaming Lord Sutch between the Wombles and Donny Osmond. The main trouble was that he was conceived as an attraction for the girls, and audiences for Jerry Lee Lewis and Gene Vincent were predominantly male. After all that publicity hailing him as a great new rock star he had quite a tag to live up to. Others on the bill fared much better – the Saints, Andy Cavell, Mickie Most – though they had less to prove. Making his entrance dolled up in the fancy black suit with white piping that Joe had chosen for him in front of a sea of leather jackets and looking, as one reporter described him, like "a search-light on a foggy night", he stood as much chance as a pig in a pork pie factory. And when they heard his voice, so cramped by nerves that it sounded like a blow-lamp, even that chance went. Nor did his embarrassed bassist, Chas Hodges, help by making teasing comments onstage about his hair and the fact Heinz's guitar was only a prop.

Heinz says that sometimes the audience were chanting "OFF" before he even got onto the stage and from there on things got worse: "I was playing Birmingham and getting blokes running down the aisle wanting to jump onstage to thump my head in, throwing cans of beans and covering the group in beans. On that same tour we played Colston Hall, Bristol and my mother came down from Southampton. She was sat upstairs. She came back-stage in tears. She could hear the blokes behind her: 'We're gonna 'ave 'im now, the bastard, we're gonna 'ave 'im. Wait round the back.' My mother's sitting there listening to it! Imagine how she felt with Teds running up, grabbing the microphone stand off the stage, trying to pull it off me and hit me with it. And Gene Vincent came up to me before that tour ended and said, 'You've got some bloody guts, I would have walked off after one

number.' He used to stand in the wings every night watching."
And Joe was watching too.

He went to the show at Birmingham and when he saw this
disgusting reception he burst into tears, putting half the blame on
the Outlaws' attitude. But though he was deeply hurt he was
angry too and as determined as ever. At another venue he attended
at Croydon's Fairfield Halls the first few front rows stood up and
turned their backs on Heinz throughout his act. Joe was there
waiting in the wings when he left the stage to push him back on
for an encore.

After the week of one-nighters was blessedly over, he was
afraid it had done Heinz's career a lot of harm. In no way though
did he see himself responsible; for that fiasco he quite justifiably
blamed the promoter, saying he should have known who was suitable for the bill. But by rights Heinz should not have been playing
anywhere at all at that time, let alone on the Jerry Lee Lewis tour.
Clocking in for filming each day at Pinewood Studios from 6.30
a.m. to 5.30 p.m. was quite enough for a day's work, without the
pressures of performing onstage around the country every
evening – a routine which had forced the nurse at Pinewood to
put him on pills to keep him awake. And there was only one person
to blame for this clash of commitments because as Heinz's
personal manager Joe knew all the schedules well in advance. But
he was in a hurry to make him a star, and as he himself was ready
to move Heaven and earth he expected Heinz to be the same.

🎼🎼🎼🎼🎼🎼🎼🎼🎼🎼🎼🎼🎼

Although most of his attention was now centred on Heinz, there
were still plenty of other irons in the fire to keep him busy. On the
Tornados front things had not been faring well either. Their
latest disc, 'Robot', had made the Top Twenty but No.17 was
nothing to dance a jig over. Heinz's departure after their
rendezvous in Paris had brought mixed blessings. On the plus
side it gave the band a chance to pull themselves together and
start afresh. A lot of jealousy and frustration had been brewing as
they saw themselves playing second fiddle to a bass player they
didn't even rate. As their drummer, Clem Cattini, puts it, "He
didn't know a crotchet from a hatchet." But it had been Heinz
getting most of the attention while they were left sitting on the

sidelines getting less and less of it.

Little things had niggled them like arriving at photo sessions to find that they were all to be dressed alike except Heinz, who was to wear something special. Of course Heinz as the group's focal point had made good business sense but that decision had not been reached till after their first record. Then as the weeks had passed, the more interested in him Joe became, the more agitated *they* became. First they had seen it as favouritism, then later concluded they had become a vehicle for Heinz's career; and Joe, never the most tactful of people and never seeing any reason why he should explain his actions to anyone, had not improved the situation. He knew of the antagonism towards Heinz and wrongly sensed it as being indirectly aimed at himself; he thought it was due entirely to their opinion of Heinz's singing and playing, so because he was the one who had discovered him, they must be against him as well. The Tornados for their part had done their best not to make their feelings felt in case he blew up and disowned them. Now hopefully they could start again.

On the negative side, when Heinz left the band he took what little glamour they possessed with him. From here on it was going to be a hard haul. And there was something else far more threatening that the Tornados as well as Heinz and all of Joe's other artistes were now having to contend with: Merseybeat.

Merseybeat had actually been around since '60 but confined to Liverpool and Hamburg, so hardly anyone else had heard of it. Many of the bands playing it had sprung up as skifflers in the wake of Lonnie Donegan, and had then absorbed other musical styles. With the benefit of Liverpool's position as a West Coast seaport they were able to assimilate the latest country'n'western, rhythm'n'blues and rock'n'roll sounds brought in by seamen from America, and by '61 it was all the rage, with about 300 groups floating around the Liverpool area. Elsewhere no one was interested, except in Hamburg where German audiences lapped it up, responding especially well when it was given a hearty beat. All these influences had merged to create a new earthy force in music which Liverpudlians and Hamburgers could proudly call their own.

By far the most popular exponents were the Beatles who regularly topped the Merseybeat polls. But even though they were being idolized in their own city, when their manager Brian Epstein had brought them down to London at the beginning of January '62 he had had difficulty getting them a recording

179

contract. Decca's Dick Rowe and Mike Smith became famous as the first men to turn them down, and the oft-quoted remark Epstein received at the time – "Guitar groups are on the way out, Mr. Epstein" – draws a smile nowadays. But Decca were not the only ones to blunder, and had it not been for Epstein's resilience his group would have taken rather longer to crack the market. Decca, Pye, Philips, Columbia and HMV all turned down the chance of signing themselves a goldmine. And so did Joe.

According to Joe, Epstein wined and dined him all over London but they could not agree on terms. Epstein, he said, wanted too large a percentage for doing too little work. This seems unlikely since by this time Epstein was growing desperate. Joe meanwhile was no more impressed with their audition tape than anyone else, seeing the Beatles as just another noisy group covering other people's songs. It seems far more likely that Joe was the one asking for the extra high percentage and that desperate though Epstein was, he was not *that* desperate!

What fruit a Meek/Beatles union might have borne is fascinating to ponder. At this point in his career Joe would have made few concessions to the Merseybeat sound. Epstein was pretty anxious, so it would have been Joe calling the shots, and no way would he have avoided making his own presence felt on their discs. Had he allowed them to record their own songs, no doubt 'Love Me Do' and the other hits would have had a fair touch of echo and compression added plus the slightly muffled quality that results from overdubbing. Overall, their natural rawness would have been replaced by a more 'produced' sound. If everyone concerned had managed to stay the course the Beatles/Meek sound would have been imitated throughout the land, whilst that of Merseybeat would probably have been shorter-lived. Considering producer George Martin's huge influence on the Beatles' product it is highly likely that Joe's contribution would have been just as great if not greater. However, given the contrasting personalities of Joe and John Lennon it is doubtful their association would have taken in more than the first two or three records, and the Epstein camp saved themselves a lot of bother when they found George Martin.

Be that as it may, none of this new music was doing his efforts with the Tornados any good at all. Much to his annoyance the Liverpool invasion was attracting immense teenage attention, with record companies snapping up beat groups like there was no tomorrow. It seemed that no sooner had the Tornados' futuristic prototype sound been unveiled than it was obsolete, as shown by the relatively poor placing of their latest disc, 'Robot'. Of course, that was not the way *he* saw it. That kind of opinion he would have described as the burblings of an imbecile, for to his mind the sound of the Tornados would still be sweeping all before it long after Merseybeat was dead and buried; Merseybeat was nothing but another craze like skiffle, trad jazz and the Twist that would just as quickly burn itself out. Furthermore he felt that its simplistic see-through style was regressive, harking back to the rock'n'roll era and doing nothing whatever to advance electronic techniques; he called it "matchbox music". Nevertheless he could not ignore the fact that, however temporarily, it was biting into his own record sales and, given for example the obvious commerciality of 'Robot', it was hard to imagine missing the Top Ten had there been no Liverpool opposition. After all, the band were still doing a roaring trade on the Continent and Australia, pulling in No.1's in countries yet to hear of Merseybeat.

Besides grappling with Merseybeat and the other million music matters, he was also digging deeper into business. Top of the agenda was the forming of no less than four new companies! The first was simply a joint publishing company with Southern Music. Called Bluebell Music it gave him a bigger share in the profits of songs he placed with them.

The next one, Joe Meek Associates, was much grander. Before it went into action in March he told the *Gloucester Journal* he was going into the personal management field soon: "I have the backing of a multi-millionaire and he is prepared to sink quite a lot of cash into the venture." The multi-millionaire was not the well-feathered Major Banks but the managing director of a noted oil and gas heating company called Valor, whose name was Michael Montague. Joe had been friendly with him for a while and through his visits to Holloway Road, Montague had started paying close attention to Joe's Greek singer, Andy Cavell. So far Cavell's recording career consisted of two flop singles, and with Joe fast losing interest in him his future had offered all the blossoming promise of an old wreath. But Montague was entranced and felt that with enough money behind him, Cavell's tide was sure to turn. Joe was also getting him to inject funds into Heinz's career, and if dreams came true the company would soon be budding out further putting it on a par with RGM Sound.

Following right behind came Heinz Burt Ltd. This one was set up to cope exclusively with Heinz and his band and would depend upon their concert, film, TV and radio appearances for its existence. Joe was going to take a leaf out of Larry Parnes's book by putting Heinz and his men on a salary; this, working out at £27.10s.0d. for Heinz along with expenses, would be deducted from the company's income. Partnering him this time and dealing with all the paperwork was an accountant he had found in the Strand, by the name of Tom Shanks. White haired, elderly looking and walking with a stick, he was the other man Joe hoped would eventually take over with Montague all Banks's work. With his clear, deep voice and totally soothing and fatherly manner heightened by an appearance that reminded one of Pinocchio's father, he at once inspired trust. Qualities such as friendliness, a sense of humour and the ability to talk at length on the music business, none of which Joe had ever found in Major Banks, were quick to win him over. Mr. Shanks was already a director of some showbiz companies whose affairs he was also accounting, including that of Petula Clark Ltd., so he was well experienced.

The last company was called Joe Meek Enterprises. Again with Shanks partnering, it would be taking his songwriting royalties and other bits and pieces.

The first week of May was to deal him mixed fortunes. On May 1 came a bolt out of the blue. The fear that every prolific songwriter has that a tune of his might accidentally resemble someone else's and get him sued for breach of copyright suddenly became an awful reality for Joe. Ivy Music's Roy Berry had been worried when 'Globetrotter' was brought in to him: the one tune of Joe's stock that smacked of plagiarism. To be sued by the writers of 'Venus In Blue Jeans' would have been vexing but no staggering surprise. The staggering surprise was that it was not over 'Globetrotter' that he was being sued – but 'Telstar'!

The trouble stemmed from an obscure piece of French film music called 'Le Marche d'Austerlitz' written in 1960 by composer Jean Ledrut. The film, *The Battle Of Austerlitz*, starred Pierre Mondy and described Napoleon's European campaigns. According to the Frenchman it was on his march that 'Telstar's' tune was based. Joe was horrified that anyone could possibly think him capable of doing such a thing, declaring that he had quite enough music of his own in his head without stealing someone else's. He had never heard of 'Le Marche d'Austerlitz' and had hardly had much opportunity since the film was yet to be

1. Joe's birthplace today (pre-plaque), Market Hall in foreground.
2. Joe on right, aged 4, with parents and Arthur.
3. Joe left, Arthur right, in 'Daffodils and Pixies'.
4. Facsimile of part of letter to his mother.
5. Radar days.

6. Lional, Biddy, Joe.
7. Joe, centre, taping a Road Show.
8. Adrian Kerridge and Denis Preston at Lansdowne.
9. Major Banks.

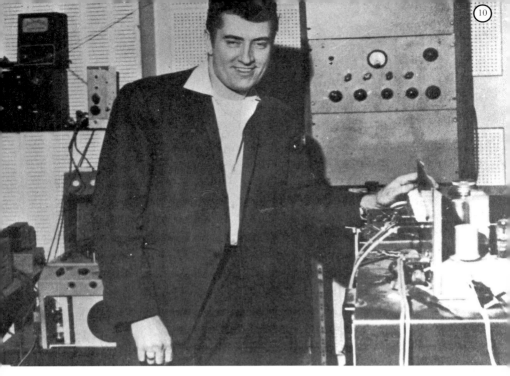

Control room on a tidy day.
A sizzling performance at West Kensington Station by Jimmy Miller & the Barbecues.
Staged photo of Chris Williams & his Monsters at 304.

Psychic News
1527   London, September 9, 1961   Price 6d.

DOES DEAD ROCK STAR GUIDE SONGWRI

'JOHNNY REMEMB ME' SENSATION

No. 1 disc in hit parade written by Spiritualist

AN AMAZING PSYCHIC STORY LIES BEHIND THE CURRENT SMASH-HIT RECORD "JOHNNY REMEMBER ME", SUNG BY JOHN LEYTON, WHICH IS TOPPING THE HIT PARADE TODAY.

Writer of words and music is 23-year-old Spiritualist Geoffrey Goddard, of 5 Ormsby Street, Reading, Berks.

"I am sure I receive my inspiration from the Spirit world," he told me last week. When I wrote 'Johnny Remember Me' it was early morning- and I had just opened my eyes. I always keep a tape recorder by my bed, and I sang that song into it without waking on it at all."

The song itself has a strong psychic theme, telling the story of a young man whose true love dies and returns to him. Here is the song

When the mists are rising
And the sun is falling
And the wind is blowing cold
across the moor,
I hear the voice of my darling
The girl I loved who died a
year ago.

"Johnny remember me . . ."

Well, it's hard to believe, I know. But I hear her singing and I feel the sighing of the wind blowing in the treetops.

Was above me?

"Johnny remember me . . ."

Yes, I'll always remember. Till the day I die . . .

by
MOLLY BLAKE

that Mr. Goddard has followed much the same success pattern as Buddy Holly.

"I did the rounds of Denmark Street publishers because I received a strong impression that I should go there." Mr. Goddard

GEOFFREY GODDARD: The tumbler spelt out Buddy's name and mine, and then I got the message which said: "Johnny would be No. 1. See you in the charts."

Goddard has just been presented with a silver disc.

Mr. Goddard has been a Spiritualist for four years, and was first intrigued by the subject when he read Hannen Swaffer's book "My Greater Story" now being serialised in *Psychic News.*

"I intend to go on with my song-writing," he said, "although it seems I must wait for inspiration from the spirit world. I find I can sit at the piano for hours

...without being able to write a note of music- and yet after a dreamless sleep I can produce a best-seller in practically the time it takes to sing it."

PSYCHIC NEWS thanks Meridian Music Publishing Co. Ltd. 2, Denmark Street, London. W.C.2, for permission to ...k words of "Johnny R... M..."

WELL, I ASK YOU!

Psychic Story Behind Eden Kane's Top Disc

JOHNNY REMEMBER ME

HE READS PSYCHIC NEWS

SO E...

13. Held up by Outlaws.
14. Psychic news.
15. John Leyton going places.

16. Mike Berry & the Outlaws, with Chas in by a nose.
17. Rod Stewart's first public performance 1961, with the Moontrekkers: Jimmy Raither on left.
18. Jack the Ripper (or is it Lord Sutch?).

19. A full house paying tribute to Buddy Holly.
20. Geoff Goddard, John Beecher, Mike Berry.

21. The Tornados, L to R: Heinz Burt, Roger LaVern, George Bellamy, Clem Cattini, Alan Caddy.
22. A favourite picture of his.
23. Tommy Scott & the Senators.
24. Glenda Collins.

25. With four Tornad
26. Joy & Dave with r
    aboard the Sunbea
    Rapier promoting
    'Chahawki'; almos
    opposite 304.
27. Billy Fury, Heinz,
    George Bellamy
    rehearsing at 304,
    early '62.
28. John Ginnett.
29. Patrick Pink.

30. The Honeycombs, Dennis D'Ell on left.

31. NME: October 3 1962 and August 26 1964.

32. With secretary Terry O'Neil

33. 'The lady with the crying eyes'.
34. Mrs Violet Shenton.
35. 'Suitcase Murder'.
36. February 3 1967.

Evening Standard

FRIDAY, FEBRUARY 3, 1967

Joe Meek in double tragedy at recording studio

TOP OF THE POPS COMPOSER AND A WIFE SHOT DEAD

'I stand

Joe Meek, 36-year-old composer of the Top Ten hit Telstar and the Kennedy March, and promoter of three pop groups, was found shot dead today at the Holloway, London, recording studio he always called The

Bathroom.
Beside him on the

Daily Mirror

Tuesday, January 17, 1967   No. 19,615

Yard men in hunt for boy's killer

CUT-UP BODY FOUND DUMPED IN 2 SUITCASES

BY TOM TULLETT AND KEVIN HUNT

THE naked torso of a youth was found in a battered suitcase lying behind a hedge in a field at Tattingstone, Suffolk, a village near Ipswich yesterday. Nearby was another suitcase containing the limbs.

A farmworker found the suitcases lying behind a hedge at Tattingstone, Suffolk, a village near Ipswich yesterday. Nearby was another suitcase containing the limbs.

The youth is believed to have been aged about 12 and a preliminary examination by the pathologist Dr. ... suggested that the body was dismembered recently.

As a boy is missing locally, police believe he was murdered in another part of the country, packed into the suitcases, dumped in the suitcases from a car.
The Scotland Yard

JOE MEEK
RECORD PRODUCER
"THE TELSTAR MAN"
1929 — 1967
PIONEER OF SOUND
RECORDING TECHNOLOGY
LIVED, WORKED AND
DIED HERE

38

39

SCREAMING LORD SUTCH
STORY

Together again after 28 years.
Lord Sutch gets his seat at last. 1991,
the 304 bathroom.
"Do you remember me?" 1992 Newent comeback.
Tribute Concert', 1991.

THE JOE MEEK APPRECIATION SOCIETY PRESENTS
THE LEGENDARY JOE MEEK
SIXTIES CONCERT

40

ONE NIGHT ONLY

SCREAMING LORD SUTCH
"Jack The Ripper"

CLEM CATTINI'S
TORNADOS

The HONEYCOMBS
"Have I The Right"

The MOONTREKKERS
"Night Of The Vampire"

HEINZ
"Just Like Eddie"

CLIFF BENNETT
& THE REBEL ROUSERS
"Gotta Get You Into My Life"

DANNY RIVERS
"Can't You Hear My Heart"

MIKE BERRY
"Tribute To Buddy Holly"

The Original Line-Up Together for the first time since 1963
The TORNADOS
"TELSTAR"

COMPERE - STUART COLMAN from CAPITAL GOLD

Friday 7th June at 7.45pm
£9.50 & £8.50

Lewisham Theatre
081 690 0002
Lewisham Leisure

41. Newent plaque unveiling by brother Eric; Lional in background.
42. Denmark Street demo, '97. Foreground, L to R: Gary Leport (of the Moontrekkers), Mike Berry, Charles Blackwell, Clem Cattini.
43. 304 plaque unveiling.
44. Geoff Goddard taking a break, 1991.

shown in this country – and he had never been to France before 1963 – while the music itself had only had one performance in the UK anyway, and that was in Northern Ireland.

When comparing the two pieces it is clear that 'Telstar' is unquestionably the better music by far, and though there is a similarity between the opening notes of each composition, it is hard when listening to them to see how anyone who wrote 'Telstar' could copy such an undistinguished piece of music as 'Austerlitz'.

At once all further 'Telstar' royalties were frozen. So far he had banked a nice fat £29,000 as RGM Sound's 5 percent of disc sales but nothing had yet come through in the way of composer's royalties; that would all have to wait. Nor could he expect much joy from Ivy Music. Like all music publishing contracts, the one he had signed with them indemnified the publisher of all responsibility in case of copyright infringement. So although Joe and Ivy had a common enemy their grounds for contesting the case were different; Ivy had their own lawyers and recommended another firm to Joe. Then it was a matter of sitting back and waiting for the Frenchman to make his next move.

Although the action-packed first week of May belonged to Heinz as far as effort was concerned, it was to Joe that all the glory went. Receiving the Ivor Novello Award on television at the BBC on May 4 had to be the proudest moment of his life. The bronze statuette was the latest and best of the bumper crop of credits 'Telstar' had dropped into his lap, and was worth its weight in gold. It was the supreme accolade from the British music industry to a composer. Nothing could have hammered home better his unparalleled success as an independent. To all the scoffers who had sniggered at the mention of his do-it-your-self, dust-laden studio; to all the smart-arses who had dismissed his music as over-produced trash; to all those carping critics who had derided his unsophisticated singlemindedness: here was his reply. And to make the occasion even more deliciously satisfying, when the big moment arrived and he walked up to collect his trophy, there waiting to present it to him was none other than David Jacobs! Perhaps those insults had been worth it after all.

♪♪♪♪♪♪♪♪♪♪♪♪♪♪

If there were three words to sum up his current lifestyle, they were either 'Music, music, music' or 'Pressure, pressure, pressure'. By anyone else's standards the recording of Heinz and the Tornados plus the managing of their careers was more or less a full time job in itself. But there were at least another twenty acts on his books to be catered for, as well as prospective pop stars knocking at the front door day and night. He had now become Britain's best known producer. His name was the only one consistently mentioned in the music press and to get an audition at Holloway Road was considered as great a feat as getting one at EMI or Decca. It meant a lot to groups that he was the one rated the best at capturing the American sound with good, thick, thudding bass instead of the usual thin clickety-click. Over the past few months communications with 304 had increased dramatically and it sometimes seemed like the whole of the music industry was descending on the man they were saying had the Midas touch: publishers, songwriters, singers, groups, managers, session men, record company men, reporters, booking agents, sponsors for musical equipment and so on. Of course, most of what he touched did not turn to gold and this was even more apparent with record companies scrambling for just about any scraps he threw their way. Because of this and the fact he could no longer spare much time on each recording, there was a sharp rise in mediocre material.

And there was a sharp rise in broken sessions. Success always brings problems and he was finding it increasingly difficult coping with his. During these months particularly he was really taking on too much and letting his mushrooming responsibilities get the better of him. There had been times in the past when he had worked excessively hard, notably in the build-up to his first recording with Jimmy Miller & the Barbecues and the inaugural weeks of Lansdowne and Triumph. If his workrate then could be described as that of a Trojan, it now had to be that of a galley slave. Always he had been a great one for moods and depressions but Geoff Goddard says they were now getting frequent: "In 1963 I got the impression that Joe seemed to be coming under an increasing strain and more temperamental. If anybody said anything critical about for example the sound that he would try to create on his records he would suddenly blow up and become very aggressive and then calm down again. He wasn't like that when I first met him; he was rather erratic, but not like that. At first he was likeable, very likeable, but then he changed about

OPERATION HEINZ!

1962. It seemed to be driving him into the ground: too bold with the music business. Joe used to get very on edge, very tense and was liable to start shouting but then he'd calm down again. I can remember once I arrived and I was a bit late, and when I got upstairs he didn't say anything. Then I sat down in the studio with all the musicians round me. Joe came in and said, 'When you came into the flat you slammed the door. Don't slam the door again.' He went marching out, I lost my temper and started swearing and we could all hear Joe shouting in the next room. He shouted, 'Everything – it's over, finished', and ran off down the stairs. And then someone said, 'Sit down and calm down and he'll come back again', which he did."

Geoff's opinion that he was getting bolder with the business was well-founded. His hard-line attitude was brought on partly by his growing mistrust of everyone, all of whom he was certain were out to fleece him, and partly by his feeling that he now had more weight to throw around with which to keep the predators in their place. His arrogant treatment of music people in general, be they bosses or backroom boys, which was characterized by his buccaneering catchphrase: "They need me, I don't need them", was not a wise one, but one he knew he could get away with as long as the hits kept coming. Heinz recalls witnessing, for example, one of his many crusty phone conversations: "I was in the office at the time when he had one hell of an argument with Sir Edward Lewis, the managing director of Decca. And Joe was speaking to him because Lewis had turned down one of his recordings and he told him to 'f—— off. I'll take my tapes some-where else', slammed the phone down, picked the typewriter up – straight against the wall. I remember that one because the typewriter hit that wall and there was a big hole in it."

Earlier in the year when Geoff gave him a gold watch to commemorate their past twenty super-successful months together, his reaction to it was not one Geoff expected. He took it, looked at it and instead of giving the customary display of tears, hurled it on the table screaming that he didn't want it because his name had not been engraved on it. So, that little gift turned out rather a waste of time.

One of his weaknesses was in believing good write-ups. Glowing reports of his achievements were swelling his head, making him bolshier than ever. True, he had always held his own abilities in the highest esteem but never before had his opinions been shared by so many.

185

Another example from his many broken sessions involved the Outlaws, and is graphically illustrated by their bass player, Chas Hodges: "You never knew how to handle Joe; you was always a bit on edge. You could never prophecy how he was going to react to anything. In this one instance he'd just bought this new mike. He was going, 'That's great, isn't it?' He was really knocked out with it. He said, 'I think I'll use it for Ken' – Ken Lundgren, the guitar player. And for some reason Ken had a way of doing the wrong thing, as far as Joe went, and Joe would fly off at him. Joe put a box down, rested the mike stand on the box. He goes out and Ken, who was a bit clumsy, turns round, knocks the mike down: crash! Oh, what have we done now? We all sort of sat there. Ken picked it up. Joe's bound to know because he's heard the crash. And he come walking in and we all looked. And he had a slight smile on his face, so we all relaxed and smiled. And suddenly he screamed, 'F— off out of it!' And he picked up these tape spools to throw at us and we run down the stairs. We'd just have to get out of it – you'd like flee for your life. We'd shoot off for a couple of hours and then ring him up or you'd just come back in and you'd say nothing, and you'd just gauge the situation by how he looked at you when he come in. When he used to get a mild attack of temper one of his favourite tricks was he would just run downstairs and put on a record at full blast: the whole building would shake. He was great, nice, quiet-spoken or when he lost his temper he had a tone of voice: it would go right through your head. He could really shout when he wanted to."

He could also be quite abusive when he felt like it, as Don Charles noticed: "He used to speak to them like shit, some of them. There were always kids in the bloody passageway waiting – you never knew what they were waiting for. Any hour of any day they were stood there, just in a dingy old passage outside his lounge; hundreds of the bastards, stood all over just waiting – absolutely incredible. And when he rowed, everybody went, everything went up in the air, everybody got out. And he used to just clear off and he'd slam the doors until they almost fell off their hinges."

Two newspaper interviews appeared at the time. Although yielding no startling revelations they did throw a little light on the high-flying Joe Meek of May '63. When asked by the *Gloucester Journal* how he summed himself up he replied, "I'm a dreamer. Very temperamental and very ambitious. But lately people have been telling me I've been working too hard, that I'm ready to crack up. I'll admit I do feel tired sometimes. Sixteen hours a day is some going but I enjoy work. I'm doing what I really want to do. Still, I'll probably take a holiday in Spain next month." The holiday though, he added, depended on whether or not he could find the time.

The interview with the *Melody Maker* concentrated on his musical activities:

What do you say to people who attack 'Telstar' as being banal?

I think it was a good tune. If it was played by the Hallé Orchestra it would be a great piece of music. What's wrong with it? It has sold three million. . . Okay, so it was a cook-up and had gimmicks. So have the trad records in this country, haven't they? I wrote 'Telstar' one midnight. I think it's good – but I suppose it could nag on people a lot.

Which artistes do you supervise?

. . . The newest one is Heinz Burt. We've just cut his first solo disc since he left the Tornados to go solo – 'Dreams Do Come True'. He will be the biggest star in the pop world within a year, rivalling Cliff Richard. This new disc is bound to top the charts.

Don't you think you are unfair, inflicting your own musical notions on artistes and moulding them all into your style instead of letting them develop naturally?

No, that's not really true at all. They all have different styles when they arrive – and they arrive in droves at the door. It's a mad scene. There are so many singers wanting to work with me. But I don't mould them into my ideas completely. I just try to cultivate any talent they have and make them sound commercial. I did it with John Leyton on his early discs, I think. I don't foist my own plans down their throats, no.

The beat scene has many critics who say the music is trash. You are fostering it. What's your answer?

The pop scene in Britain is getting better in quality all the time, in my opinion. It used to be everyone trying to sound and look like Cliff Richard. Now things are much more individual. I'd like to have a go back at the critics of the pop scene. Would Matt Monro's discs be so marvellous without good orchestral backings? No. Instrumental parts mean everything. So why not bring them to the foregound more?

Who are your favourite artistes?

Judy Garland, Les Paul & Mary Ford, some of Ella's work and modern jazz. I shall start recording jazz soon – trad, by the Dauphine Street Six. We'll try something different.

THE LEGENDARY JOE MEEK

What is your future?
I want to go into films and write a musical. As it stands, I'm quite happy with the way things are going. I have a lot of critics in the business. They are just damned jealous because one man has done so well. One thing they forget is this: my years as deejay helped me judge what the public wants. So few of the people in this business know that. Why are people so jealous at anybody who gets up and works?

He also seized his chance to lunge out at the infernal Merseybeat. While the Beatles were on top with their first No.1, 'From Me To You', having taken over from fellow Merseysiders Gerry & the Pacemakers' 'How Do You Do It', and with scores more beat groups bubbling under, a little dampening of this dangerous ardour was called for: "There's nothing new about their sound. Cliff Bennett & the Rebel Rousers have been doing the same thing for a year now and, up to a point, so has Joe Brown. I really don't understand all this fuss about the Liverpool sound. I like it, but it's not as new as everybody is trying to make out. I haven't been to Liverpool but I might make a trip up there around the end of the summer, but that depends on how it fits in with my other plans. I had hundreds of groups down here from Liverpool before the Beatles made it big but none of them had anything very different. Some of them in fact were just rubbish."

One of the Liverpool bands going into battle for him was a 20 year old Freddie Starr with the Midnighters. Joe's singing friend, Dave Adams, had been doing some talent spotting when he saw them playing at Streatham Ice Rink. He rang Joe in the early hours to tell him of his find and an audition was fixed there and then. Later a jubilant Joe told the press of the outcome: "I couldn't believe that nobody had snapped them up before. I was the first person ever to record Adam Faith, and Freddie is one of the most talented artistes I've ever worked with since then. The session was tremendous fun and Freddie was entertaining all the time. I remember Adam had this quality and I'm pretty confident that Freddie can become as big a star. He's got that extra something".

That extra something may have referred to Freddie's irreverent sense of humour, which was not entirely to Joe's taste. Once during a session he walked in to find the singer strutting about with his trousers round his ankles; nor did he find it funny the day he asked Freddie to go into the studio to test the microphones. The sound Joe heard as he checked his levels was Freddie's singing interspersed with short silent gaps; half an hour was spent

188

searching for the fault before he realized that the silent gaps came when Freddie shut his mouth. Then he nearly smashed the microphone and ran downstairs screaming. Practical jokes at his expense were not appreciated.

However, jokes at other people's expense were another matter. For example, there was the case of the terrible saxophone player. Again and again Joe was having him play his solo, full of rude blasts of wind and bum notes; meanwhile the backing band were concentrating their deepest, fearing for their lives should Joe hear them burst out laughing, and over and over the sax player played getting worse and worse with every take. Then the bass player suddenly noticed Joe around the corner looking at him doubled up, trying his best to suppress his giggles! Another day while he was watching a rehearsal of Houston Wells & the Marksmen, someone's guitar finger-pick accidentally flew off like an arrow into the bass player's nostril. The sight of the poor chap desperately trying to play on regardless had him in stitches. And often when he stopped a session to crack a joke or tell a funny anecdote he would end it staggering around with laughter. One of his own favourite stories concerned his rubber soundproofing. In earlier days when he found himself losing drum sounds through the studio floor, he had had the floorboards prized up under the drums and had tipped in a tin of liquid rubber. He would recall with wicked mirth the sight of his horror-stricken landlady, Mrs. Shenton, as she watched it seeping through the ceiling below and running down the walls. The butt of much Outlaws mickey-taking was Geoff Goddard. His weird, unsettling way of gazing at a person as if in a trance, together with the thick country accent and short, sharp bursts of laughter all put him four-square in the firing line. Even Joe thought he was a bit odd and loved to explain how a certain record was destined to be a smash hit because Geoff had said he had been talking to a cow that morning, and the cow had told him so.

When he was back in his control room, though, he generally preferred the Outlaws not laughing at Geoff or anyone else because automatically he thought he himself was their target. At those times he was pleased to find ways of getting his own back. One of the many musicians who often did not see eye to eye with him was the Tornados' drummer, Clem Cattini. During one session Joe came rushing into the studio to clip him round the ear, and when the astonished Clem asked him what it was for, since he had done nothing, he told him it was for when he did. Then there were the auditionees who would sometimes find themselves utterly castigated for their lack of talent, only to be startled on their way out by a broad grin and the news that really they were very good indeed and could record right away.

As usual despite the importance of honing Heinz into shape he was still making time for other sessions. Groups were in and out like clockwork mice. Non-stop names like the Cameos, the Beat Boys and the Puppets, all of whom mean less than nothing nowadays, were each seeking their bit of glory as they lugged their equipment up and down the narrow stairs. Amongst the many rejected were the Kon-Rads, the first group to feature saxophonist David Jones, later to find more favour as David Bowie.

His workrate was phenomenal, as was his rate of record releases: the May-July average amounted to an astounding one release per week. As always he was spreading his options wide in a bid to please everyone, and on offer he had old style pop, rock-'n'roll, country'n'western, folk, Merseybeat and instrumentals.

Of his solo singers he was pushing four girls. One of them was an attractive 19 year old Glenda Collins, for whom he had written a song called 'I Lost My Heart At The Fairground'. It turned into what one might describe as a typical Joe Meek record with everything being thrown in: sad lyrics, sound effects from a fairground, galloping beat, organ, echo, choir and heavy, solid bass.

Glenda had a good voice and was to complement several of his records over the next few years. Before meeting him she had already been contracted to Decca for three years as their 'answer' to Helen Shapiro, but she says it was not until the contract expired and her father brought her to Holloway Road that she found her potential: "It was very nice recording for Decca but it was much more exciting recording for Joe. It was his personality: he sort of inspired you. When I recorded for Decca I was only 16 at the beginning. I remember it was for Mike Smith. He was very good and he told me more or less how to sing because I was a real novice at it completely then, but he couldn't have brought out in me what Joe did. It was a different thing altogether; there was a certain something in the way Joe would get you to sing and get you to feel the music and the record. I think I possibly needed someone like Joe to bring out something a little bit more, because just merely singing the songs like I was at Decca, I don't think would have clicked with anybody. . . I thoroughly enjoyed working with Joe because he was a very alive and a very conscientious sort

190

of person and he had new ideas. He was a very unusual sort of person and consequently he had unique ideas of his own. I think possibly he was a genius; it may be an overworked word but one tended to get the feeling that he was."

He was also paid a visit by the black-clad rocker Gene Vincent. As one of the original rock'n'roll greats Vincent's career in the US had faded, but when he had later arrived in Britain he found himself hotly acclaimed by fans starved of the real thing. His career had then taken off all over again and he was still head-lining tours. Thanks to the new film, *Live It Up*, he was to sing a rock'n'roll number of Joe's called 'Temptation Baby' and went round with his band for an afternoon session. The finished song rocked along well, though Vincent was a bit taken aback to find himself recording in someone's house and seeing the producer setting microphones and messing with wires.

As soon as Heinz was back from his stint at Pinewood Studios Joe started preparing him for the first of his Joe Meek package tours. Going round seaside resorts Heinz was scheduled to top a bill including Andy Cavell & the Saints, the Outlaws and Freddie Starr & the Midnighters. Naturally the project depended on 'Dreams' bagging a place somewhere in the charts but he had no worries on that score. Already he was bluffing the press with news of Heinz singing a French version for quick release in France, and giving them more nonsense about flying to Paris the following week for negotiations on a French film part and concert dates.

Reviews of 'Dreams' were on the whole good. The record was being fairly well played on the radio and getting stacks of publicity, and he braced himself for a reasonably big hit. And nothing happened. 'Dreams Do Come True' was one that didn't and was to be the biggest turkey of his career. The next few weeks passed it by without a sound and after a month on release 'Dreams' was showing no sign whatever of breaking into any chart, and it was abundantly clear he was backing a bum steer. Nor was the Heinz-Tornados film, *Farewell Performance*, anywhere to be seen – so much for the mid-May release date. Subsequently his package tour crumbled. So all that was left was to send out a few fan club photos to those who had asked for them.

THE LEGENDARY JOE MEEK

He had no hesitation in apportioning the blame and laid it fair and square at the feet of Decca and Ivy Music for not pushing the record hard enough. Regrettably, if they were at fault they were no more so than the song itself: the words were adequate but frankly the melody was feeble, while the overall sound was by now old hat. There were already more than enough ballads to go round from a list of singers as long as your arm and this one just did not have enough going for it. After an investment of around £10,000 on the Heinz build-up the record went on to global sales of 398 copies, bringing in to RGM the grand sum of £15.19s.5d.

To add to his troubles Major Banks was fuming at the sight of all the bills for Heinz's newspaper adverts which kept landing on his doormat. And with nothing to show for those full front-page splashes he had something to fume about. All along, the Major had said Joe was spending too much on Heinz, and each new bill that dropped in was confirming it.

Joe was used to lesser disappointments and was bound to have a fair share of them since he expected every record he put out to be a hit. This one hurt like no other one had ever done and brought him right down, but he was not down and out. His hatred of depressions had long since taught him that their remedy lay in hard work, and seeing Heinz losing interest spurred him on all the more. From Heinz's point of view the Jerry Lee Lewis tour had been a washout and along with the failure of 'Dreams' plus the cancellation of his latest tour, things seemed to be going from bad to worse. He told Joe how people were saying he had been crazy to leave the Tornados and that perhaps they were right; that perhaps he would never make the grade as a singer and that he would probably be better off as a bacon-slicer.

That kind of talk brought Joe down on him like a ton of bricks. It made him angry that he should even give a moment's thought to abandoning a career almost before it had started, and no way was he about to let all that time and effort go to waste. But the cardinal factor behind his supporting Heinz went further than that.

The young man now meant a great deal more to him than a mere recording artiste. Of all his friends and all those he had signed up, there was only one who was really important: Heinz. His life revolved round him. Nor were his feelings towards him unrequited. In spite of Heinz's taking full advantage of the female fans who regularly laid themselves on a plate for him, he did not deny Joe similar opportunities. Sharing the same bed and occasionally being caught together in a compromising position, clearly the relationship was not a platonic one.

And not only had Joe grown deeply fond of him but he had a lot of faith in his ability to win over the record-buying public. So what if there had been a dreadful tour and a flop first single? There would be other tours and the next single was bound to be a winner. After all, the Tornados had flopped with their first disc, and look what had happened with their second! And if they could do it, why not Heinz? He knew he could sell Heinz if he found the right song; if he could only dig out one from all those they had tried, then a hit was sure to come of it. Heinz would be a star and everyone would live happily ever after.

That was his attitude when he took Heinz and the Saints' bass guitarist Tab Martin with him up to Newent for a weekend in June. Visits by Newent's most famous son were always common knowledge, but when he brought pop personalities along too, the queues outside his house rivalled those once outside his father's fish and chip shop. His niece, Sandra, who was 10 years old at the time describes the scene at No.1 High Street: "To me it was like a carnival without the flags when Tab and Heinz come down. That was the time that the house was open and all autographs were being signed. They sat at the table – Joe at one end, Heinz at the other, and Tab. And they just come in through the kitchen at the back and they just filed around the table and then went out again."

Then after the weekend it was back to business, and finding the right song for Heinz was top priority. But already they had sifted through dozens of demos without any luck, so where was the winner? One thing was vital: it had to get well away from the sweet, outdated pap of the first and offer something more gutsy, more on the lines of Merseybeat.

He was still keen on the tribute Geoff Goddard had written to the late rock singer, Eddie Cochran. Called 'Just Like Eddie', Geoff's demo had been knocking around for a year but as Heinz had disliked it he had not forced it on him. Now though he felt positive that if given the right treatment, it would sell well and he was determined Heinz should give it a go. Like Buddy Holly, Eddie Cochran's name had also become revered since his tragic death in a 1960 car accident, so a song dedicated to him was bound to be listened to with interest. Unlike the memorial service lyrics of its Buddy Holly predecessor the ones of this song were light-hearted, calling upon anyone feeling a bit under the weather to go out, where 'beneath the stars you can play your guitars, just like Eddie.' Geoff had made it all very subtle, not mentioning the name Cochran but with any luck saying just enough to brew up some controversy and get Heinz talked about. Joe also saw in it a chance of taking a fresh initiative with him; when the song struck oil it could make him a kind of 'answer' to Cochran, presenting him with a ready-made image and musical direction.

When Joe recorded him singing along to the Outlaws' rhythm track the voice sounded so much improved that he sang on his own with nobody ghosting. The lead guitarist, Richie Blackmore, later to become famous for his work with heavy rock groups Deep Purple and Rainbow, also came in to fire up the melody, whilst the piano accompaniment and very effective oo-ing were courtesy of Geoff. In deference to the Merseybeat sound the recording ended up very clean for an RGM production, dispensing with the usual heavily laden echo.

If one could say that Heinz's debut disc had been amongst the most crucial of Joe's career then this follow-up was even more so. His reputation was at stake, so the sooner the record became a hit and erased the memory of that first king-sized catrastrophe the better. The trouble was that ' Dreams' had not only failed but had failed for all to see, and with the news of another Heinz release reaching the press, snide stories began seeping back to him of people in the business laughing up their sleeves about Heinz: "the pretty boy, Joe's favourite and he can't even play the bass properly." It hurt but he was used to it. All his life he had had people sneering at him, so what was new?

While he again started looking forward to a Heinz harvest he piled on the pressure. Hiring a local Co-op Hall he made him buckle down to work, rehearsing the act over and over, criticizing and encouraging him all the time. What he had to give him above all was confidence. Those stage and TV appearances with the Tornados were not nearly enough, no matter how much faith Joe invested in him; it was one thing to be strumming innocently along within the security of a five-piece band, but quite some-thing else to suddenly find oneself thrust out centrestage with TV cameras focused up your nose and a thousand pairs of eyes ogling you.

And there was Merseybeat to make his Heinz assignment harder. The Liverpool sound was the one getting the attention, and precious few solo singers were evolving from it. Of his current artistes like Andy Cavell, Don Charles and Geoff

Goddard, none was selling well. British soloists of the pre-Beatles era were fast going out of fashion, and anyone whose name was not Cliff Richard was in for a bumpy ride. Stuck in the middle of his latest lean spell, with his groups looking poorly too, he would just have to keep on hammering away till one eventually clicked. And *three* did!

The first week of August was a smasher. To give him a treble chart treat were three new entries: Houston Wells & the Marksmen in one chart at No.47 with 'Only The Heartaches', while into another came the Saints at No.30 with 'Wipeout' and at last Heinz at No.29 with 'Just Like Eddie'. He was elated. For him the appearance of the Heinz record was nothing short of triumph. He felt the thrill of the marathon runner who has not only finished the race but beaten all his rivals. At last he had been proved right, whilst once again his critics' noses were being pushed out of joint. All his effort had been rewarded and he had put onto the music scene a brand new star who he intended making shine every bit as brightly as Cliff Richard himself.

Now it was action stations. First of all he had to phone Heinz's mother in Southampton because Heinz was sunning himself with one of the Saints on board a motor launch somewhere off the Isle of Wight. The boat, a twenty-four foot, six-berth sloop, was jointly owned by Joe and Heinz through Heinz Burt Ltd. Costing £2,000 it was originally called 'The Golden Heinz', till Heinz insisted on changing that to the less camp 'Globetrotter'. With pressure of work on the increase again it was anyone's guess when Joe would get the chance to sail it. Anyway, Heinz was not to spend long on it for after four days of his planned fortnight's holiday he rang home, picked up Joe's message and returned to London to receive his long-awaited adulation.

And it was also back to the rehearsal grindstone, for there could be no mistakes this time. Heinz had fallen out with his previous backing group, the Outlaws, who from here on would only agree to back his records. Rather conveniently Andy Cavell had also fallen out with *his* group, so Heinz inherited his Saints and was back in business. As well as rehearsing him, Joe had to give him plenty of briefing on what to say and what not to say to the press. The image he wanted to foster was that of a happy but tough, ambitious rebel. Some of it was there already, though not the tough, rebellious aspects. However much Joe had him talk motorbikes in interviews he never really came across other than as what he was: an ordinary boy-next-door. Certainly there was never to be the gristly Cochran quality about him which Joe was hoping for.

Still, things were going well again, and Joe's newspaper statements showed a distinct air of confidence born of victory in the field and the promise of more laurels to come: "I'm very proud that Heinz has made the charts so early in his career – I've had this feeling of certainty all the way that he's destined for very big things in the world of showbusiness. You can't keep an enthusiast like him in the background. . . Naturally I get a lot of people wanting a break on discs. But so many of them are just copying and they're conceited as well. I find that the biggest stars are really the humblest of people." Why he should suddenly start accusing people of copying seems ludicrous when there for all to see was Heinz – the latest in his squad of unoriginal artistes. Fortunately in Heinz's case Joe had decided that onstage he was not to try and take over where Eddie Cochran had left off but merely to play on the name by sporting the same enthusiasm and performing a medley of Cochran's hits. It was a wise decision since not only had Cochran been a highly rated stage performer and musician, but along with the Everly Brothers and Buddy Holly had been an innovator of the blending of rock'n'roll into pop and was one of the greatest rock'n'rollers of the lot. Yes, Heinz would have needed more than three steps into *his* shoes.

He was soon booked onto a September tour with Billy J. Kramer and Tommy Roe and another one in October with Johnny Kidd & the Pirates, Dee Dee Sharp, the Caravelles and Houston Wells.

As the weeks passed, Joe had much to be pleased about. 'Eddie's' chart position rose briskly, as did the standard of Heinz's performance. The act was automatically more appealing now that there was a hit to latch it onto, and as Heinz's self-assurance grew, so too did his pluck, and he was soon putting together quite a snappy show. Even his singing improved! Each show brought new confidence; the jeers turned to cheers and he was shortly getting the full screaming mob treatment, with souvenir hunters helping themselves to parts of his Ford Zephyr, covering the car in lipstick kisses and letting down the tyres to stop him leaving. But it was not until he played in Wolverhampton where fans presented him with a gift of two dozen cans of Heinz baked beans that he really knew he had arrived.

Of every performance Joe expected pure, unblemished super-excellence. He got round to seeing very few but one that he did

196

not miss and which fell somewhat short of expectations is well remembered by PR man Keith Goodwin: "Heinz used to have this thing in the act where at one point he'd leap onto an amplifier, then onto a speaker and then onto the piano, and the guitarist would hurl the bass across and Heinz would catch it and go twang, twang, twang. Well, Joe was getting a lot of stick because Heinz was jumping on the lids of grand pianos all over the place and they were getting scratched. It was not in the days when we all wore plimsoles and that – he had these bloody boots on. So Joe told him: 'You can't keep doing this.' One day on a show, I'd had a barney with Joe beforehand, and I went out and took the piano lid off and I had this big black cloth and put it on there instead. So Heinz in the show goes onto the amps, onto the speaker and he leaps on the piano and the first we heard was clang, cling, clang. Joe went f—— spare! He was going to sack every roadie, kill everybody. Absolutely bananas. He never found out who did it."

In fact he withdrew Heinz from the tour completely, though it was not the prank that persuaded him. Curiously it was because the promoter of the tour, Brian Epstein, had invited Heinz to a party. His decision to pull him out came after watching a show at Chelmsford when, as usual, he was less than fully satisfied with Heinz's performance and picked it to pieces. For the first time the criticism made Heinz bite back, a row ensued and Joe immediately thought Heinz was on his way to join Epstein. Joe's assumption was rather less ridiculous when considering the number of artistes that had already been enticed away from him, and warning the younger man never to trust Epstein or anyone else, he was so concerned about it that he tried to put an end to his touring days altogether. Heinz by this time was pining to get onstage morning, noon and night but he says Joe wanted him safe at home around the flat and not hundreds of miles away being adored by hordes of screaming girls: "All he wanted was records and the people he cared about round him. Joe didn't want me to go on tour – he was afraid that I'd meet somebody and drift away. He always said, 'The longer you keep out of the limelight, the better it'll be when you go back on the road.' That was his attitude. There was an enormous ballroom tour. And I couldn't go on tour. And he said, 'You've got an interview with the papers,' because the Mecca people started moaning and Joe said, 'You tell them: 'Ballrooms mean the kiss of death'.' I was like in a prison: just sessions and a flat. So the pressure got on him and I had to go out."

That next tour was to be with Bobby Rydell and Helen

Shapiro, but before joining it Joe warned him against all the vultures that might be after him. And just in case that advice was not adhered to he put someone with him to make sure it was: Lional. Good old trusty Lional was the one person he could count on to make quite certain no undesirables laid hands on his precious protégé. And Lional was well aware of the responsibility invested in him: "Joe knew that I'd keep an eye on him. It was a big decision for Joe to make – he wouldn't put *anybody* with him. He lived for nothing else, only Heinz. It was all him. I was offered good wages at the time [£20 per week] and I found it very inter- esting. It entailed doing everything for him: making sure he appeared at the theatres at the right time, possibly to drive him; always we had to spend hours in the dressing room bleaching his hair; I had to make sure he got all his clothes ready for when he went onstage and when he came off. He used to work very hard jumping all over the stage. I used to feel very proud in actual fact working with Heinz and Joe because the kids used to scream their heads off; he was a very popular boy. I'd keep him on the right tracks. Every day I had to phone Joe to let him know any news and how the show had gone down." And he might well find himself telling Joe twice because, as Heinz recalls, even when the show was way outside London Joe would insist, "Oh that's only 180 miles; you can come back tonight – Lional's driving."

Meanwhile away from all the Heinz fun and frolics the Tornados were busy at Great Yarmouth falling apart at the seams. Although for this season Billy Fury was not in sight, all was far from well. Their fourth single, a jolly little piece called 'Ice Cream Man', had only reached No.18.

Its poor placing was but one of many nails being driven into the Tornados' coffin. His most successful act was withering away through lack of attention. Whilst any other independent producer would have thrilled to the Tornados' fortunes and plunged all his efforts into maintaining them, Joe was now giving them little more time ration than to Peter Jay & the Jaywalkers, the Ramblers, the Packabeats or his string of other also-rans. Losing their Heinz appeal had indeed cost them dearly. Needling tempers more were the long, stressful months of stage and session work, and one by one they were leaving the sinking ship amidst various self accusations of greed, unprofessionalism and drunk- enness plus reports of ill health. The rhythm guitarist had departed with his back in plaster after collapsing onstage, the organist followed soon afterwards suffering from an assortment of aches and pains, the bass player was sacked and the lead guitarist had just about had enough of everything.

After an absurdly long delay their British album, 'Away From It All', was eventually released at the end of September, having been on the go for nearly a year. Intended to show off the group's versatility it was beautifully produced with some fairly good tunes, but by this time in their career it had to be exceptional to stand any chance and instead was just easy-listening.

The late arrival of the record was one more case of his mismanagement of the group, and but for his craving for more acts than were good for him it would have been on the market in the Spring while they were still at their peak. More than anything it was his hunger for fresh faces that denied them healthy sales. Had this been 1962 or earlier it would not have mattered so much; without the fearsome invasion from Liverpool to worry about, time would have been less pressing with just the Shadows to contend with. Instead they could only hope the ever-intensifying Beatlemania would hurry up and burn itself out; either that, or they should get down and pray that his latest front-page tongue-lashing in the *NME* would send all these new groups scampering back where they came from: "Don't let's kill the beat boom stone dead. At this rate the beat boom will be all over by Christmas. Liverpool characters come down here and ask for auditions and they think that just because they're from up there they run the British music business. Let's get it straight: only one or two Liverpool groups are worth bothering about. The rest are copying the Beatles or others. I appeal to the major record companies – don't clutter the market and wreck the goose that lays the golden hit. At the moment there are so many copyist groups around that the fans will wise up to it and pack it all in. They're not daft. Like everybody else in this country, I welcome the boom but managers, agents and everybody concerned have got to learn that to saturate the disc world with hundreds of tunes sounding the same is to invite disaster." And in the *Melody Maker*: "I have always been a bit of a beat merchant but a lot of the records today sound like the B-sides of my recordings of a few years ago. I don't think they deserve to be hits. The Beatles are in a class of their own but all the recording managers are trying to get a Beatle sound on other records. Sooner or later youngsters are going to realize new records all sound the same."

He was right of course to an extent, but then again just as guilty as the rest of them. He had successfully captured the

Merseybeat sound on discs by the Puppets and the Beat Boys but in so doing had made them sound the same as all the other beat groups. Likewise it would take a sharp ear to spot the difference between many of his other acts. If a band were not playing in a very distinctive style their identity on the recording could easily be spirited away in his magical bag of technical trickeries.

One artiste who had little fear of being spirited away anywhere was the ubiquitous Screaming Lord Sutch. No one else on Joe's books sounded anything like him, nor indeed wanted to! Between them earlier in the year they had recorded some more first-class BBC blacklist material called 'Jack The Ripper'. This was to be his Lordship's most infamous and the nearest he would ever get to having a hit. It opens with the approach of hurried footsteps on cobblestones, followed by a woman's breathless panting; suddenly the victim lets out a shriek, there is a dirty, ghoulish laugh and the chorus chants: 'The Ripper. . . Jack the Ripper', giving Sutch his cue to launch wickedly into Jack's grisly tale.

The latest Sutch contribution was a meaty rendering of the Coasters' 'I'm A Hog For You' backed by a spoof on 'Venus In Blue Jeans' called 'Monster In Black Tights'. With 'Monster' Joe cocked a snook at all the knockers who had dared liken 'Globetrotter' to 'Venus'; this time it was almost the same tune right through! Here, extracted from their music, the lyrics earn little credit, but writing them with Geoff during the session Joe laughed so much it gave him hiccups:

> *My monster in black tights,*
> *You've got the kind of blood that I likes.*
> *I remember the day you dragged me away*
> *And left me on a barbed-wire fence.*
>
> *My monster in black tights,*
> *You've got the kind of eye that I likes,*
> *With your wrinkled-up chin where the worms have been*
> *You make me wanna hold you tight.*
>
> *Oh I love to see you hopping along –*
> *What else can you do with three legs? –*
> *Though it may seem ever so wrong,*
> *I like you best when you're in your vest!*
>
> *My monster in black tights,*

OPERATION HEINZ!

You're everything a freak like I likes,
And if you say you won't run away
I'll untie your chains today.

By happy chance its release just happened to coincide with Sutch standing for election to Parliament. Well, it made a change from tyrannizing shoppers as the Wild Man of Borneo or being driven by hearse in his coffin as he waved serenely to horrified passers-by.

The seat he was expecting to win, under his proper name of David Sutch, was the one at Stratford-upon-Avon vacated by disgraced War Minster Jack Profumo. Offering to take care of the constituents' problems he set himself up on behalf of his newly formed National Teenage Party. "Vote for the ghoul: he's no fool" – and he wasn't. His campaigning was getting him front page coverage in all the national daily papers. However, voters were hardly likely to be impressed by such qualifications as the ability to sing 'I'm A Hog For You', so hopefully his manifesto would bring him support. The issues were not entirely preposterous. Apart from calling for more public lavatories in Stratford and the abolition of dog licences, his other proposals were for the introduction of commercial radio and for votes at 18: "You can fight for your country at 18 and you can be hung. But when it comes to voting you are still a child." Though at the time people laughed, within a few years both proposals were to become reality. In the event he got all the publicity he needed for his touring horror show but not enough votes to give him a regular booking at the House of Commons. Tory candidate Angus Maude won with 15,000 odd while Sutch lost his deposit. His own total of 208 was actually quite heartening in view of the fact that the teenagers whom he was representing did not yet have the vote.

Joe was full of admiration. Publicity was a matter very dear to his heart for he was acutely aware of the power of the press, the importance of image and the need for promotion: that you don't just stick out a piece of plastic saying, like many muttonheads still were, that records are sold through your ears not your eyes. Every record he had out he wanted someone working on, and if it was by an act he personally managed like the Tornados, then more often than not he was the one to foot the bill. Though record companies often placed adverts they were not always keen to prize open their wallets and give his discs the push he felt they deserved.

THE LEGENDARY JOE MEEK

While enviously watching Lord Sutch's masterful talents he could only console himself with the thought that the Sutch method of shouting his self-assertions from the rooftops was rather too wild for the image of his own artistes. At the same time he could not help comparing the effect of the other man's home-made publicity with what he himself was getting from the profes-sionals, and Sutch says he was not impressed: "He told me: 'I spend hundreds of pounds hiring these bloody useless publicity agents and they do nothing. You do ten times more on your own.' To advertise one of my records I suggested we get a vanload of sheep and go down Oxford Street and let them all out during the rush hour. He had the horrors: 'Oh no, I can't put my name to that! Say one of the sheep got killed: there'd be a stampede of animal lovers in here.' I had a 22-foot lifelike alligator on top of a van going round the streets and would put it on the beach to frighten the bathers. He'd suggest more straightforward things. It was Joe's idea for me to visit the streets of Whitechapel late at night dressed as Jack the Ripper; all the places frequented by Jack: pubs, clubs, back alleys. I did and it got local publicity. He did suggest that I did a whole review with this Jack the Ripper and make it into like a mini-opera and he'd have written some more music. He was saying I could make it into a big production for my stage show and stabbing women, running about with a big butcher's knife. He liked that idea. He was intrigued by horror films like I was: the Draculas and the Frankensteins and all the classic horror films and he came and saw my act. That's why I was an ideal artiste for him – we were both intrigued with horror. He loved it because it was a different approach and gave him something to get his teeth into. He was fed up with just the pretty-boy singers all the time and wanted to get away from all that."

Another of Joe's ideas was even more outrageous. At a time when the War Department were selling off old submarines at a few hundred pounds apiece, he suggested to Sutch that they buy one together and that Sutch sail it down the Thames and threaten to blow up the Houses of Parliament. "It'll still get publicity," he assured him, "even if it sinks!" Lack of funds scotched that one.

Those "bloody useless publicity agents" Joe referred to were during this period one Keith Goodwin. £10 a week was a fair old whack to be paying out in '63, but it was buying the skills of someone who could convince journalists that a certain artiste or production had something worth hearing; and besides getting especially good coverage of Heinz, there were occasional stories

202

on Andy Cavell and the Tornados plus useful mentions of various others.

Curiously those same skills that Keith used when foisting his information onto newsmen often came in handy when extracting that information from Joe. It was not that Joe was short of things to talk about but short of time to do it. Every week there was just one phone call in which Keith had to try and collect all the facts together to put out a news release: items of gossip, dates of tours, anecdotes – anything. Such a system of gathering information depended entirely on getting Joe away from whatever he was doing and into the right frame of mind to make his latest report. This was an art. Nobody could speak firmly to him and be sure of getting away with it, but Keith says his chances of success were better than most: "I had this knack. I could ring him up and he'd say, 'I'm busy, I'm busy,' and I'd say, 'Well you're f—— un-busy and you talk to me or you don't get value for the money you're paying me – suit yourself.' 'Oh, you're getting me in a corner.' 'Yes, talk to me!' I could do it with him and he'd actually go and turn a tape off or whatever and sit down and talk. We'd be on the phone sometimes half an hour, sometimes longer. Once he got going he'd come up with information for three or four good stories, snippets and so on and I'd have material for another week. Also he'd ring me up almost weekly and tell me he had a great new star; every one was the biggest thing since sliced bread – every one! And once a week: 'I've got this record and you've got to listen to it.' So maybe you'd trot over and listen to it. Sometimes you'd hear a three parts decent record, sometimes you'd hear one and think, 'You've got to be kidding.' A lot of them, I must admit, I liked. From then on, Joe was immediately into that one project until the next morning when he had another brilliant idea for somebody else. I think he treated his artistes well in the sense that he tried to do his very best for each and every one of them. His faith in them was genuine.

"Sometimes he'd ring up with some poxy story that he really believes is the front page of the *Daily Mirror* – absolute nonsense. I remember he rang up about how an artiste recorded a song and it turned out that all the musicians on the session were the same star sign, and so was he, and so was the artiste who sang on it and so was the lady who made the tea and so was the lady's cat. This, according to him, was a good story. He'd made it up. This fellow Burr Bailey was David Adams and at one point with Joe he had a record coming out as Joy & Dave, one as the Saints, one as Burr

Bailey and one as Silas Dooley Jnr: all set to come out within about three months. Joe told me we could make him the great mystery man, and when they all get in the charts we can explode the myth of who they all are. All four getting in the bloody charts! Two of them weren't even released. Another time the Tornados had a new record out and were playing a big London gig. Joe said, 'We've got to really publicize this gig. We've got to find a way.' He rang me up quite late at night at the office. He said, 'I've got a great idea. I'll hire these kids. We'll start at Piccadilly Circus and we'll draw these big arrows in white paint on the road up every street, and eventually these arrows all meet and point to this venue. People are bound to see them, and their curiosity will get the better of them and they'll have to follow the arrows.' I said, 'Brilliant. But where are you going to find all these kids to give them a fiver to do it and what compensation do you pay their parents when they're all run down?' He said, 'We'll do it in the early hours of the morning.' He phoned the next day and didn't even mention it. So I said, 'What about this wondrous idea?' He said, 'Well I talked to a couple of youngsters and they were quite prepared to do it but their parents wouldn't let them out in the early hours.'"

Keith's flair for cornering him on the phone did not however stretch to his meetings with him at 304 during the day. Arriving there at the pre-arranged time of 3p.m., he would often find himself competing for Joe's attention with a dozen or so other people: perhaps publishers with songs, artistes' managers, musicians waiting to be paid, and by the time Joe got around to talking to him about what he had got him there to talk about, three hours might have elapsed. Keith soon learnt that the way round it was to avoid the ballyhoo and make sure that future meetings were in the evening. When they met, each man would suggest ideas for publicity and, as Keith continues, Joe was never stuck for things to say: "His ideas tumbled out one after the other. God knows how many went by the board because he hadn't noted them down and had forgotten them the next day. He was always on the go; he very rarely sat in one place for long: up and down like a jack-in-the-box. He was always rabbiting about one thing and thinking about something else. You're sitting there and suddenly he gets up and walks behind you, and you hear rustle, rustle, rustle; you turn round, he's pulled out three cushions and he's diving down the back of a settee. What he's been thinking of is someone he started recording and didn't know how to finish, and has now got the finish in his head and has gone to find the tape. But he hasn't lost the thread of the conversation – he's still talking! And he sits down again and ten minutes later suddenly pulls out a picture he's been thinking of giving you: 'Oh, and by the way. . .' To keep track of him was the big adventure. He was jumps ahead of what he was saying."

When Joe tried his own hand at salesmanship his style was full of sugar-coated sincerity. But though he realized artistes needed a boost to help them along, his mistake was to boost them too far for their own good. Thus when he phoned up some writer of a teenage magazine to tell him, for example, that Andy Cavell was "definitely going to be an international star next week and must be interviewed at once", the writer would be bowled over by his enthusiasm. Unfortunately when the interview took place, Andy Cavell had no way of living up to the flattering introduction. So next time round, the writer would not be so easily duped by Joe's sales pitch. Instead those huge dollops of sincerity had the writer wondering whether Joe had the mind of a child or whether Joe thought the writer had.

Moving into the autumn, things were going very well. He had lots of new acts on disc, including Gunilla Thorne, a Swedish model cum singer who understandably looked very nice indeed, and Pamela Blue, another cracker who made Christmas crackers and who had been given Joe's phone number by Screaming Lord Sutch after meeting him at a show and singing for him. Now she was singing one of the catchiest melodies Geoff Goddard had written, another little death ditty, titled 'My Friend Bobby'. In failing to reach the charts it was to turn out one of the most eligible contenders for the Joe Meek Top Twenty tracks of 'those that got away', and give the lie to the line that you can't keep a good song down.

Another one that slipped the net, but which this time deserved to, was a trite sounding obscurity called 'Sky Men'. Written and sung by Geoff it was surprisingly unimaginatively produced, and instead of Joe lavishing it with odd spacey sound effects the best he could manage was to give Geoff a Dalek-type voice, which sounded more strange than spacey going with his Berkshire accent. In the song Geoff describes a close encounter with alien beings: 'Children of Earth, be not afraid, for we come in peace'. He says his inspiration for it was the sighting one night of a light travelling by with jerky movements. Running out into the garden he watched it pass overhead and as it drifted away he sent out all the right thoughts to bring it back again the following night. Of course, that is exactly what it did! Rumour has it that Geoff Goddard went to the Moon long before any astronaut; perhaps there is some truth in it.

In the meantime closer to home but still flying fairly high were the Tornados, for whom things were brightening up again. Thanks to the expiry of the Meek-Parnes contract, Joe was back in charge again, so now only had himself to argue with. From here on it would be him deciding when and where they played, and from that standpoint he was prepared to let them carry on backing Billy Fury.

In the midst of all this music-making, a little light relief was provided by the Outlaws. Long van rides to gigs around the country had sparked off a novel form of entertainment, which although giving Joe some worries, gave him twice as many laughs. In the thick of the action was Chas Hodges: "We was on tour with Heinz & the Saints. Anyway, we were in one van, they were in another. They were driving along in front. Suddenly Tab, he threw a cheese roll out at somebody, and it looked so funny 'cause it hit this bloke on the head. We chucked a few cheese rolls out too. I mean, it's so boring when you're on tour every day, going from somewhere like Birmingham to Glasgow. That night we was talking about it. We'd had such a good time we thought, 'Tomorrow we'll stop and get some flour bags – some little, tiny half pound ones.' We stopped in this little village somewhere, we went in this shop and we said, 'Can we have five quids' worth of flour bags and have you got anything that squirts?' And we got some eggs. One egg and flour assault raged all the way from Bournemouth to Newcastle. Our van and Heinz's would race down the Al drawing up side by side, pelting each other with eggs and flour bags. We had about eight dozen eggs at the start and he had them all at the finish. His van arrived looking like an omelette!

"The eggs and squirter got a bit played out but the flour bags really did work good. We'd make a little slit in the side. It was so funny. Richie Blackmore was a particularly good shot. That flour bag thing wasn't easy; when you're going along you've got to throw it before you feel you should throw it. And Richie just had that knack, 'cause the van's going at a certain speed. He was clever at that. I weren't too bad at it but a lot of times I'd miss. I was quite impressed with Richie 'cause he'd get spot on each time. It was such fun – we was doing it all the time. It changed the whole thing: the longer the journey, the better it was. I remember we hit this bloke once when Gene Vincent was with us. We were going to Swansea. And Gene Vincent had never seen this. We had all the flour bags and was going along and there was this geyser had his head in his engine, doing the motor. Of course, as we went past him – wallop! He must have had the fan belt going. Like an H-bomb it was. He come out. He had a beard and he was white. And Gene Vincent was killing himself! And the geyser jumped in his car and he caught us up, come up beside us and he wound down his window and he was chucking these house bricks at the van – wallop! Anyway, he chased us all round Swansea. We got rid of him in the end. And there was all these dents in the side. . .

"We got nicked for it anyway. We'd chucked a flour bag at this teddy boy at this bus stop and a policeman took our number and they traced us. They found out in time that not only had we been chucking flour bags but we didn't have any insurance for the van! Joe had bought us the van and he was supposed to have insured it. And we had to go up to the court in Shrewsbury, not for the flour bags, but every time we'd been pulled up we'd given Major Banks's company. Of course, he was getting all these letters back. He got in touch with Joe saying he don't know nothing about this van. Apparently Joe had bought the van for us and hadn't informed Major Banks about it, so consequently we all had to go to court: Major Banks, Joe Meek, all us lot. When we got there we travelled overnight – we looked like a load of gypsies. We was all sitting there. It was basically 'cause of the insurance, really. Major Banks was saying, 'I don't know nothing about it,' and Joe Meek was being really very vague. Ken had to go up into the box and say, 'We thought we were insured,' and Joe had to go up in the box. And I remember he looked sort of sheepish. We was all sitting at the back and he kept looking at us and sort of half smiling. The prosecutor was saying to him, 'Joe Meek, did you ever sign an H.P. form for the van?' And Joe said, 'No'. And he said, 'Well, look. This is the thing here with your signature.' So Joe said, 'Yes.' The man said, 'But you've just told me that you haven't signed anything.' Joe said, 'Well, I haven't.' The man said,

'But look. This is your signature here, and if it is. . .' They couldn't get any sense out of him and told him to sit down again. Then Major Banks got up and said, 'Look, we run this company. . .' and he went through all the bit. Joe was just so vague about the whole thing. It was genuine an' all – he didn't care."

However, the band were not let off lightly. They were fined £100, banned from driving the van and the driver lost his licence. No doubt they had not helped their cause much by busking on the courthouse steps that morning as the judge and his entourage passed fully robed on their way to court.

They swapped their flour bags for catapults and gooseberries! Again their scores were high but again they were caught, and Joe and the lads were paid a visit at the studio by two friendly policemen who cautioned them for "discharging missiles". And that was the end of that.

Meanwhile, away from flour and gooseberry matters it was back on the Heinz bandwagon where most of his attention was centred. The young man who was now his principal artiste was enjoying the distinction of being the only male solo singer in direct competition with Merseybeat who was actually gaining popularity. Whilst the Adam Faith's, Marty Wilde's and Billy Fury's were on a downward spiral that would soon see them swept away like so many old leaves, Heinz was positively blooming. 'Eddie' had reached No.5 and in Sweden had topped the charts. With sales high in Norway and Denmark too, Decca were giving the record full European and US release, with views to making him an international star. Singer Michael Cox had also reached the top in Sweden with 'Sweet Little Sixteen' and 'Stand Up' and was now well into a four-year star spree of concert tours plus his own TV and radio shows. For Heinz things looked just as promising because as well as new records that Joe had in the pipeline plus tours and TV spots lined up both here and in Scandinavia, there were the two film appearances set to catch the public's eye. Reviews of the newly released 'Heinz' EP were excellent, as were those for the follow-up single, 'Country Boy', which was played for Heinz's guest slot on *Juke Box Jury*, receiving the dubious honour of being voted a hit.

In order to jazz up his stage act, Joe was also toying with the idea of having Heinz's hair dyed flaming red and getting him to make his entrance on a motorbike and actually looping the loop. Bearing in mind the width of most stages it was, as Keith Goodwin described it, "a typical Joe potty idea".

And besides Heinz, Joe had more dreams a-plenty waiting to come true. Flushed with the glow of success he was getting ideas of building an organization big enough to rival Decca and EMI. Obviously it would take some while before he could seriously put plans into action but with a few more hits that should not be too long. 'Eddie' had done well, though not quite well enough to get the Major off his back – yet!

Happy days were here again. There was much to look forward to and certainly much to be pleased about with life in general. It was with a reasonable sense of well-being that he could now wake up in the morning and mull over the day's prospects. It may not have been seventh heaven, for he knew difficulties still lay ahead but it was soothing to think that despite all the hurts and irritations life had its bright side. He was winning through and knew that with more hard graft and a helping hand from Lady Luck his skills would move yet more mountains. Yes, things were looking pretty hopeful; his star was indeed once again in the ascendant. But then disaster struck!

Something happened that was to have an earth-shattering effect on his life, leaving mental scars from which he would never fully recover.

12
Incident At Madras Place

November 11 was a long, hard day. There were groups in and out, sessions, phone calls, offers, demands, problems – pressure. In fact it was a normal, regular, run of the mill Joe Meek day. Not until late that night did the unexpected happen. He was arrested for importuning.

The arrest was made in the grimly sordid setting of a dimly-lit gentlemen's convenience half a mile down the road at Madras Place. From there he was frogmarched another half-mile to Caledonian Road police station where he was summoned to appear in court the next morning. An hour later he returned home, shocked and frightened. Amongst the people he telephoned for consolation was Don Charles, with whom he had discussed lesser crises in the past: "He phoned me about 3.30 that night. The first thing he said was: 'I'm in one hell of a mess: I've been caught in a toilet.' He didn't tell me where initially. I said, 'Oh Joe, what the Christ have you done, how, what, why, where?' And he was crying. And he was terrified that his mother would find out, would it get in the press, what would they do with it, what would the profession say. I said, 'Why the bloody hell do you do this? Why? For what bloody reason? You've all the protection of your own place.' And he said he didn't know why; that he just found himself going into toilets. He used to go in parks as well. We were on the phone for about half an hour. I did my best to put his mind at rest. I told him life would soon get back to normal again afterwards, but he was still very down when we hung up."

The next day he went to Clerkenwell Magistrates Court, King's Cross, where he pleaded guilty to "persistently importuning for an immoral purpose" and commented, "I have nothing to say." The policeman who had arrested him testified that on being charged Joe protested, "It's all a pack of lies." He was fined £15.

Even so, many people were of the opinion that it was indeed a pack of lies; that it must somehow or other have been a set-up job. His good friend Lional, for example, was convinced that was the case when Joe gave him his story: "He phoned me up and told me, 'I was picked up last night. These police officers said I was smiling at an old man with a gold chain.' That was wrong for a start because he wouldn't smile at old men anyway. He told me he had done nothing and that the evidence against him had been cooked up." Stories circulated about unknown people in the music business being jealous of his success, arranging for him to meet a budding star or new friend at that spot. Some of his singers and musicians could not believe he was experienced enough to attempt soliciting, considering how shy he was and how little he went out. They declared that not only was such behaviour completely alien to his nature but totally unnecessary; should he want to expend his passions he had only to pick up the phone and ask round a willing friend or colleague. In short, they concluded, the whole business had been a tragic miscarriage of justice – he couldn't have done it.

Unfortunately he could. Had he not been arrested there on that occasion he most certainly would have been on another. It was in fact no isolated incident. Rather it was the exact opposite for he had been a regular visitor to the establishment for quite some while. Shy he may have been but not so shy as he might have had some people believe, for even though he was not the world's greatest party-goer this did not stop him going out meeting people on a casual one-to-one basis; brief anonymous encounters with like-minded males were well within his scope.

The seeds had been sown back in '56 on the Luxembourg Road Shows. After dinner at the hotel he would tell his colleagues he was "going out to pick up a fellow"; later he would bring one back to his room. The "shy" Joe had already come a long way since his Newent days. As time went by and he became more and more interested in studio work back at IBC, these fleeting affairs offered the only real attraction of working with the Road Shows. Lional, with whom he had been living at the time, puts it all down to Joe's high libido: "He wasn't like that when I first met him. In the early days when he was with me, he was with me and no one else. But he'd still go around when he was away travelling. Later it got to the stage that he had to have so many people in the day – 'Gotta find another one.' He'd come back late after a session and go out again at 2 o'clock in the morning. He'd say it was 'to ease the pressure'. He'd go round in his car for an hour or so at night. He might meet someone and say, 'Come back, I'll introduce you to so-and-so', which happens today with big impresarios and at the end of it is the casting couch. When he moved to Holloway Road, Madras Place was one of the main meeting places. There was another one at the bridge's end and another one at the back. They were three meeting places and people would go round and round and round.[28] I'd say, 'Look, don't go to these places – no need. You've got friends; you don't need to go.' I used to worry myself sick over it. I'd get in my car at night and just go and see if I could find him around. He'd leave his red Sunbeam Rapier outside the loo; all the police for miles around must have known the number. If I'd see his car, I'd say, 'Out!' I wasn't going to have him caught doing anything like that."

However in spite of Joe's propensity for such unbecoming conduct plus his pleading guilty to it, on this particular occasion there was still a hint of uncertainty about it. The assertion he gave Lional, his most trusted friend, that he had not been "smiling at an old man" may have been genuine. Lional says that Joe never once lied to him, and that he had no reason to do so on this occasion. Neither had his story changed the following day when he confided his secret to his office boy Patrick Pink (nor indeed six months later when it would still be exactly the same): "He told me the whole story. He swore blind the police framed him. He said, 'I don't go chasing old men with watch chains dangling from their waistcoats – I go after young trade. Who wants a f— old man?' He said the old man had been planted there and they'd obviously been watching him for a long time and couldn't get him, so they framed him.

"I used to say to him, 'Why the hell do you go out, Joe? The phone rings night and day. There's people there all the time want you, and yet you still go out and walk the bloody streets.' Because they used to phone him left, right and centre. It seemed they were nearly all available. I knew because I was of the in-crowd there; I knew what was what. They were all keen to get on in the profession and many were willing to go along with whatever goes. OK, I think possibly a percentage of them were homosexuals anyway or pretended to be, I dont know. But there was never any need for Joe to go out looking; it would always come to him anyway. This is what I could never understand with Joe."

It would seem that the motives behind such vagrant delights went further than merely cooling hot blood. Lurking in lavatories was not the kind of pastime one would expect from the type of person he had been in Newent. Admittedly the pressure on him now was ten times that which he had left behind at home but basically he was the same person. The subtle difference was that he was now free, unshackled, with no father to beware of and no mother close at hand to keep a watchful eye on him. So he could rebel. After 25 years of being a good boy he could at last thrill to being a bad one. If there had been any pent-up frustrations at seeing his naughty brothers misbehave, now he too could let loose and be even naughtier; if he had watched enviously as they wooed and won their girls one after another, now he could do the same his way. Of equal significance was the risk element. Every shadow presented the possibility of a policeman; every sound could be a danger signal. Therein lay the spice, the exhilaration. As Oscar Wilde once said, describing a similar situation: "It was like feasting with panthers; the danger was half the excitement." Not even a queue of lads at Joe's bedroom door could offer that.

The day of November 12 was a torturously long one. Pleading guilty was the only course. Whether or not he *had* been smiling at the old man was of less concern than the fact that he had been loitering there long enough for his intentions to be obvious. Contesting it would have been useless, and had he done so, he knew full well that the whole business would have mushroomed into a far less savoury Sunday paper scandal.

Waiting around all morning added to the torment, but when his turn came he was in and out within five minutes. It was a very worried man who stepped out of the courthouse and into the drizzling drabness of London's King's Cross Road. Everything rested on the newspapers. Were they to hang his dirty washing out for all to see, then he was in for the blackest day he had ever known and a future forever marred by this disgrace. Were they to somehow overlook it as not being newsworthy . . . he would be saved. Then he could breathe again and blast this day of dread away with a thunderous barrage of music. And never, never, never he promised himself, would he take such risks again. Now all he could do was hope for the best, but that he knew was pie in the sky. They would knock him like everyone else knocked him, the same as they always had done. His photograph would be paraded all over the front pages; the headlines would scream the news to the world plastering his name out for all to see. No way would they fail to make a meal of it. After all, he brooded, the public had to be fully informed on such a vitally important issue; not the slightest detail could be sacrificed in frankly exposing this 'heinous' crime. Already he could hear people the length and breadth of the British Isles muttering his name to each other, shaking their heads in disbelief. He felt as if a heavy, grey blanket had descended upon him, from under which a thousand and one fears reared their ugly heads: fears which had crossed his mind in the past but never lingered long enough. They had always succumbed to that well worn adage: "It won't happen to me."

For a start, how could he keep it from his family now that Britain was about to share his shame? And how would they live it down in that tiny town where everyone knew everyone else's business? His mother was the last one in the world he wished to hurt but here he was within a stone's throw of doing just that. All the humiliation he was now suffering would be doubly compounded if he knew she was being punished too.

Then there was the music business to think about. How would all this affect his standing professionally? Would he be ostracized? There were so many homosexuals in the industry who might feel he had dragged their names through the mud. Worse still, some might soon be shivering in their shoes at the thought of his being caught again and that a subsequent interrogation or raid on his premises might reveal their own names. And what about the A & R sneering brigade? After eating humble pie with 'Johnny Remember Me', etc., this new item would be a very tasty titbit for them to drool over. He could picture them all lined up ready to swoop down on him. They would make excuses for not accepting his product: that the BBC, that bastion of respectability, could not tarnish its image by playing his music; that they were very grateful but now had sufficient product of their own. And how would life go on at the studio? Would he still be able to count on drawing new acts? Could he even count on keeping the ones he had? And most important of all, with so many nagging worries, would he still find the inspiration for his creativity and the ability to cope with normal, day-to-day hassles?

On his return from King's Cross he instructed an assistant to cancel the day's sessions and went upstairs to lock himself away in the control room. Amongst the usual flood of everyday phone calls was one from singer Kim Roberts asking him to escort her to a Decca publicity reception that afternoon to which they had both been invited. He declined without explaining why; probably he would have refused anyway but this time there was no chance. Nasty childhood memories were seeping back. The finger-pointing nightmare of children calling "cissie" had returned; the only difference now was that his accusers would be older and the taunts would show in sidelong looks and waspish whispers. What a hell of a hell-hole he had dug for himself! This day had to be the foulest he had known.

Somehow he summoned up the courage to venture out and

INCIDENT AT MADRAS PLACE

buy the two London evening papers. Hoping against hope that he might yet get away with it he peeked nervously at the headlines: "RUSSIA ARRESTS YALE PROFESSOR" and "FORWARD TO '64! Peace, Prosperity, Social Progress And An Easing Of Rates Burden". He could hardly believe it and scanned them ravenously. In the *Evening News* he had indeed made the front page but only a short column of a dozen lines at the foot of it. The *Evening Standard* had not mentioned him at all. He felt that blanket lift a little. They had not exactly let him off scot-free but now with such a tepid disclosure as that, there was just a chance it might pass unnoticed. There were still Wednesday's dailies to get through but if the London papers had not jumped on it, then maybe no one else would. He spent the evening being reassured by Lional.

Next morning he bought copies of all the national papers and found . . . nothing. He could breathe again. What he now had to find out was if anyone knew. He had a session that day with the Saints. Keeping a sharp eye open for any sign that his secret was out told him nothing, but popping downstairs to the living room to listen in to the band on a bugging device revealed his worst fear: they knew. They had seen it in the *Evening News*.

The session was a strangely quiet one. Not until it was over did he mention his problem to Roy Phillips, their guitarist, who was completely hoodwinked by Joe's frankness: "I walked into the office, and Joe's got the paper out. He says, 'I've got my name in the paper – look at that. F—— 'em!' And he even cut out the piece and pinned it on the wall. So he had no secrets – no secrets at all."

It was a crushing blow. Letting his hopes get the better of him had been foolish and as he again analyzed that brief column under the heading: "The Man Who Wrote 'Telstar'", its full significance began to dawn on him. It mattered nothing that the story had missed the headlines; it was still there on the front page, and some people in the business were bound to have noticed it. They would have cut it out and shown it around. There was no escape. He read it again for the hundredth time, but now viewed in this new light it had taken on an air of menace. Simply stating who he was and what he had been found guilty of, those twelve lines could not have cut deeper if they had been razors.

Now he realized *everyone* would know, and not only about his conviction but also his homosexuality.

And suddenly he had a new dilemma: blackmail. That tiny

215

mention in the *Evening News* had stirred up a whole hornets' nest of rogues and scoundrels, all eyes a-gleam at the thought of easy pickings. People started knocking at the door demanding money, with lines like: "You've molested my brother. I shan't say anything if you give me £50" and "Give me some money now or I'll tell my father" and "Give me £5 or I'll go to the press". So he would hand out fivers here and there hoping they would do the trick. Naturally they did not and Lional, when he was around, would send the callers packing. It became a daily occurrence dealing with rascals at the door and threats on the telephone. Some people who called felt they were honourable causes. Many were the times when he had singled out a member of a group and proposed a brief encounter upstairs. For those ambitious enough a quick fling looked worthwhile for the promise of a pot of gold recording contract, but when the contract brought no more than one flop record and a badly punctured ego the bargain looked less fair and square. One spotty herbert, known as "the weasel Dave", would come from up the road at Archway and would never give up. He wanted to be a star and had done the doings and got nothing out of it. All he ever received for his efforts was a bottle of aftershave, which Joe flung at him down the stairs. Obscene abuse from all and sundry and "I'm going to come and kill you" threats became regular messages on his answerphone. He felt unsafe going out without wearing dark glasses, and the door to the street and the upstairs one to the flat were no longer left open for the world to walk in. From now on, they would first have to introduce themselves on the intercom he fitted by the front door.

So far he had actually been lucky. None of the blackmailers had yet dared seek revenge through a solicitor. If they did, they could really cane him. But doing that, their parents would hear of it – and Joe knew that; he knew that they, like him, feared their mums finding out, and this he depended on. But he realized now he was living on a knife edge. He could see his lifestyle fast becoming common knowledge throughout the music world, and that as one of the half dozen or so elite homosexuals in the British industry – some of whom shared similarly sleazy habits, secretly partaking in a repulsive trade amongst "stables" of star-struck teenage boys – he was a prime target for the most ambitious.

That he was a corrupting influence is plain. True, the choice was theirs: some were looking for any opportunity to get on in the profession and he was merely offering them one; others needed coaxing. Either way there is no escaping the fact he was using his power for sexual gain, which was totally immoral. Years later it would be the source of many a guilty conscience; where those same young men would have a wife and children – and a skeleton in the cupboard. It will be there till they die.

Then as now, the casting couch permeated the industry and, as Mike Berry recalls, Joe had gained quite a reputation: "There was this guy that worked for a very big agency. I went to see him and he took me out for dinner. And I could tell he thought he was going to get somewhere with me physically by using his influence as an agent. He figured I was easy game because I was with Joe, and Joe was homosexual . . . There was an atmosphere in Joe's place. Sometimes if you weren't actually there just to record – if you went there for some other purpose – there was always that uneasy feeling of an ulterior motive for you being there. I went there very rarely without everybody else. We were always all afraid that Joe would be trying to get us into bed; it was a permanent fear. And we suspected every boy that went up there that they were playing ball if they didn't get out of there quick or they weren't with a bunch of other fellows. And of course, quite wrongly, we all thought, 'Bloody queers' in that horrible, narrow-minded way, but then as kids you tend to. It's the start of the bigotry of life unless you broaden your mind and say, 'Hang on, there's room for us all.' Because it was an older man seducing young boys it was considered corrupt. And yet, you look at an older man seducing a young girl, you think, 'Oh, Jack the lad' . . . It was unnerving at Joe's. I think, even myself, I'd get bizarre images of a homosexual gone berserk with a pair of scissors. That sort of thing would create the fear within you because he was such an unstable person. You'd figure he might suddenly go berserk and want to have his way with you and nothing would stop him. You always felt a little bit on edge because even when you were relaxing and joking and laughing with Joe he could suddenly change. Somebody might say the wrong thing, totally unintentionally, or carry the joke too far and he would say, 'F——you, then.' He was an unpredictable man."

𝄞𝄞𝄞𝄞𝄞𝄞𝄞𝄞𝄞𝄞𝄞𝄞𝄞𝄞

During these trying times there were thankfully a couple of things from which he could draw comfort. Firstly, the record companies appeared to be completely ignoring his recent embarrassment. They were still calling round with open arms, and Parlophone were even pushing him for an LP from Houston Wells. Secondly there was Heinz whose busy career was doing much to take his mind off his troubles; an LP had to be rushed out for January and pop programme appearances were lining up. But there was not much else to smile about.

Of the twenty records Joe had out on release during November and December, Heinz's 'Country Boy' was the only one to reach the charts; and it was not doing big business. And the EP, 'Heinz', was selling about as fast as candy floss at a funeral. He was not feeling too happy about the film situation either. *Farewell Performance*, featuring Heinz's first single, 'Dreams Do Come True', had arrived seven months too late to do it any good and was now on the circuits haunting Joe with memories of a disastrous disc and a wooden performance from Heinz. *Live It Up*, going out with Norman Wisdom's *A Stitch In Time*, was not much better, having chopped out much of Heinz and showing him again as camera-shy.

During December Beatlemania was still at its height. While Mersey groups were taking turns to head the singles charts, the Beatles had been monopolizing the top spot in the LP listings with 'Please Please Me' from May to November and 'With The Beatles' since then. Though he was beginning to like the Beatles and a few of the better beat groups he didn't like them hogging his share of the market too. There should be room for everyone, with music for all tastes, but apart from Heinz none of his acts was getting a look in. Record companies were still hedging their bets by taking most of his product in case the Liverpool sound should suddenly peter out but now they were giving his records less push, reserving their budgets for the Merseyside flavour of the month.

December saw the cutting of ties between the Tornados and Billy Fury. Since Heinz's departure there had been no less than five changes in the band's line-up, each one obviously meaning extra rehearsals. These had become irritating to Billy, whose demanding work schedule and unstable health were already more than he could cope with. His decision to find himself another band came as no shock but was a disappointment for Joe, who could now wave goodbye to his chances of recording him at 304.

INCIDENT AT MADRAS PLACE

Two more singers to wave goodbye to were amongst his top artistes. Squabbles with Decca saw him refusing to hand over his latest recording of Don Charles and resulted in the exit from Holloway Road of one of his few good singers. His farewell to Mike Berry was less surprising, for Mike says Joe had already predicted it a year earlier: "He was very bitter about Robert Stigwood taking away his artistes. He said to me one day, 'Robert Stigwood's very interested in you. Do you want to sign with him?' And I was beside myself with excitement and I said, 'Christ, not half!' He said, 'Well listen. Stigwood took Charlie Blackwell away from me and he'll do the same with you.' And I probably said something stupid like, 'Oh don't be silly, I would never...' Anyway, sure enough, soon as I went with Stigwood he took me away from Joe! Mind you, Joe blew it first. 'My Little Baby' was the beginning of the end with Joe. It reached No.30 odd. It was a dreadful record as a follow-up – I think it was only a hit on the back of the previous one. And then 'It Really Doesn't Matter'; I think Stigwood said, 'This is the last straw; I'm taking you away.' But I think there was an ulterior motive on Stigwood's part in that he figured he'd make hits with me and have a lot more money. By that time I had a track record, so I would get the plugs more easily and get the publicity more easily." But he didn't get the hits more easily. Mike's hits had never been regular, and for his next one he would have a little wait of seventeen years.

As the year lumbered to a close there was one small consolation: the fact that in spite of the scene being swamped by the Northern hordes, readers of the *NME* voted Heinz into their Top Ten category of 'Best New Singers', putting him in at No.8 behind Gerry Marsden of Gerry & the Pacemakers at No.1. Now Joe could only hope that 1964 would see the whole craze bite the dust.

1963 had certainly been a mixed bag: the 'Telstar' rewards, followed by the French lawsuit which was still lying unresolved in the hands of lawyers; the setting up of the four companies; the emergence of the Merseybeat threat; the big build-up for Heinz which turned first into fiasco and then into triumph; the bitter breaking with Robert Stigwood and Mike Berry; and finally the Madras Place nightmare which he had suffered and survived.

At Christmastime, after taking round the usual batch of over-extravagant presents to publishers, record company contacts and so on, it was with some trepidation that he drove home to see the family. All they knew of was his success.

13
Major Banks Marches Off

J oe was cheesed off. It was February and every music paper he looked at was full of hoo-hah on the Beatles. Beatlemania, far from dying the death he so eagerly wished for it, was escalating out of all proportion: "THEY'VE DONE IT AGAIN", "YANKS URGE BEATLES – PLEASE PLEASE US", "YEAH, YEAH, YEAH", "YANKEE DOODLE BEATLES", "BEATLES TOP IN THE US". Why were they making so much fuss about a British group getting an American No.1? The Tornados had done it a year before and there had been no fuss then. Nor had they needed a huge publicity campaign to help them get it. And now suddenly there were the record companies bombarding US pop fans with all the Beatles flops which had been released over there in '63: 'Please Please Me', 'She Loves You', 'From Me To You' and 'Love Me Do'. If they could have only taken a tenth of the trouble when they pushed out 'Globetrotter' and 'Ridin' The Wind' together . . . There was even talk of 'I Want To Hold Your Hand' soon outstripping 'Telstar's' three million plus to take over as Britain's biggest ever single. It was all very irritating.

He was even more annoyed about Heinz's latest record, 'Country Boy'. As a follow-up to a Top Ten hit its climb to No.26 was depressingly short-winded. He decided it must be the fault of Decca's promotions department, and made sure they knew it. Meanwhile the next Heinz single, 'You Were There', had to be a No.1, and now that Heinz was back from a quick 4,000-mile tour of Sweden with Brian Poole & the Tremeloes, there was an LP in the works too. In the event the single did not quite reach No.1 but again No.26 which meant firework time. Rows with the head of Decca, Sir Edward Lewis, and anyone else who came within range resulted in a tug-o'-war between Joe and Decca with Heinz in the middle. An uneasy truce was reached before Heinz's arms could be pulled off, and the world breathed again.

Another of the 'culprits' was his music publisher, Bob Kingston, who says he was one of the many to have his knuckles rapped when records were not faring well: "He always was critical, except in times of great success, of what was wrong. He always had to blame somebody. Say for example I had a song written by Geoff Goddard, recorded by Joe, released on EMI and nobody was buying it. It would be my fault as the publisher for not promoting or it would be the record company's fault and he would have incredible stories about how they weren't pressing it because they were getting back at him for something or other: a deliberate down-tools at the factory at Hayes because there was somebody running the overnight department there who didn't like him; or he would blame Geoff Goddard because he didn't want to record that song that Geoff had written for that particular artiste or he would blame the artiste. Joe Meek blamed everybody for everything except when there was success."

It was Bob's Southern Music Joe had in mind when he offered Geoff what he called a 'shady deal'. To get round the contract which tied Geoff exclusively to Southern, he suggested that any further songs they wrote together should bear someone else's name as composer. This way their songs could be published by his favourite Ivy Music and all royalties would be safely channelled back through that person to himself and Geoff without anyone else knowing. Geoff turned him down.

The dismal response to Heinz's last two records was making him desperate to get back in the Top Ten. Interest in him from the major companies was drying up as fast as the hits, and with the Merseybeat sound prospering worldwide he now found himself back on the old hawkaround again.

Nor did things look like improving. In fact over the next few months he was to be hit by a series of sour fortunes, the first of which played on his mind throughout February and March. It seemed he had to be ever on the look-out for sharks and shysters, who when they were not trying to break in blackmailing and threatening him over the court case, were snooping in milking his ideas. The latest idea he was convinced had been seized was now high in the charts on someone else's record. It was the pronounced stomping beat on 'Bits And Pieces' by the Dave Clark Five, the concept for which he was sure had been cribbed from a session of his with a new group called the Saxons. In emphasizing the drum beat, he had got his own effect by having the drummer bang on the floor. He remembered that while this had been going on, someone connected with the Dave Clark Five had been visiting 304, and immediately concluded the obvious. He didn't give two hoots that the song's producer, a young man by the name of Adrian Kerridge, might possibly with the benefit of three years' worth of Joe's experimenting influence, have thought up the idea himself. However, there was nothing Joe could do about it (footstomps cannot be copyrighted) and he could only watch angrily as 'Bits' climbed all the way to No.2 in the charts, forcing him to take more stringent steps to see it never happened again. Along with the notice on the first staircase exhorting musicians to carry their instruments up quietly, others were pinned around declaring that the business is full of spies and that anyone entering the premises must close their ears to any sound that came their way. Sessions would often stop abruptly, either for spot checks on musicians, who he sometimes caught with hidden tape recorders, or for the ever ominous knock at the front door.

Besides pinning up notices and intensifying his usual bug-searching operations, he was also clamping down on his music publishers. A symptom of his ever deepening sense of mistrust, through which he saw in publishers and A & R men alike all the unimpeachable integrity of used-car salesmen, was in making sure his discs were pressed *before* meeting the publisher. Usually a song is published first, then the record company gets it. However, many times after giving Southern a song, he had accused them of sabotage saying he had just detected a snatch of it on someone else's record. This he hoped would seal up more leakage of secrets.

It was just as well he never heard about another suspicious event from around this time. One day while he was upstairs recording, his office assistant Patrick Pink caught two managers of a pop group in the living room quietly playing Joe's demo acetates. In spite of their protests that Joe wouldn't mind, Patrick hustled them out knowing full well that he would, and when they asked him to say nothing he agreed. Mentioning it to Joe, who was already in a "filthy" mood that day, would have caused quite a scene, though would have removed any chance of their sidling in again from the waiting room. Acetates were piled high in the living room and for those with some pluck, were there for the taking.

This particular period would hardly seem opportune for hearing from the main person he thought was stealing his sounds! But then no time ever was, so when the American record producer Phil Spector rang up out of the blue in the hope of arranging a meeting, now was as good a time as any. Joe, of course, blew his top. Somewhere amongst the flood of invective he screamed down the telephone was an accusation that Spector had been listening to his records and pinching ideas, and then he slammed the phone down with such force that it broke.

Spector, who was over here for a couple of weeks, had become a household name in Europe and America. Great records like 'Da Doo Ron Ron', 'Then He Kissed Me', 'He's A Rebel' and 'Be My Baby' had made him at 23 the darling of the American pop scene and the most famous record producer in the world. He was the one with whom people were always comparing Joe. Like Joe he had created an instantly recognizable sound that was unique. Known as the 'Wall of Sound' it was characterized by productions which seemed like they had been made in vast cathedrals with huge orchestras and no expense spared. He achieved the effect by recording instruments in unison – 2 basses, 2 pianos, 4 acoustic guitars, half a dozen drumkits – and putting them through exceptional echo chambers.

Both men were producing records that were thick and meaty but their sounds were worlds apart. Whilst a Meek record of the period is generally on the attack, with no quiet bits, so that when the vocalist stops singing everything comes up from underneath, a Spector record has far less compression, so contains loud and quiet passages. Just as noticeable are their different styles of microphone placing: Joe's close-mike technique emphasized particular instruments, whereas Spector's distant technique helped give him, with echo, a much bigger sound. And whilst Spector sessions were planned minutely beforehand so that most of the recording was done there and then, a Meek session could well be just the beginning of a long build-up stuffing and squashing one sound on another and experimenting ad infinitum. Being an engineer himself he was better suited to this method than his rival.

But they still shared some curious personal attributes. For a start, both men suffered from a king-sized persecution complex. Spector had been a loner at school, made fun of for being Jewish, short, fat and feeble, had wished he had muscles, was smothered by his mother, terrified of girls and prone to tantrums. But he started writing songs and sitting in on recording sessions, and in 1958 arranged for a high school girl to sing his 'To Know Him Is To Love Him', all the harmonies of which he dubbed on himself. Calling themselves the Teddy Bears he gave the recording to a small label who sent it to No.1 in the States. Another singer was brought in and they all went out on a tour which he soon left after suffering the indignity of being urinated upon by four men in a lavatory. Then in mid-'61, after working for a while as a courtroom stenographer and for various record companies as a fairly successful songwriting producer, he found backers to help him set up his own label: Philles. By hiring studios he was able to start fighting the big, established companies and win, and late in '62 bought out his partners to become at 21 the youngest label chief ever.

Like Joe he was a one-man-army: picking the groups, writing or choosing their material, supervising the arrangements, directing the singers in their phrasing and masterminding the whole session. The only important differences were that he relied heavily on his engineer to get the sounds he wanted and that he had no need of major companies at all, since everything went out on his own label.

Into his records with their lovey-dovey lyrics he poured his anger and frustration. If Joe's sound could be summed up as one that powered along on the wings of the wind, then Spector's was the thunderous tread of a massed army. Each man's concept of production was always more important than the artiste or group concerned – after all, groups were two a penny – and they often made them sound the same too. And like Joe, Spector was not afraid to replace singers on record: the Crystals' 'He's A Rebel', for example, was not sung by them but by a trio called the Blossoms! Both men totally dominated their artistes; they knew what they wanted and would settle for nothing less. Most musicians Joe would at least allow some scope but always within a set framework; however talented they might be, they were there solely to translate his thoughts into music.

But Joe had studied the Spector phenomenon and it had him rattled. All this talk hailing Spector as a young genius and pioneer was a load of old hogwash when it was as clear as day that the man was no more than America's 'answer' to himself. And this huge success Spector had achieved was all thanks to the so-called 'Wall of Sound' – a variation of his own; Joe recognized the fuzziness in it as the result of multiple overdubbing, sound upon sound – like his own. There too were the instruments swamped in echo. Nor did he relish hearing chains on Spector's piano strings; such gimmicky sound effects he had used himself. That was why he always snapped the radio off when a Phil Spector record came on. And that was why he broke the phone.

Happily, although he was sure Spector had filched a few ideas for sound effects he felt confident that most of them were still safely undeciphered. All that time working on them had been well spent, not only in enhancing their commerciality but obscuring their identity. Unlike other studios who were tied by time limits he could take as long as he liked, and getting an effect could take hours if necessary. On one session he spent twice as long on the funny noise at the start as he did on the backing track. For two hours he had a guitarist running a half-crown up and down his strings, whilst he played around with the sound; the effect only lasted a few seconds. For a song called 'Lollipop', he wanted a 'finger-in-mouth-pop' and as singer-guitarist Tony Dangerfield illustrates with his own first-rate finger-popping the 'pop' had to pop perfectly: "He got a drummer doing 'pop' into the mike for about an hour, and his mouth was out here, and in the end his whole mouth had gone numb. And Joe was poking his head round the door: 'More treble, more bass.' I mean, how do you put treble or bass on doing this: 'pop'? And he's running the tape backwards, forwards, echo and compression, whatever. And he still couldn't get it right. And the office boy came in for a cheque to sign, and Joe said, 'Go to the mike and do that: 'pop'. And the guy went 'pop' and he said, 'That's the one!' And he got paid a session fee for it."

'Plopping' took longer still, and for 'Three Coins In The Sewer' two days were spent dropping marbles in the bath water and coins down the stairwell into a bucket. When he caught a cold soon afterwards he was so angry that he blamed it on the singer Alan Klein for having written the song, and would not speak to him for quite a while. The bathroom-lavatory was well used for strange noises and when he was not picking up barking from outside and stopping the session because "I've got dogs in the echo chamber" it was almost ideal. Besides cramping four violinists in there or having a drummer in there bashing away, he was known to have held red-hot pokers in the bath water and dangled a £300 Neumann microphone down the lavatory while it was flushing. His microphones may have been the best around but they must surely have been the worst treated! They would be poked, stroked, rapped and slapped, have combs and other objects scraped across them and at least once he threw one down the stairs from the studio to the office, recording it through vast quantities of reverberation as it was bouncing down. A favourite drum sound, for example, would be obtained simply by balancing a plain cardboard box over a microphone and banging it on top.

Drum sounds were a speciality. People had been marvelling at the peculiar percussive noises he got ever since his IBC days when he committed heresy dismantling bass drums to put microphones inside. Now, as then, it was still a hush-hush affair, and anyone asking about it met with a stony silence. One such secret was at last revealed when one day drummer Clem Cattini dared peep inside. The outside skin had already been removed, showing a drum full of pillows and blankets which had been tightly packed into it; snugly wrapped amongst all these and held firmly against the inner skin where the foot pedal strikes was a small cardboard box. Nicely cellotaped inside this miniature echo chamber was the microphone. It was at this point in the proceedings that Clem's investigations came to an abrupt halt when Joe burst forth in one of his famous fits accusing him of spying. On another recording where he wanted more impact from the snare drum he had a drummer hitting the beat by bringing both hands down from above his head; when that still was not loud enough he angrily grabbed a chair, snapped two legs off it and, throwing a blanket over the drum, gave them to the drummer to carry on as before. After ten minutes' thrashing, the drum stand collapsed and the drum was held firm on two chairs by the rest of the band till the end of the session.

Besides drummers beating biscuit tins, shoe boxes, bass drum cases and scaffold pipes, there were endless effects to keep the pop world guessing. The crackles of two wires shorting opens the Tornados' 'Robot', whilst another of their tracks features the exquisite clicking of a screwdriver across a jagged ashtray. The piano was often the centre of attention too, and when the lid wasn't doubling as a creaky coffin in the latest Lord Sutch spinechiller, it might well be having marbles, toilet chains or sheets of paper pressed between its strings. Ideas would come to him with finger-popping frequency: anything from jabbing holes in speakers for distortion and fluttering pages for the flapping of bats wings to the plucking of a rubber band in time with the bass line to give it more sharpness. He had ears like an elephant and many a sound he would pick up while listening in on musicians' tea breaks. The noise of a signet ring tapping a saucer would bring him bounding in gasping, "That's a good sound. Come over here and do it again by the mike." And they would hear all the variations he could get out of it. Of course, any new sound had him in raptures, eyes a-sparkle with delight and with the grin of a birthday boy being given a present.

Right now he needed any sparkles of delight he could get because the view of the music scene from his angle was looking grimmer by the day. Americans in April were going Beatle barmy, ordering two million copies of 'Can't Buy Me Love' before they had even heard it and making it the first record to reach No.1 in Britain and America simultaneously. Besides putting 'Twist And Shout', 'Can't Buy Me Love', 'She Loves You', 'I Want To Hold Your Hand' and 'Please Please Me' into their Top Five chart positions in that order (a feat that has never been equalled since), they also had them at No.1 and No.2 on their LP charts with 'Meet The Beatles' and 'Introducing The Beatles'. At this rate the Americans would be snatching up all the British matchbox music they could lay hands on and making his job even more difficult. Were it not for the constant deluge of Merseybeat which had sky-rocketed the record companies' output from an average 30 to 100 releases per week, he knew his own discs would be in with a better chance. And things would be rosier still if not for the accursed Madras Place incident . . .

It still weighed heavily on his mind making him moody and forgetful, moderating his usual zest for life and musical inspiration. The blackmail threats were still coming in unabated and he viewed those around him with suspicion or embarrassment. And underlying all was that old devil of a persecution complex, pointing with the out-thrust finger. One consequence of this sense of oppression was his peculiar system of auditioning groups. Half of the audition would take place after their actual session when the band were alone in the studio and Joe was downstairs in his living room, secretly listening in on them for twenty minutes! Any mention of his homosexuality would see them swiftly booted out, while flattering remarks might earn a contract.

Someone who understood him better than most was his publisher, Bob Kingston, though that on-off relationship of theirs was now turning more off than on. Those 'Johnny Remember Me' days when they had been in almost daily contact either phoning or writing, had long gone and Bob ascribes much of the blame to Joe's big hang-up: "He was acutely conscious of his homosexual inclinations and sought to conceal that, even from those who knew him. He never ever once admitted that situation to me. I never questioned him closely about any of his personal affairs. We had such a very good business relationship. Having said that, it was very emotional as well. It varied tremendously and weeks and months sometimes would elapse without hearing from Joe before I discovered that he wasn't talking to me. It would emerge afterwards – because he always wanted to get these things off his chest – that at the last time we were together I said something which he misconstrued as meaning directed at him, and he read it as a spite. Incidents like that occurred several times."

That court case misfortune and the Mersey menace were his two sorest subjects. They were doing much, he felt sure, to throttle his chances of placing recordings. Why else, he demanded, were the majors suddenly turning down so much of his product, the calibre of which they had craved for before? This they were doing in spite of his having toned down his echo effects since the success of the echo-rationed 'Just Like Eddie'. A prime example was a recording by another group which had been rejected by EMI and Decca and which only through his dogged persistence had been finally accepted by Pye. This one was called 'Have I The Right' by the Honeycombs and, like others of his that were being cast out, had been returned by EMI with a letter saying it was "of no commercial value". They would have snapped it up six months back.

Meanwhile, storm clouds were gathering on the Decca front. The old bugbear of having his records rejected was to spark off new strife, at the centre of which was a 24 year old Welsh singer called Tommy Scott, nowadays better known as Tom Jones. Tom's stentorian voice and Elvis hip-swivelling had branded him old-fashioned by the major companies, but when he called round to 304, Joe at once recognized the man's talent and had him sign a year's contract. Over the next few weeks Tom and his group, the Senators, drove up from Wales for their first ever recording sessions, though for someone possessing the iron throat of Tom Jones, he could just as well have stayed at home in Pontypridd and sung to Joe from there. They cut seven tracks, two of which found an interested customer in Decca. But Decca did not seem interested enough and month after month were postponing the release date, telling Joe another new singer they were launching, P.J.Proby, was taking priority. So everyone was getting fed up with everyone. Jones & Co had grown tired of the long seven-hour treks up to London, one of which had seen them arrive at Holloway Road at 10 a.m., only to have to turn back again for Wales because Joe had forgotten all about the session and was recording a band in Cheltenham. Nor did they like his offhand manner towards them, brought about by his dislike of Tom's two pushy young managers, who called themselves Myron & Byron, and contempt for the Senators, whose musical attributes he rated on a par with Kenny Lord's Statesmen; and his treatment of Tom was not exactly courteous. Whether it was a practical joke or designed to make Tom and the Senators perform better will never be known, but once during a take he stormed into the studio, pulled out a gun, levelled it at Tom and fired it! There was a loud bang and Tom thought he was done for. It was a starting pistol. Joe walked out leaving a room full of shivering wrecks. Perhaps it had something to do with Tom's tight trousers which later enticed Joe into making an advance to him, sending Tom away "steaming" and leaving Joe disappointed.

Matters came to a head one day when Myron and Byron arrived telling him they had just met Dick at Decca – he had denied all knowledge of Tom and *any* release date! After a fine old row Joe duly terminated the contract by tearing it up and slinging it in the bin. Off they went and a week later he heard they had all joined Decca. He was livid. There are no prizes for guessing what conclusion he had drawn: that Dick had told them to finish with Joe so they could sign direct. It was a logical deduction though incorrect: the Jones camp had received some timely assistance from disc jockey Jimmy Savile. And it left Jones & Co convinced that their only hope of Joe ever offering anyone their recordings, was to have had Tom submit to his wicked wishes. Anyway, coming on top of Joe's increasing dissatisfaction with Decca's promotions department – provoking another tug-o'-war over Heinz – plus their new hard-to-please attitude towards his recordings, he needed no excuse for more caustic hostility. From now on, Decca would have nothing off him at all except recordings of artistes already contracted to them; then when those contracts ran out, to hell with them – he would seek new ones elsewhere.

The next stop was Pye. Their eagerness to take over where Decca left off was matched by Joe's zeal in putting his latest singing sensation, Tony Dangerfield, their way. When the 19 year old had first come to Joe's notice he had been a Savage, playing bass guitar for Lord Sutch. Impressed as much by his Black Country arrogance as by his leather clothes, cowboy boots and long bleached hair with its pink and green streaks, Joe had started grooming him for the big time. As for the multi-coloured hair-do, Joe now had that jet black, shorter and adorned by a fancy quiff. The new Dangerfield record, 'Has Anyone,' had been accepted and for a big board meeting at Pye, Joe took him along to play up his image of insolent yob. Alas, the sight of so many cigar-chewing fatties around one table took Tony's breath away and on the journey back by taxi Joe was so disgusted with the lily-livered performance he booted him out. Nor was his choice of phrase polite a month later when instead of the record going out on release it came back to him again with a request for a new title and for strings to be added.

But all the fine, fighting talk and angry scenes were bringing scant sunshine. As far as record sales went the year so far had been a non-starter and now once again he found himself riding on the crest of a slump.

The records of his biggest band, the Tornados, now had a note of desperation creeping in and with the blight of good melodies continuing, he was covering up with more outlandish effects: 'Hotpot' opened with what sounded like a herd of pigs grunting and snorting. So after reading that he was turning out "the same old thing" he decided in June to get right away from pigs and outer space and record a 'live' Tornados version of the 'Theme From Exodus' during their *Big Star Show Of '64* at Blackpool. It flopped.

He also had a new personal problem to make him curse. Much against his will he was now having to send his precious Heinz away on tour here, there and everywhere. Heinz had committed the cardinal sin of finding himself a girlfriend, a cinema usherette called Della, whom he had met whilst on tour in Bournemouth. Joe was green-eyed with jealousy and in a flash Della had leap-frogged over Dick Rowe, Major Banks, Robert Stigwood and Larry Parnes to the No. 1 spot on his list of Public Enemies. Gone were the days when he wanted Heinz locked up safe and sound at 304 away from the screaming multitudes, because he knew the fellow would soon be shinning down the drainpipe now that Della was on the loose and would be legging it to Bournemouth at every opportunity. Well, as Heinz had said he liked going touring, then touring he would go! Already this year he had played in Sweden, Finland, toured Britain with the Rolling Stones, then with Joe Brown, the Crystals and Manfred Mann and appeared on a string of ballroom dates which suddenly Joe no longer considered the "kiss of death". Right now Heinz was winning over the mums and dads in a summer season with Arthur Askey at Rhyl and after that Joe had plans to send him out to Australia, the Far East . . . anywhere; the farther the better to help Della forget him.

Good news came at the end of July. After nearly two months on release the Honeycombs' 'Have I The Right' entered the charts, giving him a welcome send-off for his fortnight's holiday, and off he flew with a new friend to Majorca. Mooching round the hotel swimming pool and soaking up the sun made a well-earned break, and apart from his songwriting and some recordings he had taken along, there was nothing to remind him of work. Besides cine filming and recording sound effects, the only semi-strenuous thing they did was smash a window; amongst the souvenirs he was taking back was a metal wall ornament and this he had asked to have altered, but on calling round later to collect and pay for it he found the shop shut. With their flight back booked for that night he was very pleased to be told by one of the locals that smashing the window and leaving the money was the done thing, so he did it.

On his return mixed fortunes awaited. The good news was that 'Have I The Right' had zoomed into the Top Ten, giving him the possibility of buying out the Major. The bad news was that Geoff Goddard was disputing the song's authorship. He was saying it was not the composers Ken Howard and Alan Blaikley who had written it, but himself and Joe. He recognized it as a song he had brought to the studio in April called 'Give Me The Chance', and which during its subsequent modification they had retitled 'Have I The Right'. Joe dismissed it as drivel. Their relationship was already strained, for since Geoff had heard from Lional of the troubles Joe had been having at 304 following the court case, the thought that he himself might be beaten up walking to the studio was frightening him away. As a result he was either arriving at the door in a taxi or, more often, sending tapes by post. Joe interpreted it differently. In his eyes Geoff was simply trying to avoid being seen associating with him after the Madras Place publicity.

This clash was to mark the end of their working together. Fittingly, the last song of Geoff's that Joe had recorded was a tribute to yet another great singer, Jim Reeves, who in July had died piloting a private plane. Sung by Houson Wells, it was doomed to stay unreleased.

And more spitting, snapping and teeth-gnashing was soon going on around Tony Dangerfield. Joe had arrived back to be faced with a much shorter-haired Tony than the one he had left behind. The perpetrator of this knavery was none other than the very man into whose safekeeping he had entrusted him: his accountant-partner Tom Shanks. When the chance of a spot on TV's *Ready Steady Go!* had cropped up, Shanks had flown him to the nearest barber then sent him off spick and span in a new regular cut suit and tie: perfect rejection material for an intensely fashion conscious pop programme that included in its line-up the trendy Kinks and the Rolling Stones! The hair, Joe screamed,

THE LEGENDARY JOE MEEK

would take months to grow. Perhaps it was just as well the record's release had again been postponed.

In the third week of August 'Have I The Right' climbed to No.2. Now his mind was made up: it was time he put Banks on his bike. A meeting of RGM Sound directors was duly arranged for the following week. Come 5 o'clock on August 27, a day that smiled on his decision when 'Have I The Right' clinched the No.1 position, Joe and the Major arrived at the Strand. In a cordial atmosphere Banks presented his final bill for £14,999.4s.6d. covering expenses. The amount was agreed upon, Banks signed out, Shanks signed in. This time, though, Joe was giving away only one of the 50 shares the Major had sold back to him, keeping an unchallengeable 99 for himself. He had learnt his lesson.

♩♩♩♩♩♩♩♩♩♩♩♩♩♩

In its first week at No. 1, 'Have I The Right' was reported to have earned a Silver Disc and by the second week it had sold half a million copies. The record was up there for a fortnight (three weeks in the *Disc* chart), creating plenty of fresh work. It also brought him a sorely annoying rumour in the press regarding the stomping rhythm which featured prominently on the disc. The accusation he had earlier levelled at the Dave Clark Five that they had pinched the idea off him for 'Bits And Pieces' was now being levelled at him, saying he had pinched it off them for 'Have I The Right'! So he told the Honeycombs' girl drummer to inform journalists he had been into heavy marching feet on Anne Shelton's 'Lay Down Your Arms' long before the Dave Clark Five were even thought of.

The story of the session itself is nowadays one of the most recounted of all amongst the people who worked at 304 and the Honeycombs' lead singer, Dennis D'Ell, remembers it like yesterday: "It was all over and done with in no time. We did about four takes of it and I did about two or three vocal tracks . . . Joe was trying for a bass drum sound and couldn't get what he wanted and came in saying, 'Stop, stop, stop', and lined us up on the stairs; Anne stayed on the bass drum. We had about four mikes to cover the length of the staircase, with bicycle pump clips under the stairs and he just clipped the mikes into them. For about an hour we all stood stomping in time with the music. His cleaner had actually been cleaning the stairs and was waiting at the bottom for us to finish. I don't think she understood what was going on."

The record was a wonder drug. Though to Joe its climb to No.1 was no mind-boggling marvel and more a case of when than whether, it could not have had a more refreshing effect. On its own it made him cast off the foul memories of past months, exciting and energizing him with the prospects that lay ahead, all of which looked ten times better now he had slipped the chains of Major Banks. Overall control was at last his. Gone with the Major were the profit-milking days and ahead lay golden years of unfettered creativity. It was like a whole new world.

The whole new world though still allowed scope for the occasional tantrum! While the record was at No.1 and during a recording session for the obligatory Honeycombs LP, a film unit from ITN headed by newscaster Peter Snow arrived to interview the group. Joe had of course already agreed to the visit but, needless to say, when all these men suddenly appeared humping lights and filming apparatus, interrupting both his train of thought and a pressing album session, he was riled to say the least. At first he told them to get out and come back another day, then giving in he stormed off telling them to let him know when it was over. While they were setting up, Peter Snow had the bright idea of having the record playing in the backbround and as no copy was to hand, he had a word with Dennis D'Ell. "I'll go down and ask Mr. Meek," he told him. – "Oh, I shouldn't do that if I were you," D'Ell advised. "Not in the frame of mind he's in at the moment." All the same, he did. He went down and knocked on the living room door and waited; there was no reply, so he tried again, but still nothing. Then he committed the fatal error of opening the door and peeping in. A piercing scream of "Get out!" rent the air and an electric razor came flying across the room, smashing into bits on the door. Snow went scrambling back up the stairs to breathlessly tell them, "That bloody man's mad!" In the end he got his way though, had the record playing in the background and then Joe resumed the session.

With the success of 'Have I The Right' the challenge was naturally to sustain the momentum but it was going to be tough. His fourth No.1 was, like the others by Emile Ford & the Checkmates, John Leyton and the Tornados, the group's first hit, so once again anything less than another chart-topper would automatically be seen as a decline. Thus all the records following in hot pursuit were nail-biters including Heinz's latest which, after two months of bargaining between EMI and Decca, was finally coming out on Columbia.

Meanwhile, he could catch glimpses of Heinz jetting in and out from Australia, Scandinavia and so on and sit back to watch himself on Granada TV's *World In Action*, giving a brief chat about being an independent producer. Characteristically he used up his segment by taking a swipe at record companies: ". . . I met with a lot of difficulties because I kept coming up with hits, and the A & R men and different people tied to these major companies were inclined to be a little bit envious and complained about the plugs my records were getting. So I have to watch these people like a hawk."

He was also the subject of a 30-minute colour film, A *Day In The Life Of Joe Meek*. This was shot one weekend in September showing him at work in the studio. Apparently it reached cinema screens but has since sadly disappeared.

The next few weeks won him none of the spoils he had promised himself. His latest multi-pronged assault on the Top Ten had the impact of a water pistol. The performance of the Honeycombs' follow-up was pathetic, worming its weary way up to No.38 and doubtless only getting that far on the back of 'Have I The Right'. Nor were Columbia ready to kill the fatted calf when Heinz's debut disc for them only managed No.39. As for his other protégé, Tony Dangerfield: his record failed to show at all. This Joe angrily attributed to bias on the part of Pye's promotions department, who he believed had spitefully withdrawn four TV spots they had secured for Tony and re-allocated them to Sandie Shaw. Perhaps that was pretty smart work, seeing how her 'Always Something There To Remind Me' went on to top the charts and launch another Sixties success story.

The alliance with Tony soon started coming unstuck. Giving a rocking Savage gooey love songs to sing and keeping him off tours till he had a hit record was not doing much for the singer's morale. For a while Joe kept him sweet allowing him any money he wanted for expenses and his ex-wife's maintenance, thus saving him from a fourth arrest for non-payment. But time was dragging for the young rock'n'roller and his impatience was not eased by the touch of intrigue in which he saw himself as a pawn in one of Joe's vendettas. Joe, he believed, had not only made him an 'answer' to Billy Fury but had poached Billy's fan club secretary from under the nose of Larry Parnes. According to Tony, Joe was convulsed with laughter on hearing that Parnes had called round to the secretary's office and that instead of finding pictures of Billy adorning the walls, was shocked to see Tony's. However, Tony found none of it funny and turned his back on 304 to take to the road again.

Honeycombs fortunes were still mixed. While 'Have I The Right' was selling well around the world and up at its highest position of No.4 in the States, helping earn a Gold Disc presentation from Jimmy Savile, their third single was doing nothing. 'Eyes', a slow, boring, bluesy exercise in how to destroy a pop group's popularity in one fell swoop, was for a change not Joe's fault but that of their co-managers, Ken Howard and Alan Blaikley. These two young men were the ones writing the material and showing little of the superb songwriting mastery that was soon to generate a string of hits for Dave Dee, Dozy, Beaky, Mick & Tich.

Had things worked out right that very string of hits might have come from Holloway Road. Following 'Have I The Right's' success, Dave Dee & Co (then called Dave Dee & the Bostons) were the next new act that Howard and Blaikley sent round, but proved less docile than the Honeycombs. After driving up from Salisbury one day, they did a few takes of another Howard & Blaikley song, 'Strange Things Happen', but found one of his unethical recording techniques hard to swallow. Revving up recordings afterwards was a favourite trick of his, with voices approaching the Mickey Mouse frequency if musicians played slowly enough. When they complained that they were getting no feeling, Joe told them not to worry but to carry on playing slowly and he would speed it all up later. The group then glumly buckled down for more takes, but during the tea break things came to a head when he objected to the rebellious attitude of Tich by throwing a trayful of coffee at him, and when Dozy threatened to ram a microphone up a certain part of his anatomy, Joe promptly made one of his dramatic exits, calling off the session.

On the 'Have I The Right' front, meanwhile, more problems were starting. Geoff Goddard was setting legal wheels in motion in preparation for a showdown.

Thumbing through the music press offered him as much comfort as toothache. The glut of Beatles jabber was raging on unabated. In the twelve months to August, they had notched up the biggest sales ever in a year with an estimated 35 million, and 'I Want To Hold Your Hand' had overtaken 'Telstar' as Britain's biggest seller. During their summer tour in America, armies of police had been required to escort their every movement and souvenir hunting had reached unheard of proportions. Amongst the more bizarre items of merchandise, bottled 'Beatle breath' was said to have sold well in New York, whilst bedlinen they had used in Denver hotels had been cut into 3-inch squares, each set on parchment with a legal affidavit certifying it as once forming part of a Beatle bed and now selling at $10 a square. The quest for souvenirs was taking on an air of worship, with audiences throwing peanuts and jellybeans onstage to be crushed under the Beatles' boots and collected in pieces afterwards. Reports that girls had been falling to their knees to eat the grass which the Fab Four had walked on hardly boosted his hopes of a quick fizzle-out of Beatlemania or Merseybeat. A glance at December's British charts revealed a big nothing in the way of RGM sounds but the usual plethora of beat groups, led again by the Beatles in top spot with 'I Feel Fine'. The number of them now operating in Britain was set at a full 27,000.

The problem had given rise to a new threat: the independent producer. Until recently Joe had had the pop-leasing game more or less tied up but since the chronic beat group outbreak, competition on his side of the fence had started. Besides Robert Stigwood, there were amongst others Andrew Oldham, who had briefly worked for Joe as a publicist and was now producing for the Rolling Stones, and new whizz kid Mickie Most. Singing in a duo, the Most Brothers, then emigrating to South Africa to produce records had given Most enough flair and confidence to start hiring studios in London, reeling off half a dozen Top Twenty hits since the summer. Unearthing material and talent were turning out to be his two great fortes, and amongst the acts demonstrating it for him were the Animals with 'House Of The Rising Sun', Herman's Hermits with 'I'm Into Something Good' and the Nashville Teens with 'Tobacco Road'.

People were at last cottoning on to the fact that anyone with a spark of imagination, a competent group and a fistful of notes could simply book a few hours in a studio and fool around till he got a new sound. The more success the Meek's, Most's, Stigwood's and Oldham's were seen chalking up, the more appealing the prospects looked. Joe's thoughts about his new rivals were negative. Intensely jealous of their success, he saw them cashing in on his groundwork, ritzing it up on the influential social circuit, which may have been opening the gates wider, but what use was that if too many independents were there to

236

squeeze in?

Rounding off another muddled year was his bleakest *NME* poll since 1960. Slipping down to No.7 in the 'Top Ten Instrumental Bands' were the Tornados, while the Honeycombs had only scraped in at No.15 in the '15 Best New Groups' stakes. No one else had got a look in. At the same time Andrew Oldham's Stones and Mickie Most's Animals and Herman's Hermits were all more popular. 'House Of The Rising Sun' was voted 'Best Record Of The Year'.

However, Joe's lacklustre chart and poll showings paled into piddling insignificance when viewed in the light of that million selling 'Have I The Right'. His second biggest seller had systematically lifted him up by the seat of his pants and flung him back into his old rapid-firing routine, giving him the heart to get on with the rest of his life. So, what else mattered when a record could do all that?

14
"You Are In One Helluva Mess"

Joe's big January highlight was the Tornados' first release in six months: 'Granada'. Their debut disc on Columbia was a prime, peppy performance of the old Latin standard and went out with the news that 'Telstar' had just clocked up its 4th million. But good though it was, the style was right out of keeping with 1965's charts and he waited in vain for the record to show up.

Nearly everyone from the pre-Merseybeat era was feeling the pinch and even the Shadows were starting to struggle. And while the Beatles were still to the fore with their "matchbox music" the Stones were rolling close behind, spearheading the rhythm'n'-blues movement. He was not exactly wild about that style either but nonetheless was tackling it with the help of groups like the Syndicats, the Blue Rondos, Bobby Rio & the Revelles and Shade Joey & the Night Owls. The sound he was getting with some of them was much cleaner, capturing the British r'n'b style perfectly and losing all links with that familiar Joe Meek ring, though rewarding him with modest sales and the usual glut of no-hit-wonders.

No doubt he could have learnt a lesson from Phil Spector whose 21st hit on his Philles label, the Righteous Brothers' brilliantly monolithic 'You've Lost That Lovin' Feelin'', was currently thundering up to the top. It was only his 24th single for the label. In contrast Joe's singles' output during that same three-year period was a whopping 141 ! Joe could still point out that in terms of domestic chart success he was marginally ahead with 25 British Top Forty hits, as opposed to Spector's 21 in the American Hot 100, but the fact was that had he been spending as much time and effort on as few acts as Spector – six – thus cutting out the other 80 percent of his product, which was mostly dead wood, he too might have been enjoying some of the latter's astounding consistency. "My belief," Spector explained to the music press, "is that every disc issued should be a hit. Big labels put out hundreds of discs, but every one I put out I intend for the charts. People are amazed by my measure of success . . . But my theory is that unless there's something worth recording, don't record. I'd sooner wait six months and come up with a good disc rather than bring out regular mediocre discs." Like Spector, he should by now have learnt to concentrate on far fewer acts instead of spreading himself so thin. But lack of discipline was a lasting weakness. As usual he was finding it incredibly hard sustaining interest in those that failed to achieve hit status; he couldn't even sit it out for long with famous names like the Tornados. The daily distraction of starry eyed hopefuls coming up the stairs with their handsome, young faces and different sounds was one temptation he could not resist, and so there was this assembly line turnover of unsuccessful acts intermingled with occasional winners, who were guaranteed his support as long as they held his fly-by-night enthusiasm.[29]

Another artiste for whom his enthusiasm was waning was Heinz. In spite of the latest record, 'Diggin' My Potatoes', enjoying a bumper EMI press reception with stalls serving hot baked potatoes and Joe elbowing a shy Heinz around for lots of interviews, it only squeezed in at No.49. As a result Heinz started losing interest in recording and taking long steps to escape from the Joe Meek sphere of influence by moving out of Joe's other flat at 54 Great Peter Street, Westminster which had, incidentally, been Petula Clark's and was now being rented to Joe by Tom Shanks as a tax dodge. When he also ceased contacting him and tried to arrange with Shanks a release from his contract, Joe exacted swift retribution by having Heinz's new Zephyr Estate and the boat 'Globetrotter' repossessed; then he started recouping some of the money he had lavished on the singer's publicity and wardrobe which included umpteen suits, shirts and shoes, and trying to pay back £2,661 worth of bills to various creditors of Heinz Burt Ltd.

Although he was still smitten by Heinz he had never liked the feeling it gave him. Much as he would have preferred being faithful to just one person it was a situation he found impossible to fall in with. On top of that, there had been many a time when he felt he was being used and had – until now – been unable to do a thing about it. A half-hearted peace treaty was finally reached, with Heinz agreeing to continue recording and Joe promising not to allow his possessiveness to keep him 'trapped' in the flat, but relations between them remained strained.

The Honeycombs, meanwhile, were in almost the same peculiar position as Michael Cox had been a couple of years back. While their releases in Britain were barely scraping the charts, elsewhere those same records were making them one of the hottest acts on the international scene! Apart from reaching Top Tens around the world, 'Have I The Right' had topped the charts in Australia, Japan and South Africa, whilst Sweden had given them four No.1's in a row. Their poor showing at home they blamed on 'Have I The Right' for giving them a happy, mums-and-dads image, losing them credibility with discerning teenagers.

It was at this time that he set up a brand new company called Meeksville Sound. Subject to his obtaining funds and permission, he intended having a neon sign placed across Holloway Road reading "WELCOME TO MEEKSVILLE". At first it was simply to be the new name of RGM Sound, but Tom Shanks had been trumpeting the advantages of a second RGM Sound ever since the 'Telstar' copyright action first raised its ugly head. Why, he asked, should they keep building up RGM with further assets when the Frenchman might win the case and nab the lot? Far better would be to start afresh with a similar company and let RGM die the death. Evidently Shanks was quite a cautious man speculating that the £100,000 plus of 'Telstar's' receipts which was piling up out of Joe's reach, would fail to satisfy the Frenchman who would still be grubbing for more. Anyway, that was what he impressed upon Joe and surprisingly collected an equal share in the new company for his trouble.

From here on, the 'Telstar' proceedings were to have a more and more crucial effect upon his life. Latest news came from eminent musicologist, Rex W. Gray. Presenting his Report – the location of which is now apparently long since forgotten – he compared 'Telstar' with 'Austerlitz', and began by pointing out on a blackboard that the two main melody lines had three things in common: the first one being that each one stayed in its same key throughout its length; the second, that they were both diatonic, meaning they were limited to the seven notes of the diatonic scale; and the third, that both used similar, though not identical, melodic outlines for their opening phrase.

Starting his analysis on such a sombre note sounded very ominous indeed and seemed all set to blast Joe's tattered hopes to Bakawanga. After all, if even an English expert was admitting similarities, what possible chance could he have of winning? As it happened, it was not a bad one.

The very fact, said Mr. Gray, that there were only seven notes to play with meant that the works of composers using this scale must always bear resemblances, especially since it has been used as a basis of melody writing for centuries. Then, spouting forth on the similarities and differences between the two pieces, he wedged in enough quavers, semi-quavers, demisemi-quavers and hemidemisemi-quavers to make a music-master get his crotchets twisted. In a Report running for ten pages he dissected every bar and beat and picked at the remains.

One vital factor, he explained, is the way in which music is used. Ingredients such as mood, words, instruments and singers all play a part in its impact on the listener. So for a start, the writing of 'Austerlitz' as a straightforward marching song for a film theme and the writing of 'Telstar' as a purely instrumental piece with an underlying 'bolero' rhythm for guitars to commemorate a television satellite showed distinct differences in their nature.

That led him into his pièce de résistance: harmonic and rhythmic structure. This would be the most critical factor in judging whether or not Joe actually had stolen 'Telstar' from 'Austerlitz'.

'Telstar's' harmony and persistent rhythm are, he stressed, as important to the piece as the melody above them. Therefore since the composition makes an impact as a whole, it has to be regarded as such. The chord pattern running all through it is a very common one – I-vi-ii-V – having been used by students and composers since the 16th Century and still being used by modern guitarists. As any composer will know, he said, it is from chord patterns like this that melodies are often put together. Mr. Meek did not need to have studied harmony and composition to know of them and, like so many thousands of others before him, had probably just sat down at the piano or with a guitar to play them over and over, letting the tune grow naturally from them.[30] The Frenchman, he added, might have done the same with 'Austerlitz' but had used completely different chords from those in 'Telstar'.

At last came the expert's long-awaited verdict. Apart from both pieces being entirely different in concept, purpose, style, rhythm, pulse and form, the only part of either of them bearing any resemblance to the other was the first phrase of each, being four bars of 'Telstar' and eight bars of 'Austerlitz'. These could hardly be called original by either composer, appearing as they already had in such compositions as 'Rule Britannia' (". . . This was the Charter, the Charter of the land . . .") and others. If someone were to isolate short threads of melody from any work and compare them with similar threads from other works, the majority of composers throughout the centuries would be found guilty of copyright infringement![31] In any case, even if Mr. Meek had in fact heard 'Austerlitz' before writing 'Telstar', the phrase in question was so short and different in rhythm and character

THE LEGENDARY JOE MEEK

and the melody proceeded along such totally differing lines that the two had no comparison worthy of being considered in terms of infringement of copyright.

A French translation of that Report, thought Joe, should take the edge off the Frenchman's appetite.

May provided Joe with the best laugh he had had for months. Since leaving Holloway Road nearly a year back, his erstwhile singer Tommy Scott had blossomed into Tom Jones and, still with Decca, had recently bellowed his way to the top of the charts with his first hit, 'It's Not Unusual', and with the record also climbing up to the Top Ten in America, young Tom was becoming a very busy boy indeed. What a charming opportunity, thought Joe, to relive those happy days of a year ago and salute Tom and all the friends at Decca by issuing some of Tom's old recordings. No doubt they would really appreciate the gesture and wish him healthy record sales. This time round, of course, he had no trouble at all finding a taker for 'Little Lonely One', and Columbia were so keen to get it on the market that they rush-released it just in time to see Tom's latest disc, 'Once Upon A Time', break into the Top Fifty. Now, he mused, with the prospect of two Tom Jones records in the Hit Parade together, wouldn't they all be raising a cheer and singing his praises? First one to fling his cap in the air was Tom: "This 'Little Lonely One' is something I could well do without. I made it a long time ago . . . and tastes have changed a lot since then. They were tough days when the group and I made 'Little Lonely One'. We were called Tommy Scott & the Senators and we really pinned our hopes on the recording session we had with Joe Meek. 'Little Lonely One' was one of seven tracks we did that day. Joe said it was great and he was going to get it released, but we didn't hear any more. We had a big row about it and in the end we got our contract back. It was two years before a chance came again – and now they bring out this relic from the past. I think it's dated and I'd like to dissociate myself from it." Joe gave as good as he got: "I have four other tapes of his which I would like to release. Tom auditioned for me and nobody wanted to know about him because it was the time when the group scene was very 'in' and everybody said he sang too well. I originally did him singing 'Chills And Fever', the record that Decca finally released re-recorded. I wouldn't have released this if I thought it was poor. I have tapes cut by Cliff Bennett, Sounds Incorporated and the Swinging Blue Jeans, but I have no intention of releasing them. I think this is a very good

242

record. It is something I am proud of and I believe it will do Tom a lot of good. He should be glad it is coming out."

Well Joe was, for it split Tom's sales in two, giving his red-hot breakthrough quite an icy dousing. Over in America a little more 'harmless' cashing in netted Joe a handy No.42 on Billboard's chart. Yes, it certainly paid to hang onto old recordings.

'Little Lonely One's' sales, though, were chicken feed compared with what he was expecting from the Tornados' latest, 'Early Bird'. Celebrating the launch of another TV satellite, this was the one with which he planned to put the band bang on top again with "a certain No.l", and having lost their last original member, drummer Clem Cattini, he renamed them Tornados '65 to hot up their fresh initiative. Exhilarating rocket sound effects introduced a compulsive beat and a better melody than of late, this time abandoning the spacey clavioline for raucous saxes and a manic guitar solo. He was so pleased with the result that he thought he had found himself another 'Telstar'. But instrumentals were having tough times and neither the good reviews nor Joe's hell-bent optimism were reflected in the charts, where it only reached the *Melody Maker's*, nosing in for just one week at No.49.

Naturally, after watching 'Early Bird's' shabby showing he was in no mood to welcome competition from members of his very first Tornados group. So when he was handed a demo disc they had produced under the name of the Original Tornados, with the titles 'Gemini'/'Goodbye Joe', he flung it across the room screaming, "Over my dead body!" If they kept the name, he threatened, he would sue them for breach of copyright. So they changed it to the Gemini and the record, good but out-dated, came out unsuccessfully a month later.

In June, the dispute over who had the right to 'Have I The Right' was at last heard in court. For two days those concerned trooped up to the Royal Courts of Justice in the Strand to decide who really had written the song. Geoff Goddard was on a sticky wicket from the start. His claim that the song had not been written by Ken Howard and Alan Blaikley but by himself and Joe would have stood a chance if Joe had at least agreed. But he didn't. He said he had had nothing whatever to do with the song till recording the Honeycombs playing it. So, was Geoff in the wrong or was he the one telling the truth, with Joe siding against him in order not to imperil his new found success with the Honeycombs?

The first two days dealt entirely with evidence presented by the plaintiffs, Ivy Music.

Obviously much depended on the date that each side said it was written. Compared with the Goddard claim that it was April '64, Messrs. Howard and Blaikley stated adamantly that they had composed it back in November '63, and that in January '64 they had offered it to the group, who were then performing three or four times a week at the Mild May Tavern in Balls Pond Road.

A demonstration recording was played that they said traced the actual stages the song went through in being composed. In fact the wealth of information they presented, plus the biting resolve of Ken Howard's solicitor father fighting for his son, sent such tremors through the Goddard camp that they advised Geoff to drop his counter-claim forthwith or it could cost him every penny he had.

That he had written the song with Joe, he had not one atom of doubt. His Counsel however thought otherwise and told him he hadn't a chance. So he gave up the fight. That meant that none of his evidence, including his own demonstration recording of the song's development, was presented. In an out-of-court settlement, Geoff agreed to admit that Ivy Music owned the copyright and to pay all costs, and was then ordered by the judge to stop alleging he had any interest in the song.

His lawyer, Frank Whitworth Q.C., said afterwards, "Mr Goddard has been persuaded to adopt this course much against his convictions. He is firmly convinced that he worked out with Mr. Meek a tune on the same terms. He is a composer of some distinction and would not knowingly seek to take someone else's song." That would be the last Joe ever heard of him.

♪♪♪♪♪♪♪♪♪♪♪♪♪♪

With work easing off, there was more time to contemplate the broader issues going on around him, a few of which could hardly fail to catch his attention. A slackening of moral standards had been triggered by the economic boom of the late Fifties and early Sixties – the time when in Harold Macmillan's famous words, people had "never had it so good" – and was fuelled by such things as the introduction of the Pill, the publication for the first time in full of *Lady Chatterley's Lover*, the release of films like *Room At The Top*, *Alfie*, *Dr. No*, *Blow-Up* and the series of sex scandals involving judges and MPs that had helped the Government lose the election to Harold Wilson's Labour Party. All this had brought about a daring new 'permissive society'.

Spending power was greater than ever before and nowhere more so than amongst the section of teenagers who called themselves 'Mods'. They were characterized by their love of dancing, fashionable clothes, motor scooters and of descending upon holiday resorts to wage beach battles with their rivals, the 'Rockers'. Helping many dance the night away were a variety of readily available 'boosters' (amphetamines), such as 'purple hearts', 'black bombers', 'french blues' and 'nigger minstrels' (black and white slimming capsules), all of which were known on the music scene and naturally to Joe as well. He had been pill-popping for years and no day went by without his downing something or other. A shelf full of aspirins, painkillers, barbiturates, amphetamines and tranquillizers occupied a cupboard in the living room and no doubt offered many a magical remedy for temper tantrums.

Less demand for his work meant more time for new pursuits. People calling round had often urged him to find a hobby to help him relax, so he finally acted on their advice by taking up painting "anything unusual". It might have helped get his mind off irritating reports in the music press, such as those proclaiming the Beatles to be more popular than ever, having drawn pop history's largest audience at New York's Shea Stadium; of Tom Jones who had just hit No.3 on *Billboard's* Hot 100 with 'What's New Pussycat', whilst a reckoning up of Heinz's chart positions so far that year placed him at No.85 in the popularity stakes, alongside plump and jolly piano player Mrs. Mills.

Confining himself between four walls day in and day out was another frowned-upon practice, but he could sometimes be tempted out in the evenings to cinemas and graveyards. Ghosthunting in reportedly haunted spots was very exciting, and he would drive off in the dead of night with a map, portable tape recorder and a friend to cling onto in case they had company. Investigations at Holy Cross Church in Basildon, where cleaning staff had reported seeing a spirit monk walking about, revealed nothing untoward, so after a few visits recording the wind, rain and creaky trees he tried the more handy Highgate Cemetery. Treading timidly amongst the gravestones with heart pounding and knees a-knocking, panic-stricken at the sight of his own shadow, it was just as well he never saw a soul. Had he glimpsed some pale, wraith-like shape rising from a grave his ensuing shrieks as he flew across the gravestones would probably have scared the poor spook back to life. Way back in his IBC days, for example, he had fled down the infamous back staircase behind the studios and into the street screaming that the place was haunted, and from then on had refused to work there alone at night.

One night at Highgate he did bump into a notorious grave-robber wandering around in the darkness – the self-styled 'High Priest' David Farrant – and probably nearly fainted with fright but recovered enough to arrange further rendezvous with him. There was also a visit to Warley Lea Farm, a deserted farmhouse outside Brentwood and the scene of some allegedly ghostly occurrences since a farmer had hanged himself from a balustrade. Arriving at midnight he and a friend walked round the house with a torch and tape recorder and were amazed when a cat came up to them to say in half human tones what sounded like "hello" and "help me". After a conversation of "hellos" between Joe and the cat, he asked it to show them a way into the house, whereupon it led them up some steps and onto the verandah. The rest was disappointing because all was locked and barred, and the cat reverted to cat language. Still, its voice was on tape and he loaned the recording to the Society for Psychical Research, who were very impressed and agreed that the dead farmer was now probably talking again.

At the same time his living room table was still serving well for the ever popular seances. One seance idea currently in vogue amongst spiritualists was to hang up a horn in the hope of coaxing spirits into floating up and speaking through it. First he tried it with an old HMV gramophone horn suspended from the ceiling over the table, and then with a paper one that he made, but nothing happened.

Besides holding seances his growing insecurity in what the future held had him visiting fortune-tellers in Soho and ringing or sometimes visiting Mrs. Smith, a medium in Essex who would tell him the best days to record. "Peter Sellers," he would say, "never makes a decision without consulting his medium." But Tarot cards or tumbler-and-alphabet sessions which he would hold at the flat with a small circle of mostly homosexual friends still carried a lot of weight. Much of his enthusiasm for them can be attributed to one man who was the epitome of the kind of person he would have sung and played like if he could, and who he was convinced was guiding him in both his songwriting and his day-to-day life: Buddy Holly.

YOU ARE IN ONE HELLUVA MESS

The singer never seemed far away. New Holly records were continually being unearthed and revamped, rising high in the charts and keeping the name so alive that some people suspected he was just that. Many records like 'True Love Ways', 'Bo Diddley' and 'Brown-Eyed Handsome Man' had done well, maintaining his position in the *NME's* Top Ten poll of World Musical Personalities, and he was now being recognized as a major influence on the Sixties beat movement. The Beatles, for example, had taken their insect name while thinking of the Crickets, and the first disc they ever cut was a version of 'That'll Be The Day'.

To Joe's avid interest, accompanying every new release were fresh facts about Holly: his and his producer's techniques, his phenomenal contribution to pop music and various facets of his personality and background. From these Joe had discovered some intriguing parallels with himself. Apart from the usual clutch of coincidences, such as both men being songwriters who were shy and quiet and both having two brothers, one sister and false front teeth – all of which for Joe held vital significance – there were other more substantial similarities. Both men were totally music orientated, innovators in their field, and their recordings were being released independently by the tape-lease process; each of them had tasted outstanding success, with Holly reaching the top, dying and becoming more highly regarded than ever – a legend. So, when on at least one occasion Joe voiced the opinion that "Buddy went the right way", it was possible to fathom his reasoning.

When musicians stayed overnight he would sometimes talk about him – how he believed Holly's creativity had never been fully realized and that it was still being channelled into music – though for reasons of his own he rarely divulged the fact they once met or what prompted the meeting.

In seances it was Holly he usually called upon first and if he were not available he would ask for Eddie Cochran or "any earthbound spirits". For an hour or more, two or three times a week, sometimes late into the night, he would relay messages back and forth, and by some accounts he was a remarkably efficient intermediary between those who were here and those who were hereafter. Occasionally sceptics have declared he was purposely steering the glass, but more often than not, participants were taken aback by results they found inexplicable. 'Signs' that were received, such as an organ playing upstairs on its own, a guitar string twanging or certain record numbers in the pile being quoted as proof that Buddy Holly was speaking, mean nothing nowadays in cold print; nor do the tales of bad seances, where apparently the glass would whizz round and furniture lift up scaring them all out of their wits. But whatever truth lay in any of it, he had certainly got enough encouragement to have had a growing fascination since 1957.

Sometimes it could be excellent therapy, for although serious seances were serious indeed – and woe betide anyone who laughed, because everything would fly off the table, the offender would be booted out and Joe would flounce off to bed – it did at least get his mind partially off his work. Were he moody and ill-tempered beforehand, starting a sitting would magically trans-form his scowls to smiles and it was not rare for the meeting to turn into a cliquey social gathering with Joe tippling his vodka and lime, disrespectfully mixing spirits with spirits.

Still, perhaps that was safer than dabbling in black magic, which was also beginning to attract his attention. Gleaning information from the works of Dennis Wheatley and Aleister Crowley revealed all sorts of tempting possibilities, besides offering as much danger and excitement as he could ever wish for . . .

As usual, bang on cue came his annual summer chart tonic. But he was going frantic because the record – the Honeycombs' 'That's The Way' – had scorched its way up to the foot of the Top Twenty and instead of the group standing by ready to play it on TV pop shows, they were 10,000 miles away seeking recognition in Japan! And when the record started slipping back down again he was grinding his teeth in impatience. Japan could sink below the waves for all he cared – as long as the group got back in time. For some misguided reason they seemed eager to get themselves known everywhere but Britain, recently visiting Australia, New Zealand, Finland, Sweden, Japan and Thailand (where they were the first pop group ever to play in that country), subsequently giving their releases here far too little promotion. When they at last arrived home for TV spots the record resumed its climb to No.12, putting the grin back on Joe's face.

The next few months wiped it off again. Though the new hit

showed British fans that the Honeycombs were no nine-day wonder after all, and even made it look like the Gold Rush days were back, with handfuls more Gold Discs from Japan and Sweden, it didn't last. Neither the ensuing LP nor the next few singles – theirs or anyone else's – even nipped the charts, a fact that was irritatingly rubbed in when one music paper commented that he had been "capped" by independent producer Mickie Most, who they said was now the more successful of the two. Joe promptly pinned it up in the office for all to see and hopefully sneer at.

As for the Tornados, they had all gone their separate ways, but he was keeping the name alive with a new group that included Richie Blackmore on lead guitar and Mitch Mitchell, who was later to become one third of the Jimi Hendrix Experience. Rehearsals were not going well though, and the abundance of free-thinking musicians in the one band was making them hard to control. In one particular session that their organist Dave Watts recalls, Joe was having problems getting the drum rhythm right: "Mitch Mitchell was playing drums and he kept doing it wrong. He was like he was with Jimi Hendrix – fantastic drummer, he was all over the place. And Joe'd come to the doorway and he'd say, 'Now do it right this time', and stamp his foot in his silly little way. He'd go back in and Mitch'd do it wrong, and he did it about three times. Joe would come and stamp his foot in the door. Then the next thing, he come in with a shotgun with the pin pulled back. He came straight across the floor, no smile at all on his face – an absolute mad look on his face – and poked it right at him. He said, 'If you don't do it properly, I'll blow your f— head off!' He really scared everyone to death. We all knew that he was a little bit unstable and it was a bit frightening 'cause he actually meant it, really. I mean, he came in and it looked like he *was* going to shoot him. Mitch really got scared of Joe and he did completely subdue and he did do it right." Joe broke the band up soon afterwards.

It was not until the end of February '66 that things started fizzing up again. By then he had made a brief visit to Rome to re-dub the Honeycombs' voices in Italian on a few hits and broken a toe in an organ-kicking tantrum. But things were looking up again when a sugary heart-breaker called 'Please Stay' by a new group of his, the Cryin' Shames, started selling thick and fast in Liverpool.

The session had been a tense one lasting all day, and putting on the vocal had gone on late into the night, with Joe performing one of his fiercest acts in order to extract a tearful voice from the singer: "He just can't get it," he laughed, telling an office assistant downstairs of his shock tactics. "I want him to cry and then he'll feel it." Then he was off upstairs again to shout and scream and throw a drum before returning with the latest news: "I've nearly got him, nearly got him!"

Over the next few weeks the record companies must have been extracting a tearful voice from Joe, because Pye, Parlophone and Columbia all turned it down and when he steeled himself to offer it to Decca, it was to be the first one they had had off him in eight months. By the time it was released, the group were the biggest draw in Liverpool and were being tipped as the "Stones of '66"; every night they were being tugged offstage by fans and two recent performances had provoked several serious injuries. Needless to say, he was delighted when a week after its release, 'Please Stay' was already Liverpool's second most popular record, but not so pleased on hearing that most of the shops in the North and all on Merseyside had sold out and that Decca were having trouble meeting demand. The following week, though, it did reach the top in Liverpool, as well as Scotland, the Lake District and other far flung regions. When Brian Epstein went along to see what all the fuss was about and offer them a management contract Joe was beside himself with excitement.

He had been getting on well with Epstein since joining him and the Beatles at a recent Bob Dylan concert at the Albert Hall, and knew full well the effect Brian's participation in their career would have on his own. The outcome was that Brian's offer of "guaranteed stardom", TV spots galore and an advance payment of £25,000 for new equipment, which would have to be paid back later, was not deemed as attractive as that from another agency dealing also with the careers of the Walker Brothers. Artfully whisking the group down to London in a large Chevrolet, they offered numerous TV spots, a lower agent's commission than Epstein was asking and the same lump sum for equipment which they could keep. So, in spite of earnest discouragement and floods of tears from Joe, they accepted. Naturally he was there at the signing-up meeting, looking on in bitter disappointment and recording all the management's promises on a bulky, ill-concealed tape recorder stuffed into his breast pocket. His next disappointment was the record.

All geared up for a smash hit, he spent the next few weeks working with the band on an LP. Unfortunately 'Please Stay' climbed no higher than No.26, so the LP was shelved till the time they won more fans.

While that group was bursting onto the scene, another one was breaking up. The Honeycombs had always seen themselves essentially as a blues band, and buckling down to the sound imposed on them had only been agreeable as long as the hits were there. Once in an effort to get round the Meek sound they managed to drag him miserably into Pye Studios to record them, but he achieved practically the same sound there! Voice speeding had always been their main complaint, but the risk of being speeded was an occupational hazard at 304 because three-quarters of his recordings, whether vocal tracks or backings or both, had suffered – or enjoyed – the technique. "There's not a record made yet that wouldn't benefit from speeding up a little bit," he often claimed, and it is safe to say that most of his do benefit from that fraction more zest.[32]

Much higher on his list of problems were money matters. Rising bills and falling bank accounts had been troubling him for months and he had done little about it apart from setting up yet another company, Meeksville Music Publishing, into which he was putting his own new songs and a few others. Thanks to one of the original Tornados, organist Roger LaVern, he was also receiving regular 'Final Notices' from the Board of Trade. Between them the band had so far collected only £7,000 in royalties and, in his desperation to extract more, LaVern had voluntarily gone bankrupt.[33] So the Official Receiver was now chasing Joe for a full account of all his companies' finances since the year dot.

This kind of trouble was bound to flare up when money was paid out haphazardly with rarely a glimpse of a royalty statement. It was fine for those who were friendly with him and asked for loans or royalties: he would hand them out and promptly forget it. For others it was not so easy. Thus some people were being paid for records that had not sold, while others had to do without.

Throughout all this Tom Shanks, his accountant-partner, was back in the Strand fighting a losing battle with figures. His relationship with Joe had always been characterized by his endlessly urgent pleas to keep costs down and juggle bills so the least threatening ones were paid last. That however was all to change. Mounting money worries were making Joe lose faith in him, and when in June Shanks made the fatal mistake of speaking uncomplimentarily about him behind his back without safeguarding against its reaching the wrong ears, their parting was swift. Shanks resigned, leaving him another bill. Apparently he had been drawing no wages, and £6,500 would now, he thought, pay them. Off Joe went to find another accountant, only to hear that Shanks was keeping an iron grip on all the accounts till his bill was paid.

No doubt the latest 'Telstar' news gave him a hint of relief. Ivy Music, in a bid to get the Frenchmen off their backsides, were now sueing Jean Ledrut for a declaration that 'Telstar' was *not* in breach of copyright. With any luck it might even force an out-of-court settlement.

The Tornados, meanwhile, had sprung to life again, this time from the Saxons. Coming from the Newent area they had long been his favourite and most trusted group. For the past two summers he had taken them up to Newent and Cinderford when opening charity fetes, where they would run through a few numbers and he would give a very long speech. Tornados sales were still ticking over, though it was ages since their last hit and he hoped their new Mod image and trendy clothes would help put things right. His own wardrobe had also undergone an overhaul, and though he was out at the elbows financially it did not show in his appearance; his new, dark, made-to-measure suits would, he hoped, lend authority on record hawkarounds.

Recordings being accepted had been dropping all the year, forcing him to slow up the sausage machine and concentrate on fewer acts. Perhaps he was also considering the style of Phil Spector, about whom he had now curiously had a complete change of heart. Instead of slamming the man for "stealing" his sounds he was now confiding that "Spector is the one man I would love to meet", buying a stock of his 'Christmas Gift For You' LPs to give away as presents. And if Spector's latest super-classic, 'River Deep, Mountain High', in which he had made Tina Turner sound like she was singing in a mausoleum with her boots on, was helping Joe realize the sense in spending months on each disc instead of churning them out on an endless conveyor belt, then it gave him better odds. As yet there had been little reward for reduction in product, though he scraped into one chart in July with a drastically revamped version of the old hit 'Singing The Blues', where Billy Fury's brother, singing calmly alongside a frantically misplaced lead guitar, offered a freakish attraction.

YOU ARE IN ONE HELLUVA MESS

Unfortunately another reason for the decline in output was temperament. Though he was still auditioning groups that hammered at his door, he was less able than ever to sustain interest in them. With his plate full of worries he would often find himself starting a session only to scrap it halfway through or cancelling sessions by turning groups away at the door. Sometimes they would arrive on his doorstep having been given strict instructions what time to be there, how many knocks to give and to carry on knocking till he answered them. Competing with the noise of heavy traffic, twenty minutes of persistent knocking could drag by before the group suddenly detected a long, muffled yell from some remote part of the building that went: "F—— off!" Rows with neighbours over late-night sessions were as regular as ever, but he was throwing more tempers now, along with dinners over walls and people, and drum-kits down the stairs and into the middle of Holloway Road. Once while racing up the M4 to fetch a parcel of demo discs which had been flown into London Airport from America, he nearly hit a car; when his nervous passenger warned him to watch out, he angrily pulled up sideways in the middle of the motorway and with traffic flashing by both sides, got out to let him drive instead.

Much of this strange behaviour arose from his feeling of persecution. A second telephone he had had installed, specially as a personal ex-directory line, allowed him to take the first one off the hook to stop it ringing all night with business and 'nasty' calls. But absentmindedly he left the number on it, so the wrong calls were soon getting through again! Sometimes during casual conversations, perhaps discussing his progress with a recording and which company he would offer it to and so on, his face would suddenly cloud over and for no apparent reason he would break down weeping.

Loneliness was another heartache. He said he had yet to find a "kindred spirit", someone with whom he could share a normal one-to-one relationship. As his office assistant Patrick Pink recalls, it would affect him in the same way: "I've known him to burst into tears in a private conversation when he's been really down and fed up and lonely – last thing at night when everybody had gone. He used to say, 'Nobody loves me. Don't you love me a little bit? Can't you find some love for me?' Things like that he'd come out with: 'Surely you love me a little bit?' He was obviously seeking love but he couldn't find it. Love was there all around him but he couldn't see it. Very sad it was. We all loved him in our own way, even though it wasn't sexual, we *loved* him. It *was* love. I loved the man. I loved everything he turned out: his music. Even though he was a bastard in many senses, there's no way I could hate Joe. There's no way that anybody that really knew Joe could hate him. He was a very temperamental bastard. I used to fear from one day to the other sometimes what mood he was going to be in; frightened for my life – throw me down the stairs or whatever, if I said the wrong thing! But we still loved him for it. He was a lovable person. He had a very nice side to him, he had a bad side to him, but don't we all?"

He said he felt loneliest when dubbing on his own in the control room. Loneliness and lost love were the subjects of most of his songwriting. His perennial advice to would-be songwriters was that they should always compose in whatever mood they were in and not write down that the sun is shining if they were feeling depressed, because it is not a true feeling. If he practised what he preached, the following lines from Mike Berry's record 'Loneliness' should say a lot and are amongst his more imaginative:

Loneliness, woh, woh - he's got his claws in me,
Loneliness, woh, woh - seems to be my destiny.
Made to cry in the night,
No one seems to treat me right,
Loneliness, woh, woh - what's to become of me?
Happiness, yeh, yeh, always seems to pass me by,
Happiness, yeh, yeh, give some to this lonely boy.
I could treat someone good with everything a lover should,
Loneliness, woh, woh - what's to become of me?
I'll keep on a-waiting and I know by and by
Out of the blue, I'll find you
And all the angels in Heaven will fly,
In happiness they'll cry for you and I . . .

Searching for a kindred spirit looked clearly like a lost cause. He had ruined the opportunities that presented themselves by his constant infidelity and if he had any chance of finding a permanent partner his liberated lifestyle would have to tighten up dramatically. Until then the only partner he could love and live with would have to be his music.

In spite of these plain facts, it was around this time he had marriage on his mind! The girl in question was the one he had been recording for the past three years: Glenda Collins. The possibility was not so absurd as it might at first sound. They liked each other very much and got on well together. Glenda idolized Joe the producer and his music, whilst for Joe it was a great regret that after eight records he had still not given her a hit. Sadly they were not in love.

He still gave it serious thought though, discussing it at length with his mother and friends, seeing it as a marriage of convenience, with Glenda's manager-father injecting a large sum into the company while he himself concentrated more on her career. However, his own conclusion was that having a wife and children would be a burden, heavily restricting his career and independence, and neither his mother's persistent advice that it would be a good stabling influence nor his faded image of having a happy family around him could win him over. Perhaps if they had loved each other the story would have been different. (Twenty years later any knowledge of these talks would be denied by the Collins family.)

Unhappily he had never yet found a woman to love, nor was he at ease with his homosexuality. He envied 'straight' people, saying on rare occasions they were lucky being as they were, and was known at least twice to have taken a couple of ladies from Southend up to his bedroom to help try and straighten him out.

August at last presented him with evidence of something he had always suspected but never proved: bugging! All those ideas of his over the years that had found their way onto other people's records could, he believed, have escaped him via a variety of channels. Groups, for example, might unintentionally give their own secrets away by performing their song onstage before the release date (as Lonnie Donegan had done with 'Cumberland Gap'), and to avoid this happening he would have bands such as Screaming Lord Sutch & the Savages continually holding their hands on their hearts, swearing not to play or discuss the song they had just done. Many a time he would accuse record companies, who had rejected his demos, of having copied them and of using bits and pieces which were now in the charts. Back at 304, meanwhile, anyone with a shred of nerve could wander out of the waiting room and steal a tape, plant a device or simply stand around clutching a portable recorder. Certainly a few tapes had 'walked', and once back in '64 he thought he had uncovered a new form of dirty work. A man driving by called in to say he was receiving music direct from the studio on his car radio! The source turned out to be a brand new tape recorder which was simultaneously relaying out anything recorded on it, and Joe immediately summoned the stockists to examine the thing. They found one of the coils faulty and seemed as surprised as him since faulty coils with their miles of wiring act as aerials and generally turn the recorder into a receiver, not a transmitter.[34] Anyway, he was still suspicious and from then on kept frequent checks on its performance by nipping downstairs when someone was playing and tuning the dial on his living room radio.

Since then there had been numerous instances when he thought his equipment was being tapped. Sessions would suddenly break off when he rushed in saying, "Those bastards at EMI and Decca!", and would start following wires everywhere and checking the walls. It seemed to happen mostly on Honeycombs sessions, as singer Dennis D'Ell recalls: "Several times he'd stop a session in the middle and say, 'I heard something on that tape. There was something on that tape. It's those bastards.' He must have heard something but I could never hear it, and then he'd get angry because I couldn't hear it: 'Put these earphones on then.' – 'I can't hear anything, Joe.' – 'It's f—— there, it's f—— there!' He'd say it was a click, as if something's been switched on. It was just a very minute click and I'd think, 'Well, I can't hear it,' and he's going, 'Well it's just after you sing – whatever it was – there's a click.' Maybe there *was* something there."

When, after nine years of barren bug-searching, concrete evidence was finally found, it seemed hard to believe. His office assistant, Patrick Pink, discovered a walkie-talkie behind the record player in the living room. With an elastic band holding it in the *on* position and the aerial sticking out, Joe was convinced it was a proper bugging job and took time dissecting it, assessing its range and life span. He then bought a tiny F.M. device, the size of a sixpence, and sent Patrick off to some shops in Holloway Road with it clipped behind his tie, while recording it all in the living room. The reception came through loud and clear, but the grim satisfaction that at last he was proved right did nothing for his fear of losing both secrets and privacy. Up until this point he had only scribbled messages on pieces of paper when his moods stopped him talking, but from here on he was to use this little dodge more and more to foil any prying microphones.

Throughout these uneasy days his most heartening recreation was the abiding interest he had in things mysterious. He had found a way, he said, of driving people mad and they wouldn't even know he was doing it! By sending out high-pitched whistles on oscillator machinery he believed it was possible to control someone's mind, and was intrigued by the thought that people who didn't like him might already be controlling his own.

His spiritual leaning gave him more peace of mind, and he was now a regular subscriber to the *Psychic News.* When the Tornados were away on tour he would always tell them that although he was not with them in the flesh, he was in spirit; that no matter where they were or what they were doing, he would know – and he often did! Minor details about the performance and reprimands for taking girls back to their digs left them flabbergasted saying, "He knows! He's got that bloody glass out and he knows what we're doing."

Besides having Buddy Holly to 'help' him, there were two more to whom he had been introduced. During the occasional visit to Essex to consult his medium friend, Mrs. Smith, she had told him of a Red Indian chieftain who had committed suicide and was now acting as one of his guides. The other one, she said, was no less a figure than Rameses the Great! As the most famous pharaoh of them all, Rameses is best remembered for his extensive building programmes – destroying monuments of the past to turn them into colossal statues of himself all over Egypt – and an intensive breeding programme: he fathered 162 children! He lived so long, reigning at least 67 years, that many of them died before he did. Well, if Joe ever found himself lacking vitality, he couldn't blame Rameses!

Whether it was a load of phoney baloney or there were such powers helping shape his life will never be known. Anyway, he believed it all and was probably quite flattered thinking so many spirits were taking an interest in him. He was certainly convinced his style of painting was being influenced by the chieftain and since hearing of Rameses he had picked up an Egyptian canopic vase, used for holding ancient entrails, and was gathering all the literature he could on pharaohs, mummies and Egyptology.

Perhaps though, he still didn't feel that Rameses was pulling his weight. Rumours, although unconfirmed, spoke of his dabbling with others in black magic rituals and that in order to attract power to themselves they were trying to make contact with the Great Beast himself, Aleister Crowley. The black magician had summed up his own philosophy in the outrageously liberal decree: "Do what thou wilt shall be the whole of the Law." If the rumours bore any truth whatever they might account for the footsteps Joe would sometimes hear coming up the stairs at night when he was in bed. And when he described such unlikely sounding occurrences as the night when the footsteps went round the bed and the spirit tripped over the cord of his electric fire, pulling out the plug, and another occasion when he came downstairs at 3 o'clock in the morning to find the chairs and tables all dancing round the living room, he imparted his news in a state of extreme nervous excitement. Far-fetched as such stories sound, the history of witchcraft and demonology is awash with accounts of poltergeist phenomena, and judging by the amount of mystic activity at 304 over those past six years dancing furniture would, by many enthusiasts, be considered perfectly in order.

Playing back tapes of the day's sessions on his own he would sometimes hear voices that should not have been there, and once told the press that on the fade-out of a Riot Squad record, 'I Take It That We're Through', "A phantom voice mutters 'hello' or something like that". The mutter is barely audible but is in there somewhere amongst the last guitar twangings. Late at night when the house was empty he was sure he could sometimes hear people talking in the studio, and it was the same when he went down to the living room where one of the voices would come from his painting of an all-seeing eye, warning him about certain people. Obvious explanations would be either that the walls were thin and that the voices were not spirits but those of his neighbours or that his ears were playing him tricks after a day full of deafening playbacks.

Rather harder to explain were his 'trances'. They had only started recently and usually occurred at the end of a 'take', when all of a sudden he would stand still and, for a period of anything from a few seconds to a quarter of an hour, gaze into space. A take would end and during the ensuing silence a member of the band would peep into the control room and see him standing, eyes transfixed on the controls. Talking to him got no response. Sometimes he would walk into the middle of the studio and stand staring or looking around, and always in a pose: right hand on chin, left hand holding right elbow, right foot sticking out from middle of left. For literally minutes the band would sit waiting in respectful silence for what they believed were his creative processes at work, until abruptly he would snap out of it saying, "Right, come on then," and go back to work. Rather more unsettling were the times when he stood in the studio doorway and stared just as vacantly at any one member of a group, often with a slight grin. Drugs would seem to have been the most likely cause, though it may have just been nervous exhaustion. Then again it might have been linked to his half-minute trances when, like Geoff Goddard, his mind wandered off while someone was talking and he came round again with some irrelevant comment like: "I often wonder what's going to become of people like me." When he made this remark to the Honeycombs' singer Dennis D'Ell, a little later Dennis questioned him on the subject: "I remember saying to him, 'What becomes of people after they've had hit records and got used to that kind of lifestyle – not particularly money, but the freedom of living like that, not having to get up in the morning 9 to 5 – and suddenly that is taken away from them through lack of success or whatever? What becomes of them?' He said, 'If they're artistic enough and they don't achieve success – because not all artistic people do achieve the success they deserve – then they die. I shall be dead and you shall be dead too if you don't keep on the right tracks.'"

𝄞𝄞𝄞𝄞𝄞𝄞𝄞𝄞𝄞𝄞𝄞𝄞𝄞𝄞𝄞𝄞

Musicwise he was fighting tooth and nail. Over half his product was now being rejected and a mere handful of groups were just ticking along outside the charts. They included the Tornados, who were maintaining a following despite changing the formula with every record, the Riot Squad who many reckoned his hottest property and the Honeycombs and the much acclaimed Cryin' Shames, who were both back in business having split up and re-formed.

This had been his first year without a big summer hit. Why his records were not selling more had a lot to do with lack of airplay. Record companies were simply not pushing his discs and were waiting for them to start selling themselves first. People were saying they were dated, though that was not true of most of them. Some were extremely commercial sounds, as shown in Glenda Collins's 'Something I've Got To Tell You', which with a modicum of exposure had all the trappings of a Top Ten hit. Better still was a ballad called 'Wishing Well' by a new group, the Millionaires. It was another sparkling Meek classic, and once again his magic touch was more than evident. Giving it the gentle treatment and sprinkling echo here and there in the background to help create the sound of trickling water, made it a most imaginative production and should have brought him in a fortune. Sadly it was hardly played.

Though some did indeed sound dated, and as one reviewer said of the Tornados' 'Is That A Ship I Hear': "Good of its kind and doubtless a hit three years ago, but not for today's market", there were many more that didn't. He had kept abreast of the music scene changing with the times and though his sound was usually still recognizable – hating as he did to sound the same as anyone else – it was now merely adding spice to the performance rather than vice versa. Others of his stock bore no trademarks at all, including some very advanced B-sides which showed a style blossoming with the flower power generation.

Many were ideal competition for the sounds of the day and good press reviews were accompanying nearly every release: "electrifying beat", "fascinating harmonies", "stimulating", "contagious", "recommended", "very well performed". But fine words butter no parsnips, and what he needed above all was airplay. With the demise of Ivy Music's *Topical Tunes* programme and the decline of interest in Radio Luxembourg since the start of the pirate ships, his hopes now rested on Radio London.

Competing with Radio Caroline in international waters four miles off Harwich, Essex, Radio London had been on the air for eighteen months, claiming millions of listeners and the best reception for South-east England. Hyping records was rife and, at around £5 a spin, his irregular £200 handouts would buy him sporadic airtime and chart placings. Sending out crates of whisky to the ship, wining and dining disc jockeys and slipping them newspapers containing wads of notes, all helped his records' chances, though it did look a bit suspicious when Tornados records zoomed straight in near the top of their chart one week and out again the next! There were also 'orgy-parties' that he would have to arrange at his flat, paying for drinks and the hire of prostitutes of either gender to entertain his Radio London contacts. Whether it was worth the costs is doubtful, especially in view of his fast crumbling financial position.

His income was drying up and the prospects did not look good. Sueing the Frenchman in the 'Telstar' case had speeded things up a bit, but as for an out-of-court settlement, the answer was "Non". The French case would be heard in December, though even if Ledrut lost he might well appeal and hold up payment even longer. It meant another visit to Paris to see his French lawyer. Already he had flown over twice for discussions and had even started studying French from Linguaphone records. So far he had learnt little but still enjoyed himself wandering round the Champs Elysées, swearing at those who couldn't understand what he was saying.

Meanwhile business affairs back home had reached crisis point. His bank manager from Lloyds next door had put him in touch with a solicitor, John Ginnett, who from his offices at Lincoln's Inn in Holborn was sifting through piles of papers, assessing which bills, royalty, tax and Board of Trade claims belonged where. With so much money being demanded and so little coming in, Joe agreed that the best way to buy time was to admit being "in one helluva mess".

Their relationship over the next few months would resemble that of a strict family doctor and his erring patient. Although they would sometimes meet or telephone, their main source of contact was to be via letter. Some of Joe's make absorbing reading, offering an invaluable insight into his current thoughts, and are included here as he wrote them. (The mention of Lord Sutch in the first one refers to an *Evening Standard* article two weeks earlier in which Sutch revealed he was sueing him for unpaid royalties. The sight of the article naturally sent Joe up the wall and he was now wondering if Sutch had had it printed to gain himself publicity or to discredit him in the 'Telstar' case. Two more names he speaks of are his ex-lawyer in the 'Telstar' proceedings, Mr. Archdeacon, and M.B. Enterprises, who were threatening action to obtain royalty accounts.)

Dear Mr Ginnett

Thank you for your letter of 27th sept, I have made carful note of its contents and would like to make a few coments befor you meet Shanks on friday.

I consider the treatment I have received by this man is another form of stealing, through his so called busness brain he has been able, or so it apears to extract from myself £6500 for his so called services provided, that have put each company he has connections with in a state of colapse, this is not a bussnes brain but a crooked one, and I hope he will be treated as such.

Please dont consider myself a stupid

persion, overworked and devoteted may be but it was my brain and work that made the money in the first place, and very littel has ever been at hand for my own use, because of the bluff pushed out by first Major Banks and then Shanks, I have no more desire to carry on with this treatment, we live and learn, I will not be used, and then treated as a half wit, Shanks has had a bad efect on my life and killed much of my desire to progress, this was his intention he wanted control of the companys, by any means.

Your sujestion of a bussness partener would apear pratical, but has been tried twice and failed, so I cannot be expected to find it easy to except, my Father ran bussnesses with succes my Mother sister and brother do so now, but there not in the rat race called show buissness, I have plan's what to do with whats mine and I want everyone working with me to get there share, and that only.

I say the artist Lord Sutch was in his rights to expect what was his, and it was my wish and instructions that this should be done, therefore Ive suffered very much through the story last week, there for every-one to read and caused by Shanks, but will he suffer, I think I have a case against this man and will not pay the fee I was forced to garrentee him, and he should know this, his guidance was fatal, and no matter what he has to say he was in a position more than I to watch every penny spent, and see that bills were paid as soon as possible, it was his actions that kept people waiting, I cant forgive and forget and pay up, till the end of my days I intend justice shall be brought against this man, if he asked for any more than what he has earned, the cost of a poor accountant and a bluffer.

Because you are a very creative persion yourself, its possible for you to put yourself in my position, and realise how I feel, please understand I am aware the helluva mess Im in, and so did Mr Archdeacon but no effort was ever made to point these things out at the time, he worked hand and glove with Shanks, I therefor even if there is extra exspenses feel it wise to obtain from him a complet break down of the Telstar case, this should be availible for myself in any event.

I feel that Lord Sutch and M.B. enterprises should be paid as in both case Im shure it not to great an amount and could be availible in the investment or at the Strand bank, in both case's they are unresnable people and will do harm to me to be kept waiting, everyone talks as if Ill never make another hit recording, I consider Im just starting but the rewards of succes must fall in my pockets, and so the flow of succes was stopped again by Shanks etc, he talks of me as a fool from Gloucester to other people who he thought were his friends, they told me finaly he was taking me for a mug and would do very well out of my ignorance and temprement, up to last week no one of any worth in this industry or any other ever had dout for my honesty now they have, I have to pay Sutch and run a story to cancel out this Im not crooked, I do my best to help people not rob them, all I live for has been almost distroyed, my anssering machine is full of people accusing me of being a crook, a con man, a pervert, Im finding it hard to have the guts to carry on, even some of the groups I record have pointed out they will expect there royalties soon, and lack the trust they had put in me.

I would be greatful if you do all in your power to keep my name clean, and prevent people sutch as Mr Shanks from winning the fee he expects to gain.

yours Sincerely

Joe Meek

Fighting Mr. Shanks though would be a waste of time. Knowing as Shanks did the sombre state of all the bank accounts, he was hardly likely to risk blowing his chances of getting his money by sueing the companies and making them bankrupt. Far more sensible, Mr. Ginnett advised, would be for Joe to concentrate on the other creditors, many of whom could now put him into liquidation. If they did, worse could follow. If money from one particular company had ever been used for another one, he could be held personally liable for mismanagement of company funds, which could earn him a prison sentence. Since demands overall amounted to around £20,000, with only £1,300 in the kitty, things were looking very dicey. "The whole of your future hangs upon this 'Telstar' case," intoned Mr. Ginnett, pointing out that even though any reasonable Court would favour his case, French Courts were not reasonable.

Further souring his hopes was the mournful news that Ivy Music were refusing to loan him £2,000 of the 'Telstar' royalties, in case he lost and had to pay it all to the Frenchman. So it was not surprising when one day he phoned Ginnett and hung up in mid-conversation, saying he was going to "shut up shop and just go home to Gloucester to forget it all." Again Ginnett warned him of his critical situation, adding that bankruptcy could well help the French drive a much harder bargain. Ginnett could, he said, get him out of the mess but Joe would have three tough months first. The tone of Joe's reply changes with the ink one third of the way through:

8th Oct 66

Dear Mr Ginnett

Thank you for your letter of the 7th Oct.

Ive thought over your remarks, and realise you are right, I regret my rudness in ringing off when you were only trying to help me.

I would like you to know because of the treatment and deception shown me in the past, its hard for me to act on any advice without some dout or feeling I may make mistakes again, but I do trust and admire you, and know deep down you will do your best to sort out and clear up the mess Im in.

There's no dout Im in a rundown state with the high pressure of work, trying to come up with a hit record and all the office work to look after, with every recording session, I have to use the patience you talk of and creat new sounds, and work with very dificult people, also try my best to premote the records get radio and TV, and put up with loads of moan's over the Telephone, but I will keep going and do my best to succeed.

I find it almost imposible to make the recordings apart from groups because there no means to pay the mususians, and even group disc's need some extras if only choir, so it will mean less releases if things remain in there present position.

I would like you to carry on with sortting my legal problems, and the apointment on thursday I will keep with the accountants, at your office, but I wish at all times to know the resions why, and not talked at as if Im not capable to understand legal matters and the running of a company.

Because even if my affairs are in a state and I have been used in the past, it will not be allowed to happen again, and you may have to wait a while for your fee to be paid, but it will be, and by myself, I may have a humble disposition, but I am employing you to do a job and expect the correct treatment, the same aplys to the accountant I am to meet on thursday, there are 100s of others if I dont like, what I find.

It was on Mr Waltons recommendation I came to your offices, and Im aware of his interest in my banking with his branch, this is as far as I wish to go, I remain the boss and the only director of my work, Ill stand for no other means to have any interests in my companys.

I am greatful for the overdraft he has given me, but my past succes is the garentee you both will not be out of pocket, I dont expect people who have spent there lives involved with £.s.d. to understand what make's me tick, I do know how I work best and where Im going, and in future if Im not happy with the situation I shall make changes, I shall check and investegate every move I make and people connected with me, and dont wish for, or expect any favours from any one, just for them to get on with there job.

I have made my point, so its now in your hands, if you take me on and the state my afairs are in I will be pleased, but at all times I intend to have control and do what I think best, and use your leagal advice when needed.

My desire to pay the rent befor the owner arrives on monday, was very pratical, I also wish not to let him know Im in a low finantial position, but as I have in the past I will do again, win his respect and try to avoid to great an increas on the rent that is due to be changed in any case, I dont wish to get my hands on whats not mine, but I intend to get what is, and carry on running my recording buissness and look after my self.

yours Sincerely   Joe Meek

The effect of that was swift: Ginnett could no longer act on his behalf. In spite of a mild, face-saving apology from Joe, he would not be dissuaded and returned what papers he had.

It seemed like life was becoming one long string of disasters.

As if things were not already bad enough, suddenly *all* his productions were being rejected. Latest recordings by the Honeycombs, Millionaires, Tornados and Glenda Collins had all been turned down as, surprisingly, had the Cryin' Shames' follow-up to 'September In The Rain', which had at least nipped one chart at No.48. The rejection for the first time of a Tornados single was particularly hurtful. It had in fact marked an entirely new Tornados approach; realizing he was no longer finding good whistleable tunes, so vital for instrumentals, he had bowed to pressure from the group and with a heavy heart recorded their first *vocal* A-side.

That one was refused because EMI wanted only instrumentals from the group! As for the others, the record companies were saying the sound was behind the times, that they had heard it all before; they wanted clean sounds without gimmicks or trademarks. He told them he had given them all that many times and was still doing so without commercial success. He dreaded doing away with those little magic touches which had brought him rewards in the past and which made recording such a joy. Without them he thought his records were sterile. Consequently he was tending to row with the record people, making it harder than ever to get product accepted. So despite being perfectly capable of producing modern sounds – as he was with the Riot Squad and others – he now found himself missing out on the lot. He had even had to re-record the latest Riot Squad offering because Pye were offended by its title, 'Gonna Have A Baby'. Why all his other up-to-date ones were being turned down he did not know, but could think of all sorts of weird and wild possibilities.

Then into the midst of all this bleak uncertainty rode his knight in shining armour: Sir Joseph Lockwood. As Chairman of EMI, his word carried considerable clout and Joe had often sought it over the years in getting rejected recordings accepted. This time Sir Joseph was able to persuade Mr. Ginnett to start again, and at the same time shrewdly renewed an offer to Joe of joining his staff and having an office at Abbey Road Studios. In the past Joe had always turned down such offers out of hand but though he still resisted this one it now looked slightly less forbidding.

Although Sir Joseph's timely intervention had faintly improved Joe's business prospects, other areas were taking a turn for the worse. Patience at the Board of Trade finally fizzled out and after all the months of getting nowhere they plumped for strong-arm tactics. As if out of a nightmare, officials arrived kicking his doors down and storming into the office to help themselves to files and loose documents. Coming when it did, the incident intensified a particularly harrowing period.

Around this time he was also mysteriously beaten up and found hanging unconscious out of his Ford Zodiac. Paintwork had been scraped off the car and the doors kicked in. Over the years, finding his cars vandalized had been common – sometimes it was petty pilfering of wheels and radios by thieves and souvenir hunters, other times malicious smearing of paint-stripper – but this seems to have been the first occurrence of such serious proportions. Perhaps others took place. Another car incident that might easily have turned out still worse had happened back in '62. His friend Lional had been driving down Harrow Road when he spotted Joe's Sunbeam Rapier parked outside a public convenience. A few moments later he had heard a scream and, on returning, saw that the Rapier had crashed into a pub nearby and Joe was standing there beside it. The story Joe told him was that whilst in the loo two Irishmen had snatched his gold Saint Christopher medal from around his neck and after a fight, had run off with it. He had given chase in his car, and as they crossed a zebra crossing he had tried to mow them down, crashing into the pub. The story he told the pub landlord was that he had avoided a dog.

Over the years he had probably had quite a few similar scrapes through lingering in such disenchanting places, for he had unwisely carried on prowling around. His composition 'Do You Come Here Often', on the flip-side to the Tornados' August release, includes a conversation between two 'homosexuals' meeting, he later confided, in a nightclub loo. Their dialogue, spoken in limp-wristedly flirty fashion, contains such lines as: "Do you come here often?" – "Only when the pirate ships go off," and "Cheerio, I'll see you down the dilly," – "Not if I see you first, you won't." Full of double meanings it was especially daring for Joe, and he was delighted to get away with it.

In another near calamity, again resulting from his promiscuous lifestyle, he had found himself in the ludicrous situation of running down Holloway Road in his pyjamas at 8.30 in the morning, screaming that someone was coming after him with a knife. Describing the unconcerned reaction of commuters passing him on their way to the tube station he complained, "None of the bastards helped me."

In a more sinister event some months back, three brawny thugs in their thirties and forties had broken into the house during a session and created merry hell with him in the living room, scattering furniture and papers. Through some protection racket they were muscling in on a share of the profits, though to judge by the way they rushed out soon afterwards, clattering down the stairs to the strains of his frenzied yelling close behind, he had no intention of giving them anything. Returning to the studio like a raging bull with face red and eyes big and bulging he calmed down after a minute and with the slightest of smiles muttered, "That's seen them off."

Naturally these various incidents were making him even more security conscious. The ease with which such people were marching in set him thinking beyond mere locks and chains, to weapons with which to frighten them off. A single-barrel shotgun that Heinz had bought a few years back had been hanging around the flat for some while; with time to spare on the way to gigs, Heinz and the Saints had often stopped off by fields to shoot birds. Characteristically Joe had always condemned their gun games as cruel and dangerous but on at least one occasion, already mentioned, had himself put its use to chilling effect and could now feel some protection by keeping it close at hand.

The major effect of all this aggravation was to make Sir Joseph's offer that much more palatable. His head was brimming with arguments for and against but it was the pro-EMI ones that were coming off best. There within the safety of a multi-million pound conglomerate he could start afresh, free of soul-destroying money troubles; bills, tax and royalty statements would be out of his hands. So too would nasty neighbours with their babies and headaches. No longer would he be out on a limb, being squashed out by other A & R men, but in there amongst them and in a prime position to get his discs properly promoted. Almost all his recordings would be guaranteed release – a very cheering thought at this moment when all but CBS (who had just taken their first one this year) looked like they had given him up.

A meeting between himself, Sir Joseph and Mr. Ginnett was duly arranged for November 22 to discuss the situation.

Meanwhile he was penning more thoughts to Ginnett and showing a distinct mellowing towards Tom Shanks.

18-11-66

Dear Mr Ginnet

There seems a never ending stream of problems, I hope and pray the daylight is near when I can feel Im not commiting some offence.

Im hurt so much over Mr Shanks but I cannot dislike him, and would not want anything done to cause him illness, if you can avoid it, it could be things pilled up so much and I can understand Im not to easy to work with at time's.

I have tremendous self control developing, and my nature is becoming as it used to be, except Im much wiser, I would not want the full amount paid Mr Shanks but a fair and worth while amount.

I remain yours Sincerely
Joe

His next letter features his charity work, rehabilitating ex-convicts. Apart from what he wrote here and the fact that he was once seen giving money and clothes to a man on his doorstep fresh out of prison, nothing is known about it, and even Mr. Kenyon – the Welfare Officer from Eastchurch Prison, Sheppey, that he mentions – nowadays barely remembers Joe's name. With the exception of murder and manslaughter his contacts would have been jailed for any offence, and the mind boggles at the thought of him giving robbers and gangsters singing and song-writing lessons. (The surname of this latest offender has been omitted for obvious reasons.)

22-11-66

Dear Mr Ginnett

I would be greatful if I could pay the £10— odd to release xxxx xxxx from prision, I know theres very littel money to spare, but in this case Im sure it would be the mean's to put this young man on the right track, and I feel Im perhaps the only persion he can turn to now he needs advice on a worth while way of living.

The letter from Mr Kenyon is with you, in which the date on which to send it and the persions name to which I send it, please believe me Im not waisting my time or money, theres a chance I can help, I have done so befor, he will get a good job and change's his ways, its worked with others I must try in this case, I will protect myself and walk with care.

Although I said I thought Mr Kenyon could have been checking on myself I feel he is a devoted man trying to straighten out these young people, who lack understanding and have a chance of doing good, he did posibly have me watched to see if I was a suitable persion to do some good in this direction, I can only say I have a list of people who are all working now, and turn to me from time to time for advice.

I have had to learn to understand teenageer's there battels against adults and there problem's of growing up, to get the best results in the recordings it was nessesary where young groups were concerned, Ive found they turn to me for other advice, I dont abuse there trust in me, a tremendous respect grose in time, as a rule I win, and only those that can't understand kindness I fail with, theres been about two, in several years, but at least 50 that have got good jobs, married, or working as musicion in the record industry, xxxx xxxx has been weak and is very lazy, but as I said I can win I feel.

I hope you understand me and feel its worthwhile work. I remain yours Sincerely

Joe Meek

He sent both that letter and the next one on the day of the EMI meeting which, due to illness, he missed. Unfortunately the second page is missing and is therefore indicated by dots.

271

22-11-66

Dear Mr Ginnett
    I hope you are well, Im writting to thank you for the great help you have given me, and the way you took over today while I was ill, and guided the ideals to the very best advantage for myself.
    Its still hard to believe its all happening after many years of feeling one is on his own and can sink or swim in what was undertaken, now I feel I have not only a very fine legal man in yourself but also a friend who came to my aid when I was realy desperate, I shall always be greatful to you.
    As far as the companys and outstanding problems go, I leave it to your expert advice and will stand by you in what ever you feel is best, its only a few of the small companys like the tape people and photographer's that I feel sorry for, because they must feel the let down, but it has been done to me several times, and I did not moan ...
    ... as you say if you have something to offer in the way of talent etc, they still wish to work with you.
    I know there's still lots of problems befor Im clear, but my thoughts are looking higher to the future and your faith in my talents will not be let down, I have written to Sir Joseph Lockwood to thank him for the oppertunities he has put my way, and said I will write again when Im well and on my feet again, I would think about friday.
    My overdraft has rissen next door where Mr Walton has helped me, quite a bit has been paid to mususians, and I think can be recovered should the masters be excepted by E.M.I., I would like my own money to go through his bank and will put any other worth while clients his way, Ive made notes, and kept

reciets on the money used.

Mr Shenton who sublet this place to me has been very good, but I do feel he's waited a very long time for the rent this time, I would like to sort this out soon.

Once again thank you for the tremendous help given me.

God bless. I remain yours Sincerely
Joe Meek

At the beginning of December the main news was his call-up for jury service, arousing old, painful memories. (The Mr. Wood he mentions was head of EMI's record division and helping to fix the offer.)

1-12-66

Dear Mr Ginnett
I hope you are well, I enclose some more head-akes, the one looks rather bad.

By the way is it OK for me to be a member of a Jury, as I have had one conviction, it was an unjust one, so I woundered if this is the law's way of saying it has not been held against me, or do you think I should inform them of my conviction.

There has been no phone call from E.M.I. and I hope to hear from them today, can something have gone wrong do you think it might help if you gave Mr Wood a call, next week from teusdays onward Im on the Jury so may not be able to atend an interviewe at E.M.I.

Well thats all for now
my best wishes
I remain yours Sincerely
Joe

The jury work was postponed for another day-trip to France. This time he was to attend a meeting of both English and French Experts. The discussion was livened up a bit by a few noisy outbursts from composer Jean Ledrut, strutting around shouting, "C'est à moi! Moi! Moi!" His performance was rated good but ineffective, and Joe was advised not to try upstaging him by putting on one of his own. The Experts' combined Report would be presented very soon at the French Hearing.[35]

Towards the end of the year came the expected bleak music paper polls. The Tornados had just scraped into the *Record Mirror's* 'World's 15 Best Instrumental Groups' at No.15 below the top-placed Shadows. In the *NME* the Beach Boys were voted best 'World Vocal Group', making the Beatles runners-up, though 'Eleanor Rigby' was 'Best British Disc'. No doubt some people voted for Tom Jones's 'Green, Green Grass Of Home', which to Joe's horror was reckoned to have notched up the year's biggest sale in Britain and was expected by Decca soon to be the first British record in their history to earn a Gold Disc for home sales. Tom was also 'Best Male Singer' and at the same time Joe's other old favourites, Dave Dee, Dozy, Beaky, Mick & Tich, had managed with hits like 'Bend It' and 'Hold Tight' to stay on the 1966 charts longer than anyone else. At least Buddy Holly was still in there at No.14 on the 'World Male Singer' list.

Just before Christmas he was off again to France for the 'Telstar' Hearing. Seated in the High Court, he was hounded by the thought of the million francs damages (£72,000) plus all 'Telstar's' royalties that the Frenchman was claiming off him. However, when the Experts' Report was presented it left no one the wiser. The only concrete points they could come up with were that the opening bars of 'Telstar' were similar but not identical to those of 'Austerlitz' and that this was a "regrettable melodious coincidence". Both tunes, they said, were sufficiently alike for one to have been copied from the other, but sufficiently different for this not to have been so; they had no means of telling. As for 'Rule Britannia' being involved, again they were vague, deciding that 'Austerlitz' was almost certainly not inspired by it in any way, while 'Telstar' might have been, though this was unlikely.

Unfortunately French Law states that "total or partial similarity constitutes sufficient presumption of infringement", so the chances of Joe and Ivy escaping with even their shirts looked slim. However, the judgment was not as expected. Since the French publisher had not declared any drop in 'Austerlitz's' sales – 'Telstar's' record buyers appeared to be different from their own – it seemed they had suffered no financial loss. Therefore they could have no award based on 'Telstar's' profits. The only profits they could have earned would have been from an agreement on the right to adapt those eight bars of 'Austerlitz'. So an Expert would have to be appointed to estimate what that agreement would have been; he would have three months to do it.

Significantly the amount agreed would be awarded not to the composer but to his publisher. Ledrut would instead be paid by Joe and Ivy the princely sum of 1,500 francs (£108) for "loss of morale" so he could advertise the judgment in the newspapers.

In one sense the result seemed satisfactory. It was soon looking like a settlement for a few thousand pounds would be arranged. In another sense French Law was an ass. After all, since the court had not found him guilty of plagiarism and 'Telstar' had not caused 'Austerlitz' any loss in sales, there ought to have been no penalties at all.

Still, the picture looked promising. It had Mr. Ginnett predicting an end to it all by early February and, after serving his three days on the jury, sent Joe away in higher spirits for his week of Christmas therapy in Newent.

15
To Be Or Not To Be?

hristmas did him a world of good. A week of happy family
life, being praised and fussed over by one and all, restored
his hopes and confidence. Better still might have been a fortnight
or a month, but a week of rustic inactivity was his limit. Eric
drove him back on New Year's Eve with his mother, who was concerned about his current troubles and loss of weight and would
be staying a few days to set him off on an even footing.

That evening he and his mother went along with office assistant Patrick Pink to welcome in the New Year with his landlady,
Mrs. Violet Shenton. Over the years he had been invited round
for dinner a few times at her home in nearby Finchley, and this
was a particularly happy way for him to be seeing in 1967.

However, his rapport with the 54 year old Mrs. Shenton had
never been an easy one and was something of a love-hate relationship. On the plus side, she would sometimes take him up a
cup of tea, offering genuinely motherly concern in his welfare,
and had even been known to take his shirts home to wash. He in
turn might tell her his troubles, and each Christmas bought the
family exorbitant presents. But all the warm feeling would be
turned icy cold by her and her husband's repeated requests for
quiet. Coming as they did in the middle of recordings and in the
form of a yell up the stairs or a rapping on the banisters, they
sometimes received an angry response. The session would
abruptly stop, with Joe darting out of the control room to set
loudspeakers on the stairs and blast the sound down at full
volume.

None of this was made any easier by his fear she was one of
the thousands stealing his ideas. In case she was listening in, he
would sometimes instruct people with him to stop speaking and
to write notes instead; anything on the subject of music would
receive a hushed whisper: "Write it down". At the same time he
would feed her misinformation by playing jumbled music down
through the living room chimney, because that was where he
thought she was picking it up.

As if all that were not bad enough he was also behind with his
rent. This debt more than any of the others was his most embarrassing. Though she never hustled him for money, she made
it clear in her firm, motherly way that he should not get too

overdue with his quarterly payments and it had caused some arguments. Her husband no doubt made his feelings felt too, for he prided himself on owing no one a penny and found it mighty hard to stomach when he was owed money.

The entire rent situation was in fact under review. Come June the whole property would be due for a new lease. Already he and the Shentons had received their six months' Notice To Quit by the society that owned the property but, subject to agreement, a new lease would be drawn up. All were apparently planning to stay on, though nothing as yet had been seriously discussed.

Anyway despite all the nagging undercurrents, their New Year's Eve celebrations flowed with wine and goodwill. It was a splendid start to the year. On the return to Holloway Road, he made sure 304 started the year right too by letting his mother walk in first.

The effect of the past week had brought one major development. The hero's welcome he had received at home had not only filled him with confidence but had made up his mind that any offer from EMI would have to include his retaining his studio. In his first letter of the year to Mr. Ginnett he is in buoyant mood and mentions two school-leavers, Dennis and Michael, who would soon be popping in from time to time to sort out tapes upstairs.

1-1-67

Dear Mr Ginnett

First, all you wish for yourself and family come your way in 1967, and I hope I play some part some way.

Well Ive had quite a nice rest, but my thoughts were with 304 and the recordings etc, Im very eagar to get started and plan to get going monday in full swing I am going to employ two people I spoke to you about who I think have the desire and ability to succed, I shall give them a month to show me if there right for the work, it apears the big meeting at E.M.I. is now the 17th of January, so I talk with Mr Wood on the phone monday about release's of disc I have ready, that could loose there power of being hits

if delayed to long in release and premotion.
    I enclose two cheque's you mentioned if there are others please let me know.
    Im very pleased with the Telstar case please keep me informed of any new events.
I remain yours Sincerely,
    Joe

By the time he wrote again to Mr. Ginnett his outlook had changed dramatically. No doubt it was partly due to a visit from Heinz which ended in a "hell of an argument" when the singer demanded royalties and threatened legal action. All such people Joe categorized as "ungrateful bastards" whom he had made stars of, but in this case he was especially bitter. His fondness for the young man, once the apple of his eye, had been the deepest of his friendships, and seeing Heinz equally bitter cut him to the quick. He believed Heinz had had far more from him than vice versa and that though Heinz had not seen it all in hard cash, the presents and investments lavished on him had – perhaps barring 'Telstar' receipts – covered all dues. As for Heinz's recordings, they had all ended nearly a year back and releases since then had only been old product.

In this letter, the meeting he speaks of is with the Ginnett family, while the letters he refers to are from the society serving Notice To Quit.

9.1.67

Dear Mr Ginnett
    I hope you are well, I look forward to seeing you on wensday, and everyone, I hope there will be no speacil preperations just let me fit in with what ever's usal.
    The enclosed letters I thought you may like to see befor hand, as you may wish to discuse there contents and the offer made, my mind has been changed over 304 this I will talk over with you Im looking for more comfort and theres been enough lousey

events here to turn me right off it.

So unless the car turns up Ill leave it untill wensday befor I contact you.

yours Sincerely
Joe

This time his car had been stolen so, of course, he could not drive his mother home. However, it seems likely that the "lousey events' included something more ominous than a stolen car or those Heinz hostilities.

This new dilemma would have stemmed from the recent October disaster when an avalanche from a coal tip had slid down upon the Welsh mining village of Aberfan, killing 144 people. A benefit concert had been held soon afterwards at the New Theatre in Cardiff, where amongst those performing were the Tornados. After the show they had returned to their hotel but were later summoned from their beds by a phone call from the notorious Kray twins advising them to meet them immediately. The gist of the meeting was that the two wanted to manage them and, through their connections in America, send them on tour over there. The group had tactfully said they would think about it, but as a result were badgered on the phone throughout their six-week show at Coventry with Mike & Bernie Winters, and were still receiving calls. Neither the police nor Joe had been informed of the gangsters' proposals, and a meeting was arranged for January 5 when, with bated breath, the organist went along on his own to The Grave Maurice public house in Whitechapel. Escorted into a back room by minders, he showed Ronnie Kray some Tornados photographs. Ronnie had already been told who the group's manager was but at this second meeting asked again. The organist remembers answering, "Joe Meek. He'll never let us go." The reply came back: "Leave that to me."

Whatever had happened, it must have been pretty harsh for Joe to want to forsake 304 completely. Up until Christmas he had always cherished the hope that EMI would let him hang onto the studio so he could carry on pottering around in his spare time, releasing the odd independent disc. After Christmas he had been keener still.

It must also have been pretty harsh for him to suddenly want to make out a will. He did not want his mother to know of it so, as his office assistant Patrick Pink recalls, they both went out for a walk in the rain so Joe could tell him about it: "We stood in that furniture shop doorway on the corner sheltering from rain and he said to me, 'I'm not going to be around much longer – I'll be leaving very soon. I must sort a will out.' He said he was going to get the solicitor to draw up a will and would make sure that I was comfortably off for my future days. I thought nothing of it – laughed."

How serious he was is difficult to judge, since his moods were growing more erratic by the day. The following week he started off his next letter to Mr. Ginnett with a burst of enthusiasm saying, "*I very pleased the insperation is coming back, to you know who, . . .*" His car was returned too – damaged but intact.

Meanwhile life at the studio was plodding along. Although he may not have been the record companies' sweetheart, the groups were still calling and the phone was still ringing as the traffic rumbled on by outside. He was still cooking up plenty of noise, though now he was getting tired more quickly, losing concentration and often cutting sessions midway. Two important meetings on January 17 he hoped would give him a boost.

The first was with the Riot Squad. He had at last got their record released, the one turned down months ago because of the lyrics. None of the Riot Squad's records had so far sold in large amounts (although curiously their 'I Take It That We're Through' was now in the Top Ten in Venezuela of all places), and everyone was getting very frustrated. This one *had* to sell. In the living room Joe, the group, their agent and management each agreed to raise £250 to stimulate the record's chances. The £1,000 could take whatever route he chose: pirate radio airplay or music paper charts or both. He was not putting in his share though till he had seen the colour of everyone else's.

Far more important was his evening meeting at EMI. He had been contacting Sir Joseph a lot lately and sending Top Secret letters via his despatch carrier Patrick Pink, with strict instructions they were for his attention only. Telephone calls were out of the question.

There is no doubt that Sir Joseph was growing desperate to get him. The loss in 1965 of one of his top A & R men, George Martin, who had gone independent taking with him many artistes and staff, had left a gap in EMI a mile wide, and Joe was the man to help fill it. However, desperate though he was he wanted full control over him and to restrict him to his usual producing-engineering, thus keeping him out of business affairs. About one thing he was adamant: all Joe's energies had to be channelled into EMI's direction. He could not have him arriving for work exhausted after a night's recording at 304, nor could he have a member of staff putting out records in opposition to EMI. That meant no more independent work.

Judging by that letter of a week back when Joe bemoaned certain "lousey events", Sir Joseph looked like getting his wish. Since then though Joe had changed his mind again! He wanted to retain some vestige of freedom, so it was no surprise when he came storming back to the flat after the meeting, declaring he had turned their offer down. Absurd as it might sound he said the bid had been upped to $£^1/_4$ million, a figure so immense it now had him thinking that since they valued him so highly, he must be able to earn it on his own.

A few hours' thought cooled him off though, and when he wrote later to Mr. Ginnett he was once again at a low ebb. (His mentioning his hopes of Tom Shanks releasing information draws attention to the fact that most of the company records were still in his hands. With £6,500 on his mind he was exercising the 'right of lien' which allowed him to hold onto all company documents.)

17.1.67

Dear Mr Ginnett

Hope you are well. Im not to well realy myself, and the first chance I can find I must take a holiday, this has been on my mind since befor Xmas, after the week on the Jury I realised my months of worry have left there mark, and minor problems become monsters and by 4–5 each day Ive had enough and the tension grow's, its because I had no break af all last year not even with the recordings, and even Xmas brought home problem's I tried to sort out by getting Mother back in London for a rest so I had more problem's and extra work to cope with, but it was worth it she is well and the other problem at home sortted out.

But as soon as I can get hold of some spare cash I will take two weeks off abroad, Spain I

think, I was happy there last time, because to go to
E.M.I. with the feeling I could loose my temper with
someone over next to nothing would kill all the good
Sir Joseph Lockwood has put my way, I do know
myself, with regards to how far I can go befor
breaking, I have tried to tell you this befor, Im on
tendare hooks and will be untill Ive rested away from it
all, Im covering up my feelings all the time, I will take
a friend with me Ive known for six years who
understands me as well as I expect any one can.

    The meeting at E.M.I. went well, but I need
more facts with regards to RGM sound contracts etc,
I believe the plan is for there Legal man to work with
you in an efort to release the information from Shanks
somehow and give them a better ideal of what is the
best way for me to work with them, the question of
304 came up I think it will be posible to keep it going
and make it pay to keep the equipment etc is another
matter, but it all depends on what belongs to what,
there feelings on RGM sound are the same as yours,
Im sure your right, so once we can get the gen we
need to safe gard the contracts and Artists and myself
(last again) we can decied what would be
needed to keep 304.

    It was like walking into a dream world in
the top offices, theres so much comfort, and the
buildings buzzing with progress, I know I would fit in, I
will meet some opposition, a couple walked by me while
I waitted in the room on the ground floor, giveing me
a look of distaste as a cat give a mouse befor the
attack, but the people that matter have shown me the
greatest respect, and given a chance Ill sort out the
best way to fit in, I supose somewhere someone will
have to move office's? to make room for me.

    I have that tremendous urge to get

started but must have the rest to be able to stand up to the mean one's, and the ever selfish Artists who seem to think Im a Robot in pink plastick skin, not all of them, thank God.

There was the constant talk of taking away the wieght from my shoulders Ive had to carry for over 7 years now, it will have to be done with care or Ill flote or fall over Im so used to doing almost the lot, I still feel I was very right to go to the man there I trust and admire so much, because he understands what make's me tick, Ill be given a chance to breath and succeed Im sure.

I like the new lyricks and tune and will be working on it soon, the patern is right lets hope with this, succes will be started, I know after a rest Ill be on form to do my best again.

I remain yours Sincerely   Joe

That week bad luck dealt him another body blow. On January 16 a tractor driver ploughing a field in the remote Suffolk village of Tattingstone noticed two suitcases lying near a hedgerow. Inside he found the dismembered limbs of a youth. And so began one of the most intensive police hunts ever mounted into what would be dubbed the "Suitcase Murder".

The news made banner headlines, though it was probably not until a few days later when first a description of the victim was released and then his name that Joe grew concerned. He was 17 year old Bernard Oliver, a warehouse worker from nearby Muswell Hill, who had been known by Joe, and press reports that police intended questioning all the boy's acquaintances were now adding to Joe's sea of troubles. His fears were no doubt doubled when further statements described the murderer as homosexual and that all known homosexual offenders in London and the Home Counties were to be thoroughly investigated.

THE LEGENDARY JOE MEEK

The strongest theory at this point was that Bernard, a shy, lonely boy who was easily led, had made one of his frequent visits to the West End, where he had been picked up and lured to his death. During the 11-day period in which he was missing, he might have been taken either to a deserted caravan or a certain cottage in an isolated lane near Tattingstone, where there had been reports of seamen and businessmen holding all-male weekend parties. At present there were two clues to the killer's identity: first, the obvious skill with which the body was severed, and second, the initials P.V.A. which had been found on one of the suitcases and which police suspected might belong to a seaman cook from the Harwich area.

Back at 304 while all this was going on, there was another new development. The time had come to take a chance on EMI. At last he accepted the offer and sent another Top Secret letter via postman Pat who had to hand it over to Sir Joseph and wait for a reply. The outcome of it was that the contract would be signed as soon as those of his artistes were dealt with.

What mattered now was what happened next, and when he wrote again to his solicitor he was back in fine, fighting form. (The first few paragraphs are omitted, since they deal only with cheques he had signed and a humdrum account of a Musicians Union agreement he was considering.)

23.1.67

Dear Mr Ginnett

... I think you will find the E.M.I. set up will develope into something good, without leaving me to the mercey of the brain pickers and cinicks, my actions have been deliberate because apart from three people there, Ive been misused, so dont under estimate my methodes of getting results when Ive something good to sell, as time gose by you will see Im very determined with the talent I have to offer and wont be kicked around to much, with you around, a good accountant and a free head it will be a succes story all over again, Ive collected some very talented people around me, some new, ready to lissen and work hard to succed, those that muck me around will have to try there luck else where, I have a couple of realy hot disc's to offer Ive recorded with new groups so a realy solid arrangment can be made with E.M.I. for world rights and publishing, after Ive met there man in charge Im going to ask for a certain amount of gareented premotion, you may feel Im going to far at times, but let me have a go.

You seem to detect the artistic streak in my actions, I can tell in your voice when your amused over the phone at some of my ways, the passport will cost me 30/- and Ill be able to hold my head up again it was worth it, Ive changed my mind about where I will go for a holiday, it should be Egypt its all I think about apart from work, and a littel play, Im very keen on Egyptian Art and mythology and its influance on most art so two weeks in Cairo and around there would do me a world of good, and broaden my desire to grasp this fanstastic subject, it could develope into something solid knowing me, Ill take a friend with me, and will pay his bill, I dout if Id go anywhere, if I cant see someone else getting pleasure and experiance from it, I'm like that, that gose for my work to, thats the lot for now, hope you succed with IVY or PRS or both – thank you.

my kindest regards yours Sincerely
Joe

Rather mysteriously his letters to Mr. Ginnett stop abruptly there. Any more he may have written were removed.

From the tone of that latest letter, one might be tempted to think things were on the mend. The tough talking showed him coming to terms with this new stage in his career, preparing for it with tooth-gritted confidence and looking forward to safeguarding the contracts and taking a well earned holiday. But he was still very up and down, becoming progressively more down than up as the days wore on, and much can be deduced from that line in his previous letter: *"I'm covering up my feelings all the time."*

THE LEGENDARY JOE MEEK

For a start he was almost flat broke. His personal bank account was overdrawn and the others were just sluggishly paying off bills, reducing the threat of bailiffs removing equipment. With no big-selling records to finance all the others, he could no longer afford Ivor Raymonde's £100 orchestra backings and had even tried, without success, to do a cheap deal with his one-time arranger Charles Blackwell. In fact he still hadn't started paying for the £1,000 four-track tape recorder he had bought a year ago, and which was vital in cutting down on overdubbing and giving him a cleaner sound. Nor, with the 'Telstar' talks suspended, had his right-hand man Mr. Ginnett been able to extract any advances from the PRS or Ivy Music. That meant that in spite of the tune having now passed 5 million sales on the Tornados' record and heaven knows how many millions on cover versions, he had never seen a penny for composing it. Dribs and drabs of other royalties were still seeping in, but these soon disappeared and he dearly missed the £20 per week that had always been his salary.

Due to the cash crisis he found himself depending more and more on food handouts from Patrick Pink. The young man, who was the friend going with him to Egypt, would often bring round things like bread, butter, steak and tomatoes – in fact anything he could pilfer from his mother's larder.

Naturally he could no longer expect those handy little £50 advances he had been used to when recordings were accepted, simply because almost nothing was getting through. As to the possible reasons for the constant rejections, he had a new suspicion: the Board of Trade. Why, he wondered, had Pye taken six months to put out the latest Riot Squad disc and then suddenly for the first time given no mention on the label to Meeksville Sound? Had they perhaps been forbidden by the Board of Trade to release his records till he got his books in order? No one had ever told him so, but it would explain the abrupt September rejection of all his productions and the omission of Meeksville on that label. Whatever it was, he was sure he smelt something very fishy.

What he needed right now, more than anything else, was a good, long rest. Gone was his youthful zest for life, and so too the full, fleshy face, giving way to a drawn, haggard look that undermined his 37 years. If he could only go and laze away somewhere for a few weeks, soaking up some sun and filming a few bull-fights and splash-arounds, he could leave the worries to John Ginnett and then burst back onto the scene with all that iron-fisted energy of old. They wouldn't know what hit them. But before he could go he wanted to get his artistes' contracts sorted out – all of which were still in the clutches of Tom Shanks – and then he could sign on with EMI and take the holiday. Meanwhile his efforts to speed up the cash flow had him tiring himself out with recordings and anxieties, keeping him stoked up the dangerous way: on 'uppers' and 'downers'. Then off he would go with his demos, trailing round publishers and record companies in a vain bid to get some advance somewhere.

But it was a vicious circle. The drugs he was taking to increase his income were actually decreasing the grade of his output. Losing his sharp reactions he was taking round work he would normally have tossed away and nobody wanted it. It had reached the stage where his contacts were avoiding him, telling their secretaries, "If Joe Meek calls round today, I'm out." So whereas once it had been: "Come in, Joe! Have a drink," he would now arrive to hear someone say, "No, he's not in today, Mr. Meek." Of course, he knew very well they were.

Not surprisingly he was getting bitter. It seemed like nearly everyone in the business was against him and he couldn't understand why; all he was doing was trying his best for people, and for his efforts he was just getting slapped. A typically caustic comment, "I'll come back and haunt the bastards," summed up his attitude to those he thought had it in for him.

Amongst those "bastards" selected for haunting he no doubt had found space for some "spies". In recent weeks he had grown convinced that not only were people listening in to 304 but watching him as well. On several occasions while walking outside he thought he had seen people in parked cars looking at him, and suspected them of tuning in to his flat with radio receivers. Evenings would find him peeping round curtains as if the road were alive with eyes and ears monitoring his every move. Perhaps it was all persecution complex poppycock, but there may have been some truth in it. At least one other person, Patrick Pink, a well-balanced 18 year old, also believed Joe was being spied on – by the police.

For a start, the "Suitcase Murder" hunt was hotting up with vital stains, dust and hair clues prompting police to swoop on four North London addresses. Besides checking all-night cafés and restaurants in Soho, detectives were visiting the haunts of known sex offenders throughout North and West London and, as the

Evening News put it, "One of the biggest-ever searchlights was turned on the twilight world of homosexuals. . ."

As well as these enquiries, he could have been subject to others. The police must have had a file on him following the Madras Place episode and one other known incident not long afterwards when friends of his were caught leaving 304 carrying drugs, and fined. On numerous occasions he had broken off telephone calls because of what sounded like phone-tapping, so if in fact anyone were bugging the place it could have been the police checking on drug abuse or other illegal pursuits.

Joe's finger was pointed at the record companies. They were the ones he had always suspected of stealing sounds and ideas. His thoughts had not changed, only his situation. Here *he* was, the man whose adventurous overdubbing techniques had done most to make the British scene shake off its dull sloth of one-track recording and push on with multi-track; whose fresh-blooded ideas and use of electronic effects on the most simple sounds had left engineers scratching their heads in bewilderment and helped liberate record production from its fossilized conventions; whose example was now being followed by many a new independent producer, realizing he didn't need a huge studio and the London Symphony Orchestra to make recordings.

There *they* were, enjoying the fruits of his labours: discovering his ideas one way or another and developing them along with their own, and on far better equipment. A lot of his secrets were now common knowledge. Thus it took no great mental agility for him to deduce that they were not only squeezing him out but might soon pass him by. The superb work of George Martin on the Beatles' 1965 recording 'Yesterday' had made him realize he had been caught up. When playing it one evening and someone said, "That's beautiful," he replied pensively, "I don't need telling that." 'Eleanor Rigby' and records by groups like the Fortunes and Walker Brothers rubbed it home.

His anguish was understandable. These were the people he had always detested, and yet soon he would be packing his bags to run along and join them. The thought appalled him.

It would mean surrendering everything he had fought for these past twelve years – above all, his independence. Painful images of his IBC days kept flashing back: memories of a world of time-keepers and tea ladies, of people nosing in on his work, picking his brains and belittling his product, of in-house bitching and mickey-taking and of lock-tight budgets and rigid regulations hampering him at every turn. Would it be the same old story all over again?

But he must not forget Sir Joseph. His great ally understood his style of working and had promised to give him scope, so he could forge ahead with their equipment creating more new sounds to amaze the music world. Sir Joseph was determined to see him succeed. He would remove all the worries and with careful control provide the right atmosphere in which he would flourish. In other words, he was offering what Joe had needed all along: someone he could actually trust to take care of all the time and energy-consuming business affairs, leaving him free to get on with the music. It sounded too good to be true but that was what was on the plate.

A few days later there was another new twist. An American disc jockey, Ed Verschure, from the WHTC radio station in Michigan, had been in contact during the past few months and on January 24 flew over to London to meet him. Verschure was enthralled by some of the music Joe had turned out – especially the Blue Rondos' 'Little Baby' – and urged him to help set up a joint record label solely for the American market. Recordings would be produced at Holloway Road, shipped over and distributed by a major company on their own personal label.

Despite having agreed to the exclusive EMI deal, Joe still had thoughts for this one! He was fascinated by the idea of having his own label and during their discussions at the studio, at Mr. Ginnett's and whilst eating out, he matched Verschure's valiant efforts by trying his best to find faith in him. But as the week progressed he grew more and more wary, admitting sadly at the end that he had been hurt too many times by people walking off with his ideas, and that though he wanted to trust him, he did not trust record companies and could not risk giving him a new master tape to hawk around in case it was stolen. He was still interested, but sent him home disappointed with some old masters instead.

On January 31 things looked promising. He called round a photographer to take passport photos and also sent off the money for a new Fairchild compressor. By this time, though, there was still no news of his artistes' contracts and no more discs had been accepted. For all the chance he had of getting anything released, he might as well have been offering them Stravinsky's 'Dumbarton Oaks'.

With mounting concern about how he would eventually be received at Abbey Road, aggravated by these endless rejections, he called round on February 2 to see his usual EMI contact at Manchester Square, Rex Oldfield. Both "hot discs" were cold shouldered.

From there he made his way to Charing Cross Road, perhaps to look up publishers in Denmark Street. Wandering down Charing Cross Road he stopped to look in the window of Zwemmer's bookshop. And who should pass by but Arthur Frewin! The producer who had given him his first big break as an engineer and had not seen him for a year chatted for a few minutes about nothing in particular, noticing he was not his usual self. To Arthur he sounded slurred and distant, talking over his shoulder. Then to his astonishment, Joe suddenly turned in mid-conversation and stepped straight out into the traffic. With car brakes squealing he walked trance-like across the road in the direction of Leicester Square.

His state of mind at this point must have been frightful. Dosed up to the eyeballs with anti-depressives he was perhaps still waging some hopeless war with the 1,001 bogeymen inside him. Maybe he had already surrendered. In the afternoon he arrived back at the empty flat. Shuffling listlessly about, his tortured thoughts writhing like a snake pit, he probably felt worse now than ever before. The rejection of these latest recordings would have bolstered another suspicion that had recently struck him: that it might not after all be due to petty jealousies, nor victimization over his soliciting incident, nor even the intervention of the Board of Trade – but the directive of Sir Joseph himself! How a record company so keen on acquiring his talent could persist in flinging it back in his face could only draw from him one explanation: that he was getting the carrot-and-stick treatment; money was the carrot, record rejection the stick. If that were the case he could see no reason why the mighty Sir Joseph should not somehow be blocking the rest of his product. His trust in him was shattered.

Where could he turn? The trust that Sir Joseph inspired had always meant more to Joe than the money he offered, and without it the deal had lost much of its charm.

But then there was 304. It would be no earthly good making recordings there if nobody wanted them, and if he now backed out of the EMI deal, that company would probably never accept anything off him again. In any case he could hardly afford to make any more recordings, unless they started being accepted and pulled in a few advance fees. As for the one record he had on release – by the Riot Squad – there had been no more word of hyping it since the meeting, so that one offered little hope. Bills were still a headache too. Although Mr. Ginnett was slowly wading through them, somehow keeping the companies afloat, there was still at least £15,000 to be found from bank accounts holding only a few hundred, and with Messrs. Shanks, Sutch, Burt and LaVern all bearing down on him like the Four Horsemen of the Apocalypse, it could be many months before he was out of debt.

On the other hand, as he said himself, the "old dump" had been lucky for him. In spite of low sales on latterday records, he could never forget those past massive sellers that gave him the glory he had always been seeking. There was also the chance of a favourable settlement in the 'Telstar' case. With what had now ballooned to over £150,000 in frozen royalties, he could hopefully buy all of these people out of his life in one swift stroke.[36]

Money might not be the answer to one problem though. With the June lease expiry fast drawing near, he strongly suspected the Shentons of wanting him out. When he recently paid his £87.10s.0d. he had been four months overdue. Since the rent was always paid out of RGM funds and that account was particularly low, priority was being given to those creditors pressing hardest; as the Shentons were not considered a threat they were lower down the list.

Later that afternoon Patrick Pink arrived with the goodies. From this point onwards it is mainly upon Patrick's account (the bulk of which appears in the Prologue) that the tracing of Joe's movements is based. To no one person, though, would Joe ever bare his whole soul, and would never talk to him about, for example, people trying to break into the premises, for fear this might frighten him away; nor would he speak ill of the Shentons in front of him, since Patrick was quite friendly with Mrs. Shenton and might be tempted to repeat what he heard. So his knowledge is limited.

That evening Joe was still languishing under the effect of barbiturates. No doubt it was partly due to such drugs that over the past few days his fear of the house being bugged had intensified, and writing messages on bits of paper was now common practice. However in spite of his stricken mental state, he still decided to go ahead and make a recording with Patrick. The fact that after six years he at last wanted him on disc is all the more striking considering the events that were to follow. If, as is likely, this was a present to thank a loyal friend it could well have been the first stage of a master-plan he was putting into action.

During the course of the session acute paranoia set in. Triggered off perhaps by a click on a tape or a movement outside in the dark, it had him defiantly trying to outwit bugs and cameras by directing Patrick to mime to the music. To someone so obsessively secretive, the feeling of being both listened to and spied on would have been hideous. Locked in a living nightmare of alien eyes and ears, where people were watching his every move and syphoning away his sounds, it's a wonder he didn't pack the session in at once. In fact it lasted till midnight when Patrick went upstairs to bed. Joe followed soon afterwards to fetch down the shotgun he had left under the bed. By itself this action may not have been significant since by this time it seems to have become fairly routine. Then, unbeknownst to Patrick, he phoned to ask over a friend.

For a couple of years he had held the lease on a flat further down the road, and was renting it out cheaply to one of his top guitarists, Richie Blackmore. In recent months, while Richie was away on tour, his German wife Margaret had sometimes called round to ward off lonely evenings having quiet, rather mystical chats. However when she knocked at his door this time things were very different: "I got a shock of my life because he was white in his face and it was like the eyes coming out of his head. Actually he looked like a devil and when I talked to him he didn't answer me. He was like a madman, saying somebody stealing something. He was dressed completely in black: black trousers and a very shiny shirt and black shoes. We went in the living room and he started running in the room like an idiot; he didn't sit, he stood and was running from one corner into the other – very restless – and was keeping his hands on his head and always said, 'I don't understand it, I don't understand it. I don't know what's happening'. He wrote but he was ripping it to pieces afterwards. He told me he was frightened somebody been stealing something of him – his ideas. He said, not to steal it from the paper – 'I know there's somebody who'd try to steal it out of my mind'. He always was afraid that somebody hypnotize him and he said, 'If I could ever get one of these hypnotists to myself, he can steal all my thinking if he sends me to sleep. Otherwise I could use one who steals from somebody else's thinking.'

"I think it must have been either this [Aleister] Crowley or somebody through black magic who disturbing his way to live. And this is what he always told me: 'I'm not by myself'. I said, 'Why, you're sitting there by yourself?' 'No,' he said, 'There's somebody around me – I can feel it. There's somebody in the air.'

TO BE OR NOT TO BE?

He mentioned it that particular evening. It was a negative spirit. He always had an 'evil' mind: everybody hate him, everybody wants to – only imagined – to kill him, everybody wants to get something off him. But it was only on the outside. In the inside of him he was a very soft person and we talked about it and I said, 'Tell me why are you so restless, why are you always shouting and get so mad about things?' And he always said, 'Listen. There's somebody in me. I can't help myself, I can't get him out. I feel sometimes I'm not myself; I'm talking but it's not my voice.' He told me that in his life before, he was a nice person but in this life he's evil: 'I have to get everybody back for what they've done before in this life.' What I think was that he was doing black magic. I think in his black magic he was wishing some other producer very bad luck. I don't know any names but I know he was wishing him failure. . . He said, 'Oh, nobody wants me. My music is no good anymore, nobody interesting in my music.' And then he started talking from Heinz and he said, 'This man has ruined my inside because I know he has only taken and taken and taken off of me but he never gives. He only takes me to get famous, and after he's famous he dropped me,' – something like this. He saw everything black. A pessimist.

"Then I turned my head and I saw this picture. And I saw that it was ruined. The day before, the painting was perfect – this lady with the crying eyes – but that evening it was like full of blood, all these colours running in between like somebody tried to get some blood in it. He painted it himself and was very proud of this picture. It was like somebody said goodbye to something. Because he loved this painting. Because everybody who came in had to look at it. It was very pretty.

"Another thing which he always said to me, and said that night, 'Margaret, you are so much like Lady Harris.' And I said, 'Who is she?' – 'No, no,' he said, 'It's OK, it's OK.' She was the girlfriend of Aleister Crowley. . . I think it must have been about half past one when I went. He said, 'I'm sorry but you have to go now.' And I went. He never said that before to me."

In the morning when Patrick awoke, Joe was still busy with the tapes. Now though his mood had changed. Gone was the nervous uncertainty of a few hours earlier, replaced by a tense, persistent anger, some of which was the effect of amphetamines. During breakfast he was still writing his messages but burning them too. He also burnt several letters and documents, though what they were exactly is unknown. Then with the firm assurance: "They aren't going to f—— get this", he took down a picture he had

293

painted, and scorched it. What significance there is in little black boys dancing naked round a fire is open to a number of theories. Since the painting was not one of his favourites – as opposed to the "lady with the crying eyes" – the likeliest possibility would at first seem to be a fear that it suggested an interest in naked boys. This in turn would lead to the theory that something had happened to make him think he might soon be subject to an enquiry. A blackmail threat perhaps alleging he had been unpleasantly involved with a child is plausible but far less likely than the current "Suitcase Murder" investigations. Three days before, in Tuesday's *Evening News*, detectives were said to have pieced together details of the boy's whereabouts during the 11 "missing" days before his death and of whom he was with. According to a spokesman, "Several people have been interviewed at the Highgate murder headquarters and positively sighted Bernard before he was murdered." If the police had not already called on Joe, the chances were they soon would. He would have wanted to destroy any clues he thought might link him with the victim.

The black arts could also have had a hand in it. Some smart jack might come along and assume those boys were voodoo dancing. A glance at the painting of the "lady with the crying eyes" would then tell him it too might have been used in similar sorcery, with the lady representing a *real* woman, or even *all* women. . .

One thing is certain. Since Mr. Ginnett had the financial problems under control, thus avoiding any immediate danger from bailiffs, Joe had no worries about either painting being seized in part payment for unpaid bills. This would therefore lead one to think that the documents and the painting of the boys could be used as evidence against him either by the police or the possible blackmailer.

Having spent half an hour burning all the 'evidence', he returned to the studio to finish Patrick's tape. When he came downstairs again about fifteen minutes later it was solely to hand Patrick a note that read: "I'm going now. Goodbye." Scribbled out before he came down, the message was at the time just as cryptic as most of the others. In retrospect its meaning is clear: he intended to take his own life.

At a stroke, this fact offers a more detailed, down-to-earth explanation for his earlier burn-up. Realizing that his suicide would provoke a police enquiry, he would have imagined them examining the painting of the boys (untampered with), and suspecting it might connect him with the murder. Their rooting through his personal letters, notes and addresses might even persuade them to pin it all on him, saying he committed suicide because the police were getting too close for comfort. After all, he apparently believed they had framed him over the Madras Place incident, so as far as he was concerned they could just as easily try it again. This time, though, he was not giving them the chance.

Then back he went to Patrick's tape. He was either still getting it finished or, more likely, gearing himself up for what lay ahead. Ten to fifteen minutes later he was still messing around with it when Michael, one of the young part-timers, arrived to do some tidying for him. Up went Patrick to let him know, noticing as he called out that the shotgun was propped up under the phone inside the control room door. Joe, it seems, had forgotten about the lad's irregular visits and had probably not planned on speaking again to Patrick either. Had Michael not arrived when he did, events might well have turned out very differently. As it happened, Joe had to break his train of thought to tell Patrick to send him away and, after a few moments, added the fateful request that he fetch Mrs. Shenton.

Mrs. Shenton came up. When she was told of the bad mood he was in, she appeared confident she would cope in her usual firm, motherly way. However, when she joined him in the control room he was soon loudly demanding from her "the book" and no amount of motherliness could calm him down. The book in question was almost certainly his rent book. Why she should still be holding onto it is unknown since, according to a later statement by her husband, no rent money was now owed. The most likely reason would be that retaining the book was her way of gently hinting at his Notice To Quit, without unleashing upon herself a storm of fury by actually telling him. It is extremely probable she wanted him out, and even if she didn't, he thought she did. Since 1965 there had been occasional rows about noise from the studio, the complaints from neighbours and his recent belated rent payments, and he had told people that were it not for his lease she would force him to leave. Come June 24 that lease would be up.

After a few minutes she turned away and headed for the stairs. He blasted her in the back. The sound of the explosion brought Patrick out. She seemed to have breathed her last in the young man's arms as he held her draped across the stairs. What is certain is that any impetus Joe might have been seeking in order to finish himself off, he found at the sight of her body and hearing Patrick say, "She's dead." Within seconds he had reloaded the gun and, to Patrick's horror, turned it on himself.

As Patrick walked back down the stairs, with the weight of the world on his shoulders, Michael returned. He had been waiting outside on the pavement for his friend Dennis to turn up and had heard the shots. Patrick told him to ring for the police, but after dialling 999 the lad panicked and ran out of the house. So Patrick rang. At this point someone else peeped in. An estate agent, Jim Wilson, had actually been downstairs in the shop with Albert Shenton discussing ways of disposing of the premises! Two or three times during the past six months Mr. Shenton had asked him round and was still unsure whether to renew the lease or sell up the business. Trade was poor, and several times he had planned to quit, only to change his mind again. Both men had heard the second shot, and when the boy came dashing out into the street Wilson decided to investigate. Ten seconds was all he needed, then he was gone too. Next Mr. Shenton tried to come in, but Patrick reached the door just in time to shut it on him, and then returned to sit waiting, sobbing in the living room.

For Patrick the horrors had only just begun. The police arrived, and in their efforts to get at the truth they accused him of killing both people and placing the gun in Joe's hand. Then he was led out, arm in arm between two policemen and through a crowd of a hundred strong that had gathered on the pavement, some spitting and shouting, "Murderer" and "Hang him". He received a grilling for five hours at Hornsey Road Police Station before the forensic report was presented and he was released. Reporters mustered outside his house and a *News Of The World* journalist harassed him for days in the hope of a scoop. When his address appeared in the newspapers, it was time for pop groups to start calling round. Thinking that as Joe's assistant he would be carrying on the business, they demanded royalties and the return of their tapes.

Someone else to come under a tough five-hour interrogation was Heinz. The gun had been his and was plastered with his fingerprints. The last time he had been seen with Joe was during their bitter row of a month back. For a while he was a prime suspect.

News of the deaths made the headlines in the London evening papers: "TOP POP MAN SHOT DEAD AT HIS LONDON STUDIO"; " TOP OF THE POPS COMPOSER AND A WIFE

SHOT DEAD".

An inquest was held on February 9 at St. Pancras Coroner's Court. Amongst those appearing was of course Patrick, who spoke of Joe's moodiness, fear of spies and the warm, mother-son relationship with Mrs. Shenton, while Heinz told the Coroner that Joe had asked for the gun saying there were a lot of people around who sometimes "tried to rough-handle" him. The pathologist in charge was the celebrated Professor Francis Camps, the "Professor of Murder", who had helped convict, amongst others, John Christie the Notting Hill strangler. He said there were traces of an amphetamine drug in the body, which was not altogether surprising since the police had counted 24 bottles at the flat, containing barbiturates, amphetamines, dexadrine and purple hearts: "He may well have been under the effect of the drug and this could have had a bearing on his behaviour. I don't think the risk of these particular drugs is fully appreciated. You can get changes in persons taking them, with delusions of persecution in particular. Having taken an overdose they suddenly get an impression that somebody is following them and that they may have been assaulted or are being attacked or ill-treated."

In spite of the evidence indicating his having been of unsound mind, the Coroner recommended the Jury return the verdict that "Meek murdered Mrs. Shenton and then commited suicide". Coroners' juries nearly always do what the Coroner tells them and, not surprisingly, this one faithfully complied. It was an unreasonable verdict. Since there was a definite area of doubt surrounding the killing of Mrs. Shenton, and a Coroner's jury does not have to come to a positive conclusion one way or the other, an Open Verdict would have been the right decision. Even if they lacked the capacity to recognize the strong possibility that Joe's mind was disturbed they should still, surely, have allowed for the chances of pure accident. After all, no one saw him deliberately kill her and no reason was found why he should have done so. As the Coroner himself admitted: "Why he should do this, we don't know. He just did it."

Next day Joe's funeral took place. About two hundred people, including his family and a handful of London friends and artistes, congregated in the small parish church at Newent. The sun was shining as he was buried in Newent Cemetery and some of his records were played quietly at the graveside.

𝄞𝄞𝄞𝄞𝄞𝄞𝄞𝄞𝄞𝄞𝄞𝄞𝄞𝄞𝄞

Whatever the verdict, it still leaves unanswered questions. If he in fact had planned to kill himself, as is the obvious assumption, why had he only three days earlier bought a new piece of recording equipment and undertaken a passport photo session for his Egyptian holiday? And why had he, the previous week, booked in Chad Carson & the Senators for a recording session on February 3? (They had appeared at the front door half an hour after the shooting.) Perhaps it was all simply to cheer himself up and nothing of any substance. If, on the other hand, they were serious considerations, then any plan he might have made would have become solid between the time of Tuesday's photo session and the early hours of Friday morning. In that case it looks suspiciously like something happened during that 30-hour period.

There were two known occurrences of importance. The first was Tuesday evening's newspaper report on the "Suitcase Murder", saying the police had information on who was with the boy and where they both were during the 11 "missing" days. Perhaps this news increased his fear of being dragged into the enquiry. The second was the EMI rejection of his recordings. He might have been depending entirely on their acceptance for cash to pay for the holiday, as well as reassurance of his faith in Sir Joseph's offer and the music industry in general. A disappointment of such proportions would have been crushing.

Its impact, of course, would have been further enhanced had he met with any other recent setbacks. A variety of grim possibilities exist: phone threats, blackmail letters, a police swoop or a visit by hoodlums; the sudden conviction that Mrs. Shenton wanted him out at a time when he most definitely wanted to stay (two members of groups who rang him during the early evening of February 2, have recalled his speaking of a "problem with the landlady"; he told them he might not be able to record at 304 in the future as he could be forced to move); the shadowy Mrs. Smith who along with all the 'guides' could have either been guiding him up the garden path or scaring him with genuine forecasts of his future; a bad experience at the seance table (in mid-January he had complained of spirit voices keeping him awake at night).

Then there was the date. Some say there is no way that

TO BE OR NOT TO BE?

February 3 could have come around without his being aware it was the anniversary of Buddy Holly's death. Given his firm beliefs concerning Holly, it is in all probability that that date had been simmering at the back of his mind at least since the first week in January when he discussed the will. It would have offered a morbid attraction, making the whole idea less galling, for not only might he have believed that sharing the same day would place him on the same spiritual level but that it could add an air of mystery too.

From these points two theories can be offered. The first one hinges on the strong occult atmosphere of the evening before he died and the indication from his clothing and conversation that he had either been practising or contemplating black magic. There are some who maintain that those who use the black arts to inflict harm upon others risk drawing that harm upon themselves. Perhaps the harm had already befallen him for, according to Margaret Blackmore's account, it would seem he believed himself possessed by an evil spirit. Who can conclusively state that he wasn't?

The second one conveniently ignores metaphysics and will find more plausibility amongst those firmer footed. In the absence of any *specific* evidence during the last few days that he was any more anxious than usual of either blackmailers, money-hunters or prophecies about his future, and assuming he was not listening in to the Shentons and their estate agent that morning on bugging equipment, the most likely cause of his killing himself was an acute paranoia brought on by an amalgam of the known factors: record rejection, the threat of eviction, an intense feeling of insecurity from intruders and prying devices, fear of evil spirits, the prospect of police interrogation in the murder case,[37] drugs and general persecution complex, all of which was shrouded in the presumed morbid attraction of February 3. As for the shooting of the landlady, this would appear to have been a spur-of-the-moment action demonstrating to grave effect his typically uncontrollable temper.

In short, death had offered a way out of all the torment. Having finally reached his decision, probably during the early evening of February 2, he started tying up loose ends. First he recorded some songs as a parting gift to a good friend; then, should his suicide arouse suspicion, he destroyed any material that could be used as 'evidence' against him in the "Suitcase Murder" enquiry. However, when the critical time arrived he could not summon up the resolve. Calling up Mrs. Shenton he probably hoped she would say the right thing regarding his tenancy, thus giving him a last-minute reprieve. She didn't, so with one tumultuous volley of anger he killed her. Evidently this act then gave him all the resolve he needed.

Epilogue

oon afterwards his companies went into liquidation. With the release by Tom Shanks of Joe's Books of Account in an "appalling confusion" plus liabilities of around £30,000 – not including legal fees and unknown sums of royalties due to various artistes – a Liquidator had to be appointed. A few weeks later the flat was cleared out; it was a matter of shifting all the stuff before the army of creditors started breaking in to help themselves. Curiously no will was admitted to probate, so by law he had died intestate and everything was loaded onto a large lorry and taken to be stored in a Balham warehouse.

In April 1968 an auction was held in Greek Street, off Shaftesbury Avenue. His vast accumulation of recording equipment with a selection of everything from microphones to music stands fetched £3,000, the old faithful honky-tonk piano and 'Telstar's' clavioline going for a fiver apiece. Most of it was bought by a band leader, Bob Potter, who was setting up his own studio at the Lakeside Country Club near Camberley, Surrey, and remained in use till 1983 when he sold it who knows where.

Also in '68 the English 'Telstar' case was sorted out. Following a Hearing at the High Court, a settlement was reached whereby the Frenchman received £8,500 of Joe's share. It was reckoned, though, that by the time Ledrut had paid all his own costs and handed over some to his music publisher, there wouldn't be much left for himself. About ten years afterwards he received roughly £10,000 more in a French settlement. The English case also provoked fresh interest from Major Banks. In an astonishing letter to Joe's solicitor he dismissed the Frenchman's claim saying, "The whole concept of 'Telstar' was mine". It turned out that the Major had made no contribution to the composition whatever; he had merely suggested Joe compose a different type of music and after hearing 'Telstar', felt that Joe had acted on his advice. (Ten years later the Major was to suddenly pop up again, saying he had not been paid in full for relinquishing his shares, and expressing an interest in taking over RGM Sound. Nothing was to come of any of it.)

As for Joe's unissued recordings, it was not until a year after the auction that a decision was made. In order to avoid a mess of tape ownership claims should he sell the recordings individually, the Liquidator had originally considered paying EMI £20 to spend ten days wiping the lot so he could then sell them off as blanks at five shillings each. Fortunately he thought again. He realized their value for future generations and saw their preservation as being something positive to come out of the profoundly negative death. So they found new owners intact. Of the 69 tea-chests full, plus enough spools of tape to fill a further 30, five were apparently donated to an orphanage by the Meek family, while the rest were sold for £400 (half the price they would have fetched as blanks) to a member of one of Joe's latterday groups, Cliff Cooper of the Millionaires, for use "in the study of the musical methods of the late R.G.Meek." 3,000 reels offered fair scope.

Eventually the various companies were taken over by the Official Receiver.

Of those who worked with Joe, several still have showbiz links. They include the evergreen Mike Berry, still recording and appearing onstage as singer and actor; Chas Hodges, who has swapped his guitar for a piano and, as one half of the cockney singalong duo Chas & Dave, is always in demand; Clem Cattini, the Tornado who keeps the Tornados' name whirling and who, as one of Britain's top session drummers, has enough credits to fill a book; Roger LaVern, happily tinkling the ivories again, with a vast and varied 6,000-tune repertoire, after his arthritic hands had been tamed by the surgeon's knife; Dennis D'Ell and Tony Dangerfield playing the clubs with the Southside Blues Band and the Savages respectively; Tom Jones, still one of the world's most popular singers; Cliff Bennett, with his Rebel Rousers, a big presence and a big voice; John Leyton, whose looks belie his years as he sets grandmas' hearts a-flutter on the rock'n'roll revival circuit; Charles Blackwell, still a musical director and mainly working in Europe; Robert Stigwood, a multi-millionaire whose organization goes from strength to strength; Mike Preston, a Hollywood actor; Jonathan King (who recorded unreleased material), the irrepressible; Freddie Starr, the unpredictable; Rick Wayne, still in fine shape, though nowadays the former Mr. Universe, Mr. World,

EPILOGUE

Mr. America, etc is publisher of *The Star* on the South Pacific island of St. Lucia; Allen Stagg, an audio-consultant; Dave Adams, poet and singer, who lives in New York and has warmed up memories of Holloway Road by recording a tribute album. And sister Joy is living near him as a Professor of Art; while Lional is managing a restaurant and looks uncannily the same forty years on.

Joe's mother, sister and brother Arthur have since died. So too have Major Banks, Tom Shanks (who never got the £6,500), John Ginnett, Jean Ledrut, Albert Shenton, Larry Parnes, Brian Epstein, Denis Preston, Alan A. Freeman, Dick Rowe, Ivor Raymonde, Sir Joseph Lockwood, Marcel Rodd, Anne Shelton, Frankie Vaughan and Alan Caddy.

The Wild Man of Rock'n'Roll and the prospective MP deemed by some to have been the best Prime Minister Britain never had, died in 1999 aged 58. Shockingly, Screaming Lord Sutch was found hanged at his home. Any hopes that it might possibly have been one of his publicity stunts, in best bad taste, were soon quashed. He had been suffering bouts of depression since his mother had died two years earlier, and also since the recent failure of his Official Monster Raving Loony Party to afford to field any candidates in the European elections. He will be missed by the Joe Meek Appreciation Society not only for some classic discs but because he was the one Meek performer who was guaranteed to pack any venue they provided.

A year later it was Heinz's turn. Years of mixing mundane jobs with back street pop revival shows had gradually ushered in the demon drink and the subsequent symptoms of motor neurone disease. More than once he had cheated death. In spite of these ailments he could always muster the strength to take to the spotlight, showing the same grit he had had in his early solo career. A prime example was his memorable performance at 1991's *Tribute Concert* at Lewisham. He died aged 57, still ranting about record royalties he felt he was owed.

The following month, the second most important person in 304's annals suddenly slipped away to join the choir invisible. Geoff Goddard, whose haunting melodies and rousing rhythms will still be echoing down the corridors of time when we are all long gone, suffered a heart attack, aged 62. He had quit the music scene in 1969, further disillusioned when a Cliff Richard song of his was spoilt in production, and settled for as creatively sterile a job as one could wish to find. Mopping floors and wiping tables in a canteen gave him something to do and people to talk to.

Though still sore at how he was treated by Joe, he admitted being lazy and requiring a set-up like that to lure him back to music: "I need someone driving me forward and Joe used to do that for me." Sadly it wasn't to be, and his remarkable talents drained away.

Holloway Road is as busy as ever. Mr. Shenton carried on running the leather shop till 1973. 304 was then taken over by Lloyd's Bank next door, which in turn handed over to Cycle-Logical bicycle shop in 1992. When tenants upstairs are asked if they have had any strange experiences, they generally say they have not. That contrasts with people who used to occupy his earlier homes in Newent. When Elsie Stranger lived at 1 Market Square, she would hear loud thumps on the first landing outside the bedroom which was once Joe's. "There's old Joe wandering about again," she would comment unperturbed. Her husband did not share her belief. However, even he couldn't explain the goings-on at their previous home, where at times they would hear the distinct sound of footsteps clomping up the stairs and open the door to – nobody. By coincidence that was over the dairy where Joe had also lived. Well, he did sometimes say that if he could find a way back he would, so who knows?

On the evening of the day he died, three friends had arranged to meet nearby and play Buddy Holly records. The evening was instead devoted to Joe's music. A plan was made there and then to collect every Meek release and keep alive the name and music. Calling themselves the R.G.M. Appreciation Society, they attracted like-minded collectors, and by the end of 1969 their rummagings through record shops, junk stalls and music papers had assembled an almost complete discography.

In 1972 another collector, Chris Knight, approached their leading light, Jim Blake, with a view to writing a biography. With one providing the tape recorder and the other the transport they interviewed thirty people who Joe had known, but then decided to scrap the project. As Knight admits: "The more we found out about him, the less we understood! It was the proverbial snowball getting bigger and bigger." Instead he contacted BBC Radio 1 with their research, and encouraged them to produce the excellent *Insight* documentary on Joe in 1976.

Prompted by such enterprise, Blake and two fellow fans, Hinton Sheryn and Alan Blackburn, petitioned Decca for an RGM album. For their pains, they were given carte blanche for a double LP, and drew up Joe's acclaimed first compilation, 'The

Joe Meek Story'. Launched in 1977 with a get-together of Meek acts, fresh interest in the music was aroused and some fanzines printed.

During the mid-Eighties, access was at last granted to the 'tea-chest tapes'. Over the years, various artistes had petitioned the owner for copies of their recordings, but he had stood firm against releasing anything. RGM enthusiast Alan Blackburn now took on the daunting task of roughly cataloguing them. What he found was a wealth of finished masters, demos, rehearsals, backing tracks, songwriting sessions and bugged conversations with groups and managers Joe did not trust; much of it was in stereo and, amazingly, in perfect condition. Amongst it are a few musical gems, though unfortunately no masterpieces to set the world on fire. It did, however, bring to light the fascinating monologue he made in 1962, describing equipment, techniques and life at the studio.

The publication of the first edition of *The Legendary Joe Meek* in 1989 was followed by a long-haul drive for media coverage. Those keenest for interviews were disc jockeys on 'golden oldie' radio shows, delighted to be part of a nationwide blitz in promoting the man behind so many of the discs they were playing. Occasional plugs on TV and numerous reviews in the press spread the word wider.

The forming of a fan club was the obvious next step. Various collectors who had compiled the discography drew up a constitution in 1990 for the Joe Meek Appreciation Society to "further the interest in the music created by Joe Meek, and to keep his memory alive." A newsletter and magazine were started, providing in-depth interviews with the artistes, news of record reissues, technical treatises and limitless chit-chat. As membership grew to nearly 400, a variety of services sprang up, including a 'radio library' comprising an ever-expanding archive of Joe talking and 'singing', of discussions with colleagues and of related documentaries long junked by broadcasters.

Further indulging the members and doing its share to promote 'live' music, the JMAS has exhumed many a Meek act and lured them back to Holloway Road. Long-forgotten names have found themselves performing to better reaction than they had in their hey-day! Amongst those rock'n'rolling back the years at The Lord Nelson and The Holloway Tavern have been Billie Davis, Kim Roberts, Danny Rivers, Gerry Temple, Neil Christian, Dave Kaye, Heinz, the Moontrekkers, Mike Berry & the Outlaws,

Screaming Lord Sutch & the Savages, Chris & the Students, the Honeycombs, the Blue Rondos, the Scorpions, the Off-Beats, the Riot Squad, Wes Sands, Bobby Rio, Ray Dexter, Mark Douglas and Johnny Parker, the boogie-woogie piano player on 'Bad Penny Blues'.

Maintaining momentum, a *Tribute Concert* was staged at Lewisham Theatre in 1991. The day began on an ominous note when a man died outside the building. Annoyed to find his car blocked in by the show's film crew he had demanded space to move it immediately. On being advised to "drop dead", he walked away and did just that!

Topping the 9-act bill was the 'Telstar' line-up of Tornados, sadly racked by ill health but together again after 28 years. The show was such a hit that it spawned a long-running mini *Telstar Tour*. All the performances that night were captured on film, but was it the dead man's curse that switched around all the microphones, delaying the show by 25 minutes, and then mysteriously caused the entire master footage to have a black stripe through it? Whether or not, the show later underwent 374 hours' remastering and was televised in condensed form on ITV's *Cue the Music*.

Around this time, a row was settled that had been raging since 1979. Royalties had continued flowing in from far and wide, with those from Joe's songwriting going to his family, and those for production to the Official Receiver. As the artistes were receiving nothing, some had offered to forego unpaid dues in return for the rights to their recordings. Others, including the Tornados, had been refused. So a litigation executive specializing in entertainment law, Graham Cole, had contacted the band to act on their behalf. Since at least £100,000 had gone to the Receiver, it was felt that Joe's bills had long been settled, and that all this income was now simply paying solicitors' and accountants' salaries. Proceedings were started and RGM sounds were put on ice.

Now in 1991, the matter was at last sorted out in the High Court. In exchange for a clean slate and a piddling "proportion of any outstanding monies", most Meek artistes were accorded the rights to their master tapes. The apparent exceptions were artistes on Pye, whose rights Joe had signed away "in perpetuity". However, such a contract would nowadays be construed as unfair, and unlikely to hold up in court.

A court case may yet put Joe's name back in the headlines. One day in 1991, Charles Ward of the Charles Kingsley Creation switched on the radio and was astonished to hear what he claims was the same snatch of melody that he had written 29 years earlier: "The opening phase of my 'Stepping On The Stars' had also become the opening phase of Jason Donovan's No.1 hit 'Any Dream Will Do'." That one had been written by Tim Rice and Andrew Lloyd-Webber for their *Joseph And The Amazing Technicolor Dreamcoat*. It was in 1962 that Ward had composed his own tune, and then taken the precaution of sending himself the manuscript in a Registered Envelope. In 1965, following the release of their 'Summer Without Sun', Joe recorded the band playing it as an instrumental and took it to EMI. That was the last any of them heard of it.

Dusting off his sealed envelope all these years later, Ward took it round to the nearest Commissoner for Oaths. "My nine notes were indeed identical to those of Messrs. Rice and Lloyd-Webber. Unfortunately my problem has been in proving access. All I know is that Tim Rice was working in EMI's A & R department in 1965, and says they wrote their song around 1965. My investigations will continue." Plagiarism or a 'regrettable melodious coincidence'?

A major coup was achieved when the prestigious BBC Television arts series *Arena* agreed to produce a documentary on Joe's life. Basing their 1991 *The Very Strange Story of Joe Meek* on the book, they spliced together sundry clips from meetings with his family and colleagues plus archive film stock. All was held together by Joe's crackling voice wafting in from 1956 and 1962 via his ancient EMI TR50. Interviews ranged from one with Lord Sutch, spouting irreverent recollections from inside a coffin, to brothers Eric and Arthur, sitting back so relaxed that one reviewer described them as still looking "dazed by what had happened 24 years after Meek's death". Also viewers could gape at the otherworldly Geoff Goddard who had fallen back down to earth into the barren landscape of Reading University's canteen, where he was now working. Meanwhile, back at the graveyard, there was Joe's old friend Tony Grinham remembering spooky nights spent wandering round cemeteries and interviewing a "talking" cat.

The programme was keen to credit Joe for breaking rules and doing things his own way. However, in spite of commendations from Jonathan King and Mickie Most, it all fell far short of acknowledging his boot up the industry's backside, conferring on him little more status than oddball bedroom boffin. Much harder to understand was the lack of explanation for his craving to succeed. How could a director attempt to make a £107,000 hour-long documentary about Joe's life without commenting on what made him tick?

Nonetheless, his *Very Strange Story* was well received and probably did his name some good. And running the closing frames over graffiti scrawled outside 304 was a charming touch: "Joe Meek Lives On".

As is so often the case, the pictures are better on radio! Another documentary, this time on BBC Radio 2, provided a much clearer image of the man and his importance. Again 1992's *The Telstar Man* employed the book as its source, this time teasingly putting John Leyton in what had been the 304 studio to present the words and music. This has been the most thorough to date.

Soon after the property was vacated in 1991, the first of many organized visits was made. Singers and musicians who had never dreamt of setting foot inside those rooms again have found themselves giving guided tours, conjuring up an image of what it was like there 30-odd years ago. Though the rooms are now residential, their structure is almost exactly the same, and picturing things as they were is not hard.

The building's empty rooms inspired thoughts of reviving it as Britain's first Museum of Vintage Sound Recording Technology. It could also exhibit Meek memorabilia, provide an educational resource and house a studio in the basement, using valve equipment.

The plan got off to a healthy start with vocal support from Schools' Examining Boards, recognizing its potential for students of GCSE and A' Level Music Composition. The thought of all those egg boxes adorning the walls, with miles of cables and tape edits to trip over, sent one man into raptures. Tony Clark, co-producer of the albums of the classical rock group Sky and technical adviser at the British School of Performing Arts & Technology, was euphoric: "We would adore to send students down. Today we've got so many systems and formulas, and none of them are coming up with the goods. So what you have to release is that 'original pioneering spirit'. I think it would give young people a different insight into the technology they've got today, and they would start to use it differently. They would see something like Joe Meek's studio, and they would relate to the equipment that *he* had." Other colleges agreed and lecturers tendered their services.

A permanent loan of vintage equipment was offered by the

National Sound Archive. More was awaiting collection at Decca, but alas not a dime of finance. Preserving their heritage and inspiring the next generation of producers and sound engineers was not on the industry's priority list. The local Borough of Islington promised £100,000, though that depended on their winning £37 million in a Government regeneration scheme, which unfortunately they didn't.

So the chance was missed. But at least the effort was made. The current lease runs out in 2017.

The following year the JMAS arranged for a commemorative plaque to be affixed outside the building. In the presence of the Mayor of Islington, it was unveiled by Joe's niece Sandra, echoing the previous year's plaque at his birthplace, which they had asked brother Eric to unveil.

In 1994, BBC Radio 4 produced the first Meek drama. Mis-titled *Lonely Joe*, it portrayed him as an aggressive, humour-less lecher and would have been more appropriately called 'Lusty Joe'. A fictional plot in which he was being interviewed by a reporter was used to tie together a batch of flashbacks, but it all lacked dramatic effect and failed to convey any sense of the torturous personal problems which fired his talent. Errors were profuse, and the actor playing him even got the voice wrong, endowing it with a broad-accented masculinity. Needless to say, this inferior play was another lost opportunity.

In happy contrast, the first drama to be *filmed* made him sympathetic. *Joe Meek shall Inherit the Earth* was acted out by a cast of tin cans! It was produced on a shoestring by a student, Simon Goddard, for his Fine Art degree at Humberside University: "Sounds peculiar but the film is meant as a light-hearted tribute, bringing comedy to Meek's often tragic life story, and with plenty of echoey Sixties sounds to boot." Running for 50 minutes, its puppet cans did indeed resemble their characters, with Joe having three to show him relaxed, anxious or raging. Complete with voices, sets and props, the cartoon was effective in scaling the heights of his career, and followed the decline via his personal problems and flashbacks to his childhood. There were also guest ghost appearances by Buddy Holly, Al Jolson and Rameses II.

As for producing a major film dramatization, interest since the first publication of the biography has fluctuated from one extreme to the other. The most up-to-date news in the latter half of 2000 is that a film company has been seriously working on the project, a script has been commissioned and an option on the book's film rights has been extended. Things are looking optimistic.

1994 was the first year when, if you telephoned a certain electronics firm, the receptionist bizarrely answered, "Joe Meek." To the receptionist though, there was nothing bizarre about it because she was simply stating the company's name. JoeMeek Ltd had just been set up by Ted Fletcher, a former RGM session singer. His trio, the Fletchers, had provided backings on scores of discs, as well as making a record in their own right as the Cameos. He had also been keen on the technical side, and Joe sometimes let him help out in the studio. Later when Joe became more anxious about people lifting ideas, Fletcher was one of those who stood accused. He has been running studios and designing equipment ever since.

With the growing interest in matters Meek, he decided to introduce a new device: the JoeMeek Stereo Compressor. Though compression went out in the Seventies and Eighties, it is now back again adding oomph to modern digitally disinfected recordings. He credits its design concept to Joe: "I modelled it on his equipment. Joe achieved a particular full-bodied noise on his records that was to do with the way he used his equipment and the fact he was a very fine engineer. The equipment that we manufacture is of such a quality that you can achieve that sound, as opposed to a lot of digital equipment today where you can't. When Joe accused me of pinching his sounds he was right, of course, but thirty years wrong!" Pinching the name was a shrewd move too.

So Joe's name is now on view in studios around the world. Gadgets such as the JoeMeek Voice Channel, Meequalizer and Meekrophone JM47 are finding their way onto recording sessions of some of the industry's top performers, like David Bowie, Tina Turner, Mark Knopfler, Peter Gabriel and the Spice Girls. It has made JoeMeek Ltd a £ multi-million company. Fletcher may well be right when he says, "There must be a hundred times the people who have heard the name Joe Meek now than when he was alive."

To find out more, one need only log onto the internet and 'search' the name Joe Meek. A prodigious list of websites shows up, offering plenty more than Fletcher wares. Here, a singer recounting 40 year old conversations as if they were last week; there, an article on the final hours drooling over murder theories. Information on the artistes abounds, with photographs and discographies forever on standby ready to be sent scudding through the ether. Answers are offered to 'Frequently Asked Questions' while RGM gems and lesser musical mush await their turn to be down-loaded in Bombay, Baghdad or Birchington-on-Sea. Clever essays and witty viewpoints fly side by side with slap-dash inaccuracies and naïve speculation. You pays your phone bill and you takes your choice: that is the nature of the beast. Most significantly, it all helps keep the name on people's lips – even if it is sometimes the name of that equally illustrious pioneer: Joe Meek, the 1840s mountain man of the Oregon trail!

The effect of publicizing all things Meek has sent his record prices skywards! Several singles sell for £100s, including the Syndicats' 'Crawdaddy Simone', the Dowlands' 'Lucky Johnny' and the Sharades' 'Dumb Head'. The 'I Hear A New World' EP goes for even more, while demand for the album has led to fake copies being pressed. At £1,500 apiece, it is no surprise that rogues' noses are twitching.

For those who can't afford the vinyl, there is another option. The Meek CD market has become a minor industry! Joe's name on a cover guarantees some thousands of sales, and few producers carry such weight. Clearly his original sound is still immensely appealing. 'Telstar', incidentally, remains Britain's biggest selling instrumental single worldwide, with estimated sales of 6 million plus. In 1997, even an album of his Fifties engineering works was issued. His CDs are mostly well mastered, well packaged and have informative sleeve notes. Nor has the voracious cult appetite for anything Meek been satisfied with mere re-releases. Fans want the previously unheard and unissued tracks of anyone who breathed into one of his mikes! They are being well catered for, and are adding to the 20-odd cassettes of all sorts washing around within the society.

What Joe would have thought about it is open to debate. Since much of what he taped he withheld from release, he would no doubt be smarting at some of the dross which has been shovelled out under his name. Still, as long as that is borne in mind when listening to the worthless stuff, he probably would have been equally thrilled that rejected gems were also getting an airing. Top of that list has to be RPM's CD release of his 'I Hear A New World' album.

Unfortunately the parasitic practice of not paying artistes has still not crawled away. Although most of Joe's squad now own their recordings that hasn't stopped compilers from sneaking tracks out without permission. It is reckoned that at least three-quarters of those artistes whose recordings have been released since 1967 have received nothing. Most are not even informed. Doug Henning, for example, who was the Flee Rekkers' bass guitarist, only heard of the band's CD when he was asked to autograph it: "I didn't know anything about it. This is becoming common throughout the music industry, and none of us know what to do about it. The MU seem pretty helpless. It is actually theft, in the same way as if you went to a concert with a DAT recorder up your shirt and recorded something and tried to sell it."

However, unscrupulous though this conduct undoubtedly is, tracing and paying at least one representative in every act would probably dull some compilers' appetites. Then little would be issued. But it is ironic that so many of his artistes who never saw a penny or a royalty statement in the Sixties, are no better off the second time around.

Far more troubling is the deteriorating condition of the 'tea-chest tapes'. As the years have passed, their plight has been of growing concern. While acknowledging they are the private collection of Cliff Cooper, artistes and fans remind him of the need to preserve them, while there is still something left worth preserving, and that hoarding them away unheard and unappreciated is denying the spirit in which they were sold to him. He in turn says he recognizes the tapes are of historic significance for British music and of importance to those studying Joe's character, but admits that some are decaying. Apparently, they have been run only once since 1967.

On 3 February 1997, the 30th anniversary, lack of response prompted a demonstration by artistes and fans outside his shop in Denmark Street. Alongside a stack of tea-chests, a skiffle band played and banners were waved. As a result he agreed to donate the tapes to the National Sound Archive – after they had been catalogued. Two years on, the NSA were still patiently waiting. As the curator there says, "It's a great collection and I'd love to have it. And at least we'd be able to make them available for people to listen to." So another demonstration was staged, this time attracting TV and radio coverage and a promise from Cooper in the *Daily Mail* that the tapes would indeed be transferred very soon. At the time of writing, not a single reel has changed hands, and all is quiet on the Denmark Street front. By the time they eventually are acquired – if ever – will they still be in a salvageable state?

Joe is still well remembered, though for various reasons. Even today his name provokes fear or anger, whilst for some it has acquired a mystique, turning him into a kind of outrageous folk hero of the music industry. But he is also recognized as having been a vast influence on the British music scene and hailed by some as the father of modern recording techniques. Not only did his innovative ideas help stimulate a more progressive way of thinking, but achieving success on his own with just talent, sheer guts and hard work inspired a whole new generation of independent producers. For a start, most of them began as sound-balance engineers. They are doing their producing on a scene where there are literally hundreds of labels dealing with the mighty major companies in much the same way as he once did, though now the majors produce little themselves and their power lies in deciding whose labels they want to press and distribute.

One of Britain's foremost music-makers harking back to the Meek sound is engineer Liam Watson of East London's Toe-Rag Studios: "Joe was a big influence because before I started as a commercial studio I was recording in my home. I admire lots of his stuff because it was so extreme for the time and the fact he was a rebel. He would have recognized much of the equipment here. I have exactly the same model speakers, amplifiers and cabinets that he had. And they are marvellous – he was right! I also have an Altec compressor. Another thing I've got that he had is an Astronic response control unit, as well as equalisers that he would use. Probably one of his best bits was an EMI BTR2. Besides my own, I only know of one other person who has it."

Watson plays guitar with the Bristols, who he describes as the "most Joe Meek sounding band around", and they have re-recorded several RGM numbers: "We really go for that Meek sound, but it isn't mainstream any more and we've had no chart positions. But we have interest in Japan, and our first album was voted the 4th Best Album of the Year in a Japanese teen pop magazine."

Another group he produces are the celebrated Shadows imitators, the Rapiers. Their guitarist, Colin Pryce-Jones, says he and Watson have succeeded in matching two starkly contrasting compositions: "My idea was to recreate the slow hymn 'The Old Rugged Cross' as an instrumental sounding exactly like 'Telstar'! 'Telstar' is the ultimate clavioline instrumental. Would the tune fit in with the galloping rhythm? It did exactly. We've got speeded-up guitar on it, clavioline, sound effects, foot-stomping, galloping beat, huge amounts of reverb, and I honestly think Joe would have liked it."

Other bands such as Stereolab, Erasure, Teenage Fanclub and St. Etienne all profess to have been influenced by his sounds. Musical tributes have come with Dave Stewart & Barbara Gaskin's 'Lucky Star', Wreckless Eric's 'Joe Meek', Graham Parker's 'Just Like Joe Meek's Blues' and Sheryl Crow's cryptically sordid Top Ten hit, 'A Change Will Do You Good'.

One of singer-songwriter Edwyn Collins's most treasured possessions is a strange looking amplifier which he claims was used on 'Telstar', and which is still in action in his own studio: "I use it regularly. Last year I was producing Space, the Liverpudlian group, and we also used the Binsen echo unit in a very Joe Meek way, I suppose influenced by 'I Hear A New World'. I think of him as this sort of space rocker!

"The fact he was the first bona fide independent pop record producer, making records on a shoestring: that parallels with the record 'A Girl Like You'. We only had a small budget of £10,000, that paid for our own recording studio and the record. I really admire that he could take on the majors and that he was the first to do close-miking techniques, like Humphrey Lyttelton's drum sound and the way he recorded trumpets. These were all breaking the rules and were quite daring things to do."

Were he alive today, what would he be doing? As things were, the EMI set-up was doomed. His state of mind could not have coped long with working for others and a showdown would have been quick in coming. It is hard though to imagine him soldiering on and on by himself, having the occasional hit and getting ever more frustrated in the lean months between. The time would surely have come when he would have felt impelled to seek psychiatric help. He had to be made to fully understand himself, to shake off the inferiority complex that was so closely linked to his homosexuality and iron out his sense of persecution by delving deep into childhood memories. Somehow someone had to win his trust, extract and examine his past and explain how it had affected the way that he was. Only then would he begin to find peace of mind.

Of course, the degree to which that peace of mind would have affected his output could have been considerable. Unbottling his anger could have cost him much fuel for his talent. Unburdened by the need to offset his complexes the world would have seen a calmer Joe, less inclined to spend his life burning up the hours on music and more at one with life around him.

However, some of that passion for sounds would have remained. It is safe to say he would still be in there somewhere conjuring up new noises and turning music inside out. Indeed it has been said that with the mind-boggling choice of digital gadgetry on today's market – which at the time of writing includes such marvels as portable keyboards that can play well over a hundred different sounds from a saxophone to a string section, 'harmonisers' which can actually raise or lower the tone of an out-of-tune voice without changing the tempo, and the incredible 'samplers' which can feed on any sound from that of a breaking saucer to a snare drum sound they have lifted from someone else's record and obtain its entire musical range – his potential was never fully realized, and that he could have advanced the futuristic sounds of such bands as Pink Floyd, Kraftwerk and Tangerine Dream ten times further. Since his day, albums have become works of art, no longer restricted to three-minute tracks, and the idea of using a whole side for one track would have thrilled him.

Perhaps he was simply too far ahead of his time. Had he arrived on the scene in 1970 he might have had the richer career his talents deserved. In fact retracing his life turns up various 'ifs' which might have provided a happier ending: if he had not left Major Banks . . .; if he had not composed 'Telstar' . . .; if he had not been sued by the Frenchman . . .; if there had been no Merseybeat, and so on.

Then again, if he had not spent so much of those first four years of his life as a girl . . .   It's all conjecture. Maybe it is better not to dwell on what might have been but to be thankful for what was. In spite of – or perhaps thanks to – a life largely spent fighting himself and those around him, he left behind a legacy of music that more than justified his efforts and while it is still being enjoyed, Joe Meek will not be entirely forgotten. God rest his soul in star-aspiring sounds.

APPENDIX

1. Shell-shock is now an obsolete term and is known more accurately as traumatic neurosis. It applied during WW1 to soldiers who had experienced overwhelming stress and who thus became hypersensitive to such things as noise, movement or light, any of which could bring on irritability and sometimes lead to violence.

2. The recording contained a highly praised piano solo and is another reason why Humphrey Lyttelton remembers it well: "It was a number we'd been doing for some time at the 'Humphrey Lyttelton Club', now the '100 Club'. The pianist, Johnny Parker, specialized in that rhythmic blues stuff and based his solos on the style of Dan Burley, who in fact originated the word 'skiffle'. After hearing the playback I wasn't happy with the drum sound and told Joe it was over-recorded. At that time the recorded sound corresponded much more closely to that produced 'live', and this of course won the approval of the people playing it. But Joe stuck to his guns, and it was too late to change it anyway because the session was over. It was plugged very strongly on the BBC's *Jack Jackson Show* and I had a great surprise coming back off holiday to find it in the Top Twenty."

3. He could have any number of microphones but they each had to be adjusted there and then, one by one, depending on how much impact was expected of them, and of course they were all headed for that one mono track. This can be compared with today's ultramodern technology which instead of just one track, now affords at the last count well over 100 of them: over 100 different sounds, each having a track to itself so it can be separately stretched, squashed and hung, drawn and quartered without eliciting so much as a whimper from the others.

4. A session would generally deliver the two sides of a single, but there could still be editing work afterwards. In the case of singers, half a dozen takes during a session would normally be the limit – if they hadn't got it by then, forget it. However, by cutting out the worst bits and joining up the best, engineers could work wonders. For example, in one song of actress Janette Scott's, Joe and his assistant Adrian Kerridge made 42 edits! She couldn't sing, so the engineers forced her to – on tape in the editing room.

5. Actually he was less abusing the equipment than using it to its full potential. After all, when a new car is taken out and really shown its paces, that is the way to get the most out of it. That is also true of recording equipment. On the same tack, when it comes to designing the next model it is obvious who the mechanics who build the stuff will turn to: not the person who always leaves his controls in the set position, because he seems quite satisfied. Instead they ask the meddler.

   For a more technical view on Joe's tinkering and tampering, here is one of his fellow engineers, Ray Prickett: "In those days recording was a lot different from today. You had to be very careful about overload points and things like that. Nowadays a desk is built in with what they call an overload factor: most desks have a 24db overload factor; it means you can overload the early stages of amplification 24db and still get zero distortion coming out. In those days you couldn't. You had to work and adjust your levels. If you went 10db over, you had to do something about it. One of the things you had to do was to get an attenuator, which was like a little plug, and you unplugged the microphone and stuck it in to give you 10db of padding – it was as critical as that! Joe wasn't worried about that because his mind was on the creative side, not on the little technical aspects of those sort of things. He was before his time. These days you can deliberately overload so that you can create distortion or whatever type of sound you want. His recordings often tended to be a little bit distorted, but it was great because that was what he was trying to achieve."

But this could cause problems. Although after Joe had finished with it the production would sound fair enough, things could go awry in the next stage. The recording would be passed on for cutting by one of the major companies which was handling it, and their technicians would sometimes even refuse to transfer it to disc because in the process it could end up unbearably distorted. Joe could get away with it if he only distorted it a bit and turned the knob just a few db, but he would often go the whole hog; if the knob could have gone round another four times he would have turned it! As Ray continues: "Basically there's a law: if you've got a tape and you copy it you always increase the distortion on it. It's a fact of life. There is no system which is 100% distortion free. So what happens is every time you copy something you create more distortion. But if you've got a clean tape to start with and can't hear it, it's fine: because you've got to get about 2% distortion before it becomes noticeable to the human ear. There's distortion there anyway: it might be about ·2%. But if you've got a tape and it's crunchy and it's just the sound that you want, one generation of copying or transferring to disc and it comes out and you've got terrible problems. But Joe wasn't interested in that. He was there and he was creating. He was probably doing a better job than some of the producers he was working with, to be quite honest . . . Sometimes to get the sound he wanted during the actual recording session he'd alter the tape recording equalisation. Then if he still wasn't happy with it, he'd tweak the replay equalisers to make it play back differently till he got the effect he wanted. But unless they knew exactly how he'd tweaked them, nobody would ever achieve that effect again."

6. Denis, incidentally, was Britain's first independent record producer. He had started off in 1947, inspired by the American jazz producer, Norman Granz, and during most of the Fifties his production company, Record Supervision, was the only one in Britain leasing recordings to the major labels.

7. Today it is well nigh impossible to check whether or not the following achievements are on a worldwide scale but they are certainly justified as far as Britain is concerned and are supported by experts in this field:

   (1)   Denis Preston: "Joe was the first man to utilize distortion; now you build it into your equipment."

   (2)   Adrian Kerridge: "Joe introduced the 'close-microphone technique' in this country. If you were recording a brass section you'd have one mike suspended fifteen feet away from them so you got a clean sound. Joe was the first to use two microphones on four trumpets, and two feet away; the sound was like a trumpet in your ear. Same for drums. Engineers would use one microphone suspended one and a half metres above the kit. Joe would say, 'No! Right on the snare drum, right on the cymbals.' Other engineers would be frightened to do this."

   (3)   Arthur Frewin: "He was the first man to take the front off the drums and put the mike inside the drums to get a drum sound so you get the impact on the skin the whole time; he'd leave the front off. The drummers didn't like it because it meant them having to do some work."

   (4)   Adrian Kerridge: "In 1955 he and producer Michael Barclay of Pye

would work what they called 'composites'. They are another word for pre-mixing; they're made track by track by track by track. Instead of the recording being laid down all at once on one track, they'd make a rhythm track – the first composite – add something else to it and then something else and finally put the voice on top; so it would end up three or four generations removed from the original. What they were in fact doing was multi-track recording by a composite method. No one else to my knowledge in England or Europe was recording music this way."

(5) Arthur Frewin: "He was the first one to phase. It came off on some of his pop records way back in '57, '58 and people wondered how the hell he did it. During the 'live' take he'd play back the previous take into the studio with a microphone by the speaker, and blend the two. He worked that out himself. He was the first in many, many things. He distorted brass by making them play against the wall; this hit the next sound coming out, breaking the sound up. They do it now and think it's the greatest thing in Heaven!"

8. Like most songs, Donegan's 'Cumberland Gap' has a story behind it: "We were guests on a 'live' TV show in a Kilburn ballroom. We were standing in the wings waiting to go on and wondering what we should do. 'Don't You Rock Me Daddy-O' was the previous big hit so I said, 'We'll have to do the old 'Daddy-O', I suppose. Because we never liked to do the same thing twice, and I started to play this 'Cumberland Gap' thing while we were standing there fiddling about. The boys joined in and the guitar player said, 'Yeh, that's a good one – let's do that on the show.' I said, 'All right.' We decided where the guitar solo came in, and so on, and then they announced: 'And here he is – Lonnie Donegan.' And we walked on and played the hit, 'Daddy-O', and then we played 'Cumberland Gap', which we'd never even rehearsed.

"The next morning the phone went – Alan Freeman, crackers: 'What are you trying to do to me? A hit record and we haven't even got it recorded.' I said, 'What are you talking about?' He said, 'You went on television last night playing a new song.' I said, 'So what?' He said, 'So what? Now everybody wants the song. Everybody else is going to be on and bloody cover it and we haven't even got it recorded!' So we rushed into the studio. And he was right. There were about six bloody covers came out before we could get ours on the market: Dickie Bishop, Wally Whyton – all the skiffle groups. Consequently we lost about 100,000 sales because the others got in first."

Never mind, at No.1 for five weeks it wasn't a complete flop.

9. Publishing the song and leasing the recording were dealt with by Denis. Suffice to say that accepting independent productions was very much frowned upon by major companies at this time, and but for the big name of Denis Preston behind it, the recording might well have never seen the light of day.

10. The piano, incidentally, was later to become a star in its own right and to feature on literally millions of discs. It was one of those old-fashioned player-pianos designed to use music rolls and play itself. Because of all the mechanism this required, the actual box of the piano was quite large, and so after he had emptied that part out it had a certain echoey sound of its own. But what made its sound most distinctive were the thumb tacks he put in each of the hammers, so on striking the strings they were sharply metallic. This made the piano more definable on recordings – especially when

some notes were de-tuned! In time it was to play an integral role in creating the sound for which he would become famous and can today be heard tinkling away on most of his discs.

11. Whilst discussing *The Legendary Joe Meek* on BBC Radio Leicester in 1990, the disc jockey John Clark was reminded of an interview he had heard in March 1958 on the BBC's *Woman's Hour*. Holly was recounting some of the "strange incidents" that had happened during his tour of Britain. In one of them, a brick had come crashing through his theatre dressing room window, with an autograph book attached to it. (This anecdote was repeated on BBC Radio 2's *Buddy in Britain* in 1998 by the tour's presenter Des O'Connor, who had been in the room with Holly at the time.) On another occasion, someone had handed him a note telling him he was going to die.

12. At that time one of the more conventional methods at his fingertips was 'tape-echo'. This he could simply obtain by running a six-inch piece of recording tape on a tape recorder that had three heads. While the tape runs round and round, the first head picks up the signal going in, then the other two play it back again in turn. This gives a 'repeat' echo, as in a cave. It was not, however, invented by Joe. Nor was the Binson echo unit he sometimes used: a thin metal disc made from a long coil of wire, giving a metallic type echo to sounds passing through it.

13. Chris Barber: "Denis was the most negative and non-producer I've ever worked with. I told him, 'Lansdowne is a rotten studio to work in for brass instruments and we can't play in it – we must go somewhere else.' He'd laugh and say,' You can't *play* in it.' I'd say, 'That's right, we can't play in it. You can get it fine technically but the acoustics are all wrong.' 'No, no, dear boy,' he'd say, 'There's nothing wrong with the acoustics – you can't play in it.' And so it would go on. Denis didn't think we were real jazz men – they were the Duke Ellington's and Louis Armstrong's, not youngsters from English public school. He was very good for commercial records – sellable commodity – but not for the artistic side. He'd say that as jazz musicians we'd be forgotten in a few years, and this made him difficult to work with. A lot of the time we didn't get that vital spark. 'Lonesome' didn't have the spark which 'Petite Fleur' had because it was made at Lansdowne. At Lansdowne we'd get them technically right without a wrong note. Often he wouldn't be interested in doing another take. He'd say. 'Don't waste time; they'll buy it if it's good Chris Barber or bad Chris Barber.' And he would want the record done in one session to save costs. One of our LPs took six 3-hour sessions and he wasn't at all pleased; that is until it did very well, and then he said we should do the same again in future!"

14. Broadening the argument further, there are those who say that worrying about commercialism is unwarranted in any case, because once you start charging people 5 bob a ticket to come and see you perform, there is no way that you are anything else but commercial. Denis had a choice: either give in to the jazz aesthetes and make records no one would buy or soak them in syrup so he lost credibility as well as musicians. Better still, he could aim to make records which satisfied both players and public – which is what he was trying to do. For his efforts he was generally praised and throughout his career was considered Britain's most ambitious and sophisticated producer of jazz.

15. Charles, like most other English arrangers, was strongly influenced by the styles of American recordings, his favourite being those of Stan Applebaum with the Drifters and Ben E. King.

16. Saga in the meantime had not turned out such a bad investment after all. Despite Banks burning his fingers when it went into receivership he still managed to make nearly 100% profit out of it. The entire repertoire he sold off to Marcel Rodd's Allied Records who resurrected the label under the name of Saga Records, which is still around to this day.

Triumph on the other hand isn't. Following Joe's departure Coupe was to soldier on through five more record releases before eventually succumbing to receivership early in '61. But in spite of the unhappy ending it had in some respects indeed been a triumph. Having started out with barely a ghost of a chance they had pooled all their skills and come up with three chart entries (one of which, given the distribution, might have made the No.1 spot), and that is a pretty good tally out of eight releases!

In a nutshell, they were blessed with first-rate productions and marketing but cursed with lack of funds, irresponsible opportunism and almost malicious MCPS bureaucracy; without those three millstones, they might have lasted longer. Joe summed it up, timidly painting less than half the picture: "Barrington-Coupe was a very classically-minded person and we never really saw eye to eye; I'm completely pop-minded and like to cater for the teenage market. The eighth record which was 'Angela Jones' became a hit and this was where the problems started. We discovered that we didn't have enough money to carry on pressing this record so we had difficulties, but anyway it got to No.7. And then I discovered that things were being misused in different ways and I was advised to leave the company and try and start up again on my own. This of course was impossible because by this time all my money had gone, and so I decided to take a partner by the name of Major Banks."

17. It was for a certain number of recordings per year from each artiste, and all those that were accepted would be financed by Top Rank; any productions by new artistes that were not accepted he would be free to take elsewhere.

18. Briefly, in order to avoid getting bogged down in contract gobbledygook, a lease at that time would run about 20 years; it gave the lessor (Joe's company) about 7% of the retail sale of each record sold (roughly $5^1/_2$ d). Out of this he would have to pay the artiste a royalty: usually 2% of sales ($1^1/_2$ d per record). The lessee (the record company) would, through Joe, sign the artiste to a recording contract for one or more records, any of which they had the option of refusing. After three refusals, the artiste could offer his talents elsewhere.

19. His deal with Dick meant saying goodbye to his singer Mike Preston, whose contract he had to hand over to Decca.

20. Joe's deal with Ivy was the usual *10-50-50*. He would get 10% of the minuscule sale of sheet music (that would be threepence per sheet), 50% of PRS royalties (due from the playing of his compositions, i.e.: on the radio, television and in concert halls, factories, etc.) and 50% of 'mechanical' royalties (these were for disc sales, and his share for each of his compositions worked out at $1\,{}^9/_{16}$% of the record's retail price).

21. That one and the Danny Rivers follow-up both appeared on Decca but only thanks to Danny's manager, who arranged the deal with Joe's Public Enemy No.1, Dick Rowe.

22. Joe was to guest on several records, usually playing a tambourine or a small toy xylophone. His most notable appearance was to be on a grotesquely over-echoed B-side monstrosity called 'Come Back To Me', where Geoff Goddard hams it up for all he is worth as a heartbroken lover wailing along to his own piano accompaniment, while Joe supplies the rhythm by

banging on the studio door. Not a pretty sound.

23. However, he did let himself be talked into signing up with two other companies whose demands were rather less. The first deal, which cast him as an executive independent producer for the small Ember label was to last but one record. The second one with Kapp Records sounded much grander. In a deal which made him the first British independent pop producer to sign direct with a major American label, he agreed to produce discs which would be issued in the States before being released over here. It soon fizzled out.

24. Unfortunately the record missed the charts, but over the next eighteen months Houston Wells & the Marksmen would have several releases, selling well enough to merit an LP and two EPs. The fact that Joe achieved even moderate success with a country'n'western outfit is an indication of his versatility. Admittedly he took steps to make the product reasonably palatable to the masses but managed to do so by striking a balance between truly authentic c'n'w and that of a commercial sound. This was to be most apparent on his next Houston Wells record, 'Only The Heartaches', which reached the Top Thirty. All this sounds reminiscent of his jazz days at Lansdowne where he was reckoned to be souping up British jazz, but the sound he got on many of Houston's tracks was not dissimilar to that of c'n'w great Jim Reeves who along with Hank Locklin was warm in his praises of Houston and his Marksmen.

25. In November '62 he sat down and recorded a potted life story for the magazine *Audio-Record Review*. It was not published but this technical, off-the-cuff description of his studio and equipment is interesting, especially since it is the only known recording still around of his talking on the subject. During it he was quite composed but it is not hard to imagine him fairly fizzing with enthusiasm when chatting to friends about this, one of his favourite topics: "I'll describe first of all the studio itself. It's on the second floor and it's the size of an average bedroom – no larger. I've covered all the walls with acoustic tiles – except one, which is covered with a thick curtain. This has a very good absorbing power and the studio is extremely 'dead'. The floor is carpeted and the ceiling is completely covered in tiles. And only the one wall has a few tiles missing and this gives me a certain amount of brightness. But basically it's completely 'dead'. I have no playback speaker in the studio and no cue lights. I have a piano which I've put drawing pins in the pads and it produces a more metallic sound which is much better to record, and is much more suitable for pop records.

"The microphones: the cables lead straight out into my control room which is about the size of a small bedroom. It was actually used as a small bedroom, I should imagine. In this control room I have a desk with the equipment piled on it and I have a table and a rack.

"Let's go back to the studio and I'll describe the microphones. The main microphones are two U47s. I think this is a wonderful microphone and I use it for all my vocalists. It has a very good characteristic for close-work, that is for instruments that you need a lot of presence on. To help this I use a small piece of foam plastic on it – this stops pops and bangs when a vocalist is very close to it . . . The others are AKG mikes – the small microphones, dynamic types that are very popular nowadays. I have about six of those. I have also a couple of Reslos. I use one on the bass drum and one sometimes for a vocal group, working on both sides of it. Really the microphones aren't all that expensive, but they're very efficient, and being such a small studio they're used pretty close to the instruments, and later in the control room I add echo to different channels. This way I get what I feel is a more commercial sound than to get the instruments to balance themselves in the studio.

"Anyway, we go into the control room now and the main recording machine is a twin-track Lyrec. I usually record the voice on one track and the backing on the other. The other recorder is a TR51 and this I use for dubbing, and I must say it's turning out to be a marvellous little machine, but I would prefer to change it soon for something like an Ampex, which will possibly be a little more reliable. This machine tends to pop just a little bit. Sometimes you get bumping in the background. I think it's to do with the bias.

"The mixers: there's a varied selection. I have a homemade mixer which has got four channels with 'top lift' on each. Then I use a Vortexian mixer, which is a pretty good solid job, and the sort of thing that you leave and sort of forget, but it has been very useful for me. Then I use a Vortexian tape recorder for delaying the echo; this gives me 'tape delay' echo, which I use. Then above my control room I have a room which I've made into an echo chamber. It's quite remarkable for the size of it. It really gives me a very, very good echo sound, which is on all my records. Also I use electronic echo and this is used quite a lot on my records too, especially on guitars and percussive sounds. The vocal mike goes through a little cooker I've made which has got bass, top and middle 'lift' in it; it was originally a small amplifier. It has three channels so I can mix in a vocal group with it and possibly the frontline instrument. And this is on top of the Lyrec . . . and is quite handy: I can mix without having to walk about the control room too much.

"The speaker is a Tannoy 'Dual-Concentric' in a Lockwood cabinet – the type they use in most studios today. I also have the same purpose speaker downstairs so I can play my acetates and records through to make sure they're cut properly and that the standard's well up. I've also got in my control room for the second channel – a vocal channel. I have another Tannoy speaker cabinet, a smaller type that fits into a corner. I don't know the model. This I find rather metallic and I only use at low levels. I can't really balance on it, I've tried but I can't seem to get a balance on it. It seems to have an artificial 'top lift' that rather misleads you.

"Well, I service my own gear. I have an advance oscillator and a small oscilloscope – the type you can pick up for £15. The oscillator is very important. I quite often use it on sound effects on some of my records. I have some bits of gear that you don't usually find with the keen recordist. That is, an old BBC limiter which I use on voice tracks quite often. It is very ancient and has got the old large pin, large bass-type valves. It must be at least 30 years old. That is very efficient and isn't all that noticeable in its operation. Then I have a compressor which I built myself. I found the design in one of the magazines, and it works very, very efficiently and I'm very pleased with it.

"For the electric bass: I feed this through an equaliser unit. On this unit I have experimented and I feed the output back. I believe it's positive feedback but when carefully done and through a choke, it gives you the effect of the string being plucked; you get a sort of metallic pluck of the string itself and this is quite effective on recordings. I don't always use it but on the Outlaws' records, for instance, I use it.

"Well, I think that describes pretty accurately the equipment. By the way, I feed my output to the speakers through Quad amplifiers. They are a wonderful amplifier. I also use a Quad downstairs for playing my records."

26. This machine would take over from the TR5I. Helping him get a cleaner sound it would at last give him the means to master recordings at 304, instead of having to finish them off at outside studios.

27. "Joe would never let me sing the way I wanted to sing. He was in two minds whether to let the accent come out because I had a Greek accent at the time. And he would make me smile as I sang – it was a terrific strain on the singing because the accent wouldn't come out and he'd say, 'I want you to sing very soft into the mike. I don't want you to punch the words out.' I always wanted to sing like everybody else – like Elvis Presley or Cliff Richard. One of the things they said at the time was that I looked like Cliff, and Joe was trying to build me round him and at the same time make me individual. But a lot of shows I did I got more screams saying 'Cliff' than screams saying 'Andy'. But it was better getting them for Cliff than not at all and getting boos. I didn't have a group at first. I think in the studio it was the Outlaws backing because I remember Chas swearing at me. The first record 'Hey There Cruel Heart' took a whole week to make because I was flat as a pancake, so he said, 'Maybe your voice is better different hours.' So he used to have me record very early in the morning: 5.30 – the Outlaws hated me! In the morning when you get up, your voice is a bit more resonant and powerful and I would run out of breath in the manner he made me sing; he used to make me smile and sing very softly into the microphone, and pound a lot of echo into it. When he had finished with it I couldn't for the life of me repeat that voice again because it was double-tracked, spliced and so on. He'd say, 'I've worked so hard on your record, it deserves to be a hit.' But whatever sound came out in the end, it was like a motor car making a noise and Joe turning it into a tune. It was Joe's work that made it, not my voice; anybody else could have done it."

28. Although only small, the Madras Place loo was certainly well frequented and several people were apprehended. One eager prospector once made his way there from Canada! When asked how he had managed to find it he replied that being homosexual entitled him to a special bus map with a selection of gentlemen's conveniences marked on it. All of them were on bus routes, and this one with no less than five major services passing by was one of the most sought after.

29. As for his oldest group, the Outlaws, a fresh start was made behind his back. After a year of having their recordings rejected, they sidled off to Lansdowne Studios to try on their own. Following their last release with him, a real rip-it-up rendition of his 'Shake With Me' featuring a classic guitar solo from Richie Blackmore, Richie had joined Heinz's Wild Boys, leaving multi-millionaire Michael Montague to go chasing after the rest of them for his Joe Meek Associates instruments. He never got them! (That had also marked the end of Joe Meek Associates, which due to Joe's indifference towards Andy Cavell, sank unnoticed.) As for the group recording in Lansdowne, Joe was having none of it, and immediately slapped an injunction on them, preventing their use of 'The Outlaws' name. They split up soon afterwards.

30. This in fact was only partly true. Although he had indeed composed the tune over a chord sequence, he first used the backing track of 'Try Once More' whose chords are quite different. It was the second backing he used, to 'Every Little Kiss', whose chords are the same as 'Telstar's'.

31. One musicologist, Sigmund Spaeth, spent most of his life doing exactly that. Perhaps his greatest claim to fame was in declaring that 'Yes, We Have

No Bananas' was stolen from four other pieces: Handel's 'Hallelujah Chorus', 'My Bonnie Lies Over The Ocean', 'In An Old-fashioned Garden' and 'I Dreamt That I Dwelt In Marble Halls'. So the first line could be sung: "Hallelujah bananas! Oh bring back my Bonnie to me".

32. But while playing around with recordings his eagerness would sometimes get the better of him and have him speeding fine solos from guitarist Richie Blackmore (as if they were not already fiery enough) and dubbing impossibly fast drum rhythms onto what would otherwise be classic rock'n'roll productions. Both Michael Cox and Reg Austin had walked off because of voice speeding, the latter's singing on 'My Saddest Day' being so feverishly fast and high that it actually sounds better at 33 r.p.m.!

33. Geoff Goddard, by the way, had agreed to play on 'Telstar' free of charge, since he was having his own composition on the B-side.

34. It is an occasional problem to this day for tape recorders to pick up police and taxi messages within a small radius.

35. What was apparently the final letter of the year to Mr. Ginnett is a long, rambling treatise, underlining his faith in the man who had now become legal adviser and confidant. Amongst the confusion, he makes some fascinating remarks.

14.12.66

Dear Mr Ginnett

I hope you are well, the resions for this letter is to give you an even better understanding of myself.

Firstly I have a naturaly feeling of being misunderstood, and attribute this to my artistic and creative abilities, it is the make up of many people who feel they have something new to offer, and could even develope stronger with the standard of work and I hope it will rise to a higher standard than the past few year's since Telstar case realy setteled in my mind, the desire and even a form of love that one puts into music, (myself anyway), has slowely been stunted with the thoughts of, why, when Im only called a liar and a thief, I know waiting inside becauces I cant even trust putting it on paper or tape, lies a very huge range of music of many form's, which will emerge in time if a fair and only one judgment can be fair that I wrote Telstar and, with what power I have to analise my own work many other composition, if they are hits or not, has no bering on the fact, to write just for the pop market would be like looking forward for today with no dream of tomorrow, compositions of a high standard, and I Im as I said only just begining, several years through this case have been waisted.

It has been said, that I borrowed from Rule Britannia, I think not, I do believe, and am even still in the proccess of finding out, that from the begining our minds start to developing and absorb information, around 1-2 years of age even, it is this information that controls every ideal, emotion, and therefor, the imagination grow's, with the persion personal experiance's added, I believe it is possible to be partley controled at time's by past beings, and am aware I am partly Psychic I am still very aware that when people say I love that music, writters, or artists paintings, (you have a love for Sheakspear) it is a fact, they like there work so much that it develope's or could into a real love for that artists work, and also a desire develope's to understand that artist often passed over continues befor, so whats taken in by the brian is in the mind and if stronley absorbed remains in the memory, I have for at least 15 years admiered the work of Tchaikovsky, love is admiration to the exstream in my opinion, and so it would be his works I would lissen, when I could, until I added at least another 10 writters to my list, I think Tchaikovsky wrote strong and lovely melodys, from the heart and because of his weakness's, as some call it, poured tremendous soul into his work, if then I have unconcisley, and this is posible it would be from such a man and my favorite work is his Symphony No 5 and the Andante Cantabile, my favorite part of the work of art, Ive been inspired this would be in my memory because I would listen for hour's to the recording of this Symphony.

Im not trying to back my case up, I am complety free of any dout to my work. I know my capabilities, my way of thinking, and the power I have developed not only over music, but over people, Ive studied Psychoanalysis for six year's and because I want to and needed to use my own methods to extract results from the group's of at time prity weak mussitionship the industry has cultivated or tried to, a teenager is a very dificult being as you know, the year's when one feels he has discovered the world and the anssers to everything, but has only just started to grow into a man or woman, so this desire to understand and control the people I work with, and my own creative talents is the resion at times I am over tempremental, people that have know me years say since the Telstar case I have not been so nice, well you know the resions now, also the fact that succes dose give anyone if not handeled with care a independants, which could apear selfish and greedy, Im niether, at heart the opisite is the case, so I have to watch my extravagance to others at times, but I have this strong desire to be liked and admiered, and to help other people from which I gain my greatest pleasure I know, I will choose with care when posible, the one's I do try to help, it is a fact from the age of about nine I had the strongest desires to be a doctor, and feel a form of help is given to many people, when needed that seem to apear sometimes in the Artist etc, or out of the blue, it is again the mind, I seem to be able to work through because this dose control our every move, so I understand myself better than people are lead to think, it is often a mood to control a situation, I wish to make this point, because you could misjudge me through my actions at times, I also realise only to well, I have much to still keep absorbing, and that you are the man that should know the workings of my mind, more than anyone, to help understand and somtimes advise when you think fit, you have said, and it is very correct, you cant be good at everything, I have found I only absorb what I think is benificial to my life, and the life best for me, so since you convinced me a more pratical buissness sense is a very important factor Im developing it fast, but it must not stunt my creative work, because I think with both, and your help and the man at E.M.I. the man next door and hard work, I could be a multi-millionair, and my work realy excepted, I wish to be a millionair because this is the only way to demand from many the respect needed to do all I want to while on this earth.

I remain yours Sincerely
Joe Meek

36. That same day, a letter arrived on the desk of Frederick Woods, Assistant General Manager of the Performing Right Society. It was from S.A.C.E.M., the French version of the society. The letter is something Woods has regretted ever since: "They spoke of the French court's judgment and said that only a minor percentage of 'Telstar's' royalties should go to Jean Ledrut. A considerable sum was therefore immediately available to Joe. At the same time I knew something of his problems and decided to ring him with the good news. Sadly, something else distracted me that day and, in the event, I did not ring him. Had I done so, I could have said, 'We can't sort things out finally yet, but if you write in and ask for an advance against royalties, we can do that for you.' He might well have listened to me. We did know each other, not well, but we did know each other, so I wouldn't have just been an anonymous voice from the P.R.S."

37. The murderer was never caught.

ACKNOWLEDGMENTS

LYRICS are reproduced by kind permission of the following:

Peer Music (UK) Ltd., 8 Verulam St., London WC1: 'Johnny Remember Me' (Goddard); 'Tribute To Buddy Holly' (Goddard); 'Son, This Is She' (Goddard); 'Monster In Black Tights' (Goddard/Meek); 'Sky Men' (Goddard); 'Six White Horses' (Duke); 'Just Like Eddie' (Goddard).

Ivy Music Ltd., 8-9 Frith Street, London W1: 'Loneliness' (Duke); 'North Wind' (Meek); 'Dreams Do Come True' (Meek).

Essex Music Ltd., P.O.Box 1425, Chancellor's House, Chancellor's Rd., London, W6: 'Put A Ring On Her Finger' (Duke); 'With This Kiss' (Duke).

PHOTOGRAPHS are reproduced by kind permission of the following:

Ena Shippam (2, 3); Sandra Meek-Williams (4, 5, 7); Alan Blackburn (6); Patrick Gwynn-Jones (8); Lester Banks (9); Peter Cozens (11); Dr Chris Williams (12); Lional Howard, Peter Iaquianidi (13); *Psychic News* (14); Mike Berry (16); Gary Leport (17); Lord David Sutch (18); David Magnus, courtesy of John Beecher (19, 20); John Repsch (1, 21, 27, 40); Peter A. Lane (22); Vernon Hopkins, Tom Jones, the Senators, Chris Ellis (23); Glenda Collins (24); The Tornados (25); Prof. Joy Adams (26); Patricia Ginnett (28); Robbie Duke (29); The Honeycombs (30); *New Musical Express* (31); Joe Meek Appreciation Society (32, 39, 41); Paulene Petchey (34); *Daily Mirror* (35); *Evening Standard* (36); Darren Vidler (37); Ron Long Photography (38); Tony Grinham (42, 43); University of Reading (44); Phil Smee/Strange Things Library (front cover).

SUGGESTED FURTHER READING

The Rise and Fall of Rock – Jeff Kent (Stoke-on-Trent: Witan Books, 1983)
The Time of our Lives – Alastair Burnet and Willie Landels (London: Elm Tree Books, 1981)
Buddy Holly, his Life and Music – John J. Goldrosen (London: Futura, 1975)
The Record Producers – John Tobler and Stuart Grundy (London: BBC, 1982)
Shout! The True Story of the Beatles – Philip Norman (London: Corgi, 1981)
The Illustrated History of Pop – Paul Flattery (London: Music Sales, 1973)
The Story of Pop – (London: Octopus Books, 1974)
The Sixties – Francis Wheen (London: Century Hutchinson, 1982)
The Guinness Book of British Hit Singles – (Enfield: Guinness Superlatives, 1981)
The Pop Industry Inside Out – Michael Cable (London: W.H. Allen, 1977)
Out Of His Head: the Sound of Phil Spector – Richard Williams (London: Sphere Books, 1972)

... AND CONTACTS

Joe Meek Appreciation Society, 89 Hardy Crescent, Wimborne, Dorset BH21 2AR. Website: www.rgmsound.co.uk

TelstarWeb: www.concentric.net/~meekweb/telstar.htm

DISCOGRAPHY

Compiled by: Jim Blake, Paul Everett and Ken Wright.

This is a chronological list of all the records he is known to have produced in the UK, plus some overseas issues. The date on the left indicates the month of release, and is followed by the label and catalogue number. The figures in brackets, after the artiste or group, refer to the record's highest chart position and the number of weeks it was in the Top 30 (until Feb 1960) or the Top 50 (from March 1960) . The chart placings for singles are taken from the *Guinness Book Of British Hit Singles*, while those for EPs are from the *Record Retailer* EP Top 20. As chart lists vary, some Meek records did not appear in these charts though they did in others. The key to composers' initials is at the end.

1956
June Parlophone R4184   Bad Penny Blues/ Close Your Eyes (this side engineered only) HUMPHREY LYTTELTON BAND (No.19, 6 weeks)
1957
Sept Columbia DB4006   Sizzling Hot (M/Blackwell)/ Freewheeling Baby – JIMMY MILLER & THE BARBECUES
Nov Pye N15115   The Land Of Make Believe (M/Blackwell)/ Over The Rainbow – JACKIE DAVIES WITH HIS QUARTET
1958
Feb Columbia DB4081   Jelly Baby (D)/Cry Baby Cry – JIMMY MILLER & THE NEW BARBECUES
Aug Decca F11053   A House, A Car And A Wedding Ring/ My Lucky Love – MIKE PRESTON
Sept Parlophone R4477   Whoopee/ My Oh My! (D) – JOY & DAVID
Dec Decca F11087   Why, Why, Why/ Whispering Grass – MIKE PRESTON
1959
Mar Decca F11120   Dirty Old Town/ In Surabaya – MIKE PRESTON
     Decca Fl1123   Rockin' Away The Blues (D/Adams)/ If You Pass Me By (D) – JOY & DAVID
May Decca F11133   Rock Around The Mailbags/ Blackout (D) – TERRY WHITE & THE TERRIERS
     Pye NPL18053   'THIS IS CHICO' LP – CHICO ARNEZ & HIS LATIN-AMERICAN ORCHESTRA (co-produced with Denis Preston) Heatwave/ La Cucaracha-Cha-Cha/ Olé Mambo/ Yashmak (D)/ Ain't She Sweet/ Para Cha-Cha/ Havana 1850/ Swing Low Sweet Cha-Cha/ Harlem Mambo/ Malaguena/ My Funny Valentine/ Charmaine
     Pye 7N15196   Yashmak (D)/ Ain't She Sweet – CHICO ARNEZ & HIS LATIN-AMERICAN ORCHESTRA (co-produced with Denis Preston)
Oct Decca F 11167   Mr. Blue/ Just Ask Your Heart – MIKE PRESTON (No.12, 8 weeks)
     Pye 7N15225   What Do You Want To Make Those Eyes At Me For/ Don't Tell Me Your Toubles – EMILE FORD & THE CHECKMATES (co-produced with Emile Ford) (No.1, 26 weeks)
Dec Columbia DB4383   The Monster (D)/ Eton Boating Song – CHRIS WILLIAMS & HIS MONSTERS
1960
Jan Pye 7N15240   Be Mine/ Action – LANCE FORTUNE (No. 4, 12 weeks)
Feb Triumph RGM1000   Just Too Late (D)/ Friendship – PETER JAY & THE BLUE MEN
     Triumph RGM1001   Magic Wheel (D)/ Happy Valley (D) – RODD, KEN & THE CAVALIERS
Mar Triumph RGM1002   Let's Go See Granma/ Believe Me (D) – JOY & DAVE
     Triumph RGM1007   With This Kiss (D)/ Don't Tell Me Not To Love You – YOLANDA
     Triumph RGX ST5000   'I HEAR A NEW WORLD – Part 1' EP - THE BLUE MEN Entry Of The Globbots (D)/ Valley Of The Saroos (D)/Magnetic Field (D)/ Orbit Around The Moon (D)
Apr Triumph RGM1008   Green Jeans/ You Are My Sunshine – THE FABULOUS FLEE-

	RAKKERS (No.23, 13 weeks)
Triumph RGM1009	Hot Chicka'roo (D)/ Don't Pick On Me – RICKY WAYNE & THE FABULOUS FLEE-RAKKERS
Triumph RGM1010	I'm Always Chasing Rainbows/ Heart Of A Teenage Girl – GEORGE CHAKIRIS (No.49, 1 week)
May Triumph RGX ST5001	'I HEAR A NEW WORLD – Part 2' EP – THE BLUE MEN Globb Waterfall (D)/ The Dribcots' Space Boat (D)/ Love Dance Of The Saroos (D)/ The Bublight (D) (not released)
Triumph TRX ST9000	'I HEAR A NEW WORLD' LP – THE BLUE MEN (above titles +) I Hear A New World (D)/ March Of The Globbots (D)/ Disc Dance Of The Saroos (D)/ Valley Of No Return (D) (not released)
Triumph RGM1011	Angela Jones/ Don't Want To Know – MICHAEL COX (No.7, 13 weeks)
Aug Top Rank JAR426*	Tell Laura I Love Her/ Goodbye To Teenage Love – JOHN LEYTON (*recorded for Triumph release)
Top Rank JAR431*	Green Jeans/ You Are My Sunshine – THE FABULOUS FLEE-RAKKERS
Top Rank JAR432*	Hot Chicka'roo (D)/ Don't Pick On Me – RICKY WAYNE & THE FABULOUS FLEE-RAKKERS
Sept Pye 7N15288*	Sunday Date/ Shiftless Sam – THE FLEE REKKERS
Pye 7N15289*	Make Way Baby (D)/ Goodness Knows – RICKY WAYNE & THE OFF-BEATS
Pye 7N15290*	Paradise Garden (D)/ Who's The Girl – PETER JAY
HMV POP789	Along Came Caroline/ Lonely Road – MICHAEL COX (No. 41, 2 weeks)
Durium – ?*	Bridge Of Avignon (trad. arr. D)/ Hey, 'Round The Corner – EVE BOSWELL (released in Italy only)
Pye 7N15292*	Early In The Morning (D)/ Cool Water – CHICK WITH TED CAMERON & THE DJs
Oct HMV POP798	The Girl On The Floor Above/ Terry Brown's In Love With Mary Dee (D) – JOHN LEYTON
Decca F11291*	My Very Good Friend The Milkman/ Doopey Darling (D) – JOY & DAVE
Nov Pye 7N15295*	Time Will Tell/ The Night You Told A Lie (D) – IAN GREGORY
Decca F11294	I'm Waiting For Tomorrow (D)/ Can't You Hear My Heart – DANNY RIVERS (No.36, 3 weeks)
1961	
Jan HMV POP823*	No More Tomorrows/ So Nice To Walk You Home – GERRY TEMPLE
Decca F11314	Will You Love Me Tomorrow/ My Baby Doll (D) – MIKE BERRY
HMV POP830	Teenage Love/ Linda – MICHAEL COX & THE HUNTERS
Feb Pye 7N15326	Blue Tango/ Bitter Rice – THE FLEE REKKERS
Mar HMV POP844	Swingin' Low/ Spring Is Near (D) – THE OUTLAWS (No.46, 2 weeks)
May Decca F11357	Once Upon A Time/ My Baby's Gone Away (D) – DANNY RIVERS & THE ALEXANDER COMBO
HMV POP877	Ambush (D)/ Indian Brave (D) – THE OUTLAWS (No.43, 2 weeks)
Pye NEP24141	'THE FABULOUS FLEE REKKERS' EP Isle of Capri/ Brer Robert/ Hangover/ P.F.B.
June Parlophone R4793	You Got What I Like (D)/ I'm In Love With You (D/Bennett) – CLIFF BENNETT & THE REBEL ROUSERS
Pye Piccadilly 7N35006	Lone Rider (G)/ Miller Like Wow – THE FLEE REKKERS
July Parlophone R4806	Lass Of Richmond Hill/ Ducks Away From My Fishin' (D) – CHRIS & THE STUDENTS
Top Rank JAR577	Johnny Remember Me (G)/ There Must Be (D) – JOHN LEYTON (No.1, 15 weeks)
Aug HMV POP905	Sweet Little Sixteen/ Cover Girl – MICHAEL COX
Sept HMV POP912	Tribute To Buddy Holly (G)/ What's The Matter – MIKE BERRY

DISCOGRAPHY

	& THE OUTLAWS (No.24, 6 weeks)
Parlophone R4814	Night Of The Vampire/ Melodie D'Amore – THE MOON-TREKKERS (No.50, 1 week)
Top Rank JAR585	Wild Wind (G)/ You Took My Love For Granted (D) – JOHN LEYTON (No.2, 10 weeks)
HMV POP927	Valley Of The Sioux (D)/ Crazy Drums (D/Graham) – THE OUTLAWS
Oct HMV POP938	Girl Bride (G)/ For Eternity (D) – GEOFF GODDARD
Parlophone R4836	When I Get Paid/ That's What I Said (D) – CLIFF BENNETT & THE REBEL ROUSERS
HMV POP939	Seventeen Come Sunday (G)/ Tell You What I'll Do – GERRY TEMPLE
Nov HMV CLP1497	'THE TWO SIDES OF JOHN LEYTON' LP Voodoo Woman (G)/ Can't You Hear The Beat Of A Broken Heart (D)/ Fabulous/ Thunder And Lightning/ Oh Lover (G)/ I Don't Care If The Sun Don't Shine/ (I Love You) For Sentimental Reasons/ That's A Woman (B)/ Walk With Me My Angel (D)/ That's How To Make Love (D)/ The Magic Of True Love/ It's Goodbye Then (G)
Top Rank JKP3016	'JOHN LEYTON' EP Wild Wind (G)/ You Took My Love For Granted (D)/ Johnny Remember Me (G)/ There Must Be (D) (No.11, 13 weeks)
Pye 7N15397	Can't You Hear The Beat Of A Broken Heart (D)/ Because – IAIN GREGORY (No.39, 2 weeks)
Parlophone PMC1155	'SING ME A SOUVENIR' LP – THE BOWMAN-HYDE SINGERS & PLAYERS (Side 1) Sing Me A Souvenir/ The More We Are Together/ The Old Kitchen Kettle/ The Fleet's In Port Again/ The Voice In The Old Village Choir/ Wheezy Anna/ Abie My Boy/ Try A Little Tenderness/ Anniversary Song/ I Love You Truly/Just An Echo In The Valley/ Ole Faithful/ Leaning On A Lamp-post/ Lambeth Walk/ Over My Shoulder/ We'll All Go Riding On A Rainbow/ Sing Me A Souvenir/ (Side 2) Sing Me A Souvenir/Jolly Good Company/ Let's All Sing Like The Birdies Sing/ I'm Happy When I'm Hiking/ Cruising Down The River/ Just A-Wearyin' For You/ Garden In The Rain/ The Very Thought Of You/ In An Eighteenth Century Drawing Room/ Dancing With My Shadow/ I'm A Dreamer, Aren't We All/ The Girl In The Alice Blue Gown/ Dreaming / The Wheel Of The Wagon Is Broken/ Goodnight Sweetheart/ Show Me The Way To Go Home/ Sing Me A Souvenir/
Dec HMV CLP1489	'DREAM OF THE WEST' LP – THE OUTLAWS Dream Of The West (D)/ The Outlaws (D)/ Huskie Team (D)/ Rodeo (D)/ Smoke Signals (D)/ Ambush (D)/ Barbecue (D)/ Spring Is Near (D)/ Indian Brave (D)/ Homeward Bound (D)/ Western Sunset (D)/ Tune For Short Cowboys (D)
HMV POP953	'Til The Following Night/ Good Golly Miss Molly – SCREAMING LORD SUTCH & THE SAVAGES
HMV POP956	Son, This Is She (G)/ Six White Horses (D) – JOHN LEYTON (No. 15, 10 weeks)
Parlophone R4855	Joe's Been A 'Gittin' There/ They Tell Us Not To Love (D) – JOY & DAVE AND THE HOT SHOTS
Pye Piccadilly 7N35018	The Donkey's Tale/ Let It Snow On Christmas Day – BRYAN TAYLOR

1962

Jan HMV POP972	Young Only Once/ Honey 'Cause I Love You – MICHAEL COX
HMV POP977	Taboo/ Midnight In Luxembourg (D) – THE CHARLES BLACKWELL ORCHESTRA
HMV POP979	It's Just A Matter Of Time (D)/ Little Boy Blue (G) – MIKE BERRY & THE OUTLAWS

329

Decca F11424	Walk With Me My Angel (D)/ Crazy Man Crazy – DON CHARLES (No.39, 5 weeks)
Feb HMV POP981	Big Feet (D)/ Pinto – THE STONEHENGE MEN
HMV POP990	Last Stage West (D/Hodges)/ Ku–Pow (D) – THE OUTLAWS
Mar HMV POP992	Lone Rider (G)/ Heart Of Stone (D) – JOHN LEYTON (No.40, 5 weeks)
Parlophone R4888	There's Something At The Bottom Of The Well (D)/ Hatashai (Japanese Sword Fight) – THE MOONTREKKERS
HMV POP1000	We're Gonna Dance/ Movin' In – DANNY RIVERS & THE RIVERMEN
Parlophone R4895	Poor Joe (D)/ Hurtin' Inside (Slow Twist) – CLIFF BENNETT & THE REBEL ROUSERS WITH THE PEPPERMINTIES
Apr Decca F11449	Love And Fury (D)/ Popeye Twist – THE TORNADOS
Decca F11459	Dear One/ There Was A Time (B) – TONY VICTOR
Electrola 22089	Wann Bist Du Bei Mir (G)/ Six White Horses (D) – JOHN LEYTON (released in Germany only)
Pye 7N15435	Mr. Lovebug (D)/ Pocket Full Of Dreams (And Eyes Full Of Tears) (B) – IAIN GREGORY
HMV POP1014	Lonely City (G)/ It Would Be Easy (C) – JOHN LEYTON (No.14, 11 weeks) (New Leyton recordings listed after this one still credit RGM Sound but have little, if any, involvement from Meek.)
May Pye Piccadilly 7N35048	Stage To Cimarron/ Twistin' The Chestnuts – THE FLEE REKKERS
Decca F11464	The Hermit Of Misty Mountain/ Moonlight Rendezvous (B) – DON CHARLES
Oriole CB1719	Striped Purple Shirt/ You Gave Me The Blues (D) – ALAN KLEIN
HMV POP1024	Hey There Cruel Heart (B)/ Lonely Soldier Boy – ANDY CAVELL
HMV CLP1534	'MAGNA JAZZ BAND' LP – BRIAN WHITE & THE MAGNA JAZZ BAND
	Babette/ I'm Confessing/ Calamity/ Ida/ Baby, Won't You Please Come Home/ Goody Goody/ You're Just In Love/ Ukulele Lady/ Misty Morning/ Softly As In A Morning Sunrise/ Marchita/ Don't Dilly Dally
July Oriole CB1737	Three Coins In The Sewer/ Danger Ahead – ALAN KLEIN
HMV POP1042	Every Little Kiss (J)/ How Many Times – MIKE BERRY
HMV POP1054	Down The River Nile/ I Think I'm Falling In Love (J) – JOHN LEYTON (No.42, 3 weeks)
Aug Oriole CB1748	Little Sue/ Julie – THE DOWLANDS AND THE SOUND-TRACKS
Decca F11494	Telstar (M)/ Jungle Fever (G) – THE TORNADOS (No.1, 25 weeks)
Sept HMV POP1065	Stand Up/ In April (B) – MICHAEL COX
HMV 7EG8747	'THE JOHN LEYTON HIT PARADE' EP
	Lone Rider (G)/ Son, This Is She (G)/ Lonely City (G)/ It Would Be Easy (C)
HMV POP1068	My Little Girl's Come Home (G)/ Try Once More (J) – GEOFF GODDARD
Pye Piccadilly 7N35077	Cha-Cha On The Moon/ May Your Heart Stay Young Forever – PAT READER
Oct HMV POP1074	Sioux Serenade (W)/ Fort Knox – THE OUTLAWS
HMV POP1076	Lonely Johnny (G)/ Keep On Loving You (D) – JOHN LEYTON
Ember EMB-S166	It Matters Not/ Upside Down (J) – MARK DOUGLAS
HMV POP1080	Always On Saturday/ Hey There Senorita (M) – ANDY CAVELL
Parlophone R4955	This Song Is Just For You/ Paradise – HOUSTON WELLS & THE MARKSMEN
Pye Piccadilly 7N35081	Sunburst/ Black Buffalo – THE FLEE REKKERS
Decca DFE8510	'THE SOUNDS OF THE TORNADOS' EP
	Ridin' The Wind/ Dreamin' On A Cloud/ Red Roses And A Sky

DISCOGRAPHY

		Of Blue (M)/ Earthy (No.2, 26 weeks)
Nov	Decca DFE8511	'TELSTAR' EP – THE TORNADOS
		Telstar (M)/ Popeye Twist/ Love And Fury (D)/ Jungle Fever (G) (No.4, 22 weeks)
	Decca F11528	It's My Way Of Loving You/ Guess That's The Way It Goes (M) – DON CHARLES
	Decca F11531	Can Can '62/ Redskins (K) – PETER JAY & THE JAYWALKERS (No.31, 11 weeks)
	Pye 7N15480	Evening In Paris (M)/ 'The Traitors' Theme – THE PACK-ABEATS
	Decca F11538	The Coalmen's Lament/ Lonely Weekend – RAY DEXTER & THE LAYABOUTS
	Columbia DB4938	The Road To Love/ The Big Beat Drum (J/Lawrence) – NEIL CHRISTIAN
Dec	Oriole CB1781	Big Big Fella/ Don't Ever Change (D/Lawrence) – THE DOWLANDS & THE SOUNDTRACKS
	Decca F11546	Magic Star (M)/ The Wonderful Story Of Love (G) – KENNY HOLLYWOOD
	Parlophone R4979	'Poppin'' Medley – Part 1 – Return To Sender/ Next Door To An Angel/ Bobby's Girl/ Part 2 – It Might As Well Rain Until September/ Ramblin' Rose/ Telstar (M) – THE CHAPS [The Outlaws]
	Parlophone R4980	Shutters And Boards/ North Wind (M) – HOUSTON WELLS & THE MARKSMEN
	HMV POP1105	Don't You Think It's Time (GM)/ Loneliness (D) - MIKE BERRY & THE OUTLAWS (No.6, 12 weeks)

1963

Jan	Decca F11562	Globetrotter(M)/ Locomotion With Me – THE TORNADOS (No. 5, 11 weeks)
	HMV POP1114	Angel Face/ Since You Went Away (D) – GERRY TEMPLE
	Decca F11571	In The Night (M/Adams)/ Little Girl In Blue – JAMIE LEE & THE ATLANTICS
Feb	Decca F11581	If My Heart Were A Storybook (GM)/ Vagabond (J) – TOBY VENTURA
	HMV POP1122	Cupboard Love/ Land Of Love – JOHN LEYTON (No.22, 12 weeks)
	HMV POP1124	Return Of The Outlaws (M)/ Texan Spiritual (G) – THE OUTLAWS
	Decca F11593	Totem Pole (M)/ Jaywalker (M/Jay) – PETER JAY & THE JAYWALKERS
Mar	HMV 7EG8793	'IT'S TIME FOR MIKE BERRY' EP
		Don't You Think It's Time (GM)/ Loneliness (D)/ Every Little Kiss (J)/ How Many Times
	Decca F11598	Jack The Ripper/ Don't You Just Know It – SCREAMING LORD SUTCH
	Decca F11602	Angel Of Love (M)/ Lucky Star – DON CHARLES
	Decca F11603	You've Got To Have A Gimmick Today (M)/ Westpoint – THE CHECKMATES
	Decca F11606	Robot (M)/ Life On Venus (M) – THE TORNADOS (No.17, 12 weeks)
	Decca DFE8521	'MORE SOUNDS FROM THE TORNADOS' EP
		Chasing Moonbeams/ Theme From 'A Summer Place'/ Swinging Beefeater (M)/ The Breeze And I (No. 9, 11 weeks)
	Columbia DB4996	There's Lots Lots More Where This Came From/ Three Cups (M) – WES SANDS
	HMV POP1135	Sidewalk/ Time Goes By (M) – TONY HOLLAND
	HMV POP1137	Don't You Break My Heart (M)/ Hark Is That A Cannon I Hear – MICHAEL COX
	HMV POP1142	My Little Baby (GM)/ You'll Do It, You'll Fall In Love (M) – MIKE BERRY & THE OUTLAWS (No.34, 7 weeks)

THE LEGENDARY JOE MEEK

Apr	Oriole CB1815	Breakups/ A Love Like Ours – THE DOWLANDS AND THE SOUNDTRACKS
	Decca F11645	Heart's Ice Cold/ Daybreak (Charles/M) – DON CHARLES
	Decca LK4524	'JUST FOR FUN' LP – VARIOUS ARTISTS (one track off it only)
		'All The Stars In The Sky' (M) – THE TORNADOS
	HMV POP1156	They Were Wrong (M)/ Don't Pick On Me (M) – CHAD CARSON
May	HMV POP1160	Saturday Dance (G)/ Come Back To Me (M) – GEOFF GODDARD
	Decca F11652	Dreams Do Come True (M)/ Been Invited To A Party (M/Burt) – HEINZ
	HMV POP1163	I Lost My Heart In The Fairground (M)/ Feel So Good – GLENDA COLLINS
	Decca F11659	Poet And Peasant/ Oo La La (M) – PETER JAY & THE JAYWALKERS
	Decca F11662	The Ice Cream Man (M)/ Theme From 'The Scales Of Justice' – THE TORNADOS (No.18, 9 weeks)
	Decca F11663	Who Told You (G)/ Peter Gunn Locomotion – FREDDIE STARR & THE MIDNIGHTERS
	Parlophone R5031	Only The Heartaches/ Can't Stop Pretending – HOUSTON WELLS & THE MARKSMEN (No.22, 10 weeks)
June	HMV 7EG8808	'A TRIBUTE TO BUDDY HOLLY' EP – MIKE BERRY
		Tribute To Buddy Holly (G)/ It's Just A Matter Of Time (D)/ My Little Baby (GM)/ You'll Do It You'll Fall In Love (M) (No.17, 4 weeks)
	Columbia DB7061	Hobbies/ Big Boys (M) – JENNY MOSS
	HMV POP1175	I'll Cut Your Tail Off/ The Great Escape – JOHN LEYTON (No. 36, 2 weeks)
	Decca F11686	San Francisco Bay/ Like A Bird Without Feathers (M/Lawrence) – BURR BAILEY & THE SIX–SHOOTERS
	Decca F11688	Union Pacific/ The Spy – THE ORIGINAL CHECKMATES
	Decca DFE8530	'DON CHARLES' EP
		Walk With Me My Angel (D)/ The Hermit Of Misty Mountain/ It's My Way Of Loving You/ Heart's Ice Cold
July	Parlophone R5046	Everybody Loves A Lover/ My Old Standby – CLIFF BENNETT & THE REBEL ROUSERS
	Pye 7N15539	Andy (M)/ There Was A Boy – ANDY CAVELL
	Pye 7N15548	Wipeout/ Midgets – THE SAINTS
	Decca F11693	Just Like Eddie (G)/ Don't You Knock At My Door – HEINZ (No. 5, 15 weeks)
	Pye 7N15549	Dream Lover/ Packabeat – THE PACKABEATS
	Decca DFE8533	'TORNADO ROCK' EP – THE TORNADOS
		Ready Teddy/ My Babe/ Blue Moon Of Kentucky/ Long Tall Sally (No.7, 13 weeks)
	HMV CLP1664	'ALWAYS YOURS' LP – JOHN LEYTON
		I'm Gonna Let My Hair Down/ On Lover's Hill (G)/ Sweet And Tender Romance/ Johnny My Johnny (M)/ That's The Way It Is/ Too Many Late Nights/ Lover's Lane/ Funny Man/ Another Man/ Buona Sera/ A Man Is Not Supposed To Cry/ How Will It End
	Dot DOA16496	March Of The Spacemen (M)/ Lost Planet – THE THUNDERBOLTS [Charles Kingsley Creation] (Not released in UK)
Aug	Columbia DB7092	Powercut/ High Low And Handsomely – THE CAMEOS
	HMV POP1194	It Really Doesn't Matter (M)/ Try A Little Bit Harder – MIKE BERRY
	HMV POP1195	That Set The Wild West Free (M)/ Hobo – THE OUTLAWS
	Decca F11723	Keep Moving (M)/ Order Of The Keys (D) – SOUNDS INCORPORATED
	Decca LK4552	'AWAY FROM IT ALL' LP – THE TORNADOS

DISCOGRAPHY

	Indian Brave (M)/ Flycatcher/ Dreams Do Come True (M)/ Lullaby For Giulia/ Costa Monger/ Lonely Paradise/ Chattanooga Choo Choo/ Rip It Up/ Alan's Tune/ Cootenanny/ Night Rider/ Hymn For Teenagers (M/Lawrence)
Pye 7N15556	Everybody's Talking/ Poison Ivy – THE PUPPETS
Sept Decca F11730	That's My Plan/ Third Time Lucky – THE BEAT BOYS
Parlophone GEP8878	'JUST FOR YOU' EP – HOUSTON WELLS & THE MARKS-MEN
	This Song Is Just For You/ Paradise/ Shutters And Boards/ North Wind (M)
HMV POP1204	On Lover's Hill (G)/ Lover's Lane – JOHN LEYTON
Decca F11745	Hymn For Teenagers (M/Lawrence)/ Dragonfly – THE TORNADOS (No.41, 2 weeks)
Decca F11747	I'm A Hog For You/ Monster In Black Tights (GM) – SCREAMING LORD SUTCH
Dot DOA16528	Surfin' John Brown/ Big Breaker (M) – THE AMBASSADORS [The Saints] (Not released in UK)
Oct HMV POP1213	Sky Men (G)/ Walk With Me My Angel (M) – Geoff Goddard
Decca DFE8545	'HEINZ' EP
	I Get Up In The Morning (M)/ Talkin' Like A Man/ That Lucky Old Sun/ Lonely River (M)
HMV POP1220	Gee What A Party/ Say That Again – MICHAEL COX
Parlophone R5069	Blowing Wild/ Crazy Dreams – HOUSTON WELLS & THE MARKSMEN
Decca F11757	~~Kansas City~~/ Parade Of The Tin Soldiers (This side only) – PETER JAY & THE JAYWALKERS
Decca F11761	My Friend Bobby (G)/ Hey There Stranger (M) – PAMELA BLUE
? HMV 7EGS296	'IN SWEDEN: MICHAEL COX' EP
	Gee What A Party/ I've Been Thinking/ In This Old House/ Say That Again (released in Sweden only)
Nov HMV POP1230	Beautiful Dreamer/ I Guess You Are Always On My Mind – JOHN LEYTON
Decca F11768	Country Boy (G)/ Long Tall Jack (M/Lawrence) – HEINZ (No. 26, 9 weeks)
Decca F11775	Dodge City (G)/ Just For Chicks – THE RAMBLERS
Pye 7N15582	Husky Team (D)/ Pigtails – THE SAINTS
HMV POP1233	If You've Got To Pick A Baby (M)/ In The First Place – GLENDA COLLINS
Decca DFE8559	'LIVE IT UP' EP – HEINZ
	Live It Up (M)/ Don't You Understand (M)/ Dreams Do Come True (M)/ When Your Loving Goes Wrong (M) (No. 12, 9 weeks)
Decca F11786	It's Shaking Time/ Baby Blue (M) – FREDDIE STARR & THE MIDNIGHTERS
HMV POP1239	Merry Go Round (G)/ Go On Then (M) – GUNILLA THORNE
Dec ——	'LIVE IT UP' Film soundtrack only:
	Temptation Baby (M) – GENE VINCENT/ Please Let It Happen To Me (M) – JENNY MOSS/ Don't Take You From Me (M) – ANDY CAVELL & THE SAINTS
HMV POP1241	Law And Order (M)/ Do Da Day – THE OUTLAWS
Decca F11791	Christmas Stocking/ Reindeer Ride – ROGER LAVERN & THE MICRONS
Decca F11796	The Kennedy March (M)/ The Theme Of Freedom (D) – JOE MEEK ORCHESTRA
Oriole CB1892	Lucky Johnny/ Do You Have To Make Me Blue – THE DOWLANDS & THE SOUNDTRACKS
Oriole CB1897	All My Loving/ Hey Sally – THE DOWLANDS (No. 33, 7 weeks)
1964	
Jan Decca F11811	Dumb Head/ Boy Trouble – THE SHARADES
Columbia DB7194	I'm Just A Boy/ Can't Make Up My Mind (M) – DEKE ARLON & THE OFF-BEATS
Parlophone	'WESTERN STYLE' LP – HOUSTON WELLS & THE MARKS-

333

PMC1215	MEN
	I Won't Go Hunting With You Jake/ You Left Me With A Broken Heart/ Call Me Another Time/ Squaws Along The Yukon/ Little Black Book/ Kissing Tree/ I'll Be Your Sweetheart For A Day/ Blowing Wild/ Best Job Yet/ We're Gonna Go Fishin'/ All For The Love Of A Girl/ I'm Gonna Change Everything/ Behind The Footlights
Decca F11813	I'll Prove It/ For Loving Me This Way (M) – KIM ROBERTS
Parlophone R5099	Anne Marie/ Moon Watch Over My Baby (M) – HOUSTON WELLS & THE MARKSMEN
Columbia DB7201	My Baby's Coming Home/ Where 'Ere You Walk – THE CAMEOS
Decca F11825	I Learned To Yodel/ Louisiana Mama – JIMMY LENNON & THE ATLANTICS
Feb Decca F11831	You Were There (G)/ No Matter What They Say (M) – HEINZ (No.26, 8 weeks)
Pye 7N15610	Tell The Truth/ Shut Up (M/Lawrence) – ANDY CAVELL
Decca F11838	Joystick/ Hot Pot (M) – THE TORNADOS
Decca F11844	Sticks And Stones/ Please Listen To Me – THE CHECKMATES
Decca F11846	Chahawki/ You Made Me Cry (J) – BURR BAILEY
Mar HMV 7EG8843	'BEAUTIFUL DREAMER' EP – JOHN LEYTON
	Beautiful Dreamer/ On Lover's Hill (G)/ I'll Cut Your Tail Off/ Lover's Lane
Columbia DB7238	Maybelline/ True To Me – THE SYNDICATS
Decca F11866	A Fool Such As I/ It's Nice In't It – DAVY KAYE
Decca LK4599	'A TRIBUTE TO EDDIE' LP – HEINZ
	Tribute To Eddie (M)/ Hush-A-Bye (G)/ I Ran All The Way/ Summertime Blues/ Don't Keep Picking On Me (M)/ Cut Across Shorty/ Three Steps To Heaven/ Come On And Dance/ Twenty Flight Rock/ Look For A Star/ My Dreams/ I Remember/ Rumble In The Night/ Just Like Eddie (G)
Parlophone R5119	~~Got My Mojo Working~~/ Beautiful Dreamer (this side only) – CLIFF BENNETT & THE REBEL ROUSERS
Apr HMV POP1277	Keep A 'Knockin'/ Shake With Me (J) – THE OUTLAWS
HMV POP1283	Baby It Hurts/ Nice Wasn't It (M) – GLENDA COLLINS
Decca F11889	Monte Carlo/ Blue, Blue, Blue Beat – THE TORNADOS
Pye 7N15634	Baby Don't Cry/ Shake With Me (J) – THE PUPPETS
May HMV 7EG8854	'TELL LAURA I LOVE HER' EP – JOHN LEYTON
	Tell Laura I Love Her/ The Girl On The Floor Above/ Johnny Remember Me (G)/ Wild Wind (G)
HMV POP1293	Rave On/ Just Say Hello – MICHAEL COX
Decca F11913	The Other Side Of The Track/ I've Got You Out Of My Mind – BOBBY CRISTO & THE REBELS
Oriole CB1926	I Walk The Line/ Happy Endings – THE DOWLANDS
Parlophone R5141	Galway Bay/ Livin' Alone – HOUSTON WELLS & THE OUTLAWS
June Decca F11920	Please Little Girl/ For Lovin' Me This Way (M) – HEINZ
Pye 7N15664	Have I The Right/ Please Don't Pretend Again (M/Lawrence) – THE HONEYCOMBS (No.1, 15 weeks)
Oriole CB1944	She's Fallen In Love With The Monster Man/ Bye Bye Baby – SCREAMING LORD SUTCH & THE SAVAGES
Oriole CB1947	Wishing And Hoping/ You Will Regret It – THE DOWLANDS
July HMV POP1323	Lollipop/ Everybody's Gotta Fall In Love (M) – GLENDA COLLINS
Decca F11944	Boys And Girls/ You'll Be On Your Way – BENNY PARKER & THE DYNAMICS
Aug Decca F11946	Exodus/ Blackpool Rock – THE TORNADOS
Parlophone GEP8914	'RAMONA' EP – HOUSTON WELLS
	Ramona/ Girl Down The Street/ I Wonder Who's Kissing Her Now/ Nobody's Child

DISCOGRAPHY

Tower190	Chills And Fever/ Baby I'm In Love – TOM JONES (released in US only)
Eric ERIC157	Have I The Right/ I Can't Stop Now – THE HONEYCOMBS (released in US only)
Sept Pye 7N15695	I've Seen Such Things/ She's Too Way Out (M/Davis) – TONY DANGERFIELD
Pye NPL18097	'THE HONEYCOMBS' LP Colour Slide/ Once You Know/ Without You It Is Night/ That's The Way/ I Want To Be Free/ How The Mighty Have Fallen/ Have I The Right/ Just A Face In The Crowd/ Nice While It Lasted (M)/ Me From You/ Leslie Anne/ She's Too Way Out (M/Davis)/ It Ain't Necessarily So/ This Too Shall Pass Away
Parlophone R5180	Blue Birds Over The Mountains/ That's When I Need You Baby – SHADE JOEY & THE NIGHT OWLS
? Vogue DV14210	Hab Ich Das Recht/ Du Sollst Nicht Traurig Sein – THE HONEYCOMBS (released in Germany only)
Oct Columbia DB7374	Questions I Can't Answer/ The Beating Of My Heart (M) – HEINZ (No.39, 2 weeks)
Pye 7N15705	Is It Because/ I'll Cry Tomorrow (M) – THE HONEYCOMBS (No.38, 6 weeks)
Decca F12009	Never Cry On Someone's Shoulder/ Just Keep On Dreaming (M) – FREDDIE STARR
Nov Oriole CB1962	Dracula's Daughter/ Come Back Baby – SCREAMING LORD SUTCH
HMV POP1359	My Johnny Doesn't Come Around Anymore/ Please Listen To Me – FLIP & THE DATELINERS
Pye 7N15736	Eyes/ If You Gotta Pick A Baby (M) – THE HONEYCOMBS
Pye 7N15734	Little Baby/ Baby I Go For You (M/Davis) – THE BLUE RONDOS
Columbia DB7426	Christmas Calling/ He Didn't Fool Me (M) – VALERIE MASTERS
? HMV HMVX8654	Love My Life Away/ Just A Gentle Word – MICHAEL COX (released in Sweden only

1965

Jan Columbia DB7441	Howlin' For My Baby/ What To Do – THE SYNDICATS
Columbia DB7455	Granada/ Ragunboneman (M) – THE TORNADOS
Pye 7N15758	Stranger In Paradise/ Anyone Can Lose A Heart (M) – JOHNNY GARFIELD
Feb Decca F12073	In My Way/ All The Stars In Heaven (M) – DAVY KAYE
Pye 7N15749	Thunder And Rain/ As Time Goes By (M) – ALAN DEAN & HIS PROBLEMS
Columbia DB7482	Diggin' My Potatoes (trad. arr. M/Burt)/ She Ain't Coming Back (M) – HEINZ & THE WILD BOYS (No.49, 1 week)
Mar Parlophone R5255	Bring It To Jerome/ I Love To See You Strut – DAVID JOHN & THE MOOD
Pye 7N15790	Boy Meets Girl/ Don't Break My Heart And Run Away (M/Davis) – BOBBY RIO & THE REVELLES
Pye 7N15827	Something Better Beginning/ I'll See You Tomorrow – THE HONEYCOMBS (No.39, 4 weeks)
Apr Pye 7N15833	Don't Want Your Lovin' No More/ What Can I Do –THE BLUE RONDOS
Columbia DB7547	Don't Make Me Over/ Someone Must Be Feeling Sad – THE DOWLANDS
HMV POP1417	Gypsy/ It Ain't Right (M) – MICHAEL COX
Pye 7N15847	Georgia/ There And Bach Again (M/Cook) – PETER COOK
Columbia DB7559	Don't Think Twice It's All Right/ Big Fat Spider (M/Davis) – HEINZ & THE WILD BOYS
May Columbia DB7566	Little Lonely One/ That's What We'll Do – TOM JONES
Pye 7N15849	Hurt Me/ It Can Happen To You (M) – JESS CONRAD
Columbia DB7589	Early Bird (M)/ Stompin' Through The Rye – THE TORNADOS
June CBS 201767	The Train Kept A-Rollin'/ Honey Hush – SCREAMING LORD

SUTCH

Decca F12179	Saxon War Cry/ Click-Ete-Clack (M/Holder) – THE SAXONS
Columbia DB7613	Every Little Once In A While/ Well Who's That – THE SHAKEOUTS
Pye 7N15885	My Saddest Day/ I'll Find Her – REG AUSTIN
July HMV POP1439	Johnny Loves Me/ Paradise For Two (M) – GLENDA COLLINS
Columbia DB7624	Tomorrow I'll Be Gone/ Ain't Got Much More To See – DAVY MORGAN
Parlophone R5301	Diggin' For Gold/ She's Fine – DAVID JOHN & THE MOOD
Pye 7N15900	The Very First Day I Met You/ Hello Heartache – JUDY CANNON
Pye 7N15890	That's The Way/ Can't Get Through To You (M) – THE HONEYCOMBS (No.12, 14 weeks)
Pye 7N15897	Everything In The Garden/ When Love Was Young (M) – BOBBY RIO & THE REVELLES
Columbia DB7656	End Of The World/ You Make Me Feel So Good (M) – HEINZ
Sept Columbia DB7693	I Don't Love You No More/ Ain't Coming Back No More (M) – THE HOTRODS
Columbia DB7686	On The Horizon/ Crawdaddy Simone – THE SYNDICATS
Columbia DB7687	Stingray/ Aqua Marina – THE TORNADOS
HMV POP1475	Thou Shalt Not Steal/ Been Invited To A Party (M) – GLENDA COLLINS
Oct Pye 7N15957	Bless You/ Baby I Like The Look Of You – PETER LONDON
Pye 7N15958	Value For Love/ I'm Not Made Of Clay (M/O'Neil) – BOBBY RIO & THE REVELLES
Pye NEP24230	'THAT'S THE WAY' EP – THE HONEYCOMBS
	That's The Way/ She's Too Way Out (M/Davis)/ Colour Slide/ This Too Shall Pass Away
Columbia DB7733	Lonely Joe/ I Was A Fool – TOM JONES
Nov Columbia DB7758	Summer Without Sun/ Still In Love With You – CHARLES KINGSLEY CREATION
Pye 7N15979	This Year, Next Year/ Not Sleeping Too Well Lately (M) – THE HONEYCOMBS
Columbia DB7779	Heart Full Of Sorrow/ Don't Worry Baby (M) – HEINZ
Pye NPL18132	'ALL SYSTEMS GO' LP – THE HONEYCOMBS
	I Can't Stop/ I Don't Love Her No More/ All Systems Go/ Totem Pole (M)/ Emptiness/ Ooee Train/ She Ain't Coming Back (M)/ Something I Got To Tell You/ Our Day Will Come/ Nobody But Me/ There's Always Me/ Love In Tokyo/ If You Should/ My Prayer
Dec Columbia SEG8464	'TOM JONES' EP
	Little Lonely One/ I Was A Fool/ Lonely Joe/ That's What We'll Do
Parlophone R5388	Whatcha Gonna Do Baby/ Come On Baby – JASON EDDY & THE CENTREMEN

1966

Jan Columbia DB7806	A Man's Gotta Stand Tall/ Fast Cars And Money – THE FOUR MATADORS
Columbia DB7819	Heart And Soul/ Who's The Girl – DIANE & THE JAVELINS
Pye 7N17041	Cry Cry Cry/ How It Is Done – THE RIOT SQUAD
Feb Pye 7N17044	Something I've Got To Tell You/ My Heart Didn't Lie (M) – GLENDA COLLINS
Decca F12340	Please Stay/ What's News Pussycat – THE CRYIN' SHAMES (No.26, 7 weeks)
Pye 7N17059	Who Is Sylvia/ How Will I Know (M) – THE HONEYCOMBS
Mar Columbia DB7856	Pop Art Goes Mozart (Mozart, arr: M)/ Too Much In Love To Hear – THE TORNADOS
Apr Columbia DB7887	You're Holding Me Down/ I've Gotta Buzz (M) – THE BUZZ
Pye 7N17092	I Take It That We're Through/ Working Man – THE RIOT SQUAD
May Columbia DB7923	Over The Hill/ The Right Girl For Me (M) – PETER CHRIS & THE OUTCASTS
June Columbia DB7942	Movin' In/ I'm Not A Bad Guy – HEINZ

336

DISCOGRAPHY

Decca F12425	Nobody Waved Goodbye/ You – THE CRYIN' SHAMES
Parlophone R5473	Singing The Blues/ True To Me – JASON EDDY & THE CENTREMEN
July Pye 7N17130	It's Never Too Late To Forgive/ Try To Realise – THE RIOT SQUAD
Pye 7N17138	It's So Hard/ I Fell In Love (M) – THE HONEYCOMBS
Pye 7N17150	It's Hard To Believe It (M)/ Don't Let It Rain On Sunday (M/Collet) – GLENDA COLLINS
Aug Decca F12468	Wishing Well/ Chatterbox – THE MILLIONAIRES
Columbia DB7984	Is That A Ship I Hear (M)/ Do You Come Here Often – THE TORNADOS
Decca F12483	September In The Rain/ Come On Back – PAUL & RITCHIE AND THE CRYIN' SHAMES
Sept Pye 7N17173	That Lovin' Feeling/ Should A Man Cry (M) – THE HONEYCOMBS
Nov CBS 202402	Too Far Out/ Rat Tat Ta Tat – THE IMPAC
1967	
Jan Pye 7N17237	Gotta Be A First Time/ Bitter Sweet Love – THE RIOT SQUAD

• •

Compiled by: Laurence Brown, Chris Davies, Nick Garrard, Bob Hill, Graham Hill, Andy Knott, Mark Newson, Norman Thompson

This extended list consists of the majority of the LP and CD releases since Meek's death. It excludes bootlegs and most of the myriad compilations that have contained only an RGM track or two. Not all the names of artistes and titles of previously unissued recordings can be guaranteed. Indeed where such information has been unavailable, it has been known for a CD compiler to make them up.

1967

Marble Arch MAL 743	'THIS IS CHICO' LP – CHICO ARNEZ & HIS LATIN-AMERICAN ORCHESTRA Reissue of 1959 LP

1972

Decca SPA 253	'THE WORLD OF THE TORNADOS' LP - THE TORNADOS Telstar (M); Love And Fury (D); Popeye Twist; Globetrotter (M); Robot (M); Jungle Fever (G); The Ice Cream Man (M); Dragonfly; Monte Carlo; Blue, Blue, Blue Beat; Exodus; Hot Pot (M)

1974

Decca REM 4	'REMEMBERING THE TORNADOS' LP – THE TORNADOS Telstar (M); Love And Fury (D); Globetrotter (M); Ridin' The Wind; Jungle Fever (G); Robot (M); The Ice Cream Man (M); Night Rider; Hymn For Teenagers (M); Indian Brave (M); The Breeze And I; Exodus
Decca TAB TB38	'HEINZ AND THE TORNADOS' LP – HEINZ/ THE TORNADOS Heinz: Just Like Eddie (G); You Were There (G); Summertime Blues; Three Steps To Heaven; Country Boy (G); Tribute To Eddie (M); Don't You Knock At My Door/ The Tornados: Telstar (M); The Ice Cream Man (M); Night Rider; Dragonfly; Jungle Fever (G); Robot (M); Globetrotter (M)

1977

Decca DPA 3035/6	'THE JOE MEEK STORY' Dbl LP – VARIOUS ARTISTS My Baby Doll (D) - Mike Berry & the Outlaws/ Walk With Me My Angel (D); Guess That's The Way It Goes (M); Angel Of Love (M) - Don Charles/ Can Can '62; Totem Pole (M) - Peter Jay & the Jaywalkers/ There Was A Time (B) - Tony Victor/ Telstar (M); Dreamin' On A Cloud; All The Stars In The Sky (M); Life On Venus (M) - the Tornados/ Jack The Ripper; Monster In Black

337

THE LEGENDARY JOE MEEK

Tights (GM) - Screaming Lord Sutch & the Savages/ Christmas Stocking - Roger LaVern & the Microns/ Who Told You (G) - Freddie Starr & the Midnighters/ Keep Moving (M) - Sounds Incorporated/ Dreams Do Come True (M); Country Boy (G); Just Like Eddie (G) - Heinz/ My Friend Bobby (G) - Pamela Blue/ In My Way - Davy Kaye/ Saxon War Cry - the Saxons/ Wishing Well - the Millionaires/ Please Stay - the Cryin' Shames

Decca REM 7 — 'REMEMBERING HEINZ' LP – HEINZ
Just Like Eddie (G); Hush-A-Bye (G); Three Steps To Heaven; That Lucky Old Sun; You Were There (G); Twenty Flight Rock; Country Boy (G); Dreams Do Come True (M); Cut Across Shorty; Summertime Blues; I Ran All The Way; Tribute To Eddie (M)

1979

Decca (Belgium) Box 622/23 — 'AWAY FROM IT ALL' Dbl LP – THE TORNADOS
The original LP tracks + all UK EP tracks

1982

Decca TAB 38 — 'ROCK ECHOES: HEINZ AND THE TORNADOS' LP - HEINZ AND THE TORNADOS
Reissue of 1974 LP

1984

See For Miles CM 127 — 'RARITIES' LP – JOHN LEYTON
Inc: You Took My Love For Granted (D); That's A Woman (B); Fabulous; Voodoo Woman (G); The Girl On The Floor Above; Goodbye To Teenage Love; Tell Laura I Love Her; Walk With Me My Angel (D); Terry Brown's In Love With Mary Dee (D)

1985

See For Miles CM 124 — '20 ONE HIT WONDERS – Vol 2' LP - VARIOUS ARTISTS
Inc: Can't You Hear My Heart - Danny Rivers/ Can Can '62 - Peter Jay & the Jaywalkers/ Please Stay - the Cryin' Shames/ Walk With Me My Angel (D) - Don Charles

1986

Rock Machine MACH 8 — 'THAT'S THE WAY IT WAS' LP – HEINZ & THE WILD BOYS
All Columbia singles

1987

See For Miles SEE 201 — 'THE BEST OF...' LP – JOHN LEYTON
Inc: Johnny Remember Me (G); Wild Wind (G); Six White Horses (D/arr: Blackwell); Son, This Is She (G); Lone Rider (G); Lonely City (G); Oh Lover (G); I Don't Care If The Sun Don't Shine; (I Love You) For Sentimental Reasons; That's How To Make Love (D); It Would Be Easy (C)

See For Miles SEE CD 201 — 'THE BEST OF...PLUS' CD – JOHN LEYTON
As per 'The Best Of...' LP + You Took My Love For Granted (D); The Girl On The Floor Above; Tell Laura I Love Her

1988

BAM Caruso KIRI 080 — 'ANYTIME' LP – THE RIOT SQUAD
Inc: all RGM singles

PRT PYL 4009/ PRT CD PYL 4009 — 'BEST OF THE HONEYCOMBS' LP + CD - THE HONEYCOMBS
Have I The Right; Is It Because; Eyes; I Don't Love Her No More; Something Better Beginning; That's The Way; This Year Next Year; Who Is Sylvia?; It's So Hard; That Loving Feeling; How The Mighty Have Fallen; I Want To Be Free; I Can't Stop; Love In Tokyo

1989

Rollercoaster ROLL 2016 — 'SOUNDS OF THE SIXTIES' LP – MIKE BERRY & THE OUTLAWS
All RGM tracks + Set Me Free (unissued)

Connoisseur Collection RPVSOP 143 — 'ROCK PROFILE – Vol 1' LP + CD – RITCHIE BLACKMORE
Inc: Return Of The Outlaws (M); Texan Spiritual (G); Do Da Day; Shake With Me (J); Keep A-Knockin' - the Outlaws/ Big Fat

338

DISCOGRAPHY

RPVSOPCD 143	Spider (M/Davis); I'm Not A Bad Guy; Movin' In - Heinz/ If You've Got To Pick A Baby (M); Thou Shalt Not Steal; Been Invited To A Party (M) - Glenda Collins

1990

See For Miles SEE 303 SEE CD 303	'THE OUTLAWS RIDE AGAIN – THE SINGLES A's & B's' LP + CD – THE OUTLAWS All RGM singles
Repertoire RR 4121-WZ	'ALL SYSTEMS GO!' CD – THE HONEYCOMBS The original LP + Not Sleeping Too Well Lately (M); How Will I Know (M); I Fell In Love (M);Something Better Beginning; Should A Man Cry (M); Can't Get Through To You (M)
Sequel NEXLP 111/ NEXCD 111	'HERE COME THE GIRLS – Vol 1' LP + CD – VARIOUS ARTISTS Inc: The Very First Day I Met You (M) - Judy Cannon/ It's Hard To Believe It (M) - Glenda Collins/ Something I Got To Tell You (issued on CD only) - the Honeycombs
Rollercoaster RCEP 109	'IT'S TIME FOR MIKE BERRY' EP – MIKE BERRY & THE OUTLAWS As per original EP
Connoisseur CSAPLP 108/ CSAPCD 108	'BEEN INVITED TO A PARTY' LP + CD – GLENDA COLLINS All RGM singles
Sequel NEXCD 125	'THE HONEYCOMBS' CD – THE HONEYCOMBS As per LPs 'All Systems Go!' + 'It's The Honeycombs'
See For Miles CM 108	'GOT TO GET YOU INTO MY LIFE' LP – CLIFF BENNETT & THE REBEL ROUSERS Inc: Hurtin' Inside; That's What I Said (D); I'm In Love With You (D/Bennett); You Got What I Like (D)

1991

See For Miles CM 126	'60s LOST AND FOUND -Vol 3' LP – VARIOUS ARTISTS Inc: What's News Pussycat - the Cryin' Shames/ Third Time Lucky - the Beat Boys/ I've Got You Out Of My Mind - Bobby Cristo & the Rebels
Sequel NEXCD 171	'INSTRUMENTAL DIAMONDS – Vol 2: HIGHLY STRUNG' CD - VARIOUS ARTISTS Inc: Music Train; Hurricane (both unissued) - the Honeycombs/ Packabeat; Theme From 'The Traitors'; Dream Lover; Evening In Paris (M) - the Packabeats/ Husky Team (D); Pigtails - the Saints
Sequel NEXCD 171	'THE JOE MEEK STORY – THE PYE YEARS' Dbl CD - VARIOUS ARTISTS Inc: Little Baby; Don't Want Your Lovin' No More - the Blue Rondos/ Value For Love; Everything In The Garden; Boy Meets Girl - Bobby Rio & the Revelles/ She's Too Way Out (M/Davis); I've Seen Such Things - Tony Dangerfield & the Thrills/ It's Hard To Believe It (M); Something I've Got To Tell You - Glenda Collins/ Sunday Date; Stage To Cimarron; Lone Rider (G); Sunburst - the Flee Rekkers/ Have I The Right; Colour Slide; Something Better Beginning; Is It Because; That's The Way; I Can't Stop; That Loving Feeling; This Year Next Year - the Honeycombs/ Make Way Baby (D) - Ricky Wayne & the Offbeats/ Andy (M); Tell The Truth - Andy Cavell/ Theme From 'The Traitors'; Evening In Paris (M) - the Packabeats/Mr Lovebug (D); Time Will Tell; Can't You Hear The Beat Of A Broken Heart (D) - Iain Gregory/ Baby Don't Cry; Everybody's Talking; Shake With me (J); Poison Ivy - the Puppets/ Bless You - Peter London/ Thunder And Rain - Alan Dean & his Problems/ Wipe Out; Husky Team (D) - the Saints/Hurt Me - Jess Conrad/I Take It That We're Through; Gotta Be A First Time; It's Never Too Late To Forgive; Cry, Cry, Cry - the Riot Squad/ Hello Heartache - Judy Cannon/ Paradise Garden (D) - Peter Jay/ Cha-Cha On The Moon - Pat

THE LEGENDARY JOE MEEK

Reader/Early In The Morning (D) - Chick with Ted Cameron & the DJs/ Georgia On My Mind - Peter Cook

See For Miles C5 564 C5 CD 564	'JOE MEEK'S FABULOUS FLEE REKKERS' LP + CD - THE FLEE REKKERS Inc: Lone Rider (G); Stage To Cimarron; Sunburst; Shiftless Sam; Blue Tango; Isle Of Capri; Brer Robert; Miller Like Wow; Twistin' The Chestnuts; Black Buffalo; Sunday Date; Bitter Rice; Hangover; P.F.B.
Connoisseur Collection RPVSOP 157/ RPVSOPCD 157	'ROCK PROFILE – Vol 2' LP + CD – RITCHIE BLACKMORE Inc: The Train Kept A-Rollin'; Honey Hush - Screaming Lord Sutch & the Savages
Repertoire RR 4098-WZ	'THE HONEYCOMBS' CD – THE HONEYCOMBS As per original LP + Please Don't Pretend Again (M/Lawrence); I'll Cry Tomorrow (M); If You Gotta Pick A Baby (M); I'll See You Tomorrow; I Can't Stop (USA version – unreleased in UK); Hab Ich Das Recht; Du Sollst Nicht Traurig Sein
Marble Arch CMACD 146	'THE BEST OF THE HONEYCOMBS' CD – THE HONEYCOMBS Have I The Right; Leslie Anne; Once You Know; That's The Way; Colour Slide; Without You It Is Night; Something Better Beginning; I Want To Be Free; Just A Face In The Crowd; How The Mighty Have Fallen; Nice While It Lasted (M); She's Too Way Out (M/Davis)
Line (Germany) TRCD 9.01081 0	'THE JOE MEEK STORY – Vol 1: 1960' CD – VARIOUS ARTISTS All Meek's UK releases on Triumph
EMI CPD 7 98044 2	'SCREAMING LORD SUTCH & THE SAVAGES' CD – SCREAMING LORD SUTCH & THE SAVAGES Inc: all RGM singles
Beat Goes On BGOLP 118/ BGOCD 118	'DREAM OF THE WEST' LP + CD – THE OUTLAWS As per original LP
Repertoire REP 4192-WZ	'ANYTIME' CD – THE RIOT SQUAD Inc: all RGM singles
1992 RPM RPMCD 103	'I HEAR A NEW WORLD' CD – THE BLUE MEN As per unissued LP
Line (Germany) TRCD 9.01082 0	'THE JOE MEEK STORY – Vol 2: 1960-61' CD – VARIOUS ARTISTS Tell Laura I Love Her; Johnny Remember Me (G) - John Leyton/ Sunday Date; Lone Rider (G) - the Flee-Rekkers/ Make Way Baby (D) - Ricky Wayne & The Off-Beats/ Paradise Garden (D) - Peter Jay/ Along Came Caroline; Teenage Love; Sweet Little Sixteen - Michael Cox/ Early In the Morning (D) - Chick with Ted Cameron & the DJs/ No More Tomorrows - Gerry Temple/ My Baby Doll (D) - Mike Berry/ Can't You Hear My Heart; I'm Waiting For Tomorrow (D) - Danny Rivers/ My Baby's Gone Away (D) - Danny Rivers & the Alexander Combo/ Time Will Tell - Ian Gregory/ Swingin' Low; Ambush (D) - the Outlaws/ You Got What I Like (D); I'm In Love With You (D/ Bennett) - Cliff Bennett & the Rebel Rousers
See For Miles SEE CD 342	'1962 – 1973: NEIL CHRISTIAN' CD – NEIL CHRISTIAN Inc: The Big Beat Drum; The Road To Love
EMI CDEMS 1450	'BEST OF THE EMI YEARS' CD - CLIFF BENNETT & THE REBEL ROUSERS Inc: all RGM singles
Repertoire RR 4097	'EMILE FORD & THE CHECKMATES' CD – EMILE FORD & THE CHECKMATES Inc: What Do You Want To Make Those Eyes At Me For; Don't

Tell Me Your Troubles

Castle
MBSCD 401

'HITS OF THE 60s' CD – VARIOUS ARTISTS
Inc: What Do You Want To Make Those Eyes At Me For - Emile
Ford & the Checkmates/ Have I The Right; That's The Way - the
Honeycombs/ Be Mine - Lance Fortune

Castle
CHC 7056 CR

'SOUNDS OF THE SIXTIES: THE ORIGINAL RGM SOUND
RECORDINGS' CD – MIKE BERRY & THE OUTLAWS
As per 'Sounds Of The Sixties' LP

1993

Sequel
NEXCD 216

'THE JOE MEEK STORY – Vol 2 – 304 HOLLOWAY ROAD'
CD – VARIOUS ARTISTS
Inc: Pocket Full Of Dreams (And Eyes Full Of Tears) (B); The Night
You Told A Lie (D) - Iain Gregory/ Who's The Girl - Peter Jay/
Bitter Sweet Love; Try To Realise - the Riot Squad/ When Love
Was Young (M); I'm Not Made Of Clay (M/O'Neil) - Bobby Rio &
the Revelles/ Midgets; Happy Talk (unissued); Parade Of Tin
Soldiers (unissued) - the Saints/ Baby I Go For You (M/Davis);
What Can I Do - the Blue Rondos/ May Your Heart Stay Young
Forever - Pat Reader/ Goodness Knows - Ricky Wayne & the
Off-Beats/ Baby I Like The Look Of You; Stranger In Paradise -
Peter London/ Fickle Heart (M) (unissued) - Johnny Garfield/ As
Time Goes By (M) - Alan Dean & his Problems/ Cool Water - Chick
with Ted Cameron & the DJs/ Rescue Me (M) (unissued) - Ricky
Wayne/ It Can Happen To You (M) - Jess Conrad/ There And Bach
Again (M/Cook) - Peter Cook/ Sing C'est La Vie (unissued) -
Glenda Collins/ My Saddest Day - Reg Austin

EMI
CDEMS 1475

'THE BEST OF THE HONEYCOMBS' CD – THE
HONEYCOMBS
Have I The Right; Can't Get Through To You (M); I Want To Be
Free; Leslie Anne; Colour Slide; This Year Next Year; That Loving
Feeling; That's The Way; It Ain't Necessarily So; How The Mighty
Have Fallen; I'll Cry Tomorrow (M); I'll See You Tomorrow; Is It
Because; She's Too Way Out (M/Davis); Something Better
Beginning; Eyes; Just A Face In The Crowd; Nice While It Lasted
(M); It's So Hard; I Can't Stop; Don't Love Her No More; All
Systems Go; Totem Pole (M); Emptiness; Ooee Train; She Ain't
Coming Back (M); Something I Got To Tell You; Nobody But Me;
There's Always Me; Love In Tokyo

Sequel
NXTCD 249

'THE SURF SET' Tpl CD – VARIOUS ARTISTS
Inc: Surfin' John Brown; Big Breaker(M) - the Ambassadors [the
Saints]

Castle
Communications
(Germany)
CLC 5117

'TRIBUTE TO EDDIE' – HEINZ
As per 1964 LP

See For Miles
C5CD 607

'20 ONE HIT WONDERS' CD – VARIOUS ARTISTS
As per 1985 LP

Sequel
NEXCD 242

'THE JOE MEEK STORY – Vol 3 – THE COMPLETE
HOUSTON WELLS & THE MARKSMEN' CD – HOUSTON
WELLS & THE MARKSMEN
All issued RGM tracks + Strangers (unissued)

Sequel
NEXCD 243

'THE JOE MEEK STORY – Vol 4 – BEST OF MICHAEL COX' CD
– MICHAEL COX
Angela Jones; Along Came Caroline; Lonely Road; Teenage
Love; Linda; Sweet Little Sixteen; Cover Girl; Young Only
Once; Honey 'Cause I Love You; Stand Up; In April; Don't You
Break My Heart (M); Hark, Is That A Cannon I Hear; I've Been
Thinking; Gee What A Party; Say That Again; Rave On; Just
Say Hello; Gypsy; It Ain't Right (M)

RPM

'FOUR DAYS THAT SHOOK THE WORLD – THE

THE LEGENDARY JOE MEEK

RPM 122	ASSASSINATION OF JOHN F. KENNEDY' CD Inc: The Kennedy March (M) - the Joe Meek Orchestra
Mooncrest CD MOON 12	'TELSTAR' CD EP – THE TORNADOS As per original Decca EP

1994

Rollercoaster RCEP 114	'TRIBUTE TO EDDIE' EP – HEINZ Just Like Eddie(G); Summertime Blues; Tribute To Eddie(M); I Remember
Rollercoaster RCCD 3008	'TRIBUTE TO EDDIE' CD – HEINZ Original Decca LP + Country Boy (G); Don't You Knock At My Door; Been Invited To A Party (M/Burt); I Get Up In The Morning (M)
Castle CLC5134/2	'DREAMS DO COME TRUE – the 45s COLLECTION' CD - HEINZ All Decca singles + following EP tracks: I Get Up In The Morning (M); Talkin' Like A Man; That Lucky Old Sun; Lonely River (M); Live It Up (M); Don't You Understand (M)
RPM RPM 121	'JOE MEEK: WORK IN PROGRESS – THE TRIUMPH SESSIONS' CD – VARIOUS ARTISTS Unissued: Please Don't Touch; Till I Kissed You; Alabama Jubilee; Blues Stay From Away Me; Sea Cruise; Be Bop A Lula; Don't You Know - West Five, aka the Cavaliers/ Shiftless Sam; Some Kinda Earthquake; Brer Robert; Buckeye; El Rancho Rock; Sunday Date; Taboo; Summertime - the Fabulous Flee-Rakkers/ North Wind; With Someone Like You - Chick Lewis/ Say Baby - unknown/ Three Cute Chicks - John Leyton/ Hot Chicka'roo (D) - Ricky Wayne/ With This Kiss (D) - Yolanda/ We Ain't Giving Nothing Away; Keep Your Sunny Side Up - Lee Sutton/ Valley Of The Saroos (D); The Beat Of My Heart (D); I'm Waiting For Tomorrow (D); My Baby Doll (D) - Joe Meek. Issued: Bridge Of Avignon (Trad. arr: D)/ Hey 'Round The Corner (Trad. arr: D) – Eve Boswell
RPM RPM 120	'TAKE IT! - SESSIONS 63 – 68' CD – RITCHIE BLACKMORE Inc: Shake With Me (J); As Long As I Live(unissued) - the Outlaws/ Go On Then (M) - Gunilla Thorne/ I've Been Thinking - Michael Cox/ Living Alone; Galway Bay - Houston Wells/ Dance To The Bop; Catch Me A Rat (both unissued) - Gene Vincent & the Outlaws/ I Get Up In The Morning (M) - Heinz/ A Fool Such As I - Davy Kaye/ It Can Happen To You (M) - Jess Conrad/ Like A Bird Without Feathers (M/Lawrence) - Burr Bailey/ The Birds And The Bees; Something At The Bottom Of The Garden (M) (both unissued) - Silas Dooley
See For Miles SEECD 401	'THE EP COLLECTION...PLUS' CD – JOHN LEYTON Inc: Son, This Is She (G); That's A Woman (B); Fabulous; Voodoo Woman (G); Wild Wind (G); Six White Horses (D); Thunder And Lightning; Goodbye To Teenage Love; You Took My Love For Granted (D); I Don't Care If The Sun Don't Shine; Terry Brown's In Love With Mary Dee (D); Walk With Me My Angel (D); There Must Be (D); Oh Lover (G); Lone Rider (G); Lonely City (G); (I Love You) For Sentimental Reasons; That's How To Make Love (D); Johnny Remember Me (G)
Music Club MCCD 161	'TELSTAR: THE ORIGINAL SIXTIES HITS OF THE TORNADOS' CD - THE TORNADOS All Decca A-sides + Jungle Fever (G); Locomotion With Me; Ridin' The Wind; Life On Venus (M); Theme From 'The Scales Of Justice'; Hymn For Teenagers (M); Dreamin' On A Cloud; Hot Pot (M); Blue, Blue, Blue Beat; Red Roses And A Sky Of Blue (M); Popeye Twist
Kenwest Music KNEWCD746	'THE MUSICAL ADVENTURES OF JOE MEEK' CD – VARIOUS ARTISTS Be Mine - Lance Fortune/ Green Jeans - the Fabulous Flee-Rakkers/

342

DISCOGRAPHY

Angela Jones - Michael Cox/ Johnny Remember Me (G); Son, This Is She (G) - John Leyton/ Tribute To Buddy Holly (G); Don't You Think It's Time (GM) - Mike Berry & the Outlaws/ Night Of The Vampire - the Moontrekkers/ Telstar (M); Ridin' The Wind (US version) - the Tornados/ Only The Heartaches - Houston Wells & the Marksmen/ Just Like Eddie (G) - Heinz/ Have I The Right - the Honeycombs/ Little Baby - the Blue Rondos/ Please Stay - the Cryin' Shames/ 'Til The Following Night - Screaming Lord Sutch

Castle Master Collection (Germany) CMC 3091-2
'THE TORNADOS' CD – THE TORNADOS
First 7 Decca singles + Exodus; Dreamin' On A Cloud

Castle CLC 5135-2
'AWAY FROM IT ALL' CD – THE TORNADOS
As per original LP

RPM RPM 140
'MOTHBALLS – GROUP SESSIONS 64-69' CD – STEVE HOWE
Inc: Maybelline; True To Me; Howling For My Baby; What To Do; On The Horizon; Leave My Kitten Alone (unissued); Don't Know What To Do (unissued) - the Syndicats

1995

Razor & Tie (US) RE 2080-2
'IT'S HARD TO BELIEVE IT: THE AMAZING WORLD OF JOE MEEK' CD – VARIOUS ARTISTS
Telstar (M) - the Tornados/ Johnny Remember Me (G) - John Leyton/ Tribute To Buddy Holly (G); My Baby Doll (D) - Mike Berry & the Outlaws/ Chicka'roo (D) - Ricky Wayne & the Flee Rakkers/ Night Of The Vampire - the Moontrekkers/ Paradise Garden (D) - Peter Jay/ My Friend Bobby (G) - Pamela Blue/ Swingin' Low - the Outlaws/ Valley Of The Saroos (D); The Bublight (D) - the Blue Men/ 'Til The Following Night - Screaming Lord Sutch & the Savages/ Just Like Eddie (G) - Heinz/ Husky Team (D) - the Saints/ Have I The Right - the Honeycombs/ Something I've Got To Tell You; It's Hard To Believe It (M) - Glenda Collins/ I Take It That We're Through - the Riot Squad/ Lost Planet - the Thunderbolts

1996

RPM RPMCD 166
'LET'S GO! JOE MEEK'S GIRLS' CD – VARIOUS ARTISTS
Hobbies; Please Don't Say Goodbye (unissued); Big Boys (M); Please Let It Happen To Me (M) (unissued) - Jenny Moss/ My Friend Bobby (G); Hey There Stranger (M) - Pamela Blue/ Dumb Head; Boy Trouble - the Sharades/ Heart And Soul; Who's The Girl - Diane & the Javelins/ This Little Girl's Gone Rockin' (unissued); I Lost My Heart At The Fairground (M); Baby It Hurts - Glenda Collins/ Mama Didn't Lie (unissued) - Flip/ My Johnny Doesn't Come Around Anymore; Please Listen To Me - Flip & the Dateliners/ Love Can't Wait (M); Mr Right (M) (both unissued) - Kim Roberts/ With This Kiss (D); Don't Tell Me Not To Love Him - Yolanda/ Little Star (Shine On Us Tonight) (M) (unissued) - Lea & Chess/ Your Love Keeps Me Going (unissued) - Denise Scott & the Soundsmen/ Merry-Go-Round (G); Go On Then (M) - Gunilla Thorne /He Didn't Fool Me (M); Christmas Calling - Valerie Masters/ Let's Go See Gran'ma - Joy & Dave/ Cry My Heart (M) (unissued) - Diana Dee

Wooden Hill WHCD004
'ANTHOLOGY 1959-65' CD – THE SCORPIONS
Inc: Two Brothers; Love On Your Lips; Summer Holiday (all unissued)

Magic 572 732
'LES EPs FRANCAIS' CD - THE TORNADOS
As per the 4 original UK EPs + Globetrotter (M); Locomotion With Me; Robot (M); Life On Venus (M); Chattanooga Choo Choo; Night Rider; Alan's Tune; Costa Monger; Hot Pot (M); Joy Stick; Flycatcher; Rip It Up

343

See For Miles SEECD 445	'THE EP COLLECTION' CD – THE TORNADOS As per 'Les EPs Francais' CD + All The Stars In The Sky (M)
Diamond GEMCD 002	'THE JOE MEEK COLLECTION – INTERGALACTIC INSTROS' CD – VARIOUS ARTISTS

Night Of The Vampire; Hatashai (Japanese Sword Fight); Return Of The Vampire (unissued); Melodie D'Amore; There's Something At The Bottom Of The Well (D); Sunday Sunset (unissued); John Brown's Body (Trad. arr: M) - the Moontrekkers/ Just For Chicks; Take It Away; Dodge City (G) - the Ramblers/ Oo La La (M); Totem Pole (M); Jaywalker (Jay/M); Poet And Peasant - Peter Jay & the Jaywalkers/ Red Rocket (unissued) - Roger LaVern & the Microns/ Green Jeans; Cerveza (unissued); You Are My Sunshine - the Fabulous Flee-Rakkers/ Westpoint - the Checkmates/ Keep Moving (M); Order Of The Keys (D) - Sounds Incorporated/ The Spook Walks - the Spooks/ Lawrence Of Arabia; Telstar 'live' (M); Exodus 'live'; Czardas 'live' (all unissued) - the Tornados/ Pinto; Big Feet (D) - the Stonehenge Men/ Saxon War Cry - the Saxons/ Union Pacific; The Spy - the Original Checkmates/ Telstar demo (M) - Joe Meek

1997

Sequel (US) 1038-2	'JOE MEEK PRESENTS: 304 HOLLOWAY ROAD' CD - VARIOUS ARTISTS

Inc: I Hear A New World (D) - the Blue Men/ Sunday Date; Green Jeans - the Flee Rekkers/ What Do You Want To Make Those Eyes At Me For - Emile Ford & the Checkmates/ Andy (M) - Andy Cavell/ Theme From 'The Traitors' - the Packabeats/ Baby I Go For You (M/Davis) - the Blue Rondos/ Shake With Me (J)/ Poison Ivy - the Puppets/ Hurt Me; It Can Happen To You (M) - Jess Conrad/ Thunder And Rain - Alan Dean & his Problems/ Wipe Out; Midgets - the Saints/ Hello Heartache - Judy Cannon/ The Night You Told A Lie (D) - Iain Gregory/ Cha-Cha On The Moon - Pat Reader/ Georgia On My Mind - Peter Cook/ The Kennedy March (M) - the Joe Meek Orchestra

Music Club (US) 50029	'THE VERY BEST OF THE TORNADOES – TELSTAR & OTHER JOE MEEK PRODUCTIONS' CD – THE TORNADOES

Telstar (M); Hymn For Teenagers (M); Jungle Fever (G); Costa Monger; Red Roses And A Sky Of Blue (M); Locomotion With Me; Ridin' The Wind; Joystick; Popeye Twist; Dreamin' On A Cloud; Blue, Blue, Blue Beat; The Ice Cream Man (M); Alan's Tune; Monte Carlo; Love And Fury (D)

Diamond GEMCD 012	'RGM RARITIES – Vol 1: THE R'N'R ERA' CD – VARIOUS ARTISTS

It Matters Not; Upside Down (J) - Mark Douglas/ In The Night (M/Adams); Little Girl In Blue - Jamie Lee & the Atlantics/ The Other Side Of The Track - Bobby Cristo & the Rebels/ Heart's Ice Cold; Angel Of Love (M); It's My Way Of Loving You; Walk With Me My Angel (D) - Don Charles/ Can't You Hear My Heart; I'm Waiting For Tomorrow (D) - Danny Rivers/ Angel Face; Seventeen Come Sunday (G); No More Tomorrows - Gerry Temple/ A Fool Such As I; In My Way; All The Stars In Heaven (M) - Davy Kaye/ They Were Wrong (M); Stop Picking On Me (M) - Chad Carson/ Don't Want To Know; Lonesome Old House - Michael Cox/ Movin' In; We're Gonna Dance - Danny Rivers & the Rivermen/ Dear One - Tony Victor/ Louisiana Mama - Jimmy Lennon & the Atlantics/ Hey There Cruel Heart (B) - Andy Cavell/ Striped Purple Shirt; Three Coins In The Sewer - Alan Klein

Diamond GEMCD 016	'RGM RARITIES – Vol 2: THE BEAT GROUP ERA' CD – VARIOUS ARTISTS

Inc: I Love To See You Strut; Bring It To Jerome; Diggin' For Gold; She's Fine – David John & the Mood/ You're Holding Me Down;

DISCOGRAPHY

I've Gotta Buzz (M) – the Buzz/ I Don't Love You No More; Ain't Coming Back No More (M) – the Hotrods/ A Man's Gotta Stand Tall – the Four Matadors/Every Little Once In A While – the Shakeouts/Wishing Well - the Millionaires/I've Got You Out Of My Mind – Bobby Cristo & the Rebels/Too Far Out – the Impac; Who Told You(G); It's Shaking Time – Freddie Starr & the Midnighters/ Whatcha Gonna Do Baby; Come On Baby; True To You; Singing The Blues – Jason Eddie & the Centremen/ Boys & Girls – Benny Parker & the Dynamics/ That's My Plan; Third Time Lucky – the Beat Boys/ Sticks And Stones – the Checkmates/ Bluebirds Over The Mountain – Shade Joey & the Night Owls/ Summer Without Sun; Still In Love With You – the Charles Kingsley Creation/ The Right Girl For Me (M) – Peter Chris & the Outcasts

RPM RPM 182	'THE COMPLETE GLENDA COLLINS – THIS LITTLE GIRL'S GONE ROCKIN'!' CD – GLENDA COLLINS All issued RGMs + This Little Girl's Gone Rockin'; Sing C'est La Vie; Run To Me; You're Gonna Get Your Way; Self Portrait; Yeah, Yeah, Yeah

1998

Calligraph CLGCD 035-4	'HUMPHREY LYTTELTON & HIS BAND – Vol 4' CD – HUMPHREY LYTTELTON & HIS BAND Inc: Bad Penny Blues
Rialto RMCD228	'THE TORNADOS (ARCHIVE SERIES)' CD – THE TORNADOS All the Decca singles + Granada; Early Bird (M); Stingray; Pop Art Goes Mozart (Mozart, arr: M); Is That A Ship I Hear (M)
Diamond GEMCD 013	'THE DAVE ADAMS STORY' CD – DAVE ADAMS The Old Red Lion demo (D) (unissued) - the Kids/ Whoopee!; My Oh My! (D); Rocking Away The Blues (D/Adams); If You Pass Me By (D) - Joy & David/ Let's Go See Gran'ma; Believe Me (D); My Very Good Friend The Milkman; Doopey Darling (D); Joe's Been A-Gittin' There; They Tell Us Not To Love (D); They Tell Us Not To Love (promo version) (D); Chahawki (unissued version)/ Diamond Joe (unissued) - Joy & Dave/ San Francisco Bay; Like A Bird Without Feathers (M/Lawrence) - Burr Bailey & the Six-Shooters/ Chahawki; You Made Me Cry (J) - Burr Bailey/ It Feels Funny, It Feels Good; You Just Can't Do It On Your Own; Clean, Clean, Clean; The Birds And The Bees; Don't Put All Your Eggs In One Basket (M/Adams); Oh What A Party; Let Me In; They're All Up To It (M); Signs And Posters; Out Behind The Barn (M/Adams); There's Something At The Bottom Of The Garden (M); The Bathroom (M) (all unissued) - Silas Dooley Jr/ Telstar demo (M) (unissued) - Dave Adams & the Outlaws
Sequel NEMCD 882	'THE JOE MEEK STORY – Vol 5: THE EARLY YEARS' CD – VARIOUS ARTISTS Sound-balanced works only, except: The Land Of Make Believe (M/Blackwell) - Jackie Davies with his Quartet/ Yashmak (D) - Chico Arnez & his Latin-American Orchestra/ What Do You Want To Make Those Eyes At Me For - Emile Ford & the Checkmates
Repertoire REP 4708-WR	'TELSTAR – THE COMPLETE TORNADOS' CD – THE TORNADOS Inc: All UK issues + Life On Venus (M) (German version)
Diamond GEMCD 022	'JOE MEEK HIDDEN GEMS – Vol 1' CD – VARIOUS ARTISTS (All unissued.) Baby Can't Sleep - the Millionaires/ A Fool In Love (M)/ Jesse James - Chad Carson/ Cyclone; No More You And Me - the Tornados/ Grandfather Clock - the Moontrekkers/ I Can't Make Up My Mind (M)/ Funny Man - Michael Cox/ Snow-White Eastern Maid - Lennie & Les/ Cry My Heart (M) - the Joe Meek Orchestra/ Summer Holiday; Two Brothers - the Ferridays [the Scorpions]/ Cocaine - Davy Morgan/ We'll Remember You (G) -

THE LEGENDARY JOE MEEK

Houston Wells & the Outlaws/ Lips Are Redder On You (M) - Bobby Ross/ Just Like You; Atlantic Twist (M/Dexter) - Ray Dexter/ Muscles (M) - Ricky Wayne/ When My Blue Moon Turns To Gold - Houston Wells & the Marksmen/ Walking On Ice - the Riot Squad/ I'll Tell Her Now - Benny Parker & the Dynamics/ You Stole My Heart Away - Malcolm & the Countdowns/ How Will I Know (M/Holder/Holder) - the Saxons/ On A Hillside (G) - the Dauphine Street Six/ He's Mine demo (M) - Joe Meek

1999

Repertoire REP 4718-WR	'THE COMPLETE HEINZ' CD – HEINZ Inc: All issued tracks
Diamond GEMCD 026	'ALL MY LOVING' CD – THE DOWLANDS Inc: All issued tracks + Never Thought I'd Feel The Way I Do; + 3 remastered to original 'natural' speed: I Walk The Line; Wishing And Hoping; Don't Make Me Over
Diamond GEMCD 029	'TRIUMPH RECORDS – HISTORY OF A LABEL' CD – VARIOUS ARTISTS Inc: All his Triumph singles + spoken introductions by Meek to excerpts from: Entry Of The Globbots (D); Valley Of The Saroos (D); Magnetic Field (D); Orbit Around The Moon (D)
Zircon ZIRC 1005	'THE JOE MEEK COLLECTION' CD – MICHAEL COX Inc: Angela Jones; Don't Want To Know; Along Came Caroline; Lonely Road; Teenage Love; Linda; Sweet Little Sixteen; Cover Girl; Young Only Once/ Honey 'Cause I Love You; Stand Up; In April (B); Don't You Break My Heart (M); Hark, Is That A Cannon I Hear/ I've Been Thinking; Lonesome Old House; Gee What A Party; Say That Again; (I Wanna) Love My Life Away; Rave On; Gypsy; For All Time (unissued); Johnny B Goode (unissued)
Deram 844892 Z	'THE ROCK'N'ROLL SCENE' CD – VARIOUS ARTISTS Inc: Rock Around The Mailbags - Terry White & the Terriers/ My Baby's Gone Away - Danny Rivers & the Alexander Combo/ It's Shaking Time - Freddie Starr & the Midnighters/ I'm A Hog For You - Screaming Lord Sutch

2000

Westside WESA 839	'THE TWO SIDES OF.../ALWAYS YOURS' CD – JOHN LEYTON As per original LPs
Zircon ZIRC 1001	'ONLY THE HEARTACHES' CD – HOUSTON WELLS This Song Is Just For You/ Paradise; Shutters And Boards; North Wind (M); Only The Heartaches; Can't Stop Pretending; Blowin' Wild; Crazy Dreams; Anna Marie; You Left Me With A Broken Heart; Call Me Another Time; Best Job Yet; Strangers; We're Gonna Go Fishin'; All For The Love Of A Girl; I'm Gonna Change Everything; Behind The Footlights; Galway Bay; Ramona; Girl Down The Street/ I Wonder Who's Kissing Her Now; + unissued: Hula Love; The Wild Side Of Life; Please Help Me I'm Falling; We'll Remember You (G)

KEY TO COMPOSERS
M = Meek
D = Robert Duke
J = Peter Jacobs
W = Dandy Ward ⎫ = Meek
B = Robert Baker ⎭
K = Knight = Meek/Dick Rowe
C = Crosley = Meek/Charles Blackwell
G = Geoff Goddard
GM = Goddard/Meek

346

Index

Joe Meek CDs available via Cherry Red Records

RPM103

Joe Meek & The Blue Men
I Hear A New World

In the growing world of Meek collectors this album stands as the most fascinating. Recorded in 1960 the album was inspired by Meek's own fascination with outer space and much of the album is devoted to 'other world' sound effects, used to their full extent on what must be both one of the earliest stereo recordings of this type and certainly the first concept album ever. Only around 20 copies pressed originally! This album is growing in status as tracks have been recently compiled and sampled by 90's artists.

1. I Hear A New World 2. Orbit Around The Moon 3. Entry Of The Globbots 4. The Bublight 5. March Of The Dribcots 6. Love Dance Of The Saroos 7. Globb Waterfall 8. Magnetic Field 9. Valley Of The Saroos 10. Dribcots Space Boat 11. Disc Dance Of The Globbots 12. Valley Of No Return.

RPM121

Joe Meek / Various Artists
Work In Progress

A collection of rare and unissued material including demo's, acetates and tapes relating to artists produced by Meek during his time working for the Triumph label. The CD includes an impressive fold-out inlay, with comprehensive notes, and even includes snatches of Meek himself at work composing.

WEST FIVE / CAVALIERS: 1. Please Don't Touch 2. Til I Kissed Ya 3. Alabama Jubilee 4. Blues Stay Away From Me 5. Sea Cruise 6. Be Bop A Lula 7 Don't You Know FABULOUS FLEE-RAKKERS: 8. Shiftless Sam 9. Some Kinda Earthquake 10. Brer Robert 11. Buckeye 12. El Rancho Rock 13. Sunday Date 14. Taboo 15. Summertime CHICK LEWIS: 16. North Wind 17. With Someone Like You UNKNOWN: 18. Say Baby JOHN LEYTON: 19. Three Cute Chicks RICKY WAYNE: 20. Hot Chicka'roo EVE BOSWELL: 21. Bridge Of Avignon 22. Hey 'Round The Corner YOLANDA: 23. With This Kiss LEE SUTTON: 24. We Ain't Giving Nothing Away 25. Keep Your Sunnyside Up JOE MEEK: 26. Valley Of The Saroos; The Beat Of My Heart; I'm Waiting For Tomorrow 27. My Baby Doll.

Joe Meek / Various Artists
Let's Go! Joe Meek's Girls

While Meek scored his biggest hits with artists like John Leyton, Mike Berry and Heinz, these have over-shadowed his work with Girl singers. Some of his finest, most collectable productions in this area - intense beat cuts and ethereal vocal melodramas - are collected here along with ten unissued tracks*, comprehensive sleevenotes, rare photo's, memorabilia, etc.

1. JENNY MOSS Hobbies 2. PAMELA BLUE My Friend Bobby 3. SHARADES Dumb Head 4. DIANE & THE JAVELINS Heart And Soul 5. GLENDA COLLINS This Little Girl's Gone Rockin'* 6. FLIP Mama Didn't Lie* 7. JENNY MOSS Please Don't Say Goodbye* 8. VALERIE MASTERS He Didn't Fool Me 9. GUNILLA THORN Merry-Go-Round 10. JENNY MOSS Big Boys 11. GLENDA COLLINS I Lost My Heart At The Fairground 12. FLIP & THE DATELINERS My Johnny Doesn't Come Around Anymore 13. PAMELA BLUE Hey There Stranger 14. KIM ROBERTS Love Can't Wait* 15. YOLANDA With This Kiss 16. LEA & CHESS Little Star (Shine On Us Tonight)* 17. DENISE SCOTT & THE SOUNDSMEN Your Love Keeps Me Going* 18. DIANE & THE JAVELINS Who's The Girl 19. JENNY MOSS Please Let It Happen To Me* 20. GUNILLA THORN Go On Then 21. VALERIE MASTERS Christmas Calling 22. FLIP & THE DATELINERS Listen To Me 23. YOLANDA Don't Tell Me Not To Love Him 24. GLENDA COLLINS Baby It Hurts 25. SHARADES Boy Trouble 26. JENNY MOSS My Boy Comes Marching Home* 27. KIM ROBERTS Mr. Right* 28. JOY & DAVE Let's Go See Gran'ma 29. DIANA DEE Cry My Heart*.

If you have any problems finding these records in record shops they can be purchased with a credit card via the Cherry Red mail order system.

Cherry Red Records, Unit 17, Elysium Gate West,
126-128 New King's Road, London SW6 4LZ
Telephone: 020 7371 5844
Fax: 020 7384 1854
email: infonet@cherryred.co.uk

www.cherryred.co.uk

Also available from

CHERRY RED BOOKS

Indie Hits 1980-1989
The Complete UK Independent Charts
(Singles & Albums)
Compiled by Barry Lazell

Indie Hits is the ultimate reference book for alternative music enthusiasts. Indie Hits is the first and only complete guide to the first decade of Britain's Independent records chart, and to the acts, the music and the labels which made up the Indie scene of the 1980s. The book is set out in a similar format to the *Guinness Hit Singles* and *Albums* books, with every artist, single and album to have shown in the Indie charts over the 10-year period being detailed.

The first Independent charts were published by the trade paper *Record Business* in January 1980, by which time they were well overdue. By that time, Mute, Graduate, Factory, Crass, Safari and Rough Trade were just a few of the new breed of rapidly expanding labels already scoring hit records. They were producing acts like Depeche Mode, UB40, Toyah, The Cult, Joy Division and Stiff Little Fingers, all to become major international sellers. Later years brought the likes of The Smiths, New Order, Erasure, The Stone Roses, James, The Fall and Happy Mondays (not to mention Kylie and Jason!) – all successful and influential independently distributed hitmakers.

The A–Z section details every chartmaking 1980s Indie act and all hit records in a detailed but easy-to-reference format. Also included are complete indexes of single and album titles, an authoritative history of the origin and development of the Indie charts during the 1980's, listings of all No.1 singles and albums with illustrations of rare original sleeves, print ads and other memorabilia of the period plus a fax 'n' trivia section including the artists and labels with the most chart records, the most No. 1s and the longest chart stays. If it was in the Indie charts of the 1980s, it's in here!

Paper covers, 314 pages, £14.99 in UK

Also available from

CHERRY RED BOOKS

Cor Baby, That's Really Me!
(New Millennium Hardback Edition)
John Otway

Time was when John Otway looked forward to platinum albums, stadium gigs and a squad of bodyguards to see him safely aboard his private jet. Unfortunately it didn't happen that way. A series of dreadful career decisions, financial blunders and bad records left Otway down but not out. This is his true story in his own words. It is the story of a man who …

- has never repaid a record company advance in his life
- once put on a benefit concert for his record company after they had cancelled his contract
- signed himself to the mighty Warner Bros label simply by pressing his own records with the WB logo
- broke up with Paula Yates telling her it was the last chance she would get to go out with a rock star

www.cherryred.co.uk

This book is Otway's hilarious yet moving account of his insane assault on the music industry, a tale of blind ambition and rank incompetence, and a salutary lesson for aspiring musicians on how not to achieve greatness. But if the John Otway story is one of failure, it is failure on a grand scale. And it makes compulsive reading too!

Hardback, 192 pages and 16 pages of photographs, £11.99 in UK

Also available from

CHERRY RED BOOKS

All the Young Dudes
Mott the Hoople and Ian Hunter
The Biography
Campbell Devine

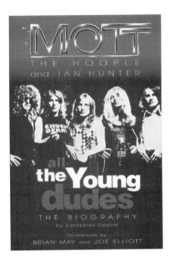

Published to coincide with the Sony 3-CD anthology of their music, *All the Young Dudes* traces Mott The Hoople's formation, their work with David Bowie, their rise to international stardom and beyond, including offshoots such as Mick Ralphs' Bad Company, Mott and British Lions, plus Hunter and Ronson's solo careers and collaborations with Van Morrison, Bob Dylan and Morrissey.

Devoid of borrowed information and re-cycled press clippings, this official biography contains new, sensational and humorous inside stories, controversial quotes and an array of private and previously unpublished views from the band, embellished with comprehensive appendices including discographies and session listings.

The author has collaborated with Ian Hunter and all of Mott's founder members, Dale Griffin, Overend Watts, Verden Allen and Mick Ralphs – who have provided their own anecdotes and photographs to illustrate and enhance the project. There are further personal - contributions from Luther Grosvenor, Morgan Fisher, Stan Tippins, Diane Stevens, Muff Winwood, Ray Major, John Fiddler, Blue Weaver and Miller Anderson.

This biography will be welcomed by both the committed and casual rock reader, and by all Dudes, young and post-young!

'This book is by far the most comprehensive work on the subject, and could well be the best book written about any band.'

– Adrian Perkins on his Mott web page

Paper covers, 448 pages and 16 pages of photographs, £14.99 in UK

Also available from

CHERRY RED BOOKS

Embryo
A Pink Floyd Chronology
1966 – 1971
Nick Hodges & Ian Priston

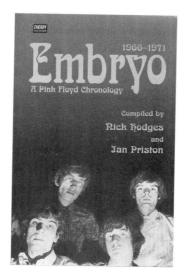

What exactly happened in 'The Massed Gadgets of Auximenes', 'Games For May' and 'The Committee' and what were Pink Floyd up to in Studio 3 at Abbey Road on 1 June 1967?

'Embryo: A Pink Floyd Chronology' is the most fully comprehensive and in-depth study of the early work of the Pink Floyd that has been compiled to date. An archetypal labour of love, the chronology draws together details of rare recordings owned by collectors, concert ads, tickets, obscure posters, unseen photographs and long-lost reviews, into a high-quality tour of the band's day-to-day work up to their first epochal work 'The Dark Side Of The Moon'.

Beginning with an evaluation of the Floyd's first tentative steps

www.cherryred.co.uk

towards their concept albums – a genre which they went on to make their own, and continuing through a painstaking commentary on the development of the band's concert, film, studio and television work, the detail of this book will achieve and surpass the high standards that Pink Floyd collectors demand.

'Embryo' also explores the solo history of the band's first enigmatic and often misunderstood leader Syd Barrett. Correcting mistakes made previously by others, the book additionally represents a fully equipped and up-to-date research resource which is made easily accessible by a detailed index and chapter-by-chapter notes. 'Embryo' is a must for every serious fan.

Paper covers, 302 pages and photographs throughout, £14.99 in UK

Also available from

CHERRY RED BOOKS

Songs In The Key Of Z
The Curious Universe of Outsider Music

Irwin Chusid

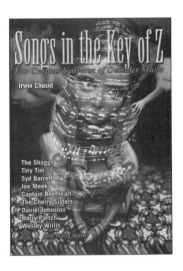

Outsider musicians can be the product of damaged DNA, alien abduction, drug fry, demonic possession, or simply sheer obviousness. But they really are worth listening to, often outmatching all contenders for inventiveness and originality. This book profiles dozens of outsider musicians, both prominent and obscure, and presents their strange life stories along with photographs, interviews, cartoons and discographies.

It contains the stories of The Shaggs, Tiny Tim, Syd Barrett, Joe Meek, Captain Beefheart, Wild Man Fischer, The Legendary Stardust Cowboy and many, many other music eccentrics. It really is a wonderful collection of wilder cards and beyond-avant talents. It also contains an extensive 'Outsider' discography.

www.cherryred.co.uk

Cherry Red Records has also released a 20 track companion CD to support the book.

"Chusid takes us through the musical looking glass to the other side of the bizarro universe where pop spelled backwards is ....pop? A fascinating collection."

Lenny Kaye

Paper covers, 300 pages, fully illustrated, £11.95 in UK

Also available from

CHERRY RED BOOKS

In Cold Blood
Johnny Thunders

Nina Antonia

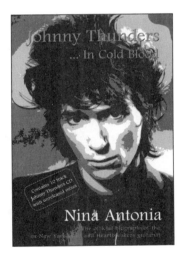

Johnny Thunders first gained recognition as guitarist with the legendary New York Dolls who recorded two albums in the early 1970's. He left the band in 1975 and, along with former Dolls' drummer Jerry Nolan and ex-Television guitarist Richard Hell, formed the Heartbreakers. Thunders and The Heartbreakers recorded prolifically and achieved great popularity in the UK. Thunders earned a reputation for his shambling stage performances owing to an excess of drugs and alcohol. The band split and reformed numerous times recording their last album in 1984. Thunders was found dead in mysterious circumstances in a hotel room in New Orleans at the age of 38.

www.cherryred.co.uk

Nina Antonia's book is a detailed, inside look at the life of Thunders, right through his career from his early pre-Heartbreakers days to his tragic death in 1991. It also contains many anecdotes from those who knew him and loved him through the years. The book includes a complete Thunders' discography and over 100 photographs, some never seen before.

The book comes with a 10 track CD. Seven tracks are alternative, unreleased mixes from the recording sessions of the remarkable 1977 Johnny Thunders and The Heartbreakers album, 'LAMF.' The two other tracks are both live, one taken from his classic live collection, 'Chinese Rocks' and the other from his 'Belfast Rocks' album. The CD is completed by a very rare 10 minute interview with Johnny recorded in 1985.

Paper covers, 270 pages and photographs throughout, £14.99 in UK

Also available from

CHERRY RED BOOKS

Random Precision
Recording The Music Of Syd Barrett
1964 – 1974
David Parker

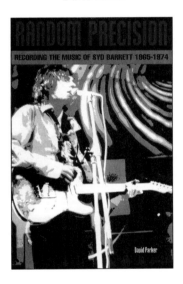

Syd Barrett was the original lead guitarist and a founder member of the group Pink Floyd, and remains one of rock music's most enduring characters. He was the principal songwriter for the first Pink Floyd album 'The Piper at the Gates of Dawn', and composed their 1967 hit single 'See Emily Play' before leaving the group in early 1968. He subsequently released two eccentric solo albums ('The Madcap Laughs' in 1969 and 'Barrett' in 1970) before withdrawing completely from the music business in the mid-1970's.

Much has been written about his life, but here for the first time are the full details of all his recording sessions - from his first semi-professional recordings with Pink Floyd in 1965 up to his last abandoned solo

www.cherryred.co.uk

recording sessions at Abbey Road in 1974.

The author David Parker was co-editor of the respected Syd Barrett fanzine 'Chapter 24', and has spent four years researching and writing the book, which is based principally on information obtained from the official archives at EMI Records and Abbey Road Studios.

The book uses a diary format, and includes exclusive interviews with many of the recording producers and engineers involved, including Peter Jenner, Andrew King, Peter Brown, Alan Parsons and John Leckie. The book also includes rare photographs and illustrations, many previously unpublished.

This is the most comprehensive, accurate and detailed account yet published of the background to the creation of Syd Barrett's unique musical legacy.

Paper covers, approx 300 pages, photographs throughout, £14.99 in UK

CHERRY RED BOOKS

We are always looking for any interesting book projects
to get involved in. If you have any good ideas, or indeed manuscripts,
for books that you feel deserve publication, then please
get in touch with us.

CHERRY RED BOOKS
a division of Cherry Red Records Ltd.
Unit 17, Elysium Gate West,
126-128 New King's Road,
London SW6 4LZ

E-mail: iain@cherryred.co.uk
Web: www.cherryred.co.uk